THE OFFICIAL BIOGRAPHY OF

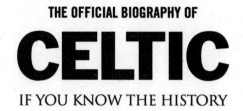

CELTIC

IF YOU KNOW THE HISTORY

ALSO BY GRAHAM McCOLL:

The Little Book of Scotland
'78: How a Nation Lost the World Cup
Celtic in Europe
The Head Bhoys: Celtic's Managers
The Essential History of Celtic
United We Stand
Celtic: The Official Illustrated History

Thirty Miles from Paradise by Bobby Lennox with Graham McColl
Lion Heart by Tommy Gemmell and Graham McColl

THE OFFICIAL BIOGRAPHY OF

CELTIC

IF YOU KNOW THE HISTORY

GRAHAM McCOLL

headline

First published in 2008 by
HEADLINE PUBLISHING GROUP

1

Cataloguing in Publication Data is available from the British Library

ISBN 978 0 7553 1585 7

Stats compiled by David McDonald.

'Celtic Club Badge' is a registered trademark belonging to Celtic FC Ltd.

Typeset in Din by Ellipsis Books Limited, Glasgow

Printed and bound in the UK by
CPI Mackays, Chatham ME5 8TD

HEADLINE PUBLISHING GROUP
An Hachette Livre UK Company
338 Euston Road
London NW1 3BH

www.headline.co.uk
www.hachettelivre.co.uk

For Anna-Maria, born 23 June 2007,
while this book was underway

Contents

Acknowledgements

I would like to thank the following for extensive interviews that were indispensable in putting this book together:

Bertie Auld, John Barnes, Alec Boden, Bobby Carroll, John Clark, Billy Connolly, Jim Craig, Dermot Desmond, John Divers, Sean Fallon, Sybolla Franje, Charlie Gallagher, Tommy Gemmell, Peter Grant, Elaine Hamilton, David Hay, Andreas Hinkel, John Hughes, Mike Jackson, Kevin Kelly, Peter Lawwell, Bobby Lennox, Ian Livingston, Joe McBride, Fergus McCann, Danny McGrain, Billy McNeill, Jack Marshall, Lubo Moravcik, Shunsuke Nakamura, Johnny Paton, Brian Quinn, Eric Riley, Tony Roper, Brian Sharp, Gordon Strachan, Brendan Sweeney, Rolando Ugolini, Dr Jozef Venglos, Jimmy Walsh, Jackie Watters, Evan Williams, Johnnie Wilson, Paul Wilson

I have also drawn on interviews I carried out with Willie Buchan, Tommy Burns, James Farrell and Jimmy Johnstone, all of whom have recently, sadly, passed away. All were exceptionally helpful, sometimes in testing circumstances

Thanks also to Iain Jamieson, Russell Kyle, Barbara Maloney, Peter McLean, Eleanor O'Neill, Jim Platt and Natalie Portelli for helping to arrange some of the above interviews

The help and advice that I received from Paul Cuddihy, editor of the *Celtic View*, and Chris Cameron, of the visitors' centre at Celtic Park, was entirely invaluable and greatly appreciated

Thanks also to Jonathan Harris and Stan, agents on this book and to Wendy McCance and David Wilson at Headline Book Publishing

If I have missed anyone out, inadvertently, please accept my fulsome apologies

Select Bibliography

An Alphabet of the Celts by Eugene MacBride, Martin O'Connor and George Sheridan (ACL & Polar Publishing Ltd, 1994)

Celtic: The Official Illustrated History by Graham McColl (Hamlyn, 1998)

Celtic in Europe by Graham McColl (Mainstream Publishing, 2004)

Lion Heart by Tommy Gemmell and Graham McColl (Virgin Books Ltd, 2005)

The Celtic Football Companion by David Docherty (John Donald Publishers, 1986)

The Essential History of Celtic by Graham McColl and George Sheridan (Headline Books, 2002)

The First 100 Years – The Scottish Football League Official Centenary History by Bob Crampsey (The Scottish Football League, 1990)

The Head Bhoys: Celtic's Managers by Graham McColl (Mainstream Publishing, 2003)

The Story of the Celtic by Willie Maley (1939, facsimile edition published in 1996 by Desert Island Books)

Thirty Miles from Paradise by Bobby Lennox with Graham McColl (Headline Books, 2007)

Foreword

BY BILLY McNEIL

The first game I can ever remember seeing at Celtic Park was Celtic playing Aberdeen and I have to say that as a game of football, it was absolutely appalling. Not that that put me off in any way because there was still plenty of excitement for a young boy in being part of a Celtic crowd. My Auntie Grace had taken me along to that match and we had found a nice viewing spot in the Jungle but, at that time, there weren't too many crush barriers on the terraces so when the sway of the crowd started, you were being swirled and carried around, almost as if a huge wave had taken hold of you. Celtic were losing for much of that match and began to turn the game in their direction only very late on and that's when the surge started, so much so that Auntie Grace lost one of her shoes. That made it memorable, as did, as I recall, a goal from Charlie Tully near the end to help Celtic win. An unusual thing I remember about that goal was that Charlie, a great ballplayer, scored with his head. When I signed for Celtic in the late 1950s, Charlie was still there – our Celtic careers overlapped briefly – and he always used to get me in front of the other players and say, 'Right, big man, tell the rest of them about the time I scored with my head.' That was my party piece.

Charlie made a dramatic impression on me that day. My dad was in the Army and had been in West Africa for a long spell; he used to carry a letter about with him that he had received when out there, telling him about this new player Celtic had signed: Charles Patrick Tully. That family tale was maybe one small thing that helped to spark my interest in Celtic. Another was hearing about the team from Dan Gallagher, one of our neighbours in Bellshill and the secretary of the local Celtic supporters' club. There was also a man called Alex Millar, who lived locally to us and who had played at Celtic and then Morton. So all of that helped me form the attachment to the club. Other than Charlie, the Celtic players who first captured my imagination were Willie Miller, the goalkeeper, and Bobby Evans.

Jock Stein was instrumental in me going to Celtic – if he hadn't suffered a bad ankle injury that persuaded him to make his way into coaching, I might have been overlooked by the club. So I was sure from my close association with him in my early years as a footballer that he would bring success when he returned as manager in 1965. I didn't realise just how extensive that success would be. I also think that if we could ever have married big Jock with this present board of directors, the success might even have been far, far greater because apart from having the Lisbon Lions, right behind them was a squad of players who were absolutely brilliant – including Kenny Dalglish, David Hay, Lou Macari and Danny McGrain. If the board had supported the manager and had been as progressive as the current board is, then what that would have done for Celtic would have been absolutely and utterly astonishing.

It wasn't a job playing for Celtic – I didn't know what a job was until I stopped playing – and being successful was a fantastic bonus. I remember in 1966 doing an interview with Jimmy Gordon and he said, 'I've always believed that there is a fairy-tale aspect about Celtic and I just have a silly feeling that it's going to manifest itself this season.' Of course, it did, with us going on to lift the European Cup.

The club has progressed enormously in recent years. It was renowned in the past for its success on the football field – only latterly has come the improvement in the ground and Celtic Park is really sparkling now. I would never have believed when I started at Celtic that it would be turned into this modern, all-seated stadium. Fergus McCann was a clever man to envisage it and carry out its construction. When you think of the average gates at Celtic in the present day and when I started out, there is no comparison. Every home game now has nigh-on 60,000 spectators. It just shows that if you give people something that they appreciate, you'll get rewarded in return.

The biggest thing that Celtic have got is a fervent support that will stay with them through the bad days as well as the good days. Celtic supporters want to win but they want to do so with a bit of style, a bit of panache. People think it's easy to play at Celtic. It's not – because the fans demand skilful, characteristic play all the time. I think Celtic's colours lend themselves to a cavalier approach and although that might sound daft, if you were to ask me about the great strips in the world, Celtic's would be right in amongst them because it's got clarity, it's got flair. The tradition of having fantastically skilled players has been maintained in the present era: if you were going to name a group of players to have really graced the Celtic shirt, someone like Henrik Larsson would be in among them.

Celtic are also very fortunate at the moment because, for me, this is the best board of directors that I can remember. They have worked to limits but the way in which, at times, they have stretched those limits I find absolutely incredible. They have been able to assist the manager in assembling a high-quality playing staff without going anywhere near bank- rupting the club – indeed keeping it profitable – and they seem to know exactly what they're doing. I'm delighted with what I see at Celtic Park today. In Gordon Strachan, Celtic also have a manager who has provided an extraordinary degree of success. There is obviously a mutual respect between him and the board and I think it's important that the fans do their part in ensuring that with their support, the club continues to enjoy such success.

It's a great club. I'm 68 years of age and it still amazes me today how vibrant the Celtic support is in faraway places such as the USA and Australia – and it seems to be growing. Celtic is a special club, with a unique and unusual history and, I'm sure, a most intriguing future.

Introduction
MATCHDAY

All shades of green mix and mingle in the pre-match minutes on Kerrydale Street, the conduit to the main entrance at Celtic Park. There are classy emerald green cardigans worn by smart, well-kempt young women and rather more scruffy fleeces and hoodies worn by young and older men. Liam Brady, a former manager, is able to pass through the verdant throng, almost unnoticed as groups of fans chat and discuss the forthcoming match among themselves. John Kennedy, Danny McGrain, Jean-Joël Perrier-Doumbé, and other players past and present, stroll towards the main entrance. 'I've been worked up all day,' says one man to his pals in anticipation of the match. The street is teeming with supporters, chatting, chinwagging.

Corporate guests advance towards the main door: green ties among some of the men, green silk scarves for the ladies. Japanese faces are dotted here and there among those milling about on the apron of tarmac outside the main entrance to the ground. The numerous Japanese drawn by Shunsuke Nakamura, the mesmeric midfield player, are fewer than in his first season at the club but they are still present, here and there, and there are occasional Afro-Caribbeans too but this is not cosmopolitan Arsenal or nouveau riche Chelsea. There are no busloads of well-dressed, clean-cut Scandinavians strolling towards the ground, as you will find at Tottenham Hotspur; or trainloads of supporters heading up from the south as at Anfield and Old Trafford. Celtic's matchday support is among the most localised of any major club, and fulsome, lived-in faces abound, topping off earthy, squat figures of straightforward, take-us-as-you-find-us Glaswegians.

A fleet of uniformly black 4x4s sit in the car park, almost exclusively the property of the players; with tinted windows to protect them from prying eyes when transporting themselves around this football-obsessed city. After the match, each car will have a steward at the wheel to manoeuvre it into position for the player to make an easy exit from the ground. The tall, raking, pylon floodlights that loomed up to make Celtic Park an easily identified landmark from the late 1950s have now gone, removed in the mid-1990s to make way for today's all-seater stadium, so enormous that its lights are incorporated in the superstructure and with the sheer height of the stadium – 34 metres at the top of the North Stand – enough to draw them up to the necessary height for illuminating the pitch.

The redbrick façade that was put in place for the 1988 centenary remains understatedly impressive. The club crest is subtly moulded into it while the exposed, wrought-iron-work for the other three stands, constructed during the Fergus McCann era, juts out high above the two ends of the ground and the north stand. Their exteriors are less handsome than the frontal façade – monuments to the can-do construction that resuscitated the club under Fergus McCann a decade ago. The turnstiles remain a connection with a time further into the past, body-wide slits in the wall that are reminiscent of those in the day when huge, snaking queues would wait to gain entry as the crowds rolled up on momentous European evenings during the Jock Stein era. The massive electronic scoreboard of the Lisbon Lions stand can be seen from as far away as the railway bridge that crosses the River Clyde and leads into Central Station in the city centre and it flickers unerringly on matchday and non-matchday alike, another sign of Celtic's high visibility within Glasgow. On the roof of the north stand flutter the tricolour and the saltire side by side, happy bedfellows within this hub of Celtic innovation and invention. Amidst such surroundings, against such a backdrop, and in front of a cacophonous, deeply partisan support, there are few players who would not feel ready to give their all when trotting out on to the Celtic Park turf.

1

THE STRACHAN STYLE

A pheasant struts majestically across the first-team training pitch at Celtic's spanking new training ground at Lennoxtown. 'It's a big one as well,' Gordon Strachan says as he observes it keenly from the manager's chair in his office on the first floor of the building that houses the gymnasium, players' canteen, changing rooms and administrative offices. The Campsie Hills, constantly changing in hue, different every day, stretch out in the background, spanning the complex and emphasising the benefits to the soul of decamping into such isolated but splendid surroundings. It seems appropriate that Strachan, a man dedicated to quality time working exclusively with players on the training pitch, should have been at the helm of Celtic when they transferred their day-to-day footballing operations to this rural idyll in the autumn of 2007.

Taking the time to observe one of nature's glorious creatures go about its business is also inimical to Strachan; visiting the world's zoos being among his various interests. He is one of the most original and most quirky of the fourteen managers in Celtic's 120-year history, and while his passion for football remains as strong as when he signed for Dundee as a teenager in the early 1970s, it is now tempered with a maturity that allows him to absorb himself in less frenzied pastimes, to drink deep of all that life offers outside the constricted world of football and return refreshed for the fray.

'I can get away from it, oh yes,' Strachan says without hesitation as he sits down to discuss at length the intricacies involved in being manager of Celtic. 'I do it in certain ways. I might not have been able to do it when I first became a manager – I know I couldn't do it at Coventry – but I can get away from it by cutting out the nonsense in my life. That means the fantasy nonsense, media wise. You can end up worrying about what everybody says about you or your team, your players. So if you cut that out, that saves a lot of problems, I assure you. People think, "He's telling a lie. He does read the paper." Not once since I've been here. I've never watched a Scottish football programme. If I've stumbled on one it's when I'm surfing through the television stations at night and I might glance at it for two minutes. So you can take that away. That allows you to get on with reality. I have other things to do. I go to the theatre and cinema, I read books. I've been reading, for the last year or so – and I'm turning into him – Rebus; Ian Rankin. I read a football book about Cowdenbeath by a pastor who supports them, Ron Ferguson; also Bill Bryson, Clive James and recently Stephen Fry's autobiography.'

As one of the most colourful footballers to have been produced by Scotland in recent decades, images of Gordon Strachan are essential to the grand panoply of the country's game. A pawky, determined character, and one possessed of oodles of skill as an attacking midfield player, he made an indelible imprint on the memories of anyone who watched him play: pretending to hurdle the advertising hoardings at the 1986 World Cup, à la Maradona, but stopping with only one leg outstretched on one, as if naturally constricted by his Scottishness in attempted imitation of the lithe and exuberant South American, after scoring a superb goal for Scotland against West Germany; the brutal foul on him by José Batista of Uruguay that led to the fastest dismissal in World Cup history after fifty-five seconds in the same tournament; of Strachan weaving in and out of opposition defences at the 1982 World Cup in Spain and the locals raving about him for days afterwards; pacing out the regulation ten yards at Hampden in a match against Bulgaria and heading straight into a too-close wall of six-foot-plus Bulgarians towering over him threateningly; of him featuring in a midweek match at Queen's Park Rangers, for Leeds United, being dismissed by the referee and Don Howe, the QPR coach, saying afterwards that the harassed official had probably decided he had had just enough of the little red-haired terrier snapping at his heels.

For Celtic supporters, memories of Strachan the player were tinged with less affection. Strachan would be best remembered as a player of scintillating brilliance who took delight in getting right under their skin when with an Aberdeen side that dominated Scottish football in the first half of the 1980s. After a 3-1 victory for the Pittodrie side at Celtic Park in spring 1980, one that did much to tear the title away from the host club and in the direction of Strachan's, he raced towards the Jungle, gleefully teasing them with clenched fists. During a match at Celtic Park later in 1980, a Celtic fan launched himself from the Jungle on to the pitch and grounded Strachan, grabbing the player around the neck, before police or players on either side could intervene. In a game at Pittodrie, after Strachan had performed a somersault on scoring a penalty, another Celtic fan jumped from the crowd and lunged at him. At the 1984 Scottish Cup final, on Strachan's final competitive outing for Aberdeen before leaving for Manchester United, Roy Aitken, the Celtic captain, sent Mark McGhee, the Aberdeen striker, tumbling to the turf shortly before half-time, and with Strachan nipping and narking at Bob Valentine, the referee, for retribution, the official flashed the red card at Aitken, leaving Celtic handicapped for the remainder of a match that Aberdeen won in extra-time.

It meant that Strachan had a bit of a battle on his hands to win acceptance from some members of the Celtic support, and some still continued to do so throughout his opening three years at the club, despite the success that flowed the club's way as a result of his hard work and inspired management of a team under circumstances that would have stretched the skills of any manager.

'It was Dermot [Desmond] who approached me when I saw him at Cheltenham Races,' Strachan says straightforwardly of how he was drawn back to Scotland in 2005 after twenty-one years in England that included working as manager of Coventry City and Southampton after his playing career had drawn to an end. 'I'd never been there before and a guy at Coventry had been asking me to go. Lesley and I were trying everything new, different places, different things, so we thought we'd go along. The box next to ours was heaving, and there was noise and singing and all that, and it so happened it was the Irish box. Eddie Jordan, whom I knew, was in there, Liam Brady, Kevin Moran. I went out for a walk and I met Eddie and Kevin Moran, and they said, "There's a guy next door would like to speak to you; Dermot Desmond's his name." It didn't mean that much to me and when I spoke to him he was speaking about Celtic and said that Martin [O'Neill] might be leaving in the summer, and if that happened would you think about taking the job? That was it. I said to him when we left, "Let's hope Martin's wife gets better," and that we might not see each other for a long time. It didn't work out that way, but in saying that, Martin's wife's a lot better now, which is great, which is fantastic.' At the time of O'Neill's departure in 2005 Geraldine, his wife, was seriously ill.

'I knew the remit,' Strachan says of taking up the reins as Celtic manager in succession to Martin O'Neill. 'We had to reduce the budget, reduce the age of the team. The team was past its peak, and I think everybody agreed with that. Great players, fantastic personalities, but past its peak, and something had to be done. I didn't have a problem because when I was out the game I was quite lucky in that people wanted me to work for them, but it was in similar jobs to what I'd had before, and I wanted to do something different, and this was definitely something different. I was a wee bit surprised at being offered this job because I thought my work would be in England from now on.'

Four months prior to that meeting with Dermot Desmond at Cheltenham, Strachan had been interviewed for the post of Scotland manager. As with anything he tackles, he did not wish to undertake the job without making a real difference. He wanted to try to improve the standing of the national team, then in a state of some stagnation, through root and branch reform at all age levels, not just lead the senior team through a dozen internationals a year. When the Scottish Football Association baulked at such revolutionary reform, Walter Smith, in December 2004, became manager even though Strachan was the popular choice among Scotland supporters. Their loss was undoubtedly Celtic's gain.

'Dermot proposed Gordon,' Peter Lawwell, the chief executive, says. 'He knew Gordon and had met Gordon and proposed Gordon to the board. There were no other candidates and the board liked him when we met him. We painted the whole picture in terms of the financial and economic constraints that we would work under and the plans that we had and he was fine with that. That's what happened with Gordon and he has been fantastic to work with because he knows our objectives and our limits.' Strachan is instinctively aware of which types of players are within his budget and is also happy to allow the mechanics of transfer negotiations to be carried out by Lawwell. 'We agree what we are going to do,' Lawwell says, 'and then I go out and do the deal. The business side and contract negotiations are all done by me.'

The logic behind the appointment of Strachan and the ongoing satisfaction with the job he is doing for the club is elucidated by Desmond, Celtic's major shareholder. 'We didn't want to lose Martin O'Neill, and unfortunate, unforeseen circumstances resulted in Martin going, and we certainly don't want to lose Gordon Strachan. He's a terrific person, a terrific manager, motivator, has done an outstanding job for the club and I think the best of Gordon Strachan is to come. At the same time, as in any business situation, you are always thinking about if you should lose the manager for any particular reason, who should be on your shortlist. So Gordon was on the shortlist when Martin decided that he would have to look after Geraldine.

'Gordon is a very good coach, he is a very balanced individual, he is a very good person, he was an outstanding footballer, he is Scottish. That was important because he didn't need any translator when he went up there . . .' Desmond laughs. 'He understands the culture. It's also an advantage and a disadvantage. People put him in little boxes because he played for Aberdeen and supported Hibernian, but there's no more committed man to Celtic and to winning at Celtic Park than Gordon Strachan. So, really, that's all history. What matters is what's present and in the future, not what's in the past. It was important he understood the passion that existed there – he had played against Celtic and Rangers so he understood the importance of football to Scottish fans. He also plays an attractive form of football. He is a terrific coach and he has a philosophy on football that meets the philosophy that we carry in the Celtic tradition.

'I think the best is yet to come from him because he is formulating, building a team, coaching young players, identifying new players and he is still in transition from an older team that he inherited to a newer team and you just can't do that overnight. You can't do that without suffering a lot of consequences. He's done it in a way that has been pragmatic. He's won Leagues, two Cups, he's resilient, honest and he's prepared to learn and he's prepared to acknowledge when he's made a mistake. He's a very competent individual. In the same way that we were lucky to have Martin, we're equally lucky to have Gordon.'

The severity of Strachan's task at Celtic could not have been brought home to him with any more stunning emphasis than during his first days as manager and in his first competitive fixture with Celtic: the first leg of a Champions League second-round qualifying stage tie played at the Tehelné Pole stadium against Artmedia Bratislava, the Slovakian champions. It was not disrespectful to Artmedia to suggest that they were one of the genuine unknown names in European football: they had undergone no fewer than eleven name changes in their history and had been given their latest moniker only in 2005 itself. Lubomir Moravcik, Celtic's Slovakian great, hooked up with the Celtic party for coffee on the day before the game, the locals were relaxed, charming and friendly, the summer sun shone, and on the night of the match the stadium was dotted with empty seats. It all looked beguilingly like the type of early-season Champions League qualifying tie in eastern Europe that Celtic had sailed through in previous seasons. That was until the game began and Artmedia time and again shimmied through a disorganised Celtic defence and sluggish midfield, slotting five goals without reply, a couple of them quite spectacular, past David Marshall, the unfortunate Celtic goalkeeper, and inflicting on Celtic their worst defeat in European competition. Strachan, by the conclusion of that match, was clearly suffering severely. On the touchline, he looked stunned, shellshocked.

'I could sit here and try and put it into words,' he says of how he felt by the conclusion of that match, 'but you'll never comprehend the hurt I was feeling that night, never comprehend it.' That sensation lasted, he says, 'about a night. We travelled back that night on the plane. In the morning you get yourself up, dust yourself down and go again. That's the way it has to be, I'm afraid.

'I look back at it now and it could easily happen. We had things like the right-back's never met anybody [at Celtic] in his life before. The centre-half is trying to do a deal to get himself to another club that afternoon on the phone. We don't really know the left-back. Chris Sutton got injured, got a broken jaw in the first couple of minutes. When you look back at it now, it was madness; the preparation.' It is the type of reverse that Strachan says could not happen again during his time as manager of Celtic. 'Not with me,' he says. 'It was circumstances. It wasn't luck; there was no bad luck about it. It was just circumstances. The club was changing.

'People don't realise that when I started pre-season training that year I had twelve recognised first-team players because fourteen had moved on. One player came in to see me on the first day and wanted a rise, a huge rise. That was the first thing: a guy that's not played for six months wanted a huge rise. He never said, "Hello, how are you doing, I'm ..." whatever; just demanded a huge wage rise and that could have been us left with possibly eleven recognised players. So there were all these things, and that wasn't bad luck. That was just the state that the club was in at the time. The club had a hangover as well from the Motherwell game [in which Celtic had lost the 2004–05 League title on the final day of the League season]. Everybody was still affected by that. So you had all these things to try and change round. To get through that was a great lesson in management. I couldn't have handled it if it had been my first job in management; that's for sure. Nobody could have.'

Despite a rousing 4-0 victory over Artmedia in the return leg at an uproarious Celtic Park, Celtic were out of European competition for a year, bitter medicine for supporters who had become used to a rich diet of European football every season in the early twenty-first century. Soon, though, a clear Strachan style began to emerge as Celtic eased into the autumn and winter while confined to plain old domestic fare. Not that they were without exoticism: Shunsuke Nakamura, the Japanese midfield player, who arrived from Reggina for £2.5 million after the Artmedia tie, brought craft and ingenuity to the team, as did Maciej 'Magic' Zurawski, a skilled, gold-booted Polish international striker, signed for £2 million from Wisla Krakow. They, together with the darting and elusive Shaun Maloney, being given his first extended run in the team by the new manager, were essential to Strachan's fast-moving passing style, in which when everything was whirring along nicely, players would be interchanging positions and pinging quick passes as the ball was whittled swiftly through midfield and on to the forwards with some fine one-touch football. Artur Boruc, the goalkeeper and another Polish international, who arrived from Legia Warsaw in the summer of 2005, helped solidify the defence, and by the time Celtic completed a sweet November double over Rangers, defeating the Ibrox club in both League Cup and League within a ten-day period, they were top of the Premier League, where they would remain for the rest of the season.

That success was interspersed by another shattering defeat, Celtic going out of the Scottish Cup in the third round after a 2-1 defeat to Clyde at Broadwood, where the eager, young First Division side were 2-0 up by half-time – and aggrieved at refereeing decisions keeping the score down – on a day on which Roy Keane, signed after being released by Manchester United, was making his Celtic debut. Du Wei, a Chinese centre-back on loan to Celtic from Shanghai Shenhua, was also making his first appearance but, after conceding a penalty, which Clyde missed, and a less than impressive overall performance, he was removed from the action at half-time. A late Zurawski goal pegged the score back to 2-1, but Celtic were out of the Cup.

An emotional afternoon at Hampden in March 2006, when the players all wore a number seven on their shorts in tribute to Jimmy Johnstone, who had passed away six days earlier, saw Celtic overwhelm an insipid Dunfermline Athletic side to win 3-0 and lift the League Cup – and the League title was duly tied up at the beginning of April. The key match had taken place on New Year's Day 2006, when, after being 2-0 down away to Heart of Midlothian, their closest challengers that season, Celtic came back to win 3-2 and left Edinburgh with a seven-point lead over Hearts when it had looked earlier in the afternoon as though they might be pegged back to one point. A second successive League title was wrapped up in April 2007, again with several matches remaining, Celtic now able to rely on goals from Jan Vennegoor of Hesselink, a Dutch striker signed for £3.4 million from PSV Eindhoven at the start of the 2006–07 season. The emergence of Aiden McGeady, an inventive, attacking, midfield player, as a regular starter was encouraging compensation for the losses of Stilian Petrov and Shaun Maloney to Aston Villa, now managed by Martin O'Neill, although the hefty sum of £6.5 million for Petrov, a record transfer fee received by Celtic, was more than adequate compensation for the loss of his skills; Celtic over the previous seven years had probably extracted the best from the player.

That 2006–07 season was also distinguished by Celtic reaching the last 16 in the Champions League for the first time since the European Cup was transformed into the new tournament in 1992. A stunning free-kick from Shunsuke Nakamura that curved unerringly into the top right-hand corner of the Manchester United net close to the conclusion of the teams' group game at Celtic Park was enough to defeat the English side and secure a match with Milan that the Italians won through a magnificent goal from Kaka in extra-time.

Nakamura has been synonymous with all that is good about Celtic during Strachan's years at the club, but the club has also done much for the player. 'The football here is quite different to Italian football,' Nakamura says, 'and I feel that all the fans here can judge and understand and know what is good play. They applaud even if I can carry out a sliding tackle and get the ball so I know then that that is a good piece of play. So I feel that all the fans teach me how to play football. I knew nothing at all about Celtic before I came here and I was surprised by the number of supporters all over the world. Also, in Japan the J-League started only about ten years ago, so I feel that there is a big history here and you have former players working in the background and people standing at the door to open the door for you, so that is completely different from a Japanese football club. I was quite surprised by that.'

The heavily physical style of play in Scotland seems unsuited to a light, lithe player such as Nakamura, whose game is based almost entirely on sophisticated nudges, dinks and pinpoint passes, plus inch-perfect free-kicks, but he has had no difficulty in accepting the way the game is played in Scotland and adjusting accordingly. 'Various countries have various types of football,' he says, 'so it doesn't matter. I don't know in which country the really good football is because, for example, in Italy you will have eight people defending and two people attacking and if you win 1-0 they might say it's good football. At the smaller clubs in Italy they will try to get a draw always and will be happy if they do and will say that's really good football, so it's all different. You can't escape the environment you are in and say, "This type of football is not me." You have to adjust – no matter the state of the grounds or their condition. By doing that I feel I can improve as a player so I think that's the important thing. I feel that I am in a really good environment at Celtic. We have a really good manager and good team-mates and supporters and everyone and all of that makes me play well.'

Dunfermline proved more resilient in the 2007 Scottish Cup final than they did in the 2006 League Cup encounter at Hampden, and although they never once threatened the Celtic goal, they kept the champions at bay until, with only five minutes remaining, Jean-Joël Perrier-Doumbé, a twenty-eight-year-old full-back on loan from Stade Rennais, who was making only his fourth appearance for the club, made his way into the Dunfermline penalty area to prod an angled shot past Dorus De Vries, the Dunfermline goalkeeper. Despite scoring a Cup-final goal, Perrier-Doumbé's subsequent experiences underlined the often transitory nature of modern football. That summer he appeared on the point of joining Sheffield United but, when they decided against signing him, he came back to Celtic Park only to be injured against Milan on his second appearance of the season in the Champions League match at Celtic Park in October. Late in that 2007–08 season he could walk through the crowds at Celtic Park minutes before kick-off to take his seat in the stand, almost unrecognised. Admittedly, his hair, close cropped at the time of the 2007 final, had now grown out but he was almost symbolic of a number of players from home and abroad who passed in and out of Celtic Park during Strachan's first three years at the club as the manager strove to construct a winning team while looking to obtain good value from players on free transfers, on loan or from those who had been languishing at big clubs with big squads and in whom the manager hoped he could spark a revival, such as Jiri Jarosik, the Czech, signed from Chelsea for £1 million in 2006 and Thomas Gravesen, a thirty-year-old Dane, brought from Real Madrid for a fee of £2 million the same year or Massimo Donati, signed from Milan for a £2 million fee in the summer of 2007.

'The turnover of players had to be done,' Strachan says, 'and also sometimes you're gambling with players because you're not guaranteed the top, top footballer. If you want the top, top footballer, if you want to buy [Alessandro] Nesta, it costs you twenty million pounds and you are going to pay a hundred grand a week. Then you know you're not going to have a problem. If you're away down at one million pounds or what-ever then you're not really sure you're getting a top, top football player. Sometimes, you're lucky. Sometimes you're not so lucky.

'I'm not fussed,' Strachan adds in relation to whether he would prefer to be spending at Celtic's level or at that of the ever-spiralling millions paid out by the major clubs in Italy and Spain and particularly England, where by 2008 the FA Premier League had become a honeypot and by far the richest in the world. 'I knew my remit when I came here. The club has now, last year and this year, made profits for the first time in I don't know how long, so that has to coincide with what they're doing on the football field. So I must admit I'm proud of what's happened since I've been here.'

It is not difficult, Strachan states, to persuade players from abroad to sign for Celtic, the club. 'No it's not hard,' he says. 'It's hard to sign players for the Scottish Premier League. It's a big difference. Do the real top players want to come and play at places where they're getting four, five thousand; where there are two stands and if you kick the ball away it goes in a field? Do players want to come on pitches that are truly horrific at times? Do players want to come into a League where you can actually be attacking for eighty-five, eighty-nine minutes? Or do they want to get tested more than that? What Celtic can give them is Champions League football, so I think we're all right that way, but on the downside it is playing in the Scottish Premier League.'

If Strachan is content to contend with the trials and triumphs of bargaining and trading for players at such a level, he has shown less tolerance, at times, for the demands placed upon him by the media. At Lennoxtown, of a Friday lunchtime, around a dozen journalists from the Scottish press will attend the Celtic manager's weekly press conference, but even though Strachan is at the heart of this matter, he pays no attention at all to its outcome, not reading the reportage or interpretation put upon his weekly musings. He can be witty with the press, intolerant of them, tetchy and condemnatory of the free-for-all nature of the phone-in, whereby anyone with any agenda can, without balance or restraint or penalty, unleash the most vicious, vitriolic and unbalanced criticisms of a person as prominent in the game as Strachan.

'This is a fantastic job,' Strachan says of being manager of Celtic. 'This is one of the best jobs in the world; the only thing you have to deal with is the stress and the media attention that goes along with it. Working with these players – it's a doddle. You could go out there and do that and enjoy that; all that bit out there,' he says cheerfully motioning towards the training pitch. 'Out there's easy; that's not a problem. The pressure comes when you walk off the coaching field. I get paid for handling the nonsense that comes with it; dealing with the turmoil around the press, whether the press create it or the fans create it; you have to deal with that. It's like being the England manager. They just get paid for the nonsense that goes with it. I don't read the press but I'm not daft. I know what's going on. It's like going up the M6. I know there's a crash and it's horrible but I don't want to look at it. It's the same thing because, if you look at it and see the dismembered body, it gives you the shakes; and it's similar to the media.

'It's easy,' he continues of maintaining his avowed avoidance of reading the newspapers. 'I have to meet them every Friday, but you have to deal with the fallout from that if you're walking about in public. Some [people in the street] can be abusive, some can be sneaky, some can abuse you when they're fifty yards away, when they've walked by you and smiled at you. So you've all that to deal with, and that I can do no problem now. I can't change the people of Glasgow's mentality. If you're rude, you're rude. It's not everyone in Glasgow but there is an aggressive side to Glasgow that they're in your face and that's not talking about Rangers supporters or anybody's supporters. I'm talking about the person themselves because I can't blame Rangers supporters for somebody behaving badly in front of me. The person I blame is the person and not the club that they support and vice versa with our supporters.'

That frenzied background contrasts with a deliberately low-key approach by Strachan to the business of football; he consistently plays everything down and focuses on each game as it comes along without being led into speculation over the long-term ramifications of each result. This is no bluff, purely for public consumption. He tends to play his strongest team in each League game, even if a midweek meeting with a seriously large European club is on the agenda for the following midweek, and this strong focus on the game in hand is echoed by Shunsuke Nakamura, the Japan midfield player, who has blended entertainment with effectiveness to a sublime degree.

'All I'm thinking about is to win each game,' Nakamura says, 'so I'm only thinking about winning the next game rather than winning the title. I don't really think about winning the title because we've got good midfield players in this team and it's really hard to maintain a position in midfield here so I just want to give 100 per cent in each game to keep that position. Being named player of the year in 2007 [when he was awarded that honour by both his fellow players and the football writers] was the highlight of my time here because I tried to maintain my level of performance throughout the year and was really concentrating so I was doing my best. When I managed to get those awards that was a great thing because it suggested that I had managed to do that.'

It was the chance to joust with the giants of European football that helped draw Strachan to Celtic Park, and it is an aspect of his time at the club that has not disappointed him; his record in European competition since the defeat in Bratislava more than standing comparison with any Celtic manager other than Jock Stein. He considers the highlights of his stint at Celtic to have been all of the European nights, with the match against Spartak Moscow in August 2007 to be the most pleasing evening of all. That match, at Celtic Park, the second leg of a Champions League third-round qualifying tie, ended 1-1 and 2-2 on aggregate, Celtic winning on penalties. 'It had everything,' Strachan says, 'and I mean everything. It had great football, chances, good players, penalty misses, a penalty shootout; it had everything. I thought that as a game, that was as good a one as we have played in. We've had performances that have been better all round for us against a team where you think, yes, that was good, that was excellent; Benfica when we beat them 3-0, I thought we were terrific that night, but as a spectacle I thought that game with Spartak Moscow was the best.' It presaged a second successive qualification from the group stage of the tournament – Strachan had taken the club into virgin territory with the first – and a knockout tie against Barcelona, in which exquisite goals from Vennegoor of Hesselink and Barry Robson, an excellent £1-million signing from Dundee United in January 2008, had Celtic 2-1 ahead in the first leg at Celtic Park before defensive errors let Barcelona back in to win 3-2 on the night; with the Catalan side concluding the tie as 4-2 victors on aggregate after the second leg.

The ambition of going one round further with the richest of Europe's clubs is, Strachan feels, a realistic one, but he holds out little hope of Celtic pushing on further in a tournament that is now heavily weighted towards Europe's three wealthiest Leagues, in England, Italy and Spain. 'If you look at the people who are through to these positions,' Strachan says of the final stages of the Champions League, 'they've spent fortunes, absolute fortunes, and that's the way it's going to stay. I think we can get to the quarter-finals, but after that, the mega teams come into play.'

Even after that exceptional stretch of results in Europe, the type of tittle-tattle and gossip that surrounds the position of Celtic manager had one of its full spates in the early spring of 2008 when, after a 1-0 home defeat to Motherwell on the first Saturday in April, Celtic sat six points behind Rangers, who had two games in hand and topped the SPL. Speculation abounded about Strachan's position, but he guided his team masterfully through their remaining fixtures, holding their nerve through two superb Old Firm victories – 2-1 and 3-2 – at Celtic Park, in which the team ethic that has prevailed under Strachan was at its strongest and in which they played some terrifically fast, joined-up football. Those matches also saw a real blossoming of Nakamura in applying his skills in the heat of an Old Firm derby. In the first of the two matches, at Celtic Park in mid-April, he eased on to the ball midway inside the Rangers half and used the outside of his left boot to whack in a shot that went swirling past the leaping Allan McGregor in the Rangers goal and reignited Celtic's quest for the League championship title. Later in the game, Nakamura worked his way into the box and angled himself away from several tight challengers before leaning back and sending in a diagonal left-footed shot that was en route to the top left-hand corner of the Rangers goal until Carlos Cuellar reached up to handle, earning a straight red card. Scott McDonald missed the resultant penalty, but the absence of Cuellar was vital when Jan Vennegoor of Hesselink took advantage of the lack of cover in Rangers' central defence to head the winner in the final minute.

It gave the lie to the suggestion that had been hanging over Nakamura that he would too often be rendered ineffective by the robust nature of the Old Firm encounter. 'Everywhere has its derby matches,' Nakamura says, 'but I was quite surprised by the Celtic and Rangers rivalry. In Italy I was with a club called Reggina, and they have a club called Messina, where Massimo Donati used to be, so that was the derby match. When I was with Yokohama Marinos we had a derby match as well. It is a really good thing for everyone. When we played against Rangers when I first came, especially in away games, we tended to put long balls in even though we could link up; through trying to go forward we looked to use long balls, but I feel that that trend is changing, and we are trying to link up and not just use long balls. So I am improving.'

The link-up play to which Nakamura refers owed much to Strachan opting, during the run-in, to go with Paul Hartley and Barry Robson in central midfield – two hard-working, clever, battling, unfussy Scots who could tackle hard and drive forward effectively or screw the ball out to the more artistically inclined wide midfield players: Nakamura and Aiden McGeady. It gave the midfield a nice balance. Gary Caldwell grew greatly as a centre-back during that final stretch, and in Andreas Hinkel, a German international defender signed from Sevilla in January 2008, Celtic had another typical Strachan full-back who would augment attacks by pushing high up the flank. Hinkel is another continental who came to Celtic for a reasonable fee because he desperately needed a change of scenery – in his case, after failing to dislodge Daniel Alves, the Brazilian widely regarded as the finest right-back in the world, from his place in the Sevilla team. In signing Hinkel, Celtic, even with their modest purchasing power, gained a thinking player with international caps and Champions League experience; another indicator of the ongoing process whereby standards are continually being increased incrementally at Strachan's Celtic.

'At youth level I played in every position – striker, midfielder, defender,' Hinkel says, describing the versatility that goes with his experience, 'and I think because of that I have a special style in my position and because of that I am not just a defender – I like to attack, to go forward. I think football is a game in which you need everything. It's not just tactics or that you need to be fast: you need pace, technique, heading, you need so many things. You can't do something with doping or something like that. Maybe you can run fast but there are so many other things – you have to play with the head, there is offside, you can be clever and that's what football is. I think there are many parts and you need many things.'

On through their remaining fixtures of the 2007–08 season Celtic travelled, winning determinedly to claw back ground on a Rangers team that was taxed through having to fulfil a testing series of fixtures that built up steadily for them through their success in reaching the UEFA Cup final. Still, Celtic had to win each game to sustain the pressure and they did so against resolute top six sides Aberdeen, Motherwell and Hibernian, taking them into their final match, at Tannadice, against Dundee United, in which they played some fine football before a Vennegoor of Hesselink header, the only goal of the game, sealed the win and the title on a night on which Rangers were simultaneously losing to Aberdeen at Pittodrie. It meant that Celtic finished three points clear of their old rivals. This had also been a season tinged with sadness because of the deaths of Phil O'Donnell, the former Celtic player, from a heart attack whilst playing for Motherwell against Dundee United in late December and of Tommy Burns, the Celtic first-team coach, from cancer, in mid-May. As Vennegoor of Hesselink celebrated his seventy-second-minute goal, he stretched an arm to the sky and gazed upwards, a moment redolent with meaning following Burns' funeral two days previously. Twenty-seven years earlier, at the same ground and end, a speared strike from Tommy Burns had been the goal that secured the 1980–81 League title for Celtic.

This was, says Strachan, the most satisfying title victory of his three with Celtic, 'because I've had to change the team. It re-jigged itself and it's a young team, and because it's a young team we still have to develop physically and mentally, and we've developed those players. The first two seasons were incredibly satisfying as well. It's hard to put into words, but as the Celtic manager you can make millions happy, and I mean millions. You can also make them depressed, and that's where the stress comes from as well: so many people are relying on you to produce a good team to make them happy, around the world. I think at times we've shown some really, really good stuff this year.

'I do all the coaching but also I like to think I man-manage. I like to get close to my players. I'm not aloof with them. I enjoy players' company and I enjoy laughing. I enjoy being close to them and I enjoy seeing them improve because basically that's my job: to make people better. Where that takes me I'm not bothered; I'm not really fussed because I can live life like that . . . from week to week, month to month. I've not got a major plan for myself. It's better that way – it's more exciting. I consider the future in terms of planning as the team manager, yes you've got to do that, but as per my future, no . . .'

It is one of the stranger facets of Celtic that none of those who have been manager at the club have gone on to surpass their achievements at Celtic Park. Strachan at Celtic has shown the potential to buck that trend through making steady, determined progress at the club under testing circumstances. Whatever the future holds, this determined, sharp, clever, spiky man has already shown himself one of Celtic's most accomplished managers through attaining three successive titles, a feat that only Willie Maley and Jock Stein, managerial giants both, had achieved before him. That alone must convince Celtic supporters that he is now indisputably a fine Celtic man.

2
BOOTS AND SUITS

It must have been disconcerting for casual telephone callers to Celtic Park during the 1960s to discover when the receiver was lifted that the person answering was none other than Jock Stein. The manager would occasionally pick up the telephone inside the office at Celtic Park and deal efficiently with the inquiry. Celtic was, in the 1960s and 1970s, when Stein was at the helm, and indeed even up until the mid-1990s, run along the lines of a small business – albeit one with a big impact on thousands of people – and as such it required only a modest level of staffing to deal with its administration. For home matches, fans would turn up, pay cash at the turnstiles and remove themselves until they were required to furnish the terraces again. That income through the turnstiles was almost the entire basis of the club's earnings.

It is different now. More than half of Celtic's £75 million turnover in the 2006–07 season, for example, was accrued from non-matchday revenue, principally from broadcasting and commercial activities, such as sponsorship and merchandising. With success on the pitch now linked inextricably to financial health off it – especially since the Bosman ruling of 1995, which allowed players to take their talents to the highest bidder without a transfer fee at the conclusion of their contract – the activities and personalities of the directors of football clubs have come under scrutiny to a greater extent than ever before. This has become even more pronounced at Celtic with the transformation of the club into a public limited company in 1995, backed by a share issue oversubscribed by fans eager to own a piece of their football club. Fans discuss, as earnestly as they talk of the football itself, the estimated wages of players, potential transfer fees, the value of incoming or outgoing players.

This is no idle chatter – the fans may not, on the whole, understand the fine detail of a balance sheet, but the effect of financial planning in the boardroom is crystal-clear in its effect on the pitch, such as in the type of success achieved by Celtic from the mid-2000s onwards under Gordon Strachan. The financial model employed in the Martin O'Neill era of 2000–05, whereby players were lured from the FA Premier League with lavish salaries comparable to those available down south, has been abandoned – after Celtic's debt had soared to more than £20 million – for a new one that requires more invention and ingenuity on the part of the coaches and management and that makes Celtic a more secure and self-sustaining institution.

It was on a freezing cold night in Donetsk, in the Ukraine, in 2004, that Celtic's second footballing and financial phase of the twenty-first century was set in motion. Brian Quinn, chairman at that time, recalls a meeting he had that night with Dermot Desmond that was the catalyst for change. 'Dermot and I sat one evening in Donetsk in Ukraine. We had just been beaten 3-0, and this was late 2004, and it wasn't going well, and we knew it wasn't going well. We just weren't doing anything commercially or financially that was sustainable – we were losing the money as we made it. So we sat that evening – Peter Lawwell sat with us too – and we agreed that we had to build a different business model. We had to organise ourselves and sustain ourselves to such a degree that we sustained ourselves year-in, year-out; in other words you don't lose money, you're trying to break even every year at worst – that was the concept that informed the business plan. Peter then went to work with the people on the finance side and the football side and fleshed it out and produced a business plan. It's a lot of work, but you find in business that once you've got a clear goal then things begin to fall into place.

'Season ticket money is forty-five to fifty per cent of your total revenues, and you're selling season tickets because you're successful in football, so you have then to say, "What kind of football squad are we going to have?" We needed a football squad that was consistent with the objective we had set ourselves of breaking even, which takes you to your cost base of the football squad. It was too high: it was running at over sixty per cent of total revenues, which was above the arbitrary, although it is arbitrary, waterline, so we said, "Let's change that." And how do we change the way we pay our players? How do we structure the payments? How do we structure the contracts? So we set ourselves a benchmark of the ratio of wages to turnover, and when it came to the question of how we pay our players, we realised that a part of the trouble was that we were paying people a high basic wage and then the bonuses came on top of that. So we changed the proportions and we said, "We aim now to pay players much bigger bonuses, which are paid only in the event of success, plus a lower basic wage." So the core of your business plan is a lower basic wage, a fixed amount, and then your bonuses on top of that.

'We negotiated contracts with Nike that improved the product and the revenue; we did a contract with T-Mobile, Carling, MBNA, CRE8, the publishing company, so contracts such as those gave us a reliable source of income. You should run your affairs so that you can pay players' wages out of your normal income. That all came out of that meeting in Donetsk, and we've turned it round. There's no doubt it's worked.'

The result in Donetsk, on a night when Celtic were pulverised by the Ukrainian team Shakhtar's attacking power, was entirely relevant to the change of course. 'Oh yes,' Quinn confirms. 'We said, "We can't go on like this." We were effectively facing an exit from the Champions League – I think we were in fourth place that year – in the group stage and so there was no more to come, and we had spent all this money, through large fixed-wage costs, and we had to meet those wage costs through domestic foot-ball. So the two were quite closely tied together: the performance on the field and the decision to adopt a different business model. We said to ourselves that the team was not good enough: the players were ageing, the players had been there for quite a while, they were being paid huge sums of money.'

As Quinn speaks, energetically and engagingly, of performing this intricate piece of emergency financial surgery on the club he has loved since growing up in straitened circumstances in Govan, the process sounds irresistibly logical and inevitable but it was one that would have enor-mous ramifications inside the club. In September 2003 Martin O'Neill stated that Celtic would have to, as he put it, 'get used to life in the slow lane' if they failed to replace the players he had brought in – for huge transfer fees and on enormous wages and, as it turned out, with little future transfer potential – with others of similar ilk. So the new policy was always likely to be a difficult one for O'Neill, especially when he was coping with the discovery of his wife's illness.

'We were as responsible as Martin for running up that very high wage bill, that very high fixed cost,' Quinn states, 'but by the same token we also had the responsibility of changing our mind about that. After the Donetsk game we said to Martin, "Look, we need to change the way things are done here because we're just eating into our capital all the time and the team is getting older," and he said, "OK, we'll do it." Then he came back some months later and said, "I'm sorry – I can't do it. I've got to go up and down [to England] to see Geraldine and I've got to be supportive of my two girls" – they were a very close family. He said, "I can't do that and make the kind of change you're talking about."'

There had always appeared a sense with O'Neill that the board were there to provide ready cash for him as and when he required it – Brian Clough, his manager at Nottingham Forest and a major influence on his managerial style, had a certain disdain for those who inhabit the boardroom, once describing as 'hooligans' the ninety-two Football League chairmen. 'When I arrived here,' Peter Lawwell, the Celtic chief executive, says as he recalls a humorous exchange after joining Celtic in 2003, 'when I first met Martin I said, "Correct me if I'm wrong, but the football people have little regard for the guys in suits?" He said, "Yes, you're right." I think we understood each other's jobs and what we had to do.

'There had been 7.8 million pounds lost in the Seville year, when we got to the UEFA Cup final. The model was bust. Maybe, there was a degree of frustration, maybe, because Martin loved the club, he loved being here, but he couldn't take it on to the next level because the financial model didn't work in Scotland.'

O'Neill's subsequent parting of the ways with Celtic in 2005 ushered in the arrival of Gordon Strachan, a different type of manager and one attuned to the new, more financially stringent era at Celtic, a manager prepared to work hard at coaching and improving the players at his disposal and willing to make the most of whatever funds might be available to him. 'Gordon's terrific,' Quinn says. 'He says, "You tell me what I've got and I'll take it from there." He doesn't make a fuss, he doesn't argue, he does the best he can with the resources given to him. Martin was quite different. Martin was always trying to persuade us to loosen up a bit.

'And Martin would be on the training ground twice a week: the coaching was done by John Robertson and Steve Walford. Gordon is much happier being on the pitch with small numbers of players or working with them individually; he doesn't want anything to do with transfer negotiations. That's down to Peter and I think that's healthy.'

Once Quinn and his colleagues had opted to rein in the spending in late 2004, some supporters quickly became agitated at the change in direction culminating, in April 2005, in Quinn being booed by a number of them at a home match with Heart of Midlothian. 'They thought that I was being parsimonious,' he says, 'if not downright mean, with the transfer budget. That was the nadir, the Hearts game in 2005, when I had to go on to the pitch and accept a plaque brought by the Villarreal Celtic Supporters' Club. They didn't speak any English and they were very excited because they were a new club. I said jokingly beforehand to Peter Lawwell, "Do you fancy doing this, Peter?" Peter said, "You must be joking." So he faded into the background, and I went on to the field and I was roundly booed. People were saying to me, "It was a small minority." It wasn't a small minority. I was there. Not everybody was booing, I wouldn't claim that for a moment, but it wasn't just a wee section stuck up in a corner – it was general disaffection . . . I had planned to say something, but when the guy handed me the microphone I didn't trust myself – I would have made things worse if I had said what was in my mind, which would have been something like, "Well, these people have come here today to receive a typical welcome from Celtic Football Club . . . is this what you call a typical welcome?" I thought, "I won't do that," and just handed the microphone back to the MC and walked off.

'Fans don't seem to realise you had no choice in the matter. If you hadn't done it, you'd have put the club back in the condition it was in 1993, 1994, before Fergus [McCann] took over. At AGMs we had people haranguing me and saying, "You've got no ambition at all. You've got no imagination," those kinds of things. We could have gone on borrowing from the bank, asking for a relaxation of the borrowing limits, but where would that have got you? You'd have just been in a deeper hole. My view was that you draw a line, you hold that line. You get a lot of objection and criticism from fans, a lot of letters from fans, abusing, and sometimes not nice stuff.

'I won't say I'm vindicated, that sounds as though I'm trying to score points, but the policy that we adopted and the way in which I pursued the policy, has been shown to be reasonable, and since then, of course, we've done well in football competitions, both domestic and European. People have said to me, "You were right. We recognise that what you were trying to do was difficult."'

The pragmatism of the second half of the noughties contrasts severely with the high-spending five years in which O'Neill was at the helm. Fees of around £6 million brought players such as John Hartson, Neil Lennon and Chris Sutton to Celtic Park, although it did seem as though Celtic were occasionally paying over the odds in certain instances. This revamping of the team, together with the arrival of a manager from England's top flight, helped raise Celtic's profile to some degree in England, as did a host of friendly matches that the club undertook to play across England in the first couple of years of the twenty-first century. All of this tied in neatly with a push from Celtic to break into the Premiership, where the available revenues and the competition would provide Celtic with greater scope for expansion.

'Football was going through a difficult time in England,' Quinn says of those early twenty-first-century years. 'The value of TV contracts was dropping – and there was a worry south of the border that the game needed an injection of freshness, and they thought Celtic and Rangers together could provide that freshness. We never said we would walk away from Scottish football – I always said that if we were to go and play in the English Premier League or something like the English Premier League, we would have to pass on some of the benefits of that to other Scottish clubs. We were not going to walk away and abandon Scottish football.

'If somebody comes to you from a very senior club,' Quinn adds, warming to his theme that Celtic were being encouraged in their efforts to join the FA Premier League by the most major clubs in England, 'and they've got clout and they can bring things about . . . When I became chairman in 2000 and for quite a bit before that, there was a lot of encouragement given to me personally by senior people in English football. Some were more guarded than others; some were saying, "It's time for a change," others, "Well, if it can be done, let's see what the proposal is, let's see what the TV contract might be worth and what it might mean for attendances." It was in prospect.'

Two things then changed the minds of the English clubs. 'They began to come out of the slump,' Quinn says. 'They began to get TV contracts that were lifting the cloud of uncertainty over them. The second thing was that a lot of their friends, in the English Premier League and below, saw what it meant for them and were saying, no way are we going to give this up. There is quite a lot of loyalty in football, and I much preferred the chairmen who said, "Look, Brian, Celtic is a great club, but I'm not going to ditch my friends just as soon as something more attractive comes along." I thought that was a better thing to hear than someone who doesn't want to say the things that are in the back of his mind.

'So it receded, and then there was a real possibility we could join the Championship. ITV Digital had failed completely [going into administration in 2002], and ITV tore up the contract, which created a real crisis in the Football League, and we were approached by people who asked us if we would bring Rangers with us, and Rangers were every bit as enthusiastic as we were. I have to tell you that because since then there have been suggestions that we were the ones making the pace and that Rangers were going along with it.' The Championship clubs proposed at this stage that the Old Firm clubs guarantee that they would remain in the Championship for a minimum period of three years, regardless of whether or not they finished in the promotion places to the Premier League. Celtic and Rangers refused to agree to that.

'It went to the point,' Quinn continues, 'that there was a vote to be taken – there was never a vote taken in the Premier League, notwithstanding what you read in the papers, but there was in the Championship. The problem was that the proposal for Celtic and Rangers to join was leaked: it appeared on BBC Television on the Saturday night and in the *Observer* newspaper on the Sunday morning, and the people who opposed it mobilised themselves during the weekend, got hold of the FA, and the FA made a statement saying that they would not agree to any change that would see the Football League admit Scottish teams. There were two or three people who were instrumental in that – I don't think I should mention their names – but they blocked it, effectively, and the whole thing was withdrawn. They had a vote, in the Championship, and the vote was against us coming in because of the FA's opposition. We got very close, very close indeed.

'A lot depends on public perception – if there had been wild applause at this, if the newspapers had said, "What a great idea! A new structure to football" ... Remember, the game south of the border was in a bad way at the time; if there had been strong public support for it, who knows what the FA would have done, but before it could be put in the public domain, it was quashed. We've given up for the present [trying to get into the Premiership] because there's no prospect of it. If there's no prospect of something then you're just wasting energy trying to work at it.'

It is not inevitable that Celtic and Rangers will eventually leave Scottish

League football. It is an idea that has been in circulation since the first day of organised League football in Britain, and 120 years later it has yet to come to pass. When the Football League was instituted in 1888, composed entirely of clubs from northern England and the Midlands, by William McGregor, a Scotsman from Perth, he deliberately did not attach the appendage 'English' to its title; it was always his hope that the Scottish clubs would eventually join their English counterparts in an expanded version of his new enterprise. If Glasgow's big two ever do join the Premiership it will, to an extent, be closing the circle.

With that particular avenue of pleasure blocked off for the moment, Celtic and Rangers must remain in what many of their followers see as the cul-de-sac of Scottish football. A European League is another suggestion that gets kicked around now and then, and in early 2008 Arsène Wenger, the manager of Arsenal, was moved to state that a European Super League, 'will still go ahead ... the European super League will happen – under UEFA's banner'. Celtic will be primed for such a development.

'Our responsibility here as a board of directors, as custodians of the club,' Peter Lawwell, the chief executive, says, 'is to grow this club. We're ambitious to take this club to its ultimate. So that's where you start. You say, "How can we make Celtic the biggest club in the world?" We are wholly committed to creating a world-class football club. If that means at some point there is an opportunity to play in a League that gives us those media values and exposure that will allow us to get nearer that, then clearly we will be interested.

'We would never leave Scottish football. We will always be a proud Scottish club. If we are playing in a European League we will be doing so as a proud Scottish club and the benefits that that will bring to Scotland will, I think, be sporting, social, economic. Celtic and Rangers and Celtic, I think, particularly internationally, is a product – a Scottish product – that can be exported and can create wealth and sporting success. Some of that wealth would be re-invested in Scotland through transfer fees, through Celtic's participation in the Scottish Cup, through Celtic potentially having another team participating in the Scottish League.

'I think the only way we can take Celtic to its full potential is to play in an environment more regularly than we are in the Champions League. That's not necessarily a bad thing for Scotland – I would hope that the Scottish nation would take pride in Scottish clubs playing at this higher level.

'I think if the market is allowed to go unchecked or to prevail, then inevitably the strong will get stronger and the weak will get weaker, and there could well be a migration of the stronger clubs away to do something themselves. They could well do it under UEFA, but there will be a polarisation; through time, potentially, people will get tired of only having Madrid or Barcelona winning the title in Spain; or Milan, Inter and Juve only winning it in Italy; or one of the top four in England. Only one club outside the big five nations has won the Champions League [in the twenty-first century] so if, through time, the major clubs in Europe see a tiredness or a lack of competition or a repetitiveness about the Champions League, and media values come back on that, they will look at the possibility of change.

'Through time, nothing stays the same, and the important thing for us as a club is to be at that table; not to be left behind. That's what I think we've created here; through our participation in Europe, from Martin's first year, is to have re-established Celtic as a European force. Milan and other big clubs love coming here, how we run the club, they love the stadium, they love the fans. They see Celtic as a big, well-run club, like it and would like to be part of anything we do. If we ever had an opportunity to play in a market like England, Italy or Spain, the restricting factors on our club would disappear and through time we would be as big as anybody in the world because the club has a global reach.'

The Champions League has regularly produced welcome revenue for Celtic since 2001, but for Celtic the unfair aspect of the competition is that the distribution of money is based on the population of the country in which the participating club is based, and for a club based in Scotland that is a serious drawback. Since the late 1990s, when four clubs from the three strongest nations were allowed entry to the Champions League, the grip held on the competition by the major nations has become ever tighter: Italy, Spain and England have dominated so much that they have all had a Champions League final contested by two of their own clubs. Sparring in the Champions League is enjoyable for Celtic, but with every passing year the odds become more heavily stacked against the club making serious progress in the competition. Given such conditions, their advancement to the last sixteen in 2007 and 2008 was remarkable and a testimony to all who created the strategy, bracing as it has made life at times, that helped bring about that achievement.

3

FAIR SHARES

Dublin in the early twenty-first century is a city of immigrants, not emigrants. Ireland's new-found wealth has attracted a host of young and eager workers from around the world but predominantly, it seems, from eastern Europe, and they appear to staff almost exclusively every service outlet from the airport to O'Connell Street. If this is one characteristic of the change in Ireland from being one of Europe's poorest countries to one of its richest, Dermot Desmond is another. A self-made man, the financier is now a billionaire, one of the world's richest people, and the major shareholder in Celtic Football Club. The club that was founded by Irish immigrants, forced to leave home for economic reasons, is for the first time influenced heavily by an Irishman who was able to make his fortune without uprooting himself from his homeland.

As a schoolboy, Desmond was captivated by Celtic's victory in the 1967 European Cup final but did not travel outside Ireland until he was nineteen and did not have the wherewithal to make visits to Celtic Park during his late teens and early twenties. 'I was lucky to find a bus fare at that stage,' he quips, 'never mind get the boat fare together to go to Glasgow.' During an era in which the money sloshing around football, particularly in England, has attracted some garish owners, Desmond has an understated and restrained presence at Celtic. If he were to be played in a movie, it would perhaps be by Donald Sutherland, whom to some degree he resembles, both in looks and in seasoned, easy charm, and as he sits down to discuss Celtic, in his lustrous office overlooking the River Liffey, he does so in a soft Irish brogue and with a dry wit lightens the talk of the serious business of Celtic.

'It was in '94 that an Irish financial person approached me and told me they were doing a fundraising in Scotland for Celtic,' Desmond says as he recalls his first involvement with the club at the time of Fergus McCann's first share issue, 'and they were trying to raise – this is terrible, but forgive me if I can't remember whether it was two million or four million – but whatever amount it was that they were trying to raise, I felt it was insufficient. I said what I'd do was that I'd under-write the whole lot and subscribe for half of it because I felt that if Celtic was being recapitalised that we should remove the financial risk there. Rather than putting up funds to meet the short-term needs, we should also meet the medium-term needs of the club. I felt, looking at the balance sheet and the profit and loss projections, that it needed more money. I was buying maybe about fifteen or sixteen per cent of the shares at the time. That made me the second-biggest shareholder after Fergus.

'I don't believe in burning pound notes or Euro notes or whatever the case is. To me, if you start that approach, you'll go bust pretty quickly. It doesn't make any sense and what you're doing is deferring a problem: you're propping up something that doesn't have a foundation and if you're propping up something in such a way it'll soon collapse.

'The way I looked upon it is I wanted to help Celtic because I'm a Celtic supporter. Second of all, I wanted to help it in a meaningful way. I didn't want to step into a temporary breach and then find out that it was going to be bigger at a later stage. Thirdly, I didn't have the view that it would give me a return per se, that it would give me a dividend return or give me capital gain. I looked upon it that, if we did the right thing with the Celtic brand, then over time it would be more valuable. That meant it had to be more valuable on the pitch because, with a football club, if it's not more valuable on the pitch, it's not more valuable on the balance sheet or on the profit and loss statement.

'I think about my investment in Celtic as an emotional investment rather than a pure financial investment. I'm not looking to sell my shares. I'm not looking to generate a return on my shares but I'm looking to participate with the other directors and the rest of the management in making sure that the club is well run and professionally run in the interests of all the shareholders.

'I think about Celtic as something that hopefully I and my family will have for a long time. People have suggested that I make a bid for the club and take it private. I'm not saying that would never happen but I'm not interested in that because I think Celtic Football Club is a family; it's not about one family, it's about the greater diaspora of Celtic supporters, and therefore I think it's better to have a broader level of ownership. It just so happens that I have been the person who has been putting in the most money and that's why I've ended up with the most shares, but I don't want to own Celtic completely and I don't really want to be a dominant shareholder there. I am dominant [because of the level of shareholding] but I want it to be a diversified shareholding base.'

Although he has investments in institutions around the world, Desmond views his shareholding in Celtic as being entirely different from them. 'The other financial investments give a rate of return,' he says, 'over a period of time, whether that's three, four, five, six, seven, ten years, and they're measured with regard to a plan for return on capital. With Celtic, I don't measure the return on Celtic, that's not on the horizon, even though the club has become more valuable, is well run, has an excellent chief executive and management team, a lot of good initiatives from the new training ground to the excellent infrastructure at Celtic Park, and we have a strategic and development programme that we will continue to implement. So I'm very comfortable that it gets more valuable every year. I often look at a major match of Celtic and I say to myself, "I'd give quite a considerable amount of money if we could just score a goal or win this match or whatever the case is." So, in terms of financial logic, it is not met . . . Celtic is unique; a unique brand; a unique football club; and you just can't recreate that. It has taken well over a century to build and that is a much longer time than I have to give to creating a new brand . . .'

With major English clubs – Manchester United, Liverpool and Chelsea among them – having been taken under new, American and Russian, ownership in the second half of the noughties and, in the case of Chelsea particularly, having had their fortunes transformed by having had around £600 million made available to it by Roman Abramovich, its owner, Celtic would appear one of the most attractive British clubs for an external bid for ownership. Desmond does not rule out entirely the possibility of a takeover but stresses that it would have to be consistent with the para-meters he sets for the club.

'If somebody came along,' Desmond says, 'and said that they were going to do something absolutely amazing, outstanding for Celtic and that they wanted to buy my shareholding, and I felt that they could do a much better job than me or that they would be a better shareholder for the club than me, then I would certainly release my shares; if that person was to come along. I don't hold my shares in Celtic for self-interest. But there would have to be evidence that they were going to do that because my interest is in the greater good of Celtic. I'd like to be of the belief that I would sell my shareholding to somebody who would do a better job and who would have the resources to do something amazing for Celtic. I would impose conditions – as far as I'm concerned talk is cheap, and people would have to do something in a tangible way. If they were theoretically going to buy my shareholding they would be buying it on the basis that they did bring major added value and they would have to commit to that.'

A prominent aspect of Desmond's time as major shareholder has been his efforts at obtaining entry for the club to a bigger League; one more conducive than the Scottish Premier League to a club that can command gates of almost 60,000. This took the form of the thwarted attempts during the early 2000s of seeking entry to the FA Premier League and then the Championship in England whilst in more recent years there has been suggestion of a European League.

'I think in time,' Desmond says, 'the world is going to become a more competitive place, and people are going to want more competitive foot-ball, and Celtic is one of the top clubs in Europe. The independent fan would prefer to see Celtic play the top clubs in England than [to see those top English clubs play] some of the minnows. If you look at TV it has evolved over the last sixteen, seventeen years. You know, we're in a mismatch situation, and that's with respect to all the other clubs in Scotland, because our budgets are so much bigger than those. That's not of my making, that's just the historical situation. It's tough for the Gretnas and the Falkirks and these other clubs whose managers have limited budgets and who have to compete against the budgets of Celtic and Rangers.

'I don't get frustrated [at Celtic playing in Scottish football], it's not frustration, but if you said what's the right thing for Celtic to do and what's in the best interests of the Celtic fans and the club, I'd say I think we should be playing in a more competitive League. I think we'd be a bigger football club and a better football club and I think that's a position that's rightfully Celtic's.

'The number of people I've spoken to about this; in the [FA] Premier League and in Europe, I would bore you. You wouldn't have enough paper to write down the number of people with whom I've had conversations on this. I should really get a masters degree on Celtic entering European football ... The monies I've spent on hiring special experts and legal opinion – I make myself tired thinking about it ... I think a lot of people are supportive of Celtic's position and Celtic's ambitions and also understand the constraints that Celtic have in Scotland. At the same time, Celtic is first and foremost a Scottish club. It's not treachery or treason or anything else. This is waving the Scottish flag and the Celtic flag in a bigger arena and I think that's the ambition of all clubs.'

Desmond's awareness of the importance of the Irish input into Celtic's history helps to imbue him with his sense of responsibility towards the club. 'I feel I hold a trust, because of the history of the thing, for the people here in Ireland and for all followers of Celtic, and that's a responsibility. That's where the roots came from. It's like when the Irish go to America or anywhere else, they are Irish-Americans but they are American probably first of all, from second or third generations, and they're proud of their tradition, and I think the same applies here: the Celtic supporters are Scottish and they are proud of their tradition. I think it's also a club that has been for the underclass and part of the history in developing it has been in showing that we can develop, we can compete and we can play a type of football that makes people stand up and acknowledge that it's a stylish way and we can support in a way that nobody else can support. So I think those two things – on the field and our support – make the club different, and that's a tradition that I want to support and I want to maintain, and it's a responsibility to past generations of Celtic supporters, because you carry the baton, you carry the torch, because they had the enthusiasm to support the club. Their aspirations have to be maintained and improved. That's what we want to do: we want to improve our support, we want to improve our football, we want to improve our facilities and we want to improve our reputation.'

During the mid-noughties, when Celtic were in severe debt, there was a clamour in some quarters for Dermot Desmond to simply erase the club's debt, at a stroke, by dipping into his personal resources. Some supporters would get quite outraged that he did not do so, suggesting that, if they were in his position, with his wealth, they would not hesitate to act in such a manner. It is a matter on which Desmond has strong opinions.

'I get all that, right, about splashing the cash or putting my hand in the pocket or giving more money to the manager,' Desmond says. 'For those people, I really have no respect and no regard whatsoever. They make absolutely no sense to me. I don't think they could even read a balance sheet or a profit-and-loss statement. Personally, I find them demotivating to me and the rest of the board because what we are trying to do is to try and build the club. Nobody has the divine right for success. It's not a formula in football; it's an art, picking a manager; and then it's an art finding players; and it's an art then of putting the right team together. So it's an imprecise art, and when people just say that you can solve all problems by throwing cash at it, it's absolutely stupid. It's an insult to my intelligence if people think that I would throw cash at it, willy-nilly. So those people, if they've got lots of money and they want to throw cash at it, we'll take it any time from them . . .'

Dermot Desmond's riches and his base in Dublin keeps him at arm's length from the influence of and pressure from the Scottish press; a strength that means that he will not be rushed into panicky decisions, regarding managers, for example, that afflict those running some other clubs. His sons attend matches alongside him and take a firm interest in Celtic's fortunes and in the club's heritage and Irish roots, and, although he has inculcated in them the responsibility that he feels towards the club, he is keen to stress that he is not creating a dynasty.

'I'm not in the business of creating dynasties,' Desmond says. 'Each of them will do their own thing, which is important to them. I don't want to create a dynasty for them to follow in my footsteps or anything like that. I think what they do recognise is that they have a responsibility to the club, outside of financial performance, outside of investment; a responsibility to see that the club is not jeopardised through any actions that they may take, through selling shares on my demise, let's say, or not supporting the club in a professional or proper manner.'

As might be expected of an accomplished, cosmopolitan businessman who has achieved success on a global scale, Desmond has no truck with sectarianism. 'First of all, we're not sectarian,' Desmond says of Celtic. 'There's no bigotry inside the club. We leave politics at the door. We're playing football. There's a history of where people come from, and every-body's entitled to history and singing historical songs as long as they conform to all those things. It depends on the level of the songs. We're living in an era, in Ireland, in Northern Ireland, in Scotland, in England; we're living in a period of globalisation, so I think the songs should reflect that – they should reflect your history but they shouldn't be antagonistic to certain parts of the community. Let's move forward, not backwards.

'The only concern I have going forward is that we retain people of the calibre of Peter Lawwell and Gordon Strachan and that we continue to improve our structure, improve our personnel, improve our playing staff. I think that we've made good progress and will continue to have hiccups along the way. I think we're brave enough and strong enough that in diffi-cult times we'll stick together and won't panic and won't have any witch hunts. I think part of what makes Celtic strong is that when times are tough we are united, not divided, and that's the way we are going forward as a club, so we're going to consolidate in challenging times and be crit-ical of ourselves in good times. We can learn more about ourselves in good times than we can learn in bad times.'

4

MATCH MAKERS

The footballers of the 1890s and early 1900s pose for us in stiff team portraits that reflect the seeming formality of the age. Smiling, it would appear, was frowned upon for these pictures, and the players of Celtic are no exception as they stare stern-faced towards the camera in their clean, starched kit; a still life for the photographer. Action images from that era are next to non-existent, and so these posed portraits serve as the pictorial record of the era and the impression given by them is of a collection of footballers always on their Sunday-best behaviour. Yet the players of that era could be as irreverent and boisterous as any of their successors, and that includes Sandy 'Duke' McMahon, who starred with Celtic throughout the 1890s and into the early years of the twentieth century.

Shortly after the New Year's Day defeat by Glasgow Rangers in 1901, Celtic decamped from Glasgow to Rothesay for a spot of training prior to facing Rangers again, in their next match, a Scottish Cup tie on 12 January. Jimmy Quinn, a shy and apprehensive twenty-two-year-old from Croy, who had signed for the club on provisional forms on New Year's Eve, joined his new team-mates in Rothesay, and on the players' first night on the Isle of Bute they invited him to join them in a 'refreshment room', where 'a few drinks were a-going', and as the evening progressed merrily, Quinn insisted he stand his round. McMahon, Johnny Campbell, the centre-forward, and other well-established Celtic players would not hear of it and insisted he could buy them a drink some other time.

Quinn happened to be sharing a room with John Divers, Campbell and McMahon, and as they conversed late into the evening, McMahon, seemingly overcome by tiredness, took to his bed and appeared to drift off to sleep. After half an hour, he began to mutter. 'Wheesht!' said Campbell to the others. 'Sandy's speaking in his sleep.' McMahon, in a low voice, began to complain in a variety of different, offended ways about what he saw as Quinn's disgraceful failure to buy a round, and eventually Quinn, shaking him awake, said, 'Sandy, I'm surprised to hear you talk that way in your sleep.' Next morning, Quinn, who had taken the incident to heart, stressed to McMahon his eagerness and willingness to buy his new friends a drink, then and there, if possible, and only then did the Duke let the new boy in on the joke.

Impishness and irreverence, on and off the field, has often been an essential component in those players to whom Celtic's supporters have taken a shine. Defenders are admired for their stolid, solid virtues but at Celtic they are there to provide a platform for the purveyors of style, and Sandy McMahon was the first Celt to embody that craved-for creativity. Robert Findlay, a Celtic team-mate in the early 1900s, described McMahon as 'the cleverest player I have ever seen', and McMahon epitomised the earliest era in Celtic's history. Quinn would later take up the baton of being Celtic's talisman and through each stage of the club's history a series of outstanding players, one after the other, have epitomised each era.

'There is an attacking style of play that is characteristic of Celtic,' Billy Connolly says. 'We have never been a clean-sheet team, although we have had our moments of getting a clean sheet when needed, but our great victories were always achieved by attacking – we were never a defensive type of team. We were always defending by attacking. I'm so proud and happy about it – attack is the best defence. Defensive teams bore me rigid and they can discuss the tactical merits for as long as they like; it is still a deadly form of football.'

Not that it has always been a matter of ease for the more artistic talents at Celtic Park to parade their talents and nor do the supporters prize excellence in the finer arts to the exclusivity of other aspects of the game. Some Celtic supporters can at times be excessively hard on those with more refined skills: as Aiden McGeady developed as a first-team player in the mid-2000s, the stands at Celtic Park were full of critics ready to scream condemnation at the slight teenager whenever he tried a trick and it didn't come off or he held on to the ball for, in their opinion, too long. Perhaps such a brittle atmosphere helps the more determined among the artists, firing them on even more to prove themselves, although a little more patience from supporters in such situations might be no bad thing.

Sandy McMahon would doubtlessly have agreed. Celtic's leading goalscorer during the 1890s, his thirty goals in the twenty-three League and Scottish Cup fixtures in the 1893–94 season made him the first Celtic player to get more than a goal a game over a season of competitive fixtures. Few players in Celtic's subsequent history would match his feat and hit 30 or more goals, while also making fewer appearances than their total goals tally: Jimmy McColl in 1915–16; Jimmy McGrory in every season from 1926–27 to 1930–31 and also in 1935–36; Joe McBride in 1966–67 and Henrik Larsson in 2000–01. Jimmy Quinn, another great Celtic goalscorer, went very close, notching 30 goals in 31 games during the 1906–07 season.

An inside-left who stood at six feet in height and weighed in at more than twelve stones, McMahon had an unusually elongated appearance for a forward in those times of small, stocky Scottish ball-players; his droopy moustache, slightly melancholic expression, stately bearing and aristocratic nickname only added to the impression of an individual out of kilter with the whirl of football. He was nicknamed after the Duke de Magenta, Patrice de Mac-Mahon, a president of the Third Republic of France in the late 1870s, whose ancestor Patrick MacMahon, of Dooradoyle, Limerick, had left Ireland after the family's lands were confiscated under the Treaty of Limerick. McMahon left behind any hint of aristocratic languor once inside the penalty area, where he showed a swiftness and alacrity – particularly in the air – at sharp odds with his overall body language. He was top scorer when Celtic won their first two Scottish League titles, in 1892–93 and 1893–94, helped them to two other championships and scored vital goals in the victorious Scottish Cup finals against Queen's Park in 1892, Rangers in 1899 and Queen's Park again in 1900. McMahon was also indispensable in constructing goals for others, most particularly his partner on the wing; the deft, darting Johnny Campbell.

'Tall, almost ungainly in appearance,' Willie Maley wrote, in summation of McMahon's qualities, 'Sandy depended on footwork and the deceptive swerve to beat an opponent. Of speed he had little. His judgement of the flight of the ball when free- or corner-kicks were being taken was simply marvellous.' The first Celtic manager appeared as bamboozled as everyone else by the contrast between McMahon's body language and his prowess on the pitch. 'To look at McMahon as he came out to play,' Maley said, 'one would have been pardoned for thinking he was an absolute misfit. His big, ungainly form, his toothless upper jaw – Sandy wouldn't have an artificial set – his enormous feet. How could this fellow play? Then would come the great surprise. McMahon on the ball was a treat. Standing almost six feet, with back slightly bent and arms spread out like wings, away he would go, weaving and swerving his way through the defence and cooperating with Johnny Campbell with the precision of a machine.' Maley's description makes McMahon sound more pterodactyl than predator.

There was no such confusion between appearance and effect when Jimmy Quinn came bustling into the Celtic team. Quinn was a very different type of footballer to McMahon but one to whom team-mates and the terraces would soon fall in thrall. A knee ligament injury to Findlay, the winger, in 1901 had provided Quinn with his chance to make his mark and in 1909, with Quinn at the height of his powers as a centre-forward, Findlay was generous in his praise for his burly successor. 'Were James Quinn in an English club he would be unquestionably the greatest goal-getter in the League.' Johnnie May, of Glasgow Rangers, who had experience of the game in England and Scotland, suggested that, as the emphasis in English football was on wingers rather than on inside-forwards, as in Scotland, Quinn would have enjoyed even greater success down south, owing to a greater number of crosses being made from wingers hitting the goal-line.

The player of whom they spoke was a battering ram with brains, a powerful player who gave it out and got it back, but back in 1901 it had been as an outside-left that he had taken the place of Findlay, and for the next three years Quinn had dotted around the forward line, featuring on both wings and sporadically at centre-forward until his hat-trick in the 1904 Scottish Cup final fixed him in a position in which he would become legendary, gathering goals unerringly and finishing as Celtic's top scorer in every one of the ten seasons from 1903–04 to 1912–13, a momentous achievement at a time when the battles between defenders and forwards reflected the heavy industrial background of the burgeoning game. Quinn, who worked as a miner before and after his stint with Celtic, would often be carrying an injury into a game. Even then when he retaliated there was often outrage among onlookers, but, as one observer suggested, 'All the men that Jimmy Quinn killed are still alive.'

Maley's assessment of Quinn was, 'Jimmy did not develop quickly, being shy. A strong, robust player, possessed of a wonderful pair of shoulders which he used to great advantage and more fairly than he was given credit for, Quinn was subject to a lot of abuse in his fourteen years' service. He seldom objected to anything done to himself but deeply resented ill-treatment to any of his colleagues less able to stand up to it, and this brought trouble on his head, which was often more harsh than circumstances demanded.'

So modest was Quinn and so strong his shyness that Maley had found it difficult to persuade the player to join Celtic in the first place. On visiting him and his family for tea at his home in Croy in late 1900, Maley was aware that Quinn, who was playing for Smithston Albion, was under surveillance by a number of major clubs, including Manchester City, Rangers and Sunderland. Despite Maley's attempts at persuasion, Quinn was adamant that he did not wish to leave Junior football, so Maley, full of tea but unwilling to leave without a result, made one final push. Telling Quinn that he needed proof to show his directors that he had pursued Quinn's signature, he persuaded the player to sign a registration form with Celtic but promised he would not hand it over to the Scottish Football Association without Quinn's permission. That, at least, ensured that if Quinn did decide to turn senior, his only destination would be Celtic Park; and that is how it turned out.

His paucity of caps for Scotland was to become a recurring theme among followers of Celtic, who felt their representatives were not given a fair chance by the SFA whom they believed at certain times during the twentieth century were not favourable towards Celtic. The Celtic Football Guide of 1946–47, when reflecting on Quinn's recent death, commented, 'It may be said that the SFA only chose him when forced by the pressure of public clamour and when they had a particularly stubborn English defence to batter through.' Seven goals in only eleven games for the national team between 1905 and 1912 suggest they may have had a point.

A radically different type of player took over from Quinn as the favourite of the Celtic support. 'If you put that wee thing on the park, you'll be done for manslaughter, so you will,' Quinn himself said to Willie Maley, on first setting eyes on Patsy Gallacher, who stood five feet five inches tall and weighed just over nine stones. A man with his own inventory of trickery, Gallacher would score 196 goals in 464 appearances for Celtic from the inside-forward position, and his impact on Celtic is encapsulated in the goal that he scored against Dundee in the 1925 Scottish Cup final: after dribbling half the length of the field, Gallacher, when blocked by a defender, was said to have improvised extraordinarily by jamming the ball between his feet and somersaulting into the net to make it 1-1, providing the platform for Jimmy McGrory to score a late winning goal with a diving header.

'Patsy was unique – until I saw Jimmy Johnstone I'd never seen a player like him,' James Farrell recalled of a player he watched perform in the 1920s. 'He was a very strong dribbler, very determined and if necessary he didn't mess around – if you fouled him, he fouled back. My father saw him in that Cup final against Dundee – and the story of how he scored that goal was true.'

Such was Gallacher's star status at Celtic Park that Maley would allow him to decide how much training he wished to do; Gallacher's light build ensured he did not pick up weight. He was also a canny negotiator with Maley when it came to establishing his pay. He had even held Celtic at arm's length when they first requested him to sign. 'I had just completed about three years out of a five-year apprenticeship as a shipwright, so there was nothing doing,' he said later, on the subject of delaying joining the club until 1911, when he was eighteen and a half.

That goal against Dundee was also the equivalent of Gallacher's farewell bow to the club's supporters. He would play just one League game the following season – a 5-1 defeat at Airdrieonians – missing most of the 1925–26 League title-winning campaign because of injury and leaving for Falkirk after the Celtic directors, sceptical about his fitness, had offered him only the basic wage for the following season. Maley had actually announced that Gallacher had retired during the 1926 close season only for the player to assure him face to face that he had not and, after declining Celtic's unsatisfactory terms, demanding a transfer, which he got, leaving for Brockville for a £1,500 fee and playing on for a further six years.

The team's new, totemic presence following Gallacher's departure was Jimmy McGrory, who had made his debut in Gallacher's inside-forward shirt in January 1923, while Gallacher was injured. During the 1925–26 season, McGrory had perhaps helped to persuade Maley that he no longer needed Gallacher, as McGrory scored forty-two goals in forty-three League and Cup matches. Far from that being a one-off freakish feat, it was the type of tally that Celtic supporters would come to expect of him as he lit up the often dim and dark years from the mid-1920s to the mid-1930s. 'My old man used to say, no matter who came up, "Ah, he couldn't lace Jimmy McGrory's boots,"' recalls Tony Roper. 'When they were choosing the Greatest Ever Celt, I voted for Jimmy McGrory. When you consider McGrory's record, of the amount of goals he scored, how hard it was to score, the kind of equipment that they had, the strength he needed, scoring in not as many games, blatantly biased refereeing . . .'

Johnny Paton recalls, with a professional's practised eye, McGrory the player. With his grandfather, Paton enjoyed a centre-stand seat at Celtic Park in the 1930s, and from their place the ten-year-old Johnny could watch the greatest goalscorer in the club's history. 'Jimmy McGrory was all strength and muscle,' Paton says, 'and he had a great bull neck. If he had been a boxer, you couldn't have knocked him out. He was the hardest header of a ball I ever saw – along with Tommy Lawton of Chelsea – and with a great shot in his right boot, but he was not a good technical player, not a player to push and pass and give and go. He was built like a light-heavyweight boxer, he was quite heavily built, so he wouldn't do much running.'

During McGrory's final year as a player at Celtic, Jackie Watters, then a teenager on the club's books, saw McGrory at even closer quarters. 'He was great with his head. He was a very, very big man. I don't think he worked on his physique – I think he was just naturally well built. In the goalmouth, he was very, very strong.'

Whatever shortcomings he may have shown in other aspects of the game, scoring goals was something at which he excelled more greatly than any other player in Celtic's history. The facts do, in his case, speak for themselves with eloquence: 468 goals in 445 Scottish League and Cup matches and almost another 100 goals altogether in other first-team matches. It is a strike rate that any centre-forward in the world would envy. It helped McGrory that, during those decades, teams were purpose-built to go forward, to get goals, to win by scoring more than the opposition. As the spearhead of a five-man forward line, he had two wingers drilled to sling over crosses continually for the centre-forward, but McGrory still needed to display bravery combined with supreme accuracy and power with head and boot to gather his goals. McGrory said of Jimmy Quinn, his illustrious predecessor, 'It was my ambition to try and follow in his footsteps. All I can say is that I tried very hard.'

The arrival of Jimmy Delaney, the winger, in the Celtic team during the mid-1930s provided McGrory with an enormous boost just as his career was drawing to its conclusion. McGrory had been Celtic's top scorer for nine seasons until interrupted in that run by Frank O'Donnell, who scored twenty-seven goals to McGrory's eighteen in the 1933–34 season. With Delaney in the side, McGrory was leading goalscorer in the next three seasons and Celtic started winning the big trophies regularly again. For the first time in more than a decade they could claim with justification that they were again the best team in Scotland.

The sight of Delaney swerving and swaying down the wing energised the Celtic support but he was a new type of winger, unconventional and innovative for the time. The winger's duty in the old five-man forward line was to hug the touchline and, on receipt of the ball, make like an electric hare for the goal-line and cross the ball for the centre-forward to thrust off attendant defenders and smack a header into the net. Delaney might do that – he always centred a great ball – or he might just as easily cut inside, diagonally, into the penalty area, causing mayhem, like a fox in a chicken coop, amongst defenders surprised at this radical departure from the norm. Delaney could then clip a short and accurate pass to a fellow forward or just as easily shoot for goal himself. He was fast, direct, and when he did score goals, they were great ones.

'My great inspiration was Jimmy Delaney,' Johnny Paton says of his fellow flank man, who habitually operated on the right. 'He was an extremely fit fellow, only because he trained as hard in the gym as any boxer. I used to try and copy that: floor exercises, abdominal exercises, using the bench, running round the park . . . I had watched him during the thirties when he was at his best and he carried Celtic on his back during the war. Delaney was an inspiration for Celtic every week during the war years, but as a player he didn't go around shouting and telling you what was what; he simply did it. When I started in the first team, they moved Delaney to centre-forward, and I went to outside-right on the team sheet. It took me about three weeks to say hello to him; that's how much in awe of him I was.

'He was one of the greatest wingers the game has ever seen and he doesn't get the credit due to him for that. I had a career with eleven clubs in fifteen years, including Arsenal, Chelsea, Manchester City and football in America, and in spite of playing for all those clubs I never met another player with the inspiration Delaney could convey on a football pitch. I played with Tommy Lawton, Stan Mortensen and Stanley Matthews, and they didn't inspire me in the same way as Jimmy Delaney did. I still put Jimmy Delaney as number one of them all.'

Two of the great Hampden occasions occurred in the spring of 1937 and Jimmy Delaney was the common factor in both. A match between Scotland and England on 17 April drew a record crowd for an international match in Europe of 149,547, and Delaney was instrumental in Scotland winning 3-1. One week later, the record crowd for a European club match was set – 146,433 – when Celtic faced Aberdeen in the Scottish Cup final, and, with Delaney on the right wing, Celtic were inspired to a 2-1 victory. Delaney was still only twenty-two, but within two years his career was under severe threat of curtailment. During a routine League match with Arbroath in April 1939, Delaney's arm was trodden on by Attilio Becchi, the Arbroath player, and the resultant injury was so severe that at one stage amputation appeared a possibility. It took Delaney two years to recover, but when he did he proved the outstanding talent in a Celtic team depleted by the absence of key players during the war years.

'Jimmy was so quiet and docile,' Rolando Ugolini remembers, 'very religious, a very good Catholic, was Jimmy. He wouldn't say boo to a cat but he could play. He crossed the ball hard, and that's the way to cross a ball. If you lob a ball it's easy for a goalkeeper. If you cross hard it's there before you [the goalkeeper] can get out.'

There would be no great reward bestowed upon Delaney with the cessation of hostilities in Europe. He asked in 1945 for his pay to be increased and consequently found himself dropped from the first team before Matt Busby, newly installed as Manchester United manager, swiftly signed him. He went on to make almost 200 appearances for the Old Trafford club. He was forty-two when he finally retired, with Elgin City, having also gathered an Irish Cup-winner's medal with Derry City at the age of forty, giving him a unique treble, of Scottish, English and Irish Cup-winners' medals.

By the time Delaney was winning that medal as an exported talent in Ireland, the Celtic supporters were savouring the talents of an imported Irish forward whose audacious approach to the game would brighten the 1950s, a decade in which Celtic were inconsistent and unpredictable and which as such seemed perfectly suited to accommodate the mercurial Charles Patrick Tully. Delaney had been the perfect professional: a self-motivated trainer, a tremendous sportsman, self-effacing and modest. Tully was in almost every respect the opposite.

The years that followed the Second World War may have been barren in terms of producing trophies, but they were fertile ones in terms of the club fielding entertainers. 'I saw John McPhail picking a handkerchief out of his sleeve,' Billy Connolly recalls of the centre-forward, 'and blowing his nose. I got to know him years later and would see him in Glasgow, and he was a complete gentleman. They were the players I always loved. I also saw Charlie Tully sitting on the ball long before anyone else in Britain did it.' Tully, signed in June 1948 from Belfast Celtic, brought humour and pawkiness to a club that needed a pick-me-up that summer, just weeks after it had come close to suffering relegation.

'I was pretty friendly with Charlie,' Jimmy Walsh, a former Celtic team-mate, says. 'He was a one-off character. I've never met anybody like him. He was on his own. When we played Rangers I used to wonder why, when he went to pick up the ball at the Rangers end, there was a big roar. This happened in two or three games, and eventually I determined that I would find out why this was. So I went up alongside him in one game and found that he was blessing himself – he was also killing himself laughing at the same time. Charlie liked a drink – in fact he liked two drinks.'

Not all of Tully's team-mates were appreciative of him. Alec Boden, the centre-half, a professional who prided himself on his physical fitness, was less than impressed by Tully's scrawny, non-muscular appearance and by his tendency to go AWOL. 'On three occasions,' Boden says, 'he agreed with me to attend supporters' functions and he didn't turn up. He was letting everybody down. Tully lived in Dennistoun – we would send a taxi driver to collect him from his house to take him to a function in the Vale of Leven or wherever, but he wouldn't be at home.' On tour in the USA in 1951, Boden recalls Tully would go missing for a couple of days at a time. 'If he had been due to go somewhere on behalf of the club it didn't bother him, didn't get to him. He'd just make an excuse.

'I was pally with Joe Baillie and John McGrory, and we didn't think he was a player at all – he was all for himself. When he got the ball he would try to show off, and that was no good when you were wanting to win.' On visits to tea-rooms on away trips, Rolando Ugolini would be first in the queue to pay for the teas; Charlie would be at the back. 'You wouldn't hear Tully talking about football,' Boden says, 'or what had happened in a game or about plans or what opponents had done. He had his own clique.

'For a genuine player who was continually good, Bertie Peacock was always a trier and always fit. He could build up quite a bit as a wing-half and he wasn't a bad wee tackler in his own box. He was a different sort of Irishman, a genuine guy, not touching the booze. You knew that if he declared himself unfit he really did have an injury. The thing is, fans see the eye-catching stuff but they don't really know what other players are trying to do, attempting.'

A bundle of frustration for some of his fellow professionals Tully may have been, but his mercurial moments became legendary. At Falkirk, in a Scottish Cup third-round tie in February 1953, Tully took a corner-kick and sent it directly into the net. An impressive feat but one seemingly spoiled by the referee insisting that the kick be retaken because the ball had not been placed correctly. Tully simply repeated the trick, again curling the ball into the goal. 'That was good,' Boden accepts. Walsh almost tarnished the myth. 'I nearly got a touch on it,' he says of Tully's retaken corner; fortunately he did not, and the ball rushed untouched on its way into the net. Another of Tully's favourites was to take a throw-in in an advanced attacking position and, if a defender had turned away from him, direct the ball off the unsuspecting opponent's back to win a corner-kick. Needless to say, his impudence did not always go down well: a Heart of Midlothian player once spat at him for sitting on the ball.

The patronage of Robert Kelly would have ensured that Tully was a regular in the team, but the winger's cheek would even be extended in the direction of the venerable chairman. After a visit to the players from Robert Kelly, Charlie Tully would mimic the chairman's mannerisms, imper-sonating him, most particularly his withered arm and the way he held it.

'I remember we went to Ireland to play a five-a-side tournament,' Johnny Paton says as he recollects his first contact with Tully, his future Celtic team-mate, 'and we played in Belfast and met Belfast Celtic in the final. John McPhail, Willie Miller, Pat McAuley, Tommy Bogan were in our team, and we used to win a lot of the five-a-sides they had at Sports Days such as the one at Ibrox. Tully played and was good – dangerous to us – so that's how I think they brought Charlie Tully in to Celtic.

'He was my inside-forward, and Charlie and I used to train together, so I got to know him quite well. Celtic bought a house – I think it was the first house they bought for a player. When I came back from Chelsea they bought a three-bedroomed semi in Clarkston, because I had a wife and baby, and when I got transferred to Brentford, Charlie moved into it. He was full of jokes and pranks and he had a bag of tricks; he was very tricky on the ball. He wasn't a very good player to play with – very much an individualist. An inside-forward's role was to make your winger play: the inside-forward was supposed to be the brains and the winger the guy with the speed, but Charlie was very much an individualist, so it was difficult to combine with him, and we used to blame each other when things broke down.

'He was still an exceptional player in the sense that he did the unexpected, and that's very rare in a football player. Most players, you can predict what they can do. His advantages by far outweighed his disadvantages – it gave you confidence when he was on the pitch that he would turn up with something exceptional but he didn't compare with Gerry McAloon, my partner during the war. Charlie, though, was an icon to the fans: some players take a trick with the fans, and the Celtic fans went crazy for him. Maybe he could have trained better, but there wasn't much of him. There was no fat on him. People like big Jimmy Mallan would come back after the summer a stone overweight and had to sweat it out by putting on three jumpers and running round the track, but that wouldn't have been right for Charlie. He would have left his strength on the training ground. It depends what type you are and how heavy you should be when it comes to training.

'Basically, Charlie was a very nice fellow, an exceptionally nice fellow. Yes, he liked a drink, but a lot of the boys liked a drink. I never had an argument with him, although he had a bit of a fiery temper, which you need as a football player to look after yourself. Every team in those days had a "killer", whose job was to get stuck into the other team's best players, so if you were a forward you had to be able to look after yourself.'

A newly professional approach characterised Jock Stein's arrival at Celtic in 1965, but there was still room for manoeuvre for the maverick members of his side. 'Bertie Auld and Jimmy Johnstone always had a great degree of humour about them,' Billy Connolly says, 'and that is unusual in football or any athletic activity, because they generally demand a seriousness of purpose. If you went to a game with Jimmy or met him before a game he would do a trick for you on the pitch, and you'd feel privileged that he'd done that for you – not only that, he'd turn and wave at you.'

The inevitable focus that was placed on Johnstone's mesmeric dribbling tends to detract from other, equally impressive aspects of his game.
He was immensely brave in an era in which defenders could sometimes
quite freely clog away repeatedly at skilled opponents before suffering
punishment from a referee. Johnstone would often take the full force of
a blow but, rather than take a tumble, would do all he could to regain
his balance and go for the ball again or, if the 'tackle' was so severe that
it forced him to fall, he would, under instruction from Jock Stein, rise
from the turf swiftly and ask for the ball again immediately from the free-
kick so that he could again take on the opponent who had fouled him,
knowing that the defender would be more cautious, in fear of a booking,
now that he had attracted the referee's attention.

The deftness and lightness of movement that was characteristic of
Johnstone also tends to draw focus away from how tough he was. On
meeting him in person the observer could not help but be struck that,
although five feet five inches in height, here was a muscular, tightly bound
individual, not slight or fragile in any way, and a player who possessed
great stamina. 'He was a good player to play with,' Charlie Gallagher
says, 'because he was the "out" ball all the time, just as Nakamura is
now. Jinky just used to dribble – he was great on the ball. If you were
playing on the right-hand side he would be the first player you would
look towards. He was one of the guys that everybody liked. Not everyone
in a dressing room gets on with everybody else, that's to be expected,
but Jimmy was a guy who was liked by everyone. He was a happy-go-
lucky, harum-scarum, carefree, great wee man.'

Another surprising aspect of Johnstone and his game was his exceptional ability in the air. One of Celtic's earliest efforts on goal in the 1967
European Cup final was a header from Johnstone that had Giuliano Sarti
in the Internazionale goal extended full-length to twist and tip the ball
up and over from under his crossbar. At Heart of Midlothian in the spring
of 1968, as Celtic chased precious points in the hunt for a third successive championship, John Hughes pelted over a pacy cross from wide on
the left, and there was Jinky climbing at the back post to send an exquisite header past Jim Cruickshank to open the scoring and send Celtic on
their way to a vital win.

'Jimmy was just a terrific wee guy,' John Divers, a team-mate in the
first half of the 1960s, says. 'I heard about him before I saw him. I heard
people at Celtic Park talk about this wee fellow, a ball boy, who comes

to training in the evening. "You want to see him – he's absolutely magic." "You want to see him – he's fantastic." "Who's that?" "Johnstone his name is; Jimmy Johnstone. He's a brilliant wee player." Then, when I saw him play, I thought, "Oh my God. This guy is so different." Then he would come and play with the first team in training, and you used to think, "Don't leave him out here up against me – he'll make a mess of me." He was just a genius. Just as importantly, as a man, Jimmy Johnstone was one of the most modest people that I've come across; such a nice man, a friendly person, not in the least big-headed.

'One person, from another club, whose name I won't give to save them embarrassment, in a game against Jimmy said, in the dressing room, at half-time, "Tell me, did he do a 360 – a complete circle – in front of me?" To which, and this is even funnier, the reply was, "I think he did." Not only was the person he did it to not sure he did it, but neither were the people who were watching. The only person I saw like Jimmy was Garrincha [the mercurial Brazil winger who inspired their World Cup wins in 1958 and 1962]. I could see things in Jimmy in him; fabulous full stop.'

The pleasure of playing alongside Johnstone during the early 1970s fell to Danny McGrain, whose role was to support the winger from the right-back position. 'In my first game I must have overlapped wee Jimmy about twenty-five times,' he says, 'and I think I must have got the ball three times. Wee Jimmy was so unpredictable to play with, and that's what made him a great player, because if I had been able to predict what he was going to do, other people in other teams would have been able to do so too. You just couldn't tie him down. He had great feet, a great brain and great bravery on the park.'

On leaving Celtic, Johnstone had his problems and at Sheffield United and Dundee, despite being still relatively young, he failed to spark before meandering through a succession of unsatisfying jobs in those hazy, post-football years. 'The person that was really most helpful to him was Jock,' John Clark says, 'whom Jimmy adored. Maybe Jimmy needed, when he went away, another figure like that; not to correct him but just for a bit of guidance.' His final five years were spent combating motor neurone disease and Jimmy died in March 2006 at the horribly young age of sixty-one. 'I think he put on a brave face for people, but he must have been really down inside, and you can understand it as well,' John Clark suggests. 'He single-handedly raised the profile of motor neurone disease,' Jim Craig says, 'and never complained at all; I never ever heard him complain.

He was terrific. You couldn't have asked for a braver wee man; just as he was brave when he was playing.'

Johnstone's closest friend at Celtic was Bobby Lennox, whose fast and direct spurts of speed on the left wing complemented Johnstone's intricacies on the right. 'He was the funniest wee guy in the world,' Lennox says. 'He was great company, he was a really good chanter, a wee prankster, and he had his moments of pessimism when things weren't going for him. He was all round a great guy to know and to be around. We always had great fun. I've got a million funny memories of him. He loved a laugh. If you could get him started laughing, you'd be there all night.

'At training, if he came up to you, he'd drop his shoulder, and you knew he was going to go the other way, and he'd do it anyway. He'd go past you as if you weren't there. When you went on to the park, you always thought, "Jimmy will do something for us today." He scored loads of goals. I think big Jock loved him because of his bravery, because of his ability, because of his cheekiness. He never ever showed favouritism but everybody had a soft spot for the wee man. If anything was going to go wrong, Jimmy would be the one who would get caught, but I'm quite sure the gaffer would be laughing at it sometimes. He became as strong as an ox – he really worked hard in training.'

Johnstone was a great admirer of the next Celtic icon: Kenny Dalglish. 'He got a lot of goals that maybe lesser people who weren't as brave as him wouldn't have got,' Johnstone said. 'He took some horrific kicks from boys hitting him from the back and what not. You should have seen his legs sometimes. He was always in the right place at the right time and he always knew where he was going, even when he had his back to goal, throwing people. He hadn't tremendous pace, he never took the ball up to anybody and went past them but he was always in the box, turning, dummying, playing his wee one-twos.'

Another of the Lisbon Lions, Jim Craig, provided the young Dalglish with a lift in his car to and from Celtic Park during Dalglish's early days at Celtic. 'Kenny had astonishing confidence,' Craig remembers. 'Off the park he could be not very communicative but on the park he'd be shouting to Bertie Auld, "What kind of pass is that?" He would hold the ball up and wait for people running. He was a really great player.'

In his style, Dalglish was a player of a type never previously seen at Celtic Park. A regular goalscorer but not a centre-forward, he would prove elusive to opposing central defenders by lying deep, in front of midfield, where he could find space to work with the ball or ping shots goalwards. His silky style also disguised the amount of effort he would put into a match – Kenny would always be red-faced through working constantly. 'Some of his positioning was good,' Alec Boden, a Celtic coach and scout, says of seeing Dalglish playing youth football in Glasgow prior to joining Celtic, 'and he was very exuberant. He wanted to get into the game. He wasn't standing there watching. He had something different.'

It was also evident to Bobby Lennox on initial sighting of Dalglish that he was possessed of a special talent. Lennox states that Dalglish's innate ability was clear 'from the first training session – and I know that's very, very easy to say, looking back, but Kenny joined in the pre-season training sessions and he was wanting the ball, he would make a pass, he would have a shot at goal, and you'd say, "This boy's not scared of anything." He had just started training with us, after we had just won the European Cup, and he was right at home. You knew Kenny was going to be a player – he had terrific ability. Kenny liked a laugh and a bit of humour and a singsong. See, if you are in a dressing room and you can't laugh at your-self, you'll never make it. You've got to be able to have a laugh, give a laugh and take a laugh, and he was witty.'

Paul Wilson, a winger with Celtic, has fond recollections of him and Kenny and Danny McGrain, fellow Celtic trainees, at the age of fifteen or sixteen, using the summer weeks to build up fitness before the season started by going for runs two or three times a week behind Milngavie to the Khyber Pass and Loch Abie. 'I met Kenny when he was thirteen, and he's never changed,' Wilson says. 'Kenny was always outstanding – even in schools and amateur football. He was very clever – he was actually a better defender than he was a striker. You couldn't get by him if he was playing as a defender when we were training as reserve team players. He just read everything; he'd take the ball off you. He just knew what you were going to do. He was about the same size as me but he was strong. You could never get him off the ball.

'We knew each other's play. If I was taking the ball up the line, I didn't even need to look up; I knew he was going to be there. You knew that he would take people far post but that if you hit the ball near post he was going to come on to it. I remember one game at Parkhead, Danny back-headed it on to me, and the ball was actually almost going out, after I had run flat-out to get it and I reached it just before it went dead. I must have run about fifty yards to get there and I leathered it from the corner flag without looking up and Kenny got on the end of it. You just knew he was going to be there.'

McGrain, Dalglish's closest friend at Celtic, suggests that tremendous as he was for Celtic, leaving the club for Liverpool, the European champions, was of great benefit to him. 'He was double the player he was when he was up here,' McGrain says. 'That's not disrespectful to the players up here – the game is just different down there, and at Liverpool, through winning so many European trophies and championships, they were proved to be the best team of their time. Kenny made them do that. We had Aberdeen and Dundee United pushing us, a wee bit, and Rangers always as our main rivals for the title, but down south, I take it, every week you play in a big, big game. So that's going to make you a better player. Kenny had all the ingredients to do what he did and took it with both hands and both feet and conquered it.

'Kenny had such a quick brain. He had two great feet, could score with headers. He would make great runs to create space for himself and his team-mates. He had the authority at fifteen or sixteen of someone who knew what they were doing. He had great ability to make great passes for other people. Kenny scored some amazing goals, but I think the goals he scored would be outweighed by the goals he created for people – he was so intelligent. People can run and shoot but if they've got something between their ears it's a great help.'

When Paul McStay threw his shirt into the Jungle at the end of the final home game of the 1991–92 season, it marked more than ten years of service to the club. It also seemed to signal the departure of a player who symbolised all that was good about Celtic during the 1980s and early 1990s. That gesture appeared to suggest he would be quitting Glasgow, perhaps for a club in Italy. Instead the pull of home and family helped to persuade this modest, family-orientated man to remain at Celtic and lighten the load of supporters who were enduring some trying times.

A decade earlier, Johan Cruyff had expressed admiration for the teenage McStay after the seventeen-year-old's performance against Ajax in a 1982 European Cup tie, and his performances for Scotland at the 1992 European Championships made him his country's prime performer on that elevated stage, and yet critics carped that he never fulfilled his potential. It was perhaps closer to the truth to suggest that Celtic never quite managed, during those times, to surround him with the type of talents that would have responded in style to his subtle promptings.

'Paul was a good player in the sense that I played with George Best after I stopped playing with Celtic,' Danny McGrain says, 'and George Best would move into a position where it would just be so easy to find him, and Paul was like that. Paul could stand still or move back or come towards you, and he would just be so easy to find. I think to have that ability is great, because if I'm on the ball I need somebody to pass to, and Paul had that inbuilt, because when he did get the ball he made good passes, because he saw things. We had a reserve game recently, and [Koki] Mizuno made some passes that reminded me of Paul McStay's, because a young boy, Kevin Cawley, kept the space open for Mizuno to play the ball into. It was great to see that mental awareness, and Paul had the awareness of everything on the park. He wasn't the quickest, but his head was quick. He could see things, score goals, support people. He had the ability to make passes seem easy. Paul would always be in space for the ball and would work hard.'

Many of Celtic's triumphs during the 1980s featured moments of inspiration from McStay. On clinching the League title with the 5-0 victory against St Mirren in May 1986, he was simply sublime, combining his desire to win for Celtic with precision and artistry and a stunning goal, smacked home from the edge of the penalty area with the outside of his boot. During the 1987–88 centenary season, he was on fire throughout, pushing and prompting his team-mates and helping out with spectacular goals scored at crucial times. Perhaps the pass of his career was the one on 2 January 1988 against Rangers, when he pinpointed a fifty-yard ball into the path of Chris Morris, the full-back, instantaneously wrong-footing the entire Rangers midfield and defence and making it easy for Morris to find Frank McAvennie, who scored the opening goal in a game that swayed the title towards Celtic.

On being made captain in the 1990s, his style of leadership was to provide the right example, working effectively and hard in service of the team before a recurrent ankle injury forced his retirement at the age of thirty-two in 1997, a particular shame in that, with a style of play reliant on brain rather than brawn, McStay could have continued to delight those who appreciate the finer aspects of football for many more years.

That summer of 1997, as Paul McStay retired gracefully, proved to be an eventful one at Celtic: with a new head coach in Wim Jansen, and the arrival of Henrik Larsson, a Swede, who had appeared at the 1994 World Cup and who had subsequently joined Feyenoord, but who had found himself being played in midfield there and had decided by 1997 that it was time either to return to Sweden or to switch to a club that would make more of his abilities. 'I knew a little bit about his contract,' Wim Jansen said with characteristic understatement when describing how he brought Henrik to Celtic. Jansen had taken the player to Feyenoord from Helsingborgs in 1993 and consequently knew of a clause that would allow Larsson to move from Holland as long as a transfer fee of £650,000 was paid for the player. It would prove to be the most magnificent piece of transfer business ever completed on Celtic's behalf.

The start of Larsson's time at Celtic proved less than illustrious. At Easter Road, for the opening fixture of the 1997–98 season, a misplaced pass backwards from Larsson, on as a substitute, led directly to Hibernian's winning goal. Later that August, the supporters saw Larsson put the ball in the net at Celtic Park for the first time, although the net in question was his own, his clipped shot from six yards making it 2-2 and tipping the balance in a UEFA Cup tie towards SC Tirol Innsbruck. That match eventually righted itself in Celtic's favour, concluding quite spectacularly with a 6-3 victory to the home side, and Larsson's Celtic phase, after those early, uncharacteristic lapses, was soon also on track. 'He's a very good trainer,' Larsson said of Jansen, 'and he made sure that my confidence came back, letting me play – and as a striker as well.'

A home match with Aberdeen early that 1997–98 season epitomised Larsson's excellence. His first goal saw him brush the ball almost imperceptibly, on the run, into the net. His second, a made-to-measure free-kick, had just enough on it to clear the defensive wall and dip down under the crossbar. Neatness and a lack of extravagance were essential to Larsson's game, and his sharp judgement in tight situations, his almost unerring choice of the correct option and the ability to carry it out with fine precision made him as close to perfection as possible for a striker. 'He is calm when he has goal opportunities,' as Dr Jozef Venglos puts it.

A goal against Rangers at Ibrox at New Year 1999 encapsulated those qualities. A powerful twenty-five-yard shot from Lubomir Moravcik came whacking down off Stefan Klos' crossbar and bounced, spinning, out from goal and high into the air in the vicinity of Larsson. With a Rangers defender close to him and aware that Klos was in the process of regaining his feet and moving across goal, Larsson had to keep his nerve until the ball dropped. He did so and, where other players might have panicked and given the ball too heavy a touch or tried to get it under control, the Swede made the most of the situation, applying only the most delicate of touches with his head, for the ball to curl into the net just inside the post, a bare instant before Klos came hurtling across goal, a fraction too late to make a save.

Larsson loosely epitomised 'Janteloven', the Jante law, a fundamental concept in the egalitarian type of society found in Scandinavia, as laid down in *A Fugitive Crosses His Tracks*, the 1930s novel by Aksel Sandemose. This law, which still predominates in Sweden and the other Nordic countries, demands that citizens work together for the greater good, subverting ego and individualism for the benefit of their fellows. Larsson may have disliked being stereotyped as a typical Swede, but in his play, despite his inordinate talents, he unselfishly worked for the benefit of the team rather than himself.

A player with a permanent spring in his step, Larsson was close to impossible for defenders to mark. There is nothing a defender likes better than a player who stands still until the ball comes to him, but Larsson was a figure of perpetual motion, ready and on his toes to bend his run or play his pass. Lithe and pliable, he was also expert at anticipating and hurdling the heftiest of challenges. It was terrible, then, for Larsson to suffer a double fracture of his left leg in a challenge during the UEFA Cup tie at Olympique Lyonnais in October 1999. It ended his season, but when he returned to action the following summer he was even sharper, hitting fifty-three goals that 2000–01 season, the most memorable his angled run, nutmeg of Bert Konterman and towering disguised chip over Klos, while on the run, for the fourth goal in the 6-2 demolition of Rangers in August 2000.

It was quite amazing that Celtic managed to hold on to Larsson's services for seven years, and when in April 1999 he signed a new four-year contract that made him the highest-paid player in Celtic's history – at a reputed £40,000 per week – it was a huge relief to the support, who feared, correctly, that he could easily have switched to a variety of leading clubs, where he would have been even better rewarded. He and his family liked living in Scotland, which was, in Larsson's opinion, 'much more like Sweden' than Holland in terms of its landscape and countryside. Being at Celtic was not only good for Larsson's home life but for his career as well, his resurgence at Celtic as a goalscorer getting him back into the Swedish international squad in the late 1990s.

'This is the club for me,' Larsson says of Celtic, for whom he scored 242 goals in 315 games. 'This is where I made myself as a player, this is where everybody got to know me. This is the club I am going to be eternally grateful to for giving me that opportunity, when other clubs didn't believe in me. This is where I got back into the Swedish national team, playing in European Championships and World Cups, delivering for Sweden. I couldn't have done that without Celtic.' On his departure in 2004 he joined Barcelona, laying on both of Barcelona's late goals, for Samuel Eto'o and Juliano Belleti, in the 2006 final of the UEFA Champions League against Arsenal, instantaneously silencing for ever those English people who had consistently questioned whether the talents Larsson displayed in Scotland could be transferred to a more highly rated level of football.

Even then, in helping Barcelona to that victory, Larsson was doing Celtic a favour, Barcelona's victory guaranteeing the Glasgow club direct entry into the group stages of the following season's UEFA Champions League. 'You feel like a child on his birthday,' is how Larsson sums up the feeling of scoring. 'It's such a special feeling it's very hard to describe.' When he joined Celtic, it was as if the birthdays of everyone with the club at heart had all arrived at once.

5

A LURING ALLURE

Nothing embodies the allure of Celtic more dramatically or distinctly than the beautiful sheen of the emerald-green-and-white hooped jersey. It does not seem too fanciful to suggest that this is a strip with such a special, eye-catching, out-of-the ordinary design that it is filled best by cavalier, colourful, individualistic players, those unlikely to conform to the norm, a uniform for the non-uniform: a design to match the designs of mavericks such as a Charles Patrick Tully or a Jimmy Johnstone, players in whom mesmeric flair always seemed more important than fitting into a plan. There is an undoubted thrill in seeing Celtic trot out in those colours from the players' tunnel, and for Billy Connolly, the Glaswegian comedian and actor, the colours have such an allure that it would be worth turning up solely to see the team take the field. 'I love the clean green and white,' he says. 'There's something about Celtic I've loved and that is that there's a lot of brightness about them, and that is partly to do with how they look. Those hoops . . . when I see them in various away strips I get slightly depressed. When I was a boy I also loved being a supporter of the only team without numbers on their shirts and then the only team with numbers on their shorts. They've always had a wee degree of originality about them.

'Something happens to me when they run on . . . for me that is the highlight. I'd show up just for that. My heart just sings a song when I see them running out. Georges Simenon, the novelist, wrote a lovely line: "I got your letter yesterday and I had a little party in my heart." That's how I feel when Celtic come out on to the park. They make me think they are on my side, that they represent part of me, my having an immigrant Irish background. Not only do they represent me, but I feel well represented by them.'

It was not always hoops – although the green and white was always there. The first Celtic team to take the field, for the match with Glasgow Rangers on 28 May 1888, did so wearing a white shirt, with a green, shirt-type collar and the jersey laced up from navel to neck, while the first badge worn was not the green four-leafed clover of today but a red and green Celtic cross. The players, moustachioed to a man, had Penman Brothers, a sports shop in Bridgeton, to thank for their donation of the strip. The rigout had altered to green and white tops, but striped vertically, by the beginning of 1889 – in time for Celtic's participation in the first season of the newly formed Scottish League in 1890–91 – and with, blue, yes blue, knee-length pants. A badge no longer featured on the players' tops; it would not return to the first-team strip until the 1977–78 season, by which time the fashion was reviving for Scottish clubs to feature the club badge on the shirt.

The four-leafed clover that has been adopted by the club as its standard, identifiable symbol, on stationery and correspondence, was co-opted on to the shirt. Its design resembles closely the bus plaque that is used by the Bonnybridge Celtic Supporters' Club and was adopted by Celtic after Tom White, the chairman, and Robert Kelly, a fellow director, had met representatives of that supporters' club in the 1940s and had asked if Celtic could use it. Permisson was granted, freely, by the Bonnybridge branch.

The clover has remained, other than during the 1987–88 centenary season, when, appropriately, a Celtic cross reappeared on the jersey in tribute to the very first team; and the Celtic cross was again incorporated in the shirt design in the 2003–04 season to celebrate a century of the hooped jersey. Yet the place of the four-leafed clover as the club's symbol has not always been secure: the badge design was the subject of planned modification with the arrival of Fergus McCann in 1994, and in the autumn of that year, Peter McLean, his press spokesman, stated, 'We are a Scottish club, and would hope some sort of Scottish element will be incorporated in the new crest. There is a question mark over the two or three different logos currently being used for different purposes, and we are looking for one which will fairly depict Celtic Football Club. There are two or three being considered at the moment, although we haven't yet reached a final decision. We would like a Scottish/Irish image, because we are very proud of our history, and I don't see us moving far away from our traditions.' It came to nothing – the plans for an altered image being quietly shelved and the prospect of a thistle entwined with the clover faded away.

The hooped jersey itself was first introduced for the opening match of the 1903–04 season – a 2-1 home victory over Partick Thistle in the League – and as any fashionista will tell you, hoops make you look fat, or fatter, and for the likes of Jimmy Quinn the hoops certainly emphasised his bulk and possibly added to his mystique, his burly, rumbustious presence on the field of play. The hoops quickly became associated with a team of serious substance: this was the Celtic that was about to go on a run of clinching a record six Scottish League titles in succession between 1905 and 1910. The association with that great success, which attracted growing numbers of people to follow Celtic, helped the hoops to remain almost completely unchanged for most of the subsequent century. It was from the mid-1990s that there were alterations in the strip, as in most things; with a modification of the shirt to incorporate a design that saw a thick hoop then a thin hoop, then a thick one, then a thin one again, and so on. This variation lasted from 1995 to 1997, but since then the hoops have reverted to their normal even width.

The shorts have remained white since the 1890s, but the socks have had their moments of modification. During the early 1960s the Celtic socks changed from green and white hoops to all-white – a streamlined, symbolic break with the pre-1950s era of heavy strips and steel-toe-capped ankle football boots, although in the mid-1990s, the socks were changed again, this time reverting to the traditional hoops.

'Celtic, of course, is a special, special club,' Andreas Hinkel, the German full-back signed by the club from Sevilla in January 2008, says. 'Stuttgart is a big club in Germany but not around the world. In Spain, Sevilla is a big club, but Barcelona and Real Madrid are big clubs around the world and I think that Celtic is like that. It is like a marque. Everybody knows the green and white around the world. If you ask someone, they say, "Ah, Celtic Glasgow." Rangers, I don't think they know it exactly, what the colours are, because the colours are not so unusual.'

It was Fergus McCann who was first to talk of Celtic being one of the few British clubs that are instantly recognisable as a 'brand', and it is the strip that is the most immediate manifestation of the club's distinctive identity, but other, more intangible matters of identification also draw people close to the club – and maintain the fascination with Celtic. Billy Connolly puts it vividly and in a manner that will strike a chord with many supporters: 'Celtic is important to me inasmuch as it's one of the only constants in my life over the years. I have changed and become various things but it is the one constant. Religion, friendships have come and gone, likes and dislikes have come and gone, but Celtic has remained. I'm not a great one for reflection and thinking back on the past – only when held down and forced to do so – but when I thought about that, it is quite profound, really. It's a very pleasant idea. It's part of me and it doesn't have the power of blood and religion and is unforced by relationships. It has been pretty voluntary, although I got it from my father, as most people tend to do. He wasn't actually too keen on me going to see Celtic, for reasons best known to himself, but when I was a boy I thought supporting Celtic had to be a great thing because if your father did it, it had to be a good thing.

'My father didn't try and encourage me, but when I was about six or seven or eight, a very wee boy, he took me to see Celtic and Forfar, of all teams. This would be at the end of the forties or beginning of the fifties; it must have been a Cup match, because I can't think of them playing under other circumstances. I remember very little except the hustle and bustle of it all and everybody being enormous and I loved being part of it. It was like rock 'n' roll; it had that immediate excitement about it. It was also an amazing distance to go to do anything. Remember, back in those days, going to somewhere like Helensburgh for the day was like visiting the dark side of the moon.

'Funnily enough, Celtic is one of the few things that didn't shrink in enjoyment with time. The anticipation of a game and sense of occasion has stayed with me when I'm getting ready at my home in Aberdeenshire. It's a three-and-a-half-hour drive to Celtic Park and a three-and-a-half-hour drive back, and it seems like no effort at all, whereas, if someone were to tell me they had arranged a meeting for me in Glasgow, I would say, "Behave yourself – it's three and a half hours to get there and back. That's like a driver's working day!" On a day for the football, though, I am happy to drive there and back and have a fish supper and I'm totally happy.

'It's being in love,' Connolly adds with regard to the allure of Celtic. 'It's like falling in love. You can talk to someone about how awful his girl-friend is, but if he's in love he's not going to hear you. You feel great about yourself when you're in love, and that's how it is being a Celtic supporter. When they run on and do what they do you feel you've made a good choice of what to do with your time and your money. The club has also in the past couple of decades changed and made the more bigoted people unwel-come, and they don't get the recognition for that that they deserve. Not only were they never a bigoted organisation but they have made enor-mous strides and they deserve great credit for that.'

The style of play is also in the forefront of Dermot Desmond's mind. 'It's passionate and energetic,' he says as he sums up the ideal essen-tials involved in Celtic's football, 'and it's stylish and creative. At Celtic Park, they really acknowledge that piece of magic, that piece of brilliance. They don't want defensive football. They want attacking football, fast foot-ball, they want to play skilful football. We don't want to be that break-away team. We want skill more than size but if we can have both so much the better.'

Billy Connolly and Rod Stewart, perhaps the club's two most famous supporters, were given seats for life when Fergus McCann was managing director at the club in the mid-1990s, after they had performed the opening ceremonies for the new North and Lisbon Lions stands. The seats do not remain empty when they are not present; they each have to ask in advance to use their seat and, strangely, in more than a decade, the two had yet to attend a home match at the same time. 'I am still not used to it,' Billy Connolly says of having his own seat in the director's box. 'I'm delighted. My whole thing when I go to watch matches on TV in Australia or America is when the people who are watching the match with me say, "Let's see if there's anybody in your seat." Not only is it a joy but it's a source of great fun.'

Stewart once gave Celtic a mention, in his late-1970s hit 'You're In My Heart'; Glen Daly, a popular Glasgow music hall singer of the 1950s and 1960s, who extolled in song the twin beauties of Scotland and Ireland, had gone further with his 1961 record 'The Celtic Song', entirely dedi-cated to encapsulating the greatness of the club, and which has been sung ever since at Celtic Park, most notably immediately prior to the teams taking the field. Daly would sing at concerts and dances players attended and would go to every game at home and some away. They say that the devil has all the best tunes; not so, Celtic have quite a few too. During the 1990s 'The Fields Of Athenry', a mournful ballad related to the Irish famine, found favour with the Celtic support; 'The Willie Maley Song', a tribute to the club's first manager and his legacy, is a catchy twenty-first-century ditty, albeit one based on Brian and Michael's 1978 hit 'Matchstalk Men And Matchstalk Cats And Dogs'. One of the biggest tributes to the potency of songs such as these is to hear supporters of clubs in England adopt them and set their own words to them.

The club's name itself is another distinctive element in its DNA – even in its pronunciation it maintains a special identity, with the use of Celtic with a soft *s* for the first letter rather than a hard *k* being a reflection of the club having been founded in the late nineteenth century, when the word 'Celtic', relating to the people and their society, was generally pronounced in this fashion. Since the mid-twentieth century, English speakers have developed a tendency to pronounce the word with a hard *k*; although both pronunciations are acceptable. As Celtic culture is often discussed in academic circles, one interesting theory is that a form of intellectual snobbery has developed in the UK that has led to the pronunciation of Celtic, when referring to the culture and the history, with a hard *k*, purely to distinguish it from the football club. This subtly separates those who associate the word with football and those who are more involved in highbrow matters. In France, for example, 'Celtic', a Latin word that has been incorporated into modern Indo-European languages, is still pronounced universally with a soft *c*.

Charitable traditions also make Celtic stand out from the herd. The club has been run on businesslike lines since 1897, when, after a sometimes bitter struggle, it was formed into a limited company, but its origins have never been forgotten, even if some of the club's custodians at various times in its history have wavered in their commitment to that ideal. Willie Maley, the hard-headed secretary-manager who was among the foremost beneficiaries of the switch to limited liability status in 1897, said, during the First World War, 'As everyone knows, the Celtic club was founded for charity's sake. The club founded thirty years ago to provide dinners for hungry little ones still keeps up the good work: Smyllum, Nazareth House, St Joseph's Home have reason to know this. Broken men and jaded women know also that a Celtic "line" has enabled them to get over a bad accident or long illness and secure a new lease of life in one or other of our convalescent homes.'

A century after Celtic had become a limited company – in 1996–97 – more than £89,000 was distributed from funds raised by the new Celtic Charity Fund, instituted by Fergus McCann. Nor have the deserving causes always been of a parochial nature: a friendly match with Real Madrid in 1962 generated a crowd of 76,000, the highest attendance until that point for a midweek evening game at Celtic Park, with the Blue and White Committee giving support to the JNF (Jewish National Fund), a charitable trust that had been established to purchase land for Jewish settlement in Palestine to the exclusion of Arabs. The funds were said to be for the benefit 'of refugee women and children from Europe and north Africa'. Celtic's sponsorship of this politically charged organisation appears to have passed by without much comment in those less politically sensitive days.

'We have more charitable community projects today than we have ever had in our history,' Peter Lawwell, the chief executive, says, briskly bringing things up to date. 'We've got 110 coaches in the community, for 4,500 kids per week. We've got fifteen full-time staff in the Celtic Foundation and we have the Charity Fund. There is Celtic Learning, where we bring in kids with classroom difficulties who are referred to us; we have Celtic Against Drugs; long-term unemployed projects; a Well-Being Clinic in association with the Royal College of Physicians and Surgeons; we have anti-sectarian and anti-bigotry projects for children and adults. Where people with social issues have failed in other programmes and projects they will come to Celtic. It's the power of the brand; making a difference in the community.

'A small example is the Well-Being Clinic, where we wrote to a number of our fans between forty and sixty and asked them about their health: blood pressure, diabetes, heart. We've brought these guys in to use the facilities, and the Royal College provides the care and assessment, and the dietary advice. These guys would never go to their GPs but they're in here every Friday getting their diets right; getting assessed, being educated in terms of health.'

Celtic fans have always been keen to distill their passion for the club by organising themselves into supporters' groups. In the early days there were the brake clubs – men young and old organising themselves to share a new-fangled charabanc to away matches – but in general, crowds remained largely local. After the Second World War, for the 1946–47 season, membership of the supporters' association embraced eleven branches extending from Greenock to Cowie to Dumbarton and to

Shieldmuir; each of those places being the furthest point west, east, north and south wherein Celtic supporters' clubs could be found; organised groupings of fans were still not too far-flung during those times, when travelling from one part of Scotland to another made for a drawn-out day. Still, those four postwar geographical points, two of which host senior professional clubs, showed how the Celtic network was beginning to spread in organisation; a process that, six decades later, sees Celtic supporters' clubs dotted across the globe.

'I attended a function in the Hilton in London, held by Chelsea, shortly before Christmas [2007],' Johnny Paton, a Celtic winger of the 1940s who also played for the London club, says, 'when they had me posing with the FA Cup and I told the Chelsea people there, I said to them, "I hope you don't think I'm being aggressive in any way, but if Chelsea had the ingredient Celtic have got they would win the European Cup," and they said to me, "What's that?" I said, "The passion of the supporters." They have the most passionate supporters in the world. Chelsea have wonderful players, a great stadium and the finances to buy players for thirty million pounds – you could buy a whole football club for that – and full houses, but I never felt the passion coming down from the terraces every week when I was a player with Chelsea that I felt when I was at Celtic.'

Tony Roper is a man given to analysis of people's motivations and following five decades and more of supporting Celtic, has some thoughtful offerings on the reasons why Celtic has such an exceptionally strong pull and hold over the club's followers. 'It's got to be somewhere deep in your psyche,' he says. 'I wouldn't argue this in a court of law but I think it's a tribal thing. I think it goes way, way, way back to the cavemen. All these tribes were like extended families, wandering about trying to protect themselves and proliferate and expand. I think that's where the football supporter comes from – we're trying to protect ourselves. You know your history of Celtic is going back not that far, only a hundred or so years, a relatively short period of time, but in modern-day living, that kicks in; this is my tribe, this is my extended family. I think that is what gives you the addiction; it's innate inside you to protect you and your kind. It's just a comfort as well sometimes.

'It's a very strange thing to think, "Why do I turn up every Saturday to watch eleven guys – or sixteen counting the bench – who are carrying my hopes and dreams?" A long time ago, when Celtic were set up, they did carry the hopes and dreams of the Irish influx that came here. The players were maybe paid a bit more than the normal person going to see the game, but it wouldn't be much more, so they had a strong connection. That went on up until quite recently. Now highly successful football players are paid huge, huge sums, vastly greater amounts of money than most fans, and they will leave your team and go somewhere else. So they are almost guns for hire, but the strange thing about that is you are now addicted. I don't think your love is for those particular players. You'll cheer them on at the time, but they are responding to market forces; but you, as a fan, are the one constant in the whole set-up. Players can come and go, but, if the fans ever say, "We're up for transfer," Celtic fans would command absolutely exorbitant amounts of money because they are way, way above everything else . . .

'I think that's because in the early times of the club people were against us. They were upstart Irish people. What makes the fans valuable to Celtic is their persistence. I turned up here for a thing called "Blowing The Blues Away Day", which was the end of the old Jungle. I played for this charity football team called Dukla Pumpherston, and we turned up that day to play Coronation Street – I think there was a Celtic-Manchester United select [of 1960s players] on that day too – but it was raining heavily. The rain was bouncing and 19,000 fans turned up to watch old players playing each other. We won that cup that day, so Dukla Pumpherston was the last team to win a trophy, not Rangers – we called it the Coronation Street Cup – in front of the Jungle.' The 1993 Scottish Cup final, in which Rangers defeated Aberdeen, had been played at Celtic Park in May 1993. 'To actually see 19,000 fans turning up for that!' Roper continues. 'You tell me any other club in Europe where that amount of people will turn up on a wet Sunday to watch an event like that. There is a loyalty there that is indefinable, unfathomable.'

There is also always the potential for fun at Celtic Park. Roper says, 'I remember taking my nephew Patrick Roper to see Celtic play Red Star when Jock Stein said Jimmy wouldn't have to fly if we beat them by a certain amount – and he played out of his skin. He was turning people left, right and centre, and I had my nephew with me, who would only be six or seven or eight, and he identified with Jimmy Johnstone because they were both wee. He saw this wee guy turning these people inside out, upside down, and he obviously thought, "That's us wee guys that are doing that," and the delight and squeals of laughter that came from him set me off laughing as well. As a wean he was kind of ba' faced, and when it laughed it laughed, and that made me laugh, and a lot of people round about me were laughing as well.'

A regular modern complaint is that there is no longer such a great atmosphere at Celtic Park, but it would be closer to the truth to suggest that the atmosphere is simply different to how it was in the past. A myth appears to have grown up that Celtic Park was always an all-singing, all-dancing enclave prior to it becoming an all-seated arena, but singing at the football would appear to have been a relatively recent development, becoming widespread perhaps only from the 1960s onwards; indeed, old-timers in the 1960s and 1970s would wonder why supporters would want to spend their time singing at all rather than being consumed and absorbed in watching the action on the field of play. 'They didn't sing as much as they do today,' Jimmy Walsh, a Celtic star of the 1950s, says in relation to the crowds in front of whom he performed, 'although at Celtic then they maybe didn't have as much to sing about . . .'

Perhaps the apex of the singing at Celtic Park was reached in the 1970s when popular music hits and advertising jingles were raided for inspiration. A British Airways tune, with the lyrics 'We'll take more care of you/Fly the flag' became, at Celtic, 'We've won the League again – fly the flag, fly the flag'; a Gary Glitter hit, from his wholesome period, was subverted to 'Hello, hello, nine in a row, nine in a row'; and 'Magic' a hit for Pilot became 'It's magic, you know, it's going to be nine in a row'.

'Nostalgia is always better than it used to be,' Ian Livingston, who was a teenage supporter of Celtic in the 1980s, says. 'People forget some of the games in the eighties and what it was like.' He is right – run-of-the-mill matches in that era would see crowds of 12,000 or 15,000, with large patches of bare terracing at the two ends of the ground. 'One of the things that has probably happened,' Livingston continues, 'is that people are used to seeing football so much on their TV. I remember walking up the steps to the Jungle and seeing the light appear and then the pitch, and it was a special sight. Back then, apart from Scotland–England games and the occasional Cup final, you didn't see football on TV.' The all-seater arena appears to have subdued a lot of supporters – it is harder to be boisterous and noisy in a seat, and when season ticket holders are sitting beside the same people every week, much of the anonymity of the foot-ball crowd is lost, in contrast to the days of roll up on the day and pay in at the gate if the match takes your fancy. Returning to the same seat game after game also means that supporters can turn up closer to kick-off; in the past, those who arrived in advance of the start would get the singing going – this is how Bertie Auld, a Partick Thistle supporter as a boy, got to know the words of 'The Celtic Song'; through hearing it belted out in the stands and on the terraces as he awaited kick-off in the dressing room. He, in turn, used it to fire up his team-mates in the tunnel prior to the 1967 European Cup final.

Celtic supporters in the mid- to late 2000s were also surprised to see a pipe band entertaining supporters prior to some matches, but it was not unprecedented: at half-time in the 1962 match with Real Madrid, the crowd was entertained by the pipe band of the 277th the Argyll and Sutherland Highlanders. 'Scotland The Brave' was played at half-time, and such entertainment was common at big matches in the period prior to the 1970s.

'You can become passionately involved in something different,' Ian Livingston says of attending Celtic matches as a means of relief from the pressures of being chief executive of British Telecom, 'although it can't always be described as relaxing – the game against Spartak Moscow could not be described as relaxation. Thirty years ago, nobody in the senior echelons of business would have admitted to being involved in football, but I was at a business lunch recently where I found myself chatting to a director of Spurs, one of Chelsea and one of Ajax – it's far more interesting than talking about opera . . . I also like to hoop-spot when I travel around the world: walking though a street in Florida you will be liable to see a Celtic shirt more often than several of the major English clubs.

'The tradition of fast, exciting play, great, exciting football,' drew Livingston to the club, he says, 'but I think that has become dissipated. When I grew up it was about pace, attack, Jimmy Johnstone, Bobby Lennox. I don't think the O'Neill era was about that.'

The communal memory of Celtic playing in their attack-based style remains strong enough for there to be aspirations among the support to seek to see Celtic use it even in the more pragmatic world of modern football, in which a more tactical, cautious style of play predominates. As long as they play in the hoops and stir the dreams of those who are imbued with a love of the club, there are no limits to what the support believe they can achieve.

6
IDENTITY TAGS

There have been few occasions on which Celtic have merited little more than a footnote in the columns of Scotland's sporting press. That, though, was the case in November 1887 when a mere eight lines on page 11 of the *Scottish Umpire*, a popular paper set up to reflect and report on the rapid expansion of organised sport in the late Victorian era, informed its readers, 'that the efforts which have lately been made to organise in Glasgow a first-class Catholic football club have been successfully consummated by the formation of the "Glasgow Celtic Football And Athletic Club", under influential auspices. They have secured a six-acre ground in the east end, which they mean to put in fine order. We wish the "Celts" all success.'

The tone of the piece is friendly and well-meaning and yet it peddles glaring inaccuracies. The club has never been 'Glasgow Celtic', as the writer suggests. Instead 'The Celtic Football And Athletic Club' had been advanced as suitable for the new institution by Brother Walfrid, the club's founder: a name that would encompass a wide constituency, unconstricted by the narrow bounds of a city. The desire would also appear to have been to avoid a clear classification as an Irish club – the names 'Emerald', 'Emerald Harp' and 'Glasgow Hibernians' had been put forward as alternative suggestions of name for the new club and rejected; 'Hibernia' being the Latin name for Ireland. Hibernian, the Edinburgh club, had fielded a strictly all-Catholic team after having been formed in 1875 by Canon Edward Hannan, a Limerick-born priest, who was also the club's first manager, and they had become renowned as a distinctly Irish club. Had Celtic adopted a similar name, they would immediately have been seen as classifying themselves in the same mould. It seems possible that Walfrid was influenced in his choice of a more expansive name by Michael Davitt, an Irish land reformer and republican who felt kinship with Scots, particularly the Highlanders, who were suffering similar types of problems to those that afflicted Ireland.

Most controversially, Celtic is labelled in that early *Scottish Umpire* report as a 'Catholic' football club. This has always been something of a hot potato, not least in the liberal late twentieth and early twenty-first centuries, when the idea of a club being strongly associated with one particular religion is widely seen as undesirable. It is beyond dispute that the vast majority of Celtic supporters are of a Roman Catholic background, but the same supporters would also roundly defend the ecumenical nature of Celtic. Haven't Celtic, the argument goes, always been non-discriminatory in terms of the players fielded by the club?

A century after Walfrid's era, the issue suddenly flared to life in the mid-1990s. With Fergus McCann having taken over at the club and with Celtic rebuilding almost from the ground up, with a new ownership, fans becoming shareholders and spanking new stands rising to jut into the skyline in the East End of Glasgow, the club in the mid-1990s was setting its face firmly against sectarianism and bigotry and attempting to project a corporate identity that was modern, slick and not hidebound by the past.

'Walfrid's aim,' McCann, the Celtic chairman, stated confidently in September 1995, 'was to bring people together and create an appreciation and understanding between Scottish and Irish cultures, hence, the name of "Celtic" representing a bridge of cultures across the Irish Sea. Celtic has a proud history as a non-sectarian club. It is disappointing that some people cannot distinguish between religious bigotry and the positive connections that Celtic has with Ireland. When the club was formed, Glasgow had a new Irish population developing, and tensions were high between the native Glaswegians and the new influx. Brother Walfrid formed Celtic as a cultural link between the countries, something positive both communities could share and be supportive of. It was a vehicle for bringing people together and creating understanding.'

A rare document from the early days of Celtic, issued by the club's founders in January 1888 in an appeal for financial help in constructing a stadium, makes it clear that the club was rooted strongly in the Catholic community. It is clearly an appeal for help from those in that same community but it does not state or suggest anywhere that Celtic is in any way an exclusively Catholic organisation:

> Celtic Football And Athletic Club, Celtic Park, Parkhead (corner of Dalmarnock and Janefield Streets). Patrons His Grace the Archbishop of Glasgow and the Clergy of St Mary's, Sacred Heart and St Michael's Missions, and the principal Catholic laymen of the East End.
>
> The above Club was formed in November 1887, by a number of Catholics of the East End of the City. The main object is to supply the East End conferences of the St Vincent de Paul Society with funds for the maintenance of the 'Dinner Tables' of our needy children in the Missions of St Mary's, Sacred Heart and St Michael's. Many cases of sheer poverty are left unaided through lack of means. It is therefore with this principal object that we have set afloat the 'Celtic' and we invite you as one of our ever-ready friends to assist in putting our new Park in proper working order for the coming football season.
>
> We have already several of the leading Catholic football players of the West of Scotland on our membership list. They have most thoughtfully offered to assist in the good work. We are fully aware that the 'elite' of football players belong to this city and suburbs, and we know that from there we can select a team which will be able to do credit to the Catholics of the West of Scotland as the Hibernians have been doing in the East.
>
> Again there is also the desire to have a large recreation ground where our Catholic young men will be able to enjoy the various sports which will build them up physically, and we feel sure we will have many supporters with us in this laudable object.

The idea of using the proceeds from the football club to provide food for the needy children of the area had been that of Brother Walfrid, born Andrew Kerins in Ballymote, Sligo, in 1840; the Marist brother widely credited as being the major driving force in the formation of the club. His efforts in founding Celtic were given extra impetus by the practical necessity of providing food to the poverty-stricken Irish-Catholic immigrant children in the East End – not least because of a fear on his part that, if those children were not fed by the Catholic community, Protestant organisations might act to put bread in their mouths and, in so doing, purchase their religious loyalties. Walfrid had seen this tactic being operated in his native Ireland in the wake of the Great Famine of the mid-nineteenth century and was determined to act to prevent, as far as possible, its repetition in his new domain, where, as headmaster of the Sacred Heart school in Bridgeton, he was one of the most determined defenders of Catholicism in that part of Glasgow.

When Celtic chose a team for their first match, a friendly against Glasgow Rangers on 28 May 1888, it would appear to have been an all-Catholic one. That policy, if it was indeed one, rather than coincidence, did not last long. Willie Maley, a player in the first Celtic team and the club's first manager, looking back from the 1930s, suggested that the club's founders 'decided they would make still another effort to build a Catholic club in Glasgow on the lines of the never-to-be-forgotten Hibernians of Edinburgh of those far away days', before musing, 'We have always been a cosmopolitan club since our second year . . .' and, writing in 1939, 'for forty-eight years we have played a mixed team . . .' thus dating the inception of that concept to 1891, which, even allowing for artistic licence, slippage or inaccuracy, would suggest that Maley was pointing to Celtic having been an all-Catholic side, by accident or design, in its very earliest years.

Non-Catholic players would be prominent contributors to Celtic's successes down the decades, but the perception of Celtic as a Catholic club in the public mind would persist. Willie Buchan, a native of Falkirk, on joining Celtic in 1933 discovered to his complete surprise that 'everyone now thought I was a Catholic, but the only chapel I had ever seen was the one I passed on the way to the public park'. Buchan had actually had a choice of joining Celtic or Rangers, but when his great friend Archie MacAuley joined Rangers, Buchan, not wishing to compete for an inside-forward's jersey with a man he considered a 'smashing player', opted for Celtic, and that random choice saw him immediately assumed to be a Catholic. It is a sign of the lack of advanced communications at the time that, prior to signing for Celtic, Buchan, out in Falkirk, had been blissfully unaware which of the Old Firm clubs was identified with which religion.

A couple of decades later, Czeslaw Muchiewski, a Pole living in Glasgow, fell into conversation with a fellow eastern European in Marks and Spencer in Sauchiehall Street, Glasgow, in December 1954. This individual, by chance, turned out to be Ferenc Puskas, the Hungarian who was then the world's most renowned footballer, in town for a friendly match against the Scotland national team. Puskas soon expressed to Muchiewski discontentment with life in communist Hungary and intimated that defection might be on his mind. 'He asked what Scottish footballers were paid and was very surprised when I said some of the big clubs paid fifteen pounds a week. He told me he was a Roman Catholic, and I spoke to him about Celtic. He was very interested ...' This almost casual link between Catholicism and Celtic seems an almost impermeable one, although it might have worked hugely in Celtic's favour in this instance – unfortunately, when Puskas did eventually defect from communist Hungary a few years later, it was to join Real Madrid. Another great footballing name had also slipped through Celtic's hands during an earlier era. Matt Busby, a deeply religious Roman Catholic from Orbiston in Lanarkshire, had a trial in the 1920s, as a teenager, with Glasgow Rangers, then, at a later date, with Celtic, who, when they learned that he had been at the club on the other side of the city, immediately informed him that he was no longer welcome at Celtic. It was not always Rangers who were guilty of intolerance.

Tommy Gemmell, a Protestant who joined Celtic in the early 1960s, stresses that 'never in my life have I thought of Celtic as a Catholic club. It was founded, back in 1888, by people who were of an Irish Catholic background, and the club has had a lot of tremendous Catholic players, and players of other religions, stretching back over the decades. If you look at Celtic, if only in the years immediately before I joined the club in the early 1960s, they had Bobby Evans, Bertie Peacock and Jock Stein as captains, and they were all Protestants. These were footballers first and foremost. They didn't go to Celtic to go to chapel; they joined Celtic to play football. I never at any time heard a Celtic director say anything against any other religion.

'Things were sometimes less proper among members of the playing staff. Right at the start of my time at Celtic, there weren't many Protestants on the club's books. Ian Young joined at the same time as me, and early in the 1963–64 season we formed a full-back partnership in the first team, with Ian on the right-hand side and me on the left-hand side. Ian had replaced Dunky MacKay, and I had replaced Jim Kennedy, and some of the more experienced players resented us, two Proddies, the only two in the first team, coming in and taking over from MacKay and Kennedy, who were big, big favourites in the dressing room. Jim Kennedy, if he was selected for the team, would be pushed forward to allow me to remain at full-back and at other times he would be left out of the starting eleven entirely. At that time, if either of us had had a bad game, one of the other players might say, "What do you expect of an Orange b*****d?" They would say it directly to you. It would be straight from the shoulder; they were not joking or having a lark. It was serious stuff. Sometimes, in matches, when things were not working for you, you would hear a couple of similar comments from other players. I don't know why they called me an Orange b*****d because I've never been in an Orange Lodge in my life.

'Obviously some players are more bigoted than others, and these were the ones who would make comments. There was no more than a tiny amount of players at the club who could be described as real bigots; this small number of players would have liked to have seen a Celtic side that was always a hundred per cent Catholic.

'My former team-mates in the Lisbon Lions also asked me about it,' Gemmell continues, 'and they asked me for the names of the perpetrators. Once I had named them, they could see how it fitted into place. Those guys were real bigots, but they never lasted that long as players at the club after my arrival anyway. They just didn't like the idea of Proddies in the team, but the guys with whom I played after that and who formed the Lisbon Lions and who wore the hoops alongside me from the start of the 1965–66 season never bothered me with anything like that. If there had been anything like that, the team spirit might not have been as good as it was. We never had that problem.'

At boardroom level and in and around Celtic Park, Celtic was, during that era, imbued with a strong Catholic influence, simply in terms of the make-up of its major components. 'The majority of players had Catholic connections,' James Farrell, a director in the mid-1960s, said, 'and the three other directors were Catholic: Bob Kelly went to Mass daily; Desmond White was a Catholic, although I don't know how fervent; and Tom Devlin was a Catholic – his brother was a Benedictine priest at Ampleforth.'

With Celtic's strong Irish lineage it might have been hoped that when Charlie Gallagher, a Glasgow-born midfield player with Celtic throughout the 1960s, received international recognition from the Republic of Ireland in 1967, he would be welcomed with open arms. Events did not go as smoothly as might have been hoped. Gallagher had Irish parents, and it was only in that year that FIFA approved parentage as grounds on which a player could adopt a country different to the one in which he had been born. 'I played two games and never really got a chance,' Gallagher says of his Irish caps. 'My first game was in Turkey, and that was anti-football; it was scratching and biting. Al Finucane was my room-mate, and when I first went there, he said, "Charlie, we'll stick together because they're very clannish." I asked him what he meant. He said, "There's Dublin guys and Cork guys, and they don't get on and they stick together and don't talk to anybody else." It was very, very clique-ish. Sean [Fallon, Celtic's Irish assistant manager] said to me, "You'll get another game, Charlie, but don't expect any more, because they're not keen on outsiders coming in." I was an outsider although my people were Irish. Johnny Carey was the manager, a kind of "name" manager, Noel Cantwell . . .; they made you feel as if you weren't very welcome, but I did play another game, against Czechoslovakia, and that was where it ended . . .'

Gallagher recalls no sense of Celtic being an Irish or Catholic club being made manifest in the dressing room or inside the club although, as Gallagher recalls, 'Jock Stein used to say, "Right, Catholics against Protestants today." If a team was short, he would say, "Right, you, you and you are Protestants today." It might also be married men against single men, Lanarkshire against Glasgow, under-25s against over-25s; different ways to create a team at random and without picking one.'

Then, during the early twenty-first century, there was the case of Aiden McGeady, a prodigiously talented forward, born to Scottish parents, and first capped by the Republic of Ireland in 2004, only weeks after his first-team debut for Celtic at the age of eighteen. The Irish were clearly determined to get McGeady on the books before Scotland could make a late bid for his services, and that decision to play for Ireland has seen McGeady booed vociferously around Scotland by some non-Celtic supporters. As he explains, though, SFA intransigence was to a great degree responsible for the loss of a player who had originally been open to representing the country of his birth.

'I had first begun playing for Ireland at schoolboy level,' McGeady says. 'I had wanted to play for Scotland schoolboys when I was fifteen, but, because Celtic didn't let you play for your school, it meant I was not eligible to play for Scotland schoolboys. I thought, "Fair enough." Then Packie Bonner phoned me up and asked if I was interested in going across to Ireland for training because he knew my grandparents on my dad's side were Irish. We had a practice match, I did quite well, and ever since then I have been involved in the Irish international set-up.

'I played for the under-15s, under-16s, under-17s, under-19s and then the first team. The Irish do let players play for their schoolboy team even if they are not playing for a school in Ireland because a lot of their young players of schoolboy age have already moved over to England. I was always going to play for Ireland rather than Scotland at full international level, if chosen, because by the time I was capped I had already been part of the Irish set-up for around two years.'

Davie Provan, a winger purchased from Kilmarnock for £125,000 in 1978, then a record between two Scottish clubs, and a Rangers supporter as a boy, also encountered a certain undercurrent in the Celtic dressing room. 'Basically, I had been signed to replace Johnny Doyle and I was really wary of meeting him, but as it turned out he became one of my best pals at the club. Johnny was at the wind-up right away, saying, "There's another 'currant bun' in the dressing room." There were other players from a Rangers background at Celtic such as Danny McGrain and Tom McAdam, while Murdo MacLeod signed about eight weeks after me. The other "currant bun" was Alfie Conn, who had played for Rangers. There was always religious banter at Parkhead, most of it started by Johnny, but it was always good-natured, never anything more. I travelled to Parkhead with Mike Conroy, who was Celtic through and through and had wanted to play for the club all his life. He would give me stick about being a Rangers man but it was just a laugh, no more than that.'

Overt and more provocative connections with Catholicism have been made by Celtic players in more recent times. Maurice Johnston, on being dismissed during a particularly highly charged League Cup final in 1986, made the sign of the cross as he trotted from pitch to tunnel. It seemed a gesture made less in piety than to goad the Glasgow Rangers supporters, who, from their half of Hampden Park that October day, would have had a full-frontal view of Johnston's action. Peter Grant, a year later, during another hectic Old Firm clash, skidded on his knees towards the Celtic support in the Broomloan Road stand at Ibrox Park and, again, made the sign of the cross.

The identification by some supporters with Catholicism and Ireland has had serious overtones. During the 1970s, when the 'Troubles' in the north of Ireland were at their height, a regular chant from the Jungle terracing, where stood the most fanatical supporters, was 'I-I-I-R-A/I-R-A Rule OK', the initials belted out, rat-a-tat-tat, with the chillingly cold and emotion-less relentlessness of a firing squad. The same fans sang of being 'off to Dublin in the green . . . to join the IRA'; although they did always seem to return in time for the next home game. On 3 January 1996, when a minute's silence was held before a Celtic–Rangers match at Celtic Park, in remembrance of the Ibrox Disaster of twenty-five years previously, in which sixty-six supporters had been crushed to death at the Rangers end of that ground, the hush was interrupted by a single but piercing cry of 'Sunday, Bloody Sunday', a reference to the 1972 shooting by British Army soldiers of thirteen civil rights protesters in Derry; the shout seemingly from someone among the Celtic supporters in the new north stand.

One week later, on 10 January 1996, Fergus McCann launched 'Bhoys Against Bigotry', when, as the club itself put it, 'Celtic Football Club came out and openly challenged the bigots in Scottish society.' McCann, Celtic's managing director following the rights issue of early 1995, stated, 'It is important for Celtic to proactively discourage sectarianism. The club's role as a major social institution carries with it a responsibility to work against individuals or groups who use football, and particularly Celtic's matches, as a medium for promoting their extreme political and/or reli-gious views. Celtic has a greatly diversified supporter profile in terms of age, sex, religion, social and political background. It is the club's respon-sibility to aim to create a positive and acceptable environment for all supporters, particularly the young children who attend our matches. The image of the club is very important and, regrettably, in some areas – and not just in Scotland – the club is perceived wrongly to harbour support of a sectarian divide . . . As Celtic, Scotland and the people of the world plan towards the new millennium we witness people in Ireland striving for peace. Now is the time for the people of Scotland to work against bigotry of all kinds. Let's no longer hear the chants for the IRA or UDA at football matches. Let's hold out the hand of friendship and show respect for other beliefs or principles.'

McCann's sentiments were admirable – although his critics quickly suggested that his aim was to sanitise the club's image to make it more attractive to sponsors. It was a brave stance to take and required vision and a monumental determination to try to change attitudes, especially as there were some supporters whose perception of Celtic and its purposes were diametrically opposed to McCann's point of view. There was no guarantee that McCann's changes would be absorbed by the support as a whole; it was one thing for the managing director to make a policy; another one to cajole thousands of supporters into acting as he wished them to do. His words also make it clear that he saw this as a matter not just for Celtic; although it would take some years for others to follow his lead.

'Fergus felt that there was a chance that Celtic might be taken over by people with an extremist viewpoint,' Brian Quinn, a Celtic director at the time, suggests. 'He also felt that it was wrong. Fergus held some very deep convictions, and he felt that Celtic should revert to the idea of raising money through charitable activities that could be distributed to people regardless of what religion they represented or where they came from. Fergus wanted to go back to the roots of the club and he wanted to nourish them and feed them. He didn't like hearing songs from the terracing mentioning "Orange b*****ds' and so on.

'The club has never been one that says, "This is just a club for Catholics," or "This is just a club for people with Irish antecedents." We've never taken that narrow, narrow view. In terms of gender mix or ethnic mix, I'm sure the mix is as wide as it has ever been. We've always rejected the suggestion that we are the political wing of anything. We were never going to let ourselves become associated with a political movement, far less a militant political movement, and that's been resented by some sections of the support. I've had letters from people asking, "Why won't you allow us to sing these kinds of songs at Celtic Park?" Oh, people feel very strongly about it.'

There was also an insistence from McCann at this time that the club's closeness to Ireland would always be maintained. 'I was amazed last year,' he said in late 1995, 'when the club was criticised for wanting to fly the Irish tricolour along with the Scottish saltire. The white of the tricolour stands for peace between the green and orange factions of Ireland. I cannot think of a more responsible message for Celtic to promote . . . We are first and foremost a football club and a thriving business but that must be balanced with the realisation that Celtic is a major social institution and the responsibility that brings with it.' When Celtic had gone to Queen's Park to rent Hampden Park for the 1994–95 season, they found the amateur club to be awkward landlords, not least in using a Glasgow lawyer to tell McCann bluntly, when drawing up the agreement to rent the national stadium, that on no account would Celtic be allowed to fly the tricolour from the stadium roof on matchdays, and that if Celtic refused this condition it would be a dealbreaker. Celtic had little choice but to agree as they needed the temporary use of the high-capacity national stadium and had no other option for a stadium in which they could be resident for that season.

This balancing act for Celtic directors between asserting and celebrating Celtic's Irish-influenced identity and publicly dissociating the club from support for political causes has always been a difficult one to maintain, as Robert Kelly, one of McCann's predecessors, had discovered four decades previously, when he found himself at the centre of what came to be known as the great flag flutter.

Small talk tends to be high on the agenda when guests are ushered into the plush and hospitable confines of the directors' box at Celtic Park. So when George Graham, the secretary of the Scottish Football Association, was a guest of Celtic during a match in 1951 and turned to Jimmy McGrory with a seemingly innocent question, the Celtic manager was only too happy to assist. Graham had spotted a distinctive flag flying from the roof of the covered enclosure opposite the directors' box in the south stand and inquired of McGrory what the flag might represent. It is impossible to know whether the SFA secretary's question was genuine or disingenuous – it could quite easily have been either – but McGrory was happy to inform Graham that it was the tricolour; the flag of the two-year-old Republic of Ireland.

This conversation planted a seed in the mind of George Graham that suddenly blossomed with an ugly bloom after the events of New Year's Day 1952, when, during an Old Firm match at Celtic Park that saw Celtic succumb to a 4-1 defeat, several hundred spectators at the 'Celtic End' of Celtic Park shrugged off the confines of the terraces and spilled on to the running track and the fringes of the field of play at that end of the ground. Bottles and fists were thrown in the mêlée. Something had to be seen to be done in the wake of the outrage that followed, and Glasgow's magistrates came up with several suggestions for the SFA to consider to improve spectator behaviour on such occasions. One of those was that 'the two clubs should avoid displaying flags which might incite feeling among the spectators'. The SFA, spearheaded by George Graham, seized on this minor edict to demand that Celtic remove 'any flag or emblem which has no association with this country or the game' and that, if they continued to display such flags, and there was trouble from their supporters at further matches, the SFA would have the options of closing Celtic Park and suspending Celtic from its competitions.

Anyone with any sensitivity to the sporting politics of Scotland would have realised that this equated to an opportunist attempt to pick at Celtic's Irish identity; it was an illogical nonsense to suggest that there was a connection between random violence and the fact that a flag was flying over a nearby terracing's roof. Robert Kelly, the Celtic chairman, in responding to the SFA, drew himself up to his full height, both figuratively and literally, to reject entirely the demand to remove the tricolour. Privately, he countered with his own threat to remove Celtic, one of Scottish football's major attractions, from the Scottish League. The might of right, Kelly felt, was on his side, and as the matter rumbled on for months during the second half of the 1951–52 season, he drew strength from his sureness in his moral stance and from seeing his opponents failing to sustain support for their demand. Eventually, the SFA quietly backed down; many of its member clubs had been unwilling to see Celtic and its lucratively substantial, if occasionally unruly, support, absent from the Scottish game.

Kelly had, interestingly, been backed throughout by Rangers, although, opposed by Harry Swan, the Hibernian chairman, who had made it his business to do all he could to prise that club away from its Irish identity. The episode had an interesting sting in the tail: in 1957, Robert Kelly, then president of the Scottish Football Association, discovered a clear connection between George Graham and the misappropriation of ticket money at the SFA and told Graham, 'You either resign now or I call in the police.' The 'great flag flutter' as it was punned, established Kelly's reputation as an upholder and defender of Celtic's traditions, but it would not signal the conclusion of attacks on the club for its espousal of its Irish identity.

Jimmy Walsh, an inside-right with Celtic in the early 1950s and an indispensable member of the side as a creator and taker of goals that 1951–52 season, offers a humorous take on the episode. 'I'd never noticed it before, the Irish flag. It was too dirty! When that was talked about they took it down and washed it and put it back up. Once they had washed it I then noticed it because you could see the colours then! So I don't think it would be true that the supporters had been goaded into fighting over the flag because they wouldn't have been able to see it. Bob Kelly went to town on that flag and Bob would have loved that – fighting tooth and claw . . .'

Concerns on the part of the club about its image and the rebellious nature of some of its supporters have often arisen down the years. Before the 1973 Scottish Cup final with Glasgow Rangers, to be attended by Princess Alexandra and Angus Ogilvy, her husband, Jock Stein and Desmond White, the chairman, penned an open letter to the supporters not to cause embarrassment to the club, such as in jeering 'God Save The Queen', which was then played on such occasions. After the final of the Scottish Cup in 1989, again an encounter with Glasgow Rangers, Billy McNeill, the Celtic manager, expressed his happiness that the Celtic support had not used sectarian chants or songs during the match. The difference under McCann was that not only did he acknowledge the problem but he put forward a long-term solution to eradicate it fully from Celtic Football Club. Previous regimes had seemed to feel that such a thing was impossible; that only temporary measures on certain occasions could persuade certain individuals to desist from their habitual behaviour for a short time, while accepting that they would inevitably return to form in due course.

It would be folly to deny that during much of the twentieth century, Celtic was viewed by many of its supporters as a major Catholic institution and one that could provide a feeling of security, comradeship and solidarity for people of that religion, often at times when they felt under threat or saw discrimination against them, either in Scotland or elsewhere. This is also a club that did not have a non-Catholic manager until 1965 – Jock Stein – although Stein was only the fourth manager of Celtic. The club also did not have a non-Catholic director until 1989 – David Smith – but most of the directors before him had family links which went back to the club's formation. Equally, it was a sign of how far Celtic and the Catholic community had come that, as the twenty-first century dawned, they, the club of the minority, had shown the way in doing much to eliminate the type of bigotry inside football grounds that had been taken for granted for many years. Celtic can take some pride in that they have clearly led the way and that Celtic Park has now been largely free of sectarian chanting for some years now, even at Old Firm matches.

It helps that Scotland in the early twenty-first century is a very different place to that when Celtic was being established. The Irish who settled in Scotland in the second half of the nineteenth century were easily distinguished from the natives by their poverty, low literacy levels and lack of technical skills. They were widely despised by the locals and responded by creating a ghetto community. That community no longer exists. Social surveys in recent times show that there is no discernible difference in the socio-economic status of Catholics and non-Catholics.

It greatly assisted McCann that he was establishing himself at Celtic in the new era of all-seater stadiums. During the decades when vast crowds piled on to the terraces in amorphous masses, it would be harder to pick out and identify offenders. Now, with close-circuit television, stewarding, individually numbered seats occupied by registered season ticket holders, the isolation of miscreants is so much simpler. The demography of the home support also changed because, with seats all round, it was a more pleasant atmosphere for families, more pleasant for children, a more expensive thing to buy into and with which to feel involved.

'Then when Celtic got into Europe again,' Peter Lawwell, the Celtic chief executive, suggests, 'there was a joy, a reputation being formed for fun behaviour the Celtic way and the terms of reference of joining that environment didn't include sectarianism. It was like the Tartan Army; further back they wrecked Wembley, but then their reputation was transformed when the peer pressure was to behave and enjoy yourself rather than tear up pitches. I genuinely believe that Celtic's are the best supporters in terms of their connections with the club – at times it's frightening if you sit on the board here and think what you are responsible for, something that means so much to so many people; it is not only a privilege but quite daunting.'

The dying embers of bigotry have still to be extinguished. Following Celtic's final home match with Rangers in the 2006–07 season, the section of Celtic Park occupied by the Rangers support was found to have been 'decorated' with numerous Ku Klux Klan stickers; most ironic given that the only goal of the game had been scored, quite spectacularly, by Ugo Ehiogu, the black Londoner newly signed by Rangers. A couple of years earlier, Rangers supporters at an Old Firm fixture at Celtic Park had quite dangerously rained down potatoes on to the pitch from their end of the ground, a less-than-subtle reference to the Irish famine. Celtic supporters, celebrating qualification for the UEFA Cup final in Seville in 2003, had gently lobbed inflated beach balls – symbolic of their forthcoming visit to the south of Spain – on to the Ibrox pitch during a preceding Old Firm match. Vive la différence?

Occasional incidents continue to occur. Artur Boruc, Celtic's Polish goalkeeper, found himself the subject of police action following a match with Rangers at Ibrox in 2006, being cautioned by Strathclyde Police for making gestures in the direction of the Rangers supporters: police reports of the incident mentioned a V-sign, a hand gesture and a blessing. Once the police action was made public it prompted a frenzy of fury on both sides of the Old Firm divide. Some Celtic supporters decided immediately, without being in full possession of the facts, that the police action had been unfair in that Boruc blesses himself before every match and leaped upon this incident to claim persecution of Catholic practices even in the twenty-first century. The Procurator Fiscal, in his report, had stated that Boruc 'was seen by members of the public and police officers to bless himself. Witnesses describe him smiling or laughing at a Rangers section of the crowd and making "come on" gestures. This action appeared to incense a section of the crowd to react in such a way that police officers and security personnel had to become involved to calm the situation. The police reported that it took ten minutes to restore normality in the crowd.'

A spokesman for the Catholic Church soon weighed merrily into the fray. 'It is quite worrying, firstly that some spectators saw fit to complain, but even more so that police felt it merited investigation. Incitement to religious hatred normally involves demeaning the signs and symbols of a person's faith. It would be interesting to know how a gesture of reverence falls into any of these categories.' The Crown Office was forced to clarify the matter by stating that Boruc had been cautioned not for making the sign of the cross, which he does prior to every match in which he participates, but for the other, provocative hand gestures. Boruc was soon dubbed 'The Holy Goalie' by some Celtic supporters although those who relished that nickname seemed to do so more because of the way the goalkeeper had riled the Rangers support rather than for any spiritual empathy with the undoubtedly genuine strength of the Pole's religious faith.

Old Firm sectarianism hit the headlines again in August 2007 when Glasgow Rangers supporters were heard, during their opening League match of the season at Inverness, to be singing sectarian songs, routinely mentioning being 'up to their knees in Fenian blood', which they clearly were not in the spotless Invernessian stands, and abusing the Pope. Offensive these chants certainly were, and, under new Scottish Premier League rules introduced that summer, such bursts of sectarianism immediately placed their club in danger of being deducted points. Rangers, within days, consequently announced that they were prepared to take the step of no longer selling tickets for away matches to supporters. Celtic independently took action of their own to address the club's away support which tended to contain individuals who appeared determined to rap out their repertoire of rebel songs into infinity, regardless of peace processes in Ireland or any other extraneous circumstances.

Subsequently, in a letter sent to Celtic fans with tickets for the match at Falkirk on 11 August 2007, the club warned of the implications of sectarian singing. 'We should not underestimate how serious this could be. Your support has earned the club worldwide recognition for its good nature and the passion with which you get behind the team, let's ensure that this is maintained this season. We are a non-political and non-sectarian organisation and we ask in the strongest possible terms that you do not indulge nor encourage songs or chants or any other form of behaviour which could in any way bring the club into disrepute.' The club have also warned they will take season-ticket passes away from any supporter who is identified as an offender, and issue indefinite bans from future matches. It worked – sectarian chanting was notable for its absence that day and that augured well for the future.

'The Irishness is part of the DNA of the club,' Peter Lawwell says. 'It is not offensive in any way and is something that should be celebrated. We cannot allow that dimension to be misunderstood and seen as sectarian but even today I don't believe that that Irish identity and Irish culture has been accepted in Scotland.

'At Celtic Park, we believe, with a margin for error, that we have virtually eliminated sectarian chanting over the past number of years. Our problem is that there is a minuscule minority, in the context of the Celtic family, but a sizeable minority in terms of the travelling support, who hang on to political chanting, which is offensive, mainly around the Provisional IRA, and we as a club are saying that is our problem, it is offensive and we will be doing all we can to get rid of that. Ronnie Hawthorne [Celtic's security adviser] devised a five-point plan, and we implemented that for our away support, and I've got to say to date it's been pretty successful. We have seen a major improvement but we will not be complacent; we've got to keep on top of it.'

For some Celtic supporters, the Irishness of the club is bound tightly and inextricably to their association with the club. For others, it is an interesting and romantic artefact related chiefly to the foundation of the club. Whatever the individual outlook, the Irish strand is one of the most colourful threads in the richly woven fabric that has made Celtic the club it is today.

← The earliest known picture of a Celtic team, in front of the new pavilion in 1888: (middle row left to right) Willie Groves, Tom Maley, Paddy Gallagher, Willie Dunning, Willie Maley, Mick Dunbar; (front row) Johnny Coleman, James McLaren, James Kelly, Neil McCallum, Mick McKeown.

← With four out of their groundbreaking six in a row titles in the bag, Celtic, in April 1908, show off three other trophies from that season: the Charity Cup, the Scottish Cup and the Glasgow Cup.

↓ Jimmy Quinn, the burly, bustling centre-forward and the focal point of the six-in-a-row team, when the team still played in stripes.

↓ The players of Celtic and Glasgow Rangers leave the Hampden Park pitch at the conclusion of the 1909 Scottish Cup final replay, which ended in a 1–1 draw … and a riot.

COLORSPORT

DAILY RECORD

DAILY RECORD

↖ A seriousness of purpose helped John Thomson, the 'Prince of Goalkeepers', make the position of Celtic custodian his own.

↑ In the Old Firm game of 5 September 1931, Thomson punches the ball clear of Sam English, minutes before the two players collide.

← Thomson is stretchered on to an ambulance outside Ibrox Park for the journey to the Victoria Infirmary.

← Jimmy Delaney, a smooth-moving and graceful winger during the 1930s and 1940s, in action against Partick Thistle shortly before his transfer to Manchester United. Matt Busby, the United manager, would rate Delaney as one of his best ever signings.

← One of the first foreign players to feature for Celtic, Gil Heron, a Jamaican, was signed in the summer of 1951. He was a professional photographer and a full-time footballer, but had a severe dislike of playing in the Scottish rain.

↓ Shades, sunshine and a sports car help Celtic players look a million dollars on tour in booming postwar America. The players enjoying their Stateside visit in the summer of 1951 are (left to right) Charlie Tully, Neilly Mochan, John McPhail and Jimmy Walsh.

↓ What's the time? It's seven past Niven. Willie Fernie strokes home the final goal in Celtic's 7–1 victory over Glasgow Rangers in the 1957 League Cup final.

← Willie Maley, the secretary-manager of Celtic from 1897 to 1939, was a stern, formidable individual and one of the greatest managers the British game has seen.

↑ Jimmy McGrory, the powerful Celtic centre-forward, set numerous goalscoring records during the 1920s and 1930s.

← Jimmy McGrory (left), Celtic manager, and Robert Kelly, chairman, admire the Glasgow Charity Cup, which Celtic won 27 times before the tournament's demise in 1961.

↙ Happy Celtic supporters, some holding up seven fingers in recognition of the record 7-1 victory over Rangers in the 1957 League Cup final.

↓ Jock Stein provides a defensive shield for Johnny Bonnar, the goalkeeper, in the 1954 Scottish Cup final victory over Aberdeen.

GN-SMX
CELTIC OUTSIDE RIGHT JIMMY
JOHNSTONE

← Jimmy Johnstone was inspired to work hard at his wing play by Stanley Matthews before becoming Celtic's very own wizard of the dribble.

↓ The tensions of an Old Firm derby are etched on the faces of Ron McKinnon, John Greig and Alex MacDonald of Glasgow Rangers as Greig attempts to dispossess the brilliant Jimmy Johnstone.

↯ Quique, the Atletico Madrid player, attempts unsuccessfully to intimidate Jimmy Johnstone in the turbulent 1974 European Cup semi-final at Celtic Park.

← Jock Stein shakes hands with Giacinto Facchetti, Internazionale's most renowne defender, before a training session on the eve of the 1967 European Cup final. Billy McNeill, the Celtic captain, is in the background.

← A 22-yard shot from Tommy Gemmell, not in picture, hurtles past Giuliano Sarti, the Internazionale goalkeeper, and into the net for Celtic's equaliser in the European Cup final at the National Stadium, Lisbon.

↙ Stevie Chalmers (right) turns away in celebration after diverting Bobby Murdoch's pass into the Internazionale net for the winning goal in Celtic's 2–1 European Cup final triumph.

↓ Celtic supporters prove too much for the Portuguese police as they swarm on to the pitch.

PA PHOTOS

ACTION IMAGES

ACTION IMAGES

PA PHOTOS

← The mass of people on the pitch meant that Billy McNeill had to go under police escort to collect the cup, while his team-mates, in the dressing room, missed out on the presentation of the trophy.

↓ The European Cup takes centre stage as the Celtic party celebrate at the official post-match reception.

↙ A senior Celtic supporter holds up for display a souvenir. An estimated 12,000 Scottish supporters had made the journey to the Portuguese capital.

↓ On the day after Celtic's greatest triumph, a lorry carries Jock Stein and his players around Celtic Park with the greatest club trophy of all.

DAILY RECORD

← After Jimmy Johnstone's cross, Bobby Murdoch (third Celtic man from left) sweeps a powerful shot past David Harvey, the Leeds United goalkeeper, to make it 2–1 to Celtic in the second leg of the 1970 European Cup semi-final.

← Tommy Gemmell indulges in his speciality of scoring exceptional long-range goals; here hitting the opener in the 1970 European Cup final against Feyenoord, the Dutch champions. It makes Gemmell one of a small band of players to have scored in two European Cup finals.

↓ Jock Stein assists in the aftermath of Scottish football's greatest tragedy: the Ibrox Disaster of 2 January 1971, in which 66 people died and 145 were injured. Stein markedly bore the strain of what he had witnessed long after that terrible day.

7

SHADES OF GREEN

Few institutions have as strong an identity as Celtic whilst remaining entirely non-exclusive and open to anyone with an inclination to become involved. No person, of whatever background, is likely to feel as though they are an outsider inside Celtic Park. The club was established and built determinedly by people outside the mainstream, so it is, by inclination, unlikely to lean towards exclusion. Celtic's open outlook, best expressed in the team's traditionally positive style of play, means the club has always found it easy to attract a diversity of supporter.

The idea that Celtic is a broad church that welcomes followers of every background is embodied in the jolly personage of Brian Sharp. An active Presbyterian in the Church of Scotland, and one of the senior Kirk elders at Bothwell parish church, where he runs the Bible class, he is a freemason to boot. He has also been supporting Celtic for five decades. 'When I was nine or ten,' he says, 'I had an uncle, a Queen's Park supporter, who took me to a football match in Glasgow every Saturday afternoon throughout the 1950s: my father was a sailor who was away at sea nine or ten months of the year. So I saw Clyde, Partick Thistle, Rangers, Third Lanark and Queen's Park themselves.

'The two teams that really appealed to me were Celtic and Partick Thistle, simply because these two teams in the 1950s were so exciting. I liked the sheer passion and atmosphere at Celtic Park, and the idea that Brother Walfrid founded the club in order to give money to the children of the starving Irish poor also really appealed to me as a Christian and as a historian, and that all helped me develop a love and passion for Celtic Football Club. On top of that, the sheer excitement of some wonderful players; chaps like Bobby Evans and Bertie Peacock and Willie Fernie and Billy McPhail. Celtic was formed on the great Christian principle of charity; St Paul spoke of faith, hope and charity and that the greatest of these is charity. '

Finding that there was never less than a welcoming atmosphere inside Celtic Park, Sharp became a committed supporter, but he has also discovered that this, when combined with his religious beliefs, has produced some strange incidences of confusion among those who find it difficult to deal with anything that fails to fit with their stereotypical, black-and-white view of the world.

'My business was printing and publishing,' Sharp says, 'and, of course, selling printing in the west of Scotland and in the Central Belt means that, really, you meet a few guys who are not particularly thrilled by the existence of Celtic Football Club. I would always state that I am a Celtic supporter and I would stand by the club in every way but early on I realised it is something you don't shout from the rooftops in terms of business life in Scotland and particularly in the printing industry, which, over the years, was very pro-Protestantism and freemasonry as well, which was rife in the printing trade. I experienced a lot of bigotry in my working life, things like I was a disgrace as an elder in the Kirk to be supporting a club that supported Irish terrorists, which is absolute rubbish, of course.

'I remember being stopped four or five years ago in Bothwell Main Street and this well-spoken chap said to me, "You're an elder in this church here" – we were more or less just outside the church. I said, "Yes, yes, you're right," with my elder's voice, expecting a pleasant inquiry on some matter of church procedure; how to arrange a daughter's wedding at the church or something pleasant such as that, but no. He said, "I thought so but I saw you getting on a Celtic supporters' bus in the Main Street last week." I'm a member of the Bothwell Emerald Celtic Supporters' Club. I said, "Yes, you're absolutely right." He said, "Yes, I thought so. You're an absolute disgrace. As a matter of fact, I've a good mind to report you to one hundred and twenty-one." One hundred and twenty one George Street in Edinburgh is the head office of the Church of Scotland. He said,

"You know, you're one of the reasons the Church of Scotland is in the state it's in today, consorting with Papists." I said, "You're entitled to your opinion." He then stormed off. That is one of many incidents over the years.

'These attitudes are still there – in business life it is under the surface. I know one or two folk within the Church who supposedly joke, but you know that behind the scenes they are seething – they are just anti-Celtic and anti-Catholic and they link one to the other. There is a real confusion between the two. There is this bitterness in some people because I support Celtic. The feeling is, in many instances, that I "should know better" than to be "consorting with Papists". It's incredible.

'As Christians, the Catholic tradition, the Presbyterian tradition, the Episcopal Church in Scotland, the Church of England, we should all be together. Yes, we have different backgrounds, we have different aspects to theology, but to my mind these differences are not all that important. Maybe I am slightly different in that I do have a great love and respect for the Catholic Church. I go to Mass quite often because I just enjoy it – as a non-Catholic I cannot take communion but I do go down to the altar and the priest will give you a blessing.

'On only a very, very few occasions have I come across a bit of animosity from real nationalists within the Irish community in Glasgow, guys that believe that, if you're not Catholic and you're not Irish, you've got no business supporting Celtic – only on two or three occasions in my entire life; minimal in comparison to the animosity I have experienced from the folk on my side of the great divide. Yes, I would say there is a greater sense of bigotry on the Protestant side. There has always been a fear of Catholicism.

'On another occasion, I was being introduced to Robert Davidson, who was the Moderator of the General Assembly of the Church of Scotland, and he came to visit us in Bothwell and was being introduced to the elders. When he came to me, one of my fellow elders said, "Moderator, I don't think we should introduce you to this man." Of course, Robert Davidson stood back, wondering why, and my fellow elder said, "Moderator, he's a Celtic supporter." And, of course, all my fellow elders shook their heads and said, "Moderator, sorry about this. We didn't want you to meet him."

'Then Robert Davidson said, "Brian, let me shake your hand. I too am a Celtic supporter." It was great to see the Moderator of the General

Assembly of the Church of Scotland there, in all his regalia, a Celtic supporter. Then he explained that he had been in Parkhead parish church and that Celtic had sent him a letter to say that as a member of the local clergy he was very welcome to come along to Celtic Park. At one time, if you turned up at the turnstiles with your [clerical] collar, the chap on the turnstile would let you in. Invariably, a Church of Scotland minister would be called "Father" – "In you go, Father". You would be allowed in free of charge – and into the stand. Robert Davidson took up that offer and became a Celtic supporter.'

A life of professional excellence has rewarded Ian Livingston with the position of chief executive of British Telecom as well as with a non-executive directorship of Celtic Football Club. The call to support Celtic came earlier than the one from BT when, at the age of ten, Livingston found himself drawn to Celtic Park to witness, among other things, the tail end of Jimmy Johnstone's career as a Celtic player. Livingston emanates from a Jewish background, and his ancestors arrived in Glasgow from eastern Europe at around the same time as Celtic was being formed, his great-grandparents rubbing shoulders with some of Celtic's first supporters in the Gorbals, the area of Glasgow in which they first settled. For him too it was the feeling of inclusiveness at Celtic that helped to develop his affection for the club.

'It was synagogue on a Saturday morning and the game in the after-noon,' Livingston chuckles as he recalls those early days in support of Celtic. 'It's not particularly a family thing. My parents have no particular interest; my father supports Queen's Park, if anyone, but from the age of nine or ten I remember going to Bellgrove station with a friend to watch Celtic. I couldn't afford the stand so we would go in the Jungle. From the age of thirteen or fourteen I would start to go more regularly.

'It is a broad church, Celtic, and it still retains its very strong chari-table aims. For a supposedly Catholic club, many of the greatest players and managers were Protestant – creed or colour didn't come into it.

'Coming from a religion that has probably suffered more from discrim-ination and exclusive attitudes, I feel passionately about the principle that everyone is given a fair chance. Celtic may have had a predominantly Catholic base, but it was open to many and all. It's always been the inclu-sive club and, in common with Barcelona, more than a football club. Particularly from my background, part of being inclusive is that people are judged not on their background but on what they do.

'Did I like the Republican politics of some people on the terraces at Celtic in the seventies and eighties? No, but that represented a minority of people. It can have its funny moments – I got a phone call from the *Scotsman*, puzzling over how a person of Jewish background who had attended Kelvinside Academy, a Protestant school, was a Celtic supporter.'

It is rare for any individual to be a part of life in Glasgow and be entirely unaware of the Old Firm, but that was the case with Mak Purewal, a Sikh who arrived in the city from the Punjab in India, in 1963, while still in his early teens, to seek his fortune. 'I was about thirteen and a half,' he says, 'and had started working in a restaurant called the Taj Mahal in Park Road. The owner of the restaurant was a Rangers supporter, and he used to go to the Rangers games so, just to keep him company, he would take one of the staff with him. One week, my turn came up, and my first game in Scotland was Partick Thistle–Rangers, at Firhill. At that time, I didn't know much about football. We went there and the crowd was OK, but when Partick Thistle scored, the atmosphere became very bad in the sense that they began shouting, swearing, pushing. I didn't like it at all. I can't remember exactly but I think Rangers scored five or ten minutes before the end and it finished 1-1.

'That was my first game, so when he asked me again, I said, "I'm not going to go back – I'm not interested." Six months passed, and a customer, Tom, and I got talking, and he was asking me about hobbies and whether I liked football. At that time, my English wasn't very good, so I answered him in broken English, "Went there once – didn't like it." He asked me, "Where did you go?" So I told him, "Partick Thistle–Rangers." He said, "Ah, you have had a bad experience – you went to the wrong game." He said that one day he would take me to see Celtic. At that time, I didn't even know where Celtic Park was.

'A couple of months later he took my brother and me to Parkhead to see Celtic play Clyde – this was just before Jock Stein came. I can't remember the score exactly, but Celtic scored quite a few goals, and every time they scored everybody was kissing and hugging and there was a great atmosphere, no hassle, and my brother and I said, "This is the place where we want to be." Ever since that day, my brother and I have been Celtic supporters. It was just so much more friendly and whatever pocket money we were able to save up, we would go there.

'We came to Celtic as supporters at the right time because Jock Stein arrived shortly afterwards. We saw the best. We used to go to the Jungle

– there was just a great atmosphere: singing, people selling macaroon bars. We used to love it. At that time our English wasn't very good, and it wasn't easy to communicate, but we loved the football.

'There were some great European nights at that time, but to get tickets you used to have to queue for three or four hours and then you would find, with only about ten people in front of you, that they would tell you it was sold out. Someone at Celtic Park, who used to do the tickets, saw us standing there a couple of times without tickets, and I think he just felt sorry for my brother and me and one day he said, "If you don't have a ticket, then come early and I'll let you in." Later, he would keep tickets for us, which was nice of him. It just got better and better from there, and we just kept following Celtic. Once we started earning better money, we started going to the stand in the 1980s and for the last ten to fifteen years we have been in the executive club, the Jock Stein lounge, which is quite nice, but I do miss the Jungle. You had a good laugh in there.

'I have never at any time felt uncomfortable at Celtic. That's the beauty of Celtic. I can't even remember one incident where I could say, this happened or that happened. I've got a lot of good Rangers friends as well. It doesn't matter if we lose or win against each other; the next day we will have a laugh at each other and talk for half an hour. I think it's a great healthy thing to have that. My son used to cry after we lost to Rangers – he wouldn't eat for two days. He's a fanatic – he would lock his door and not come out. My youngest daughter, you couldn't speak to her for two days. They're getting better now. There are a couple of thousand Indian supporters here, and we've talked a few times about setting up a supporters' club – I don't know if Celtic would like that or not. I think it would be a good thing, having a group of Celtic fans with big turbans on and playing drums . . .'

With grandparents from Donegal, Tony Roper, the Glaswegian comedy actor and writer, is from a less unusual background as a Celtic supporter and has witnessed progressive developments in the support since the 1950s. 'The feeling in Scotland,' he says of the mid-twentieth century, 'was "They've come over and taken our jobs" sort of thing. Orange Walks were violently anti-Catholic, obviously, so if you've got a bunch of people marching up and down the streets screaming about how hateful you are, it's a fair assumption on your part to say, "I don't think this country likes me very much." I don't think it's the same now, nowhere near it. It was very hard to get a job, in the shipyards or anywhere, if you were a Catholic.

My family certainly felt that – they were not only all Celtic fans but big, big Catholics as well. Nevertheless, although I have no Catholic affiliation now I still have my affiliation for that team. At Celtic Park, there are two Proddies at the front, two Muslims at the side of me. That breadth lets me know that we are now a very, very healthy club. That type of "catholic" fan base, and I'm not using the word in a religious sense, is, I think, really positive and if it wasn't that way, I don't think, intellectually, I could be a Celtic fan.'

8

A GRAND NEW TEAM

Once the serious business of fielding a football team got underway Celtic became renowned for a rapacious ruthlessness that would have made many a Dickensian factory owner's heart sing. Charity may have been at the club's core, but it was set aside when dealing with other clubs. Their first and most prominent victims were none other than Hibernian, the Edinburgh football club that had been the very inspiration behind Walfrid's idea to set up his own footballing institution. He had seen Hibs, with a team largely composed of players from the west of Scotland, impressively defeat Dumbarton in the 1887 Scottish Cup final to take the trophy to the capital for the first time. The immediate post-match celebrations of Hibs' victory had been orchestrated by their Glaswegian followers, largely from the Irish-Catholic community, and had taken place at St Mary's Hall, East Rose Street, where, at the end of that year, the meeting would be held from which would spring the Celtic Football and Athletic Club.

One year on from that Scottish Cup victory, Hibernian graced Celtic Park to play a match against Cowlairs, a club from north Glasgow, for the opening of Celtic's new ground. Four months after that, those friendly relations with the Edinburgh club were in tatters as Celtic began their competitive fixtures in their inaugural 1888–89 season with a 5-1 Scottish Cup victory over Shettleston that saw Celtic field no fewer than five players plundered from that fine Hibernian side: Michael McKeown, Paddy Gallagher, Jimmy McLaren, Willie Groves and Mick Dunbar. Tom Maley, a former Hibs player but now with Celtic, had been his new club's chief recruiting agent and those individuals had deserted a Hibernian side that in August 1887 had beaten Preston North End in a game that had been described as the Association Football Championship of the World decider – a match billing that had the official blessing of both the Scottish Football Association and the Football Association. Celtic's actions in removing half of this team from Edinburgh led to fractiousness between the supporters in succeeding years and remains a bugbear for the many historically minded Hibernian supporters, a fact that was acknowledged by a cheeky banner sported by Celtic fans at the League match at Easter Road between the two clubs in September 2007, which read, 'Hibs – Celtic's Feeder Club Since 1888'. Celtic that twenty-first-century day once again fielded no fewer than five former Hibernian players.

Another club that had recently been declared the world's best also contributed to Celtic's personnel in that first full season of their exis- tence, as the Glasgow club fought to field the very best team possible. Renton, the 1888 Scottish Cup winners, had defeated West Bromwich Albion, holders of the FA Cup, in May 1888 to declare themselves, albeit unofficially, world champions. In the immediate aftermath of Renton claiming that title, Celtic swooped to pluck James Kelly, Renton's domi- nant centre-half, and Neil McCallum, their winger. Both men had pledged their immediate footballing futures to Hibernian, but the Edinburgh side was gazumped when the players decided instead to throw in their lot with Celtic. John Glass, Celtic's persuasive president, was given much of the credit for this audacious recruitment policy, which brought the cream of Scottish football talent to Celtic Park, and it is also certain that the money on offer at Celtic must have played its part, even though Scottish foot- ballers were at that time supposed to be strictly amateur. This could easily be circumvented by paying players for 'broken time' – the amount of their own working hours they had to pass up in order to spend time on their football commitments – and the calculations for such payments would always err on the vastly generous side: sometimes amounting to four or five times their workaday wages.

This team-building project worked beautifully – Celtic's first venture into the Scottish Cup took them all the way to the 1889 final, in which, just nine months after they had sprung into life with their inaugural match against Glasgow Rangers, they would meet Third Lanark, competing in their third Scottish Cup final, at Hampden Park, not yet on its modern site but on Cathcart Road on Glasgow's south side. An hour before kick-off that early February day, a snowstorm swept the field, and officials of the Scottish Football Association decided that, although the pitch was clearly unplayable, the match should still go ahead, as the crowd was now inside the ground. Both clubs played 'under protest', a common procedure at the time, which meant they wished a replay to be considered, regardless of how the game might go, and so both sets of players and the match officials, if not the spectators, proceeded on the understanding that they were participating in a 'friendly' match. So light-hearted was the atmosphere that the players of both sides indulged in a game of snowballs before proceedings got underway.

Third Lanark won the 'snow final' 3-0, but at a meeting of the SFA after the game it was agreed that the match should be declared void – even though Third Lanark now demanded the result should stand – and a fresh final was scheduled for 9 February 1889, one week after the original one. Midway through the first half, with 13,000 looking on, Johnny Marshall, the Third Lanark winger, shot for goal, and, although James Kelly knocked it clear, the referee upheld Thirds' claims that the ball had crossed the line, and Celtic were behind to their Glasgow rivals. A Neil McCallum header provided an equaliser for Celtic in sixty-seven minutes but with Celtic pressing for a winning goal, they fell victim to a break-away move that concluded with James Oswald of Third Lanark snatching the winner.

It had been remarkable for Celtic to reach the Scottish Cup final while still in their infancy, but the Celtic committee refused to rest on their laurels, and in 1890 the club threw its weight fully behind a proposal to form a Scottish Football League. Scottish football had been haphazard in its organisation, with clubs getting by on friendly matches, Scottish Cup ties and local competitions – an arrangement that hampered any club wishing to budget for regular revenue. Celtic in September 1889 had drawn the biggest crowd ever seen for a Scottish football match until that point – 25,000 – to Celtic Park for a Scottish Cup tie with Queen's Park, emphasising the potential of their support, but when Celtic were eliminated in the replay that was the conclusion of their 1889–90 season in national competition. With the need to harness and maintain the regular interest of such a support, Celtic wanted to formulate a League that, in common with the one established in England in 1888, would ensure clubs could be guaranteed a certain number of regular and competitive fixtures throughout the season.

Queen's Park, the amateur club that had dominated Scottish football until then, was set against this measure, seeing in it little that was good for clubs such as Renton and themselves who had thrived on the less formal arrangements that had been in place until that point. They also saw this as a likely route towards professionalism, which had been frowned upon in official Scottish football circles, despite this stance having led to a flood of players heading south to earn reward for their talents.

John McLaughlin, the Celtic club secretary, was emphatic in his backing for the formation of a Scottish League when twelve clubs met at Holton's Commercial Hotel, Glassford Street, Glasgow, on 20 March 1890 to discuss the idea. McLaughlin was the driving force behind the League's formation. Five months later, the first season of the Scottish League got underway, with ten clubs involved. Mr McLaughlin's reward for piloting through this pioneering innovation was to become its first secretary.

For a club that had so eagerly chivvied for change, Celtic's opening Scottish Football League fixtures were far from auspicious. A healthy 10,000 crowd rolled up at Celtic Park for their first League match, on 16 August 1890, with Renton, but it resulted in a 4-1 defeat for the home side. Worse was to follow. Celtic, on 31 May 1890, had played in a match with Renton that had been for the benefit of James McCall, a Renton player. Benefit matches were allowed under Scottish Football Association rules only if the player in question was being forced to retire from football through illness or injury, and McCall had been doing neither. Celtic pleaded ignorance – they stated that they had been unaware that the match was for McCall's benefit, and indeed Celtic had given their share of the takings to four charities. The upshot was that Renton were suspended from football indefinitely; not the best start for the League, whose detractors were waiting for it to fail.

Celtic then lurched into the arms of another calamity. Their next two fixtures yielded ten goals for them – in a 5-0 victory away to Heart of Midlothian and a 5-2 win at home over Cambuslang – but the four points that the club had accrued were immediately removed from their maw. Jimmy McLaren, a superb left-half, had been fielded in the Celtic goal for the Renton match but had turned in a shocking performance in conceding four goals. Jamie Bell, a genuine goalkeeper, had been an emergency signing from Hurlford and had been fielded against Hearts and Cambuslang, but he had been ineligible for Celtic. Bell, at the time of those matches, had not yet been a full fortnight clear of his last appearance for Hurlford, and that breach of the new League's rules left Celtic empty-handed after their opening three fixtures. They managed to recover well, finishing third at the conclusion of that first League season, eight points behind joint champions Dumbarton and Glasgow Rangers, and at the end of the subsequent, 1891–92, season Celtic got closer to the top spot, finishing runners-up and only two points behind Dumbarton, the League's first outright champions.

The League had proved to be a success, guaranteeing regular income for the clubs, but it was still the Scottish Cup, with the death-or-glory excitement attached to each tie, that captured the imagination of supporters across the land, and in the spring of 1892 Celtic reached their second Scottish Cup final, with Queen's Park their opponents. A crowd of 40,000 was crammed into Ibrox Park, venue for the final, two hours prior to the four o'clock kick-off time, prompting the gates to be closed, leaving thousands locked out. Those inside the ground passed the time before the game began in singing popular songs. It was a clash between the old and the new in Scottish football – Queen's Park as resolute amateurs had refused to participate in the Scottish League competition and were determined to show themselves still superior to the slick, money-hungry upstarts. Celtic were on fire from the start of the match, with Johnny Campbell and Sandy McMahon, an 1890 signing from Hibernian, causing havoc on the left wing, and although Queen's Park held out until the interval, Campbell put Celtic ahead shortly after the break. With no further scoring, it appeared to those present as though Celtic had clinched the cup.

Instead, in one of those scenarios typical of the times, it was revealed that the clubs had agreed during half-time that the match was to be classified as a friendly: the teeming crowd had on several occasions spilled on to the pitch, causing delays in play deemed to have been enough to make the match an improper one for the settling of a Cup final. A replay was arranged for 9 April, the following Saturday, and the cost of admission doubled to reduce the crowd. On a fine afternoon, a more sedate attendance of 22,000 kept their distance from the action and witnessed the first half end 1-0 to Queen's Park thanks to a Tommy Waddell goal. After the break, the Celts re-emerged bristling with intent to seize hold of the game, and with Campbell and McMahon working harmoniously, two goals from Campbell and two from McMahon, plus an own goal, provided Celtic with a 5-1 victory and their first national trophy. In the words of Willie Maley, Celtic's right-half on the day, McMahon had scored the third goal after 'indulging in one of those mazy runs – head down, arms outstretched – [he] simply walked through the Amateurs' defence.'

The very clumsiness of the near-mechanical actions of the gangly McMahon endeared him to the support – that and his effectiveness in creating and scoring goals from the inside-forward position – but it also alerted Nottingham Forest to his abilities, and in the summer of 1892 the English club whisked McMahon and Neil McCallum, his fellow forward, to the Midlands. Celtic were prepared to put up with the departure of McCallum but not of McMahon. Club representatives were despatched south and through investigation discovered that the player was being kept at a countryside retreat as he awaited his Forest debut. They got there only to find he had been taken into Nottingham city centre for the day but doggedly they caught up with him on a railway platform. Quickly persuading McMahon that he would obtain a better deal by returning to Celtic, they completed their act of subterfuge by spiriting the great forward back to Glasgow, where he would remain for the rest of his career.

The left-wing partnership of McMahon and Campbell, restored after that brief summer interlude, purred smoothly throughout the 1892–93 season, yielding twenty-three of Celtic's fifty-four League goals. A seven-game run of victories in the spring, including a 3-0 victory over Rangers at the end of April, with goals from Kelly, Campbell and McMahon, in front of 14,000, a large attendance for a League match, was key to Celtic's first League championship title, which they secured by defeating Leith Athletic 3-1 at Celtic Park on 9 May 1893 in front of a 5,000 crowd, Celtic finishing the season one point ahead of Rangers.

That championship-winning side was, notionally at least, an amateur one, but, in tandem with the celebrations of Celtic's first title win, professionalism, in that May of 1893, was finally incorporated into the Scottish game. It was championed at a meeting of the Scottish Football Association by John McLaughlin, once again the agent for change and progression in the Scottish game, who stated that everyone who was anyone in Scottish football knew that under-the-counter payments were being made to players and that despite the SFA's best efforts to extinguish professionalism in the previous five years, they had only grown more prevalent. The only way forward, he suggested strongly, was to accept professionalism, to make it legal and to harness it. With players formally tied to their clubs by professional contracts, he argued, a greater discipline and control could be effected on them, and this would produce a better standard of play. 'You might as well attempt to stop the flow of Niagara with a kitchen chair as to stem the tide of professionalism,' he said in response to fears from Queen's Park that the League would encourage players to be paid. Following McLaughlin's impassioned speech, the motion was carried by a large majority, and at the behest of McLaughlin, the Celtic committee man and the Scottish League's secretary, professional football in Scotland was born.

McLaughlin had personal experience at Celtic of the effects of 'shamateurism'. Shortly after Dan Doyle, an explosive and entertaining left-back, joined Celtic from Everton in 1891, he spearheaded a strike among the players over pay; an odd situation at a nominally amateur club but one that the Celtic committee had to confront and which they resolved by conceding the players' demands for increased wages.

There was an immediate impact made on McLaughlin's own club following this most profound change. Celtic had carried a squad of thirty in winning the League title in the 1892–93 season, but the following year they drew on only nineteen players, a reflection of the increased cost in having a set of formally and regularly paid professional players on the books. There was still room within this process of rationalisation for some forward-thinking: one of Celtic's first moves on the legalisation of professionalism was to sign Joe Cassidy, a Lanarkshire-born centre-forward, from Newton Heath, the club that was the predecessor to Manchester United. Strong in the air, useful at link-up play and with a sharp eye for goal, Cassidy was a key signing and chipped in ten goals as Celtic retained their League title, finishing three points clear of Heart of Midlothian in the spring of 1894 and reaching the final of that year's Scottish Cup, in which they faced Glasgow Rangers.

Rangers had floundered in Celtic's wake during the six years since the two clubs had participated in the friendly match that had heralded Celtic's birth. While Celtic were making their fourth appearance in the final, Rangers had only twice, in their longer, twenty-one-year history, reached that stage of the competition, losing on both occasions. This final bucked the trend: a crowd of 17,000 at Hampden Park saw Rangers dominate and score three times shortly after half-time; Willie Maley scored for Celtic with fifteen minutes remaining but the Cup was on its way to Ibrox for the first time.

Celtic's squad expanded again for the 1894–95 season, but this proved counter-productive. Defeats home and away to Hearts tipped the title race in favour of the Edinburgh club, who finished the season five points clear of Celtic. 'Possibly our failure was due more to a superfluity of talent rather than a scarcity,' Willie Maley opined, 'as, while we had won the flag in the previous season with nineteen players, we found ourselves unable to repeat the performance with thirty-five – three goalkeepers were required to keep us going, four backs, twelve half-backs and sixteen forwards.' Order was restored for the 1895–96 season, when a pared-down squad of twenty-one finished top of the League, four points clear of Rangers and with a club record total of sixty-four League goals to their credit. Allan Martin, a signing from Hibernian in the summer of 1895, was the top scorer with eighteen goals in eighteen appearances that season. He scored one of the goals in the 6–2 victory over Rangers on 14 December 1895, watched by 20,000; not only was this a record victory over Rangers and Celtic's equal-highest League attendance of that 1895–96 season but the win clinched the title for Celtic.

One match in which, oddly, Martin failed to score was the game with Dundee on 26 October 1895, in which Celtic scored eleven times without reply from Dundee to record not only Celtic's record victory but what remains a record win in the top-flight of the Scottish League. Dundee were a fair side and in good form – they would finish fifth in that season's ten-team First Division – and had recently beaten both Rangers and a Hearts side that had won 5–0 in the League at Celtic Park the previous month. One newspaper reporter suggested that, on losing the third and fourth goals, to Jimmy Blessington and McMahon, through slack defending, Dundee were in tatters. By half-time it was 6–0. They had lost Bill 'Plum' Longair, their centre-half, to a severe head knock that left him with concussion and double vision in the first half, and, with substitutions still decades away from being introduced in the Scottish game, this reduced them to ten men. Frank Ferrier, the Dundee left-half, was unable to resume after the interval owing to an ankle injury, leaving two major gaps in the Dundee defence and a Celtic team that was flying was in no mood to ease off out of sympathy for their opponents. Dundee, according to one reporter, performed more creditably with nine men than they had done with eleven. McMahon suggested that Celtic had 'outplayed their opponents at every point' and that he 'felt as fresh as a daisy at the finish. The forwards combined to perfection and were strong at goal. Pleased at the whole show but sorry at Dundee accidents.' Dan Doyle, the exuberant full-back and another of the goalscorers on the day, exclaimed, 'Another record! Delighted at having a hand in the pie.'

An expansion of the squad to thirty for the following season continued a familiar pattern for Celtic, the club emerging from the 1896–97 season not only trophyless but as patsies in what Willie Maley described as 'the greatest sensation ever known in Scottish football'. It occurred in the Scottish Cup, the tournament that truly lit up every season for supporters of all clubs and which was still prized more greatly than the League. During the 1895–96 season, when Celtic were winning the title in style, attendances had still dropped as low as 1,000 for certain home League matches, those against Dumbarton and St Bernard's, clubs near the foot of the table. After the record 11-0 victory over Dundee, a match watched by 11,000 spectators, an even larger crowd might have been expected for Celtic's next League match, a home game with Third Lanark, but only 3,000 attended. During the previous season, just 600, the equal-lowest recorded home attendance for a Celtic match, had turned up for the League encounter with St Mirren in tempestuous weather three days before the Christmas of 1894. In contrast to those poor turnouts, a Scottish Cup tie in January 1896 with Queen's Park, a non-League club, had attracted a crowd of 28,000, the largest of the 1895–96 season, to Celtic Park.

That match ended in a 4-2 defeat, but such was Queen's Park's pedigree and status and reputation in Scottish football that that was regarded as being no disgrace. Not so a reverse by the same scoreline at the same stage of the competition, the first round, to Arthurlie, another non-League club from the south side of Glasgow, but one entirely without the standing of Queen's Park. It was truly one of the worst results in Celtic's history, as Maley suggested, and as much of a shattering blow in the January of 1897 as any of the seismic defeats that have periodically punctured morale at the club in the century-plus since.

Celtic did not have their troubles to seek even before kick-off. Dan Doyle, the headstrong, iconic left-back for almost the entirety of the 1890s, was again in dispute with the club over money and failed to appear for the match. Pat Gilhooly, a temperamental winger, was likewise absent. Injuries forced the replacement of John Madden and Sandy McMahon, both highly creative forwards, and of Tom Dunbar and James Orr, regular right-backs, Davie Russell, the centre-half, and Dan McArthur, the goalkeeper.

Three other players were missing, for more controversial reasons.

Peter Meehan, a full-back, Barney Battles, a half-back, and John Divers, a forward, had told Celtic officials shortly before kick-off in a match with Hibernian at the end of November 1896 that they would refuse to take the field until reporters from the *Scottish Referee* and the *Glasgow Evening News* were removed from the press box. Those reporters had been critical of what they had described as certain Celtic players' excessive aggression in a Glasgow Cup final with Rangers the week before. The committee told the players that they would take up their complaint with the newspaper in question after the match, but this was not enough for the Celtic players in question, who were adamant that they would not take the field unless the reporters were ejected. The Celtic committee were unwilling to yield to this demand, and, instead, Willie Maley, by then club secretary, got stripped and trotted on to the pitch even though he had officially retired as a player. Barney Crossan, a reserve player, was swiftly drafted into action, and Tom Dunbar, who had been playing for the reserves against Queen's Park at Hampden, was summoned to Celtic Park in the emergency and took the field during the second half, helping Celtic to an unlikely 1-1 draw. Battles, Divers and Meehan were immediately suspended indefinitely by the club, and hours before the tie with Arthurlie, Meehan was transferred to Everton.

It meant that Celtic could field only four first-choice first-team players against Arthurlie, and it was symptomatic of the state of disorganisation with which the club approached the match that only seven Celtic players were on the field as the match began; Barney Crossan, one of the late arrivals, was pulling his jersey over his head as he took to the field and played the match in his everyday trousers. With a patched-up defence and patchy forward play, Celtic found themselves 2-1 down at half-time. Instead of rallying after the interval, Celtic, in Maley's words, 'practically collapsed' as Arthurlie used to best effect the slope at Dunterlie Park. Celtic were soon 4-1 behind and hurtling out of the Cup. Willie Ferguson scored for Celtic late in the match, to add to Henry McIlvenny's first-half goal, but both of Celtic's scorers on the day were among those made to carry the can for the defeat – neither player was considered for selection again, and both were swiftly moved out of Celtic Park to English clubs.

A trophyless season for Celtic always tends to have far-reaching repercussions, and the 1896–97 season would prove to be no different. Celtic, after the Arthurlie defeat, lost their final two League matches and duly finished four points from top, in fourth position, conceding their League title once again to Hearts. The indiscipline that had plagued the club over that season could not be allowed to continue. John McLaughlin had taken over from John Glass as chairman, and, with the season over, and Celtic having become a limited company, the new board of directors appointed, in the summer of 1897, their first manager, Willie Maley, on a salary of £150 per annum. He had a template ready for a new Celtic that would sculpt into shape teams that would eclipse even the outstanding efforts of the club's earliest sides.

9

HOME-MADE HEROES

The wind of change that accompanied the appointment of Willie Maley as Celtic manager was more akin to a bracing and blustery gale than a gentle breeze. Of the squad of thirty that had been on Celtic's books for the disappointing 1896–97 season, only seven of those players made it into the first season under Maley's charge. His freshening-up of the team, backed by a board cash-rich after the recent flotation of shares in the club, included the audacious signing of a trio of players from Aston Villa, England's premier team, who had in the spring of 1897 clinched the League and FA Cup double. The three new signings comprised Jim Welford, a roistering full-back and native of County Durham; Jack Reynolds, a right-half who had been capped by both Ireland and England and who had also been an FA Cup winner with West Bromwich Albion; and Johnny Campbell, back at Celtic Park after a hugely successful two-year period with the English club during which the Villa had transformed him from being a left-winger into a centre-forward, so effectively that, in 1895–96, he had been the leading goalscorer in Britain with twenty-seven goals. Villa had a deserved reputation as ruthless plunderers of other clubs' talent, but they had nothing on Celtic. Hugh Goldie, another half-back, joined from Everton; George Allan, a forward who had helped Liverpool win promotion to the First Division in 1896 and had newly won his debut cap for Scotland against England, was another useful signing; as was Willie Orr, a promising half-back from Preston North End, who had finished fourth in the Football League.

It is not hard to imagine the Celtic support bubbling with excitement over such an array of signings, and the 17,000 who watched the match with Hibernian at Celtic Park in early September 1897 – and who witnessed a 4-1 Celtic win – made it the highest attendance for an opening-day fixture of a League season up to that point. With such stiffening of the substance of their side, Celtic coursed through the 1897–98 Scottish League season, thumping Rangers 4-0 at Ibrox in front of 31,000 on Glasgow's September weekend and becoming the only Celtic team to remain unbeaten throughout a Scottish League season, winning fifteen and drawing three of their fixtures; the first Scottish club to clinch the League title without defeat. The capturing of their fourth Scottish League championship title was still tinged with some dismay for the directors of the club as Celtic's form in the more prestigious Scottish Cup had tailed off severely since the early 1890s. By one of those curios of the Cup, in January 1898, a year to the day after their traumatic defeat at Arthurlie, Celtic revisited Dunterlie Park to face the same club, again in the opening round. This time, with Maley sternly steering Celtic's affairs, there were no mistakes and a 7-0 victory was duly obtained. Less happily, in the following round Third Lanark, a fellow Division One club, eliminated the Celts.

The situation was remedied the following year by Celtic sweeping into the 1899 Scottish Cup final and brushing Rangers aside once they got there; while a 25,000 crowd remained impeccably behaved despite Celtic dominating the final from first to last. Barney Battles, Harry Marshall and Alex King, the three Celtic half-backs, seized hold of the midfield, their clever interpassing establishing a tight grip on the game, while Welford, at the back, excelled in dousing the fire of the Rangers forwards. Goals from Sandy McMahon and Johnny Hodge gave Celtic a much-prized and praised 2-0 victory. One year later, the first Scottish Cup final of the twentieth century, on 14 April 1900, also featured Celtic, this time facing Queen's Park, their other great Glasgow rivals, but this was a dying rivalry: the amateurs remained resolutely outside the structure of the Scottish League – they were not even members of the newly established Second Division – and cut off from the oxygen of regular top-level compe-tition, this would be their twelfth but also their last appearance in the Scottish Cup final.

The Hampden club still gave Celtic a game of it in front of 18,000 at Ibrox Park, Queen's Park taking the lead before a beautifully judged, curling shot from Sandy McMahon provided an equaliser for Celtic. McMahon set up the second, heading the ball to John Divers, who, in turn, headed it into the net. Incessant Celtic pressure produced goals from Jack Bell and another from Divers that sent Celtic into a 4-1 lead, but a late rally from Queen's Park made the score 4-3 at the end.

Celtic entered the new century as Scotland's most successful club. They had won the League championship four times, a greater haul than anyone else, and only Queen's Park had lifted the Scottish Cup more often than Celtic. It was at this point, when it would have been easy to surf a wave of success, that Maley, the secretary-manager, and the board of directors took the hard decision that radical change was essential to maintain Celtic's status. The Victorian era had seen a pick-and-mix approach to squad selection at Celtic Park. The best of players from leading English and Scottish clubs had been lured to Parkhead through handsome remuneration, and, although this had been a successful method of building sustained success, its days were numbered. Not only was this policy expensive, but it could not be guaranteed to continue working indefinitely.

Several of those who had served Celtic with reliability and flair and who had seen out the previous decade together were now at the stage at which their careers were drawing to a conclusion. This included McMahon, Dan McArthur, a goalkeeper par excellence, Campbell and Divers, who all reached their early thirties at the beginning of the 1900s. In replacing them, Celtic would now recruit young players from within Scotland, where a host of newly formed Junior – or semi-professional – clubs had been formed as the country found itself in a frenzy for football. Maley would choose those with the ability to play the attractive, passing game that had become a hallmark of the club. This was a massive gamble, and it would take some time to hit the jackpot. Celtic reached a couple of Scottish Cup finals, losing 4-3 to Heart of Midlothian in 1901 and 2-0 to Hibernian in 1902, and remained a leading club in the League championship, but by 1904, as they prepared to meet Glasgow Rangers in the final of the Scottish Cup, they had gone four years without winning a national trophy, a severe drought in comparison to the club's early years.

It was an exceptionally young team that was fielded to face Rangers on that April day in 1904 and one with an entirely different and fresh complexion in comparison to its famous predecessors. Nine of the team were aged twenty-five or under, and the bulk of the side had joined Celtic from the Junior and amateur ranks around central Scotland, clubs such as Dunipace Juniors, Denny Athletic, Woodside Annbank Juniors, Rutherglen Glencairn, Smithston Albion, Cambuslang Hibernian. Two of Maley's earliest signings, in 1897, Peter Somers and Willie Orr, remained in the team, providing it with experience, Somers having been an eighteen-year-old when brought in from Hamilton Academical, a club that had then newly entered the Scottish League Second Division. Two other players in that 1904 Cup final side, Jim Young and Bobby Muir, had been recruited in one fell swoop by Mick Dunbar, a Celtic director, on a visit to Bristol, where the duo had been playing for Rovers, then a non-League club. Dunbar and James Kelly, now also a club director, worked closely with Maley, and the secretary-manager could trust those former team-mates to back him and help him in his new role.

This dramatic change in Celtic's signing policy was no temporary fad – it would remain the Celtic way throughout Willie Maley's four-decade-long stint as manager and for years beyond, into the 1950s and 1960s – several Lisbon Lions would be signed from Junior clubs – and on into the 1970s and up to the mid-1980s, when Celtic remained a club that would sign players of promise almost exclusively from other Scottish clubs and then only for fairly modest fees.

'I always felt,' Maley commented, 'that what we gained in the services of seasoned players was lost to us by the fact that their possible time of service to us was very limited, and during it we had no chance of raising lads to fill their places. This it was that induced me to try and get our board to go out for the young ones and, by recruiting these right from their Junior club, ensure for our team youth with all its vigour and the esprit de corps which has always been to me one of the greatest assets in our players. Another point against the engagement of players who had previous long service was that, when they left us, their value in League rights was nil; whereas there are very few Juniors of any standing but a club like ours can recover some of the cash spent on them.'

The amount of talent with which Scotland was teeming as football grabbed hold of the country's imagination, particularly in the central belt, is indicated by the decision of the club to abolish their reserve side at the same time as Maley was formulating this new policy. It seems a contradictory decision, when the club was opting to rely more greatly on raw youth rather than experience, but the logic within the club was that, if Celtic needed a new young player, they could easily recruit one, ready-made, from a Junior club, rather than indulging in the cost of rearing their own.

Once at Celtic, the players came under the strict control of Maley, who presented them with diet sheets and a training and disciplinary regime. 'The player who cannot conduct himself on and off the park,' Maley said, 'has no peg for his suit at Celtic Park.' Maley, a stern individual, always turned out smartly, was not only a former Celtic player, with more than 100 appearances for the club and three League medals, but also a trained accountant, and in his role as Celtic secretary-manager his tasks were to carry out the administration at the club, recruit players and keep control of costs. The secretary-manager became a key figure in British football as it settled into organised ways to fit the twentieth century – when it became more and more obvious that football was no passing fad. The board of directors at a club required someone to deal with the players on a day to-day basis while they attended to their money-making professions, but it was not seen as being in the secretary-manager's remit to coach or train the footballers in his charge; that was the province of the trainer. Even he would have little input into improving the players – it was understood that they knew how to play the game otherwise they would not have been recruited by Celtic. They were left to get on with their various jobs on the field, improving by associating with equal talents.

If the secretary-manager's work on the training field was almost non-existent, so too were his dealings with the players on matchdays. All football teams used the 2-3-5 formation, and no substitutes were allowed, so there was little chance of a manager being able to influence a match tactically once it had begun. The players were set down opposite each other on the park, and the better eleven on the day would win. Maley would still be sitting silently in the stand during the ninety minutes of action, scrutinising the players' every move; to them, he was a distant, stand-offish person, not a man to offer encouragement or advice with regard to the game of football, but few players would have relished getting closer to their manager if he felt a confrontation with them was necessary.

For all his isolation from the players, Maley's influence on a match would still be felt strongly at that 1904 Scottish Cup final with Rangers, which drew a record Scottish attendance of 65,323 to the new Hampden Park at Mount Florida. Alec Bennett, the centre-forward, had been fielded in every game up to the final, but Maley was aware that the player had been approached discreetly by Rangers and that the Ibrox club was actively seeking to recruit him. Maley pondered for days whether to field Bennett, one of his leading goalscorers, finally deciding that the player might be distracted by the attention from Rangers and that it might affect his commitment. So, feeding the press a story that Bennett was suffering from the 'flu, he slotted Jimmy Quinn, an outside-left, into the centre-forward spot. Quinn had scored five fewer goals than Bennett over the season, and on the afternoon of the final, Rangers rolled into a 2-0 lead after twelve minutes. Disaster looked to be looming but was diverted by two goals from Quinn prior to half-time, and in the second half a fine run and shot by Celtic's burly new centre-forward secured victory. Celtic had found a talismanic goalscorer – and a team-building formula that worked.

That triumph in the Cup meant that Celtic were on a high when, that summer of 1904, they became the first Scottish club to tour Europe; they enjoyed that venture abroad so much that the club would undertake no fewer than five tours during the next decade. Their destiny would be most often middle Europe and cities such as Prague, Budapest, Dresden, Vienna, the citizens of which were of a bent that was particularly receptive to the short-passing Scottish style, as evinced by Celtic, still that nation's most prominent team.

Rail travel was the only way to speed around Europe in the early twentieth century, and the extensive journeying to cross the continent to Prague and Vienna would have enhanced the togetherness of the squad. On their return from that first European tour, they set off on a different journey, one that would lead them to a record six successive League championship titles. The youth of the team that had seized the Cup in 1904 was such that the players whom Maley had fielded that day at Hampden would form the core of the side throughout that run: players such as Davy Adams, the goalkeeper, 20 at the time of the 1904 final; Donnie MacLeod, 21, and Willie Orr, 30, the full-backs; 'Sunny Jim' Young, 22, Willie Loney, 24, and Jimmy Hay, 23, the half-backs; and the forwards Jimmy McMenemy, 23, Jimmy Quinn, 25, Peter Somers, 25, and Davie Hamilton, 21. Alec Bennett, the 22-year-old centre-forward who had missed the final because of Rangers' interest in signing him, was given a reprieve when he opted to remain at Celtic Park, although he would now have to settle for a place on the wing, Quinn's peerless performance in the final having established the burly collier's lad as unarguably Celtic's first-choice centre-forward.

The first of those League titles was the hardest to win. The First Division had, by the 1904–05 season, been expanded to include fourteen clubs, and both Celtic and Rangers finished their fixtures with forty-one points. Goal difference would have given the title to Rangers, but neither that system nor goal average had been introduced, so the title would be settled by means of a play-off. The Celtic team that took to the field at Hampden Park for that match on 6 May 1905, in front of a 30,000 crowd, featured two changes from the Cup final that had attracted more than double that attendance to the same venue one year previously. Alec McNair, a twenty-one-year-old signed from Stenhousemuir in summer 1903, replaced Young at half-back, while Bennett was at outside-right rather than Bobby Muir, who had left Celtic for Notts County after the 1904 final.

Mr Kirkham, an English referee from Preston, was brought in to referee the play-off as there was a degree of tension between the clubs following the Scottish Cup semi-final six weeks previously. Quinn, in that Old Firm encounter at Celtic Park, had been dismissed eight minutes from time after Tom Robertson, the referee, had ruled that he had kicked Alec Craig, the Rangers player, in the face. That had sparked a pitch invasion, the second of the day, and the referee had been forced to abandon the match. Celtic, who had been 2-0 down, conceded the tie. Craig, after the match, stated that Quinn had been blameless. The League championship play-off, which took place more than two months after Celtic's final League game, was a more untrammelled, less controversial affair; goals from McMenemy and Hamilton providing Celtic with a 2-1 victory and the title.

Celtic notched a new club record seventy-six League goals in smoothing their way to the 1905–06 title, finishing six points clear of Hearts, and were en route to their third successive title when, in April 1907, they faced the same Edinburgh club in the final of the Scottish Cup. No Scottish club had previously managed to do the 'double', although both Aston Villa and Preston North End, bolstered by Scottish talent, had done so in England. Hearts, in front of a 50,000 crowd, kept Celtic at bay for the opening forty-five minutes, but Celtic's pressure told when they won a penalty shortly after half-time that Orr stroked into the net. Bennett soon smoothed his way past three defenders to cross for Somers to sidefoot the ball home, and the same duo combined again for Somers to make it 3-0, ensuring that Scotland had its first double-winners. Quinn, with thirty goals, would end that 1906–07 season as Celtic's top goalscorer for the fourth successive year, but it would be folly for any opposing team to focus solely on stopping him: all of the forwards in that Celtic team were adept at putting the ball in the net.

'They played the game wholeheartedly,' Maley said of the team that he had created and that would go whirring on to three further successive championships, 'and seemed to enjoy every game in which they participated ... Young, Loney and Hay will go down to history as one of the most perfect half-back lines of all time, both for vigour and science, whilst the Bennett, McMenemy, Quinn, Somers and Hamilton front line was a treat to watch in their sinuous movement and deadly attacks.' The glittering whirl of Celtic's attacking power helped the team to break its own League goalscoring record in successive seasons, finishing with eighty goals in 1907 and eighty-six in 1908, a year in which Celtic attained a second successive double, defeating St Mirren 5-1 in the Scottish Cup final.

George Robertson of Clyde, after participating in his club's semi-final replay defeat to Celtic in March 1909, said, 'What do I think of the Celts? They are a very clever team, powerful and pushful, but are showing some small signs of distress on account of the season's wear and tear. All round the team is good, but the best division is the forward division. Behind, slowness is a little marked, but that is counteracted in large measure by the judgement and resource of the defenders.' It is little wonder that Robertson might have seen signs of the Celtic players pacing themselves at that stage of the season: they were about to launch into eleven games in twenty days that would decide the destiny of the 1909 Cup and championship.

A combined total of 75,000 had watched the two semis with Clyde, and the final with Rangers would attract 70,000 to Hampden; the largest crowd up to that point to have witnessed a match in Scotland. It prompted 'Sunny Jim' Young, the Celtic captain, to comment presciently, 'One cannot fail to observe that the game of football has not yet reached its height. This year the interest shown in League and Cup tie matches has been greater than ever and the enthusiasm, generally speaking, has been in many respects extraordinary.'

Young's positive comments about the game's future were counterbalanced by his lament for 'the decline in charging' an opponent, a point of view that can be heard echoed a century later in the more gnarled managers and exponents of the game at the lack of tolerance for the physical in the modern game of football. 'Men are too shy to charge with the shoulder or body nowadays,' Young commented in 1909, 'because more often than not a free-kick would be given against them. Fair catch or foul bash is all the same to some judges, which is a pity, as it is leading to a drawing-room style of football that, though very pretty, is yet wanting in the old-time vigour.'

That 1909 Old Firm final between Celtic and Rangers would see the Scottish Cup withheld after the Hampden Riot, but following a sixth successive League title in 1910, Celtic would clinch the Cup in 1911 and 1912 with wins over Hamilton Academical and Clyde respectively, each win by 2-0, with the victory over Hamilton coming in a replay after a 0-0 draw in the first game. As at the beginning of the century it would take another four years of reconstruction for Celtic to form into existence a team to take the championship after the win in 1910, but Maley and Co. held firm to mould a side that could stand comparison with his first. It was another vindication of their visionary policy, especially as the championship win would be part of another double, pairing up with a 4-1 victory over Hibernian in the replayed Scottish Cup final. Even that superb achievement, accomplished in the spring of 1914, would soon be overshadowed by more serious matters that were looming on everyone's horizon.

10
CHALLENGING CHANGES

When the First World War intervened in football it did so very much in Celtic's favour. Heart of Midlothian had won their opening eight matches of the 1914–15 season and were looking strong at the top of the Scottish League when their entire squad enlisted for active service in November 1914, the only British football club to see such an exodus. It says much for Hearts, who had defeated Celtic 2-0 in the season's opening fixture, that they concluded that 1914–15 season only four points behind champions Celtic, after League football had been allowed to continue unhampered despite Britain's participation in the conflict from the late summer of 1914.

The war also produced the longest delay Celtic would ever experience between winning a trophy and being presented with it. A three-week European tour undertaken by Celtic in the spring of 1914 had included a match organised by Ferencvarosi Tarna, the Budapest club, who put up a trophy to be contested at a charity match on 20 May 1914 in aid of funds for the unemployed, to be played between Celtic and Burnley in the Hungarian capital. It proved to be a bruising match that ended 0-0, but there was no possibility of Celtic fitting a replay into a busy schedule that saw the Celtic party leave the following day on a tour in which they were being whisked across Europe at speed, with stops in each city that were frequently just long enough to allow them time to play their match before hitting the trail again: Inter-railers long before that became hip. It meant an agreement was made to replay the match with Burnley on British soil and to forward a percentage of the gate money to a Hungarian charity. Burnley won the toss for venue and hosted the replay, in September 1914, a match that Celtic won 2-0, only to discover that Ferencvarosi had by then given away the trophy as a prize to raise Red Cross funds. Despite several requests from Celtic, the trophy was never sent to the Glasgow club.

They had other things to think about in Budapest for the next four years – such as being involved in starting the war – and it probably didn't help that the Austro-Hungarian Empire, in which Celtic had toured in 1914, went spectacularly out of business with the redrawing of territorial boundaries at war's end in 1918. There the matter seemed to end until, in 1988, the year of Celtic's centenary, Ferencvaros officials arrived in Glasgow and, after the title-clinching victory over Dundee in April of that year, presented their Celtic counterparts with an ornate white porcelain vase, with handles that make it look more like a football trophy than a mere intricate work of art.

Unlike in England, Scottish League football, in the top division, continued as normal throughout the war; it was seen as a means of kindling morale in the populace, and Celtic played their part enthusiastically. They flung open their doors to help the war effort, with Celtic Park used for fund- and spirit-raising ventures, such as a baseball match between two teams supplied by the crew of a ship of the US Navy, when it was berthed on the River Clyde close to Greenock; and a display of trench warfare in 1916, with the participation of enlisted soldiers, on the Celtic Park playing surface, which began with the detonation of a land mine on the centre spot and the soldiers then being put under attack by a variety of fake bombs. The performance was received enthusiastically by the assembled crowd, but the tragic side of conflict was never far from the minds of the people in a war that produced huge human casualties which penetrated almost every family in the land. Celtic would not be untouched: Peter Johnstone, who had made more than 200 appearances for Celtic as a centre-half and who had been a first-choice first-team player in the title-winning sides of 1914, 1915 and 1916, died at the Battle of Arras in 1917; former Celt Donnie McLeod, a regular member of the six-in-a-row side, died in Flanders in 1917; Bobby Craig, another ex-Celt, died in France in 1918; Frank Kelly, who had made a couple of appearances for Celtic and who was the son of James Kelly the former centre-half and chairman, was killed in a train accident while on service in France in 1919, shortly after the conclusion of hostilities.

Those players who remained on the home front were obliged by a government ruling to take jobs in factories or yards to provide an extra contribution to the war effort – and to supplement a universal wartime reduction in footballers' wages – but even such energy-sapping work could not drain them of their enthusiasm for their footballing work, and it soon became clear that Maley had constructed a new Celtic, using the blue-print from which he had designed his six-in-a-row side. His grand new team would come within a hair's breadth of repeating that feat. As with the 1904 version, the recast 1914 model had as its bedrock some older, experienced players whom Maley could trust implicitly. Jimmy McMenemy, an inside-left nicknamed 'Napoleon' because of his mastery of strategy, was thirty-three when the championship was won in 1914 and had been key to all of the successes of the previous decade. 'The football pitch to him was a chess-board,' Maley noted. 'He was continually scheming and plotting and seldom if ever troubled himself with the physical side of the game – he had no need.'

'Sunny Jim' Young, an ironically nicknamed man with an expression so dour it would have sent the blazing orb scurrying behind the nearest cloud, was thirty-two. 'Celtic have never had a more wholehearted player,' was Maley's verdict on him. 'He was a half-back of the rugged type, but there was class in his ruggedness, whilst for stamina he stood in the front rank. His enthusiasm inclined him sometimes to excess, but a kinder-hearted fellow never wore a Celtic jersey.' Alec McNair, the full-back, at thirty was only halfway through a Celtic career that would see him go on to become the oldest player to represent the club, playing on just past his forty-first birthday in 1925. Described by Maley as 'the outstanding defender of his day' and 'the coolest and most intelligent and thoughtful player I have ever seen', he was nicknamed 'The Icicle' and was famed for his cool in reading the game and dispossessing opponents through smart positioning and anticipation rather than launching into tackles, an element of his game that must have helped his longevity. He was also a freemason and an educated man, a stockbroker.

These players' experience of the Celtic way of play made them perfect mentors to another clutch of young players plucked from near-obscurity by Maley before establishing themselves in the first team. Joe Dodds, the left-back, who had joined Celtic from Carluke Milton Rovers for the final two seasons of the six-in-a-row era, was twenty-six by 1914, while Charlie Shaw, the goalkeeper, a recruit from Queen's Park Rangers, then a non-League club, was twenty-eight; the others were all twenty-five or under. The tragic Peter Johnstone was twenty-five; Jimmy McColl, the centre-forward, nicknamed suitably for those times as 'The Sniper' for his pinpoint accuracy in hitting the target, was twenty-one, while Andy McAtee and John Browning, the wingers, were twenty-five. Patsy Gallacher, the livewire entertainer in the side, was twenty-one, as was John McMaster, the left-half. Browning, ironically nicknamed 'Smiler' for his dour aspect and 'Sunny Jim' were the only gloomy elements in a colourful side that won five out of six League titles between 1914 and 1919. They won those titles in style – in all but the last of those years they finished clear of their rivals by a considerable distance and when they did lose the title, in the 1917–18 season, to Glasgow Rangers, Celtic finished the season just one point behind their by now well-established principal rivals; undone by a 1-1 draw at home to Motherwell on the final day of the season. One factor in that setback was that conscription had just been introduced, and several of Celtic's team had been called up, while Rangers were virtually unaffected.

With the Scottish Cup suspended for the duration of the war and football matches allowed to take place only on Saturdays and public holidays, crowds rushed to obtain their weekly fix: attendances for Celtic's League matches remained ruddily healthy; the temporary conflict of the football match providing welcome relief from the real thing. Celtic's most mighty effort came during the 1915–16 season when, in a First Division now comprising twenty clubs, they scored 116 goals in their thirty-eight fixtures; the first time Celtic had scored more than 100 League goals in a season. McColl notched more than a goal a game with thirty-four goals in his thirty-two appearances, followed closely by Gallacher, who played in thirty-seven games and scored twenty-eight times. An eleven-point gap separated Celtic from Rangers, the runners-up at the end of the season.

A tally of sixteen Scottish League championships – more than half of those that had been available to win since the tournament's inception – and nine Scottish Cups meant that Celtic, by the end of the second decade of the twentieth century, were by far the most successful club in Scotland. Strange, then, to flip forward a little more than ten years, to the beginning of the 1930s, and find Willie Maley, by then secretary-manager of Celtic for more than three decades, struck with a sense of bafflement on witnessing the continuing successes of Glasgow Rangers as the Ibrox club maintained their new dominance of Scottish football seamlessly from the 1920s into the 1930s. Bill Struth, since 1920 Maley's counterpart at Glasgow Rangers, was, in common with Maley, a man whose greatest sporting interest had been initially in athletics not football, and Maley puzzled over how such a man could produce such inspired and relentless success on the football field.

Although Struth was similar to Maley in many ways, such as in being remote from the players and passing on little in the form of advice or coaching, he gave Rangers the edge by relentlessly stressing, with an obsessive's insistence, iron discipline, the importance of physical fitness, good diet and correct dress. Maley had, in his early days as Celtic manager, emphasised some of these elements, but Struth took it to a new level and Rangers' fielding of strong and powerful players, sometimes at the expense of artistry, gave them a professional edge. With every team still playing 2-3-5, tactics varied little from one club to the next, and it was the off-the-field approach of Rangers that transformed them into the dominant club in Scotland for the first time. Struth put the emphasis on matters that seem like fripperies but which inculcated in his players a sense of professionalism and superiority over their fellow players at other clubs: an insistence on pristine garb off the field, such as wearing a bowler hat to training; and neatly pressed, nicely designed strips on the field. Away from the game, Struth insisted on his players having the best of everything – the most luxurious hotel accommodation, prime tables at superior restaurants and the best seats in places of entertainment. It all went towards making the Ibrox Park men feel special, and with religious division in Glasgow particularly bitter in the economically harsh 1920s Rangers fielded rigidly all-Protestant sides that fulfilled the sense of supe-riority that imbued everything under the Struth regime at Ibrox, where the new main stand, constructed in 1929, with its 10,000 seats in two tiers, dwarfed, by comparison, the 4,800 seats in the new stand that, coincidentally, Celtic had also constructed in the final year of the 1920s.

These were tough times for Celtic and their followers. The *Glasgow Observer* in December 1925 reflected on hard times in the city, 'How often you and I have seen and pitied the forlorn groups hanging around outside Celtic Park gazing longingly and enviously at lucky fellows able to plank down their shillings at the turnstiles, the "great excluded" shivering in the rain outside the barricade and trying to figure out what was happening within, reading a meaning into the crowd's cheers, yells and groans and visualising Gallacher, McLean, McGrory or McFarlane shining like demigods in the unseen fray.'

In tandem with Rangers' sudden sure touch, Celtic's pre-eminence in the Scottish game was also eaten away by a series of internal disputes. Although Maley continued to bring through good players for the first team, arguments over money began, during the 1920s, to dog relations between him and key players at the club. Four decades after Celtic's inception, the squad for the 1927–28 Scottish League championship reflected emphatically Maley's blueprint for the playing staff at the club. All players were in their teens and twenties except Adam McLean, at thirty, and Willie McStay, at thirty-two, and all had been brought to Celtic from Scottish Junior or juvenile sides. It was a club identity that seemed set to stretch into infinity, but Maley's undisputed power over the players, their fates and fiscal matters had unpleasant side-effects.

Willie Cringan, the centre-half, was the keystone in Celtic's winning the League title in 1919 and 1922 and the victory over Hibernian in the Scottish Cup final of 1923, but when he was nominated as spokesman by the players in August 1923 to ask for an all-round wage rise, he was quickly demonised as an agitator by Maley and within weeks hustled out of the club to Third Lanark. Adam McLean, one of Celtic's greatest outside-lefts and a player recruited from juvenile football, had also been involved in those League and Cup triumphs together with helping to clinch the Scottish Cup in 1925 and the League title – Celtic's last for ten years – in 1926. At his peak, in 1928, he went to Maley to discuss payments on behalf of the players only to find, subsequently, his wage offer for the 1928–29 season suddenly reduced by Maley. Within weeks, he was en route to Sunderland. The departure of Patsy Gallacher, one of the greatest Celts of all, came in 1926, when Maley and the board, unconvinced of his fitness at the age of thirty-three, decided to offer him only the minimum wage for the following season. Patsy refused their offer, was transferred to Falkirk and played for a further six seasons.

The League title went to Ibrox eight times in the 1920s – but at least Jimmy McGrory, Celtic's great goalscoring discovery of that decade, continued to thrive, on the playing field at least, where, as the 1920s ended, he remained the most prolific forward in Scottish football despite the sterling efforts of Willie Maley secretively to spirit McGrory away from the club. McGrory, in January 1928, had surpassed even his own previous scoring feats, when, in a match with Dunfermline Athletic, he had stuck away eight of Celtic's nine goals, en route to becoming again Scotland's top scorer that season, with fifty-three goals in the League and Scottish Cup. That summer of 1928, Willie Maley invited McGrory, a devout Catholic, to accompany him on a trip to the shrine at Lourdes, but there was a nefarious side purpose in Maley's invitation. On arrival in London, the men were met on the railway station platform at Euston by Herbert Chapman, manager of Arsenal, and Sir Samuel Hill-Wood, the Highbury club's chairman. McGrory had had no prior warning from Maley as to the meeting having been arranged but, following a few pleasantries, McGrory was left alone with Chapman, who had led Huddersfield Town to two successive Football League titles in the mid-1920s and who was now seeking to emulate that feat with Arsenal.

Chapman badly wanted McGrory as his centre-forward and had promised Maley a fee of £10,000 to procure his transfer. Now, alone with McGrory, the Arsenal manager tried to persuade him to switch to the London club. McGrory's answer was emphatic and in the negative. Chapman did all he could to change the Celtic man's mind, and eventually, wearied by the Englishman's persistence, McGrory stated that he would join Arsenal for a signing-on fee of £2,000. As McGrory had expected, this brought a sudden conclusion to the meeting. Chapman was not done, though. He was awaiting McGrory and Maley again when the two men passed through London on their return journey from France. This time, Chapman was armed with the agreement from his board of directors to match McGrory's demand and, if necessary, to go even higher. McGrory simply declared his lack of interest in joining Arsenal, and even Chapman finally had to concede defeat. 'McGrory of Arsenal just never sounded as good as McGrory of Celtic,' the player would later comment. There was an appalling coda to this episode. The Celtic board of directors, dismayed at not receiving a transfer fee that would have been a British record and that they had urgently required to help finance the construction of the new main stand, decided that they would now pay McGrory one pound a week less than his team-mates, and this they did for the remainder of his time with Celtic, even though the goals would continue to flow from the player throughout the next decade. Celtic, the big-buying club of the Victorian era, had become very much hawkers and sellers and self-made poor relations to Rangers.

For all McGrory's ongoing scoring feats, the League title would elude Celtic entirely during the early 1930s, while Rangers' roaring twenties extended into the following decade. Still, the Scottish Cup held a cherished place in the hearts of supporters – the drama of the knockout competition still regularly attracted attendances for Cup matches that far outweighed those for non-Old Firm League matches – so when Celtic won the Scottish Cup in 1927 by beating East Fife, and in 1931, through a dramatic 4-2 victory over Motherwell in a replayed final, the supporters could convince themselves that the following season would go better. In those days before European competition rewarded the previous season's feats, every club began a new season afresh, with the slate wiped clean. Nor was there any serious media pressure on the manager: the newspapers reported matches and transfers and had occasional friendly pieces on players, but there was no hysteria transmitted via the back pages. Maley might have the occasional word with a friendly pressman, but he was not obliged to perform at a weekly press conference or to provide post-match interviews.

A flavour of those genteel times can be found in a gently humorous menu printed in tribute to the players who had won the Cup in 1931 by the Anchor Line, on whose SS *Caledonia* Celtic sailed for their North American tour in May 1931, the month after topping off the 1930–31 season in style with that Hampden victory. Titled 'Celtic Dinner', it read, 'Before the kick-off we quaffed a Paradise Cocktail from the Scottish Cup, then play began amidst great Parkhead Frivolite. J. Thomson almost turned Clear Turtle when saving a "stinger" but McStay, being the Sole Diplomate headed out from under the bar. After half-time when we had Prime Backs of Beef Cook(ed) McGonagle style, Peter Wilson sure showed he knew his Vegetables and Potatoes by cutely passing to B. Thomson, who flew down the wing like a Devilled Spring Chicken and combining with Alec [Thomson] sent over a Peach Melba of a cross, which was sure to bear Fruit, for McGrory scored after clever play by Scarff and Napier, which made them the Whole Stilton Cheese and the Cream of Willie Maley's Coffee. And that's how the Bhoys win medals.'

Medals did not come their way often enough, though. For the next three seasons Celtic were so far adrift of the Scottish League winners that they might as well still have been floating on the SS *Caledonia*. A 1-0 victory over Motherwell, the 1932 League champions, in the 1933 Scottish Cup final, was Celtic's only win in a major competition in the five years before 1936. A stabbed shot from close range by McGrory, two minutes after half-time, took the Cup to Celtic Park.

Maley was a man in his mid-sixties when Rangers, in 1935, gobbled up the fifth of the six championships available until that point in the decade. By then Celtic were nearing a ten-year drought in terms of titles. The appointment of 'Napoleon' McMenemy as trainer in October 1934 had seen Celtic immediately win nine successive matches and push Rangers close for the championship and in the following, 1935–36, season, with the assistance of his highly regarded former player, Maley's third great Celtic team finally materialised. It was a Celtic side that lived up to the traditions of the club, with dynamic young wingers in Jimmy Delaney and Frank Murphy and inventive inside-forwards in Willie Buchan and Johnny Crum. Flanked by such talent, all of whom were in their early twenties and all signed from tiny non-League clubs, McGrory banged in an incredible fifty goals in thirty-two League appearances, almost half of Celtic's total of 115 title-winning goals. Victories in all eleven of their final League fixtures saw Celtic complete the season five points clear of Rangers.

Momentum was maintained the following season, but in the Scottish Cup, not in the League, in which Celtic finished third, nine points behind champions Rangers. A 76,000 crowd at Ibrox Park saw Celtic beat Clyde 2-0 in the Cup semi-final, but even that crowd was dwarfed by the 146,433 – still a record attendance for a club match in Europe – that turned up on 24 April 1937 to see Celtic contest the final with Aberdeen, who had finished one place above them in the League. It was estimated that another 5,000 'broke in' on the afternoon, and Willie Buchan recalled vividly being rocked from side to side by the noise from the crowd inside the teeming arena when he ran out with the team before kick-off. Maley – exactly forty years on from his initial appointment as secretary-manager and now on the eve of his sixty-ninth birthday – showed he could still be as gruff and rough with the players as ever. One not given to extensive team talks, he did make an exception on that day to provide a quick word to the eleven stripped Celts prior to kick-off on this special occasion, telling them that, although it would be an honour for Aberdeen to take the trophy, for Celtic players it was simply what was expected of them.

That pep talk may or may not have boosted morale, but Buchan, a nimble player, was soon darting and dodging effectively in the early stages, and after eleven minutes George Johnstone, the Aberdeen goalkeeper, was unable to hold Buchan's shot, allowing Johnny Crum to slip the rebound into the net. Matt Armstrong equalised for Aberdeen only one minute later, but twenty minutes from full-time, McGrory controlled the ball on his chest and slipped a perfectly judged pass into the path of Buchan, whose scoring shot clipped the inside of Johnstone's right-hand post on its way into goal. 'It took ages to get across the line,' Buchan said, looking back seven decades later. 'I missed a heartbeat!' As a triumphant Buchan left the field, exuberant at having made his mark so effectively on such a day, a Celtic director pulled him aside for a quick word in his ear, angrily chastising the player for having scored the winning goal, when a replay would have guaranteed Celtic another massive dividend from another huge crowd.

There would only be a brief period in which the star of the final could bask in glory. Six months later, Maley hauled Buchan into the Bank Restaurant, Maley's own establishment in Glasgow city centre, which advertised Maley as its proprietor on its façade, and from which he conducted much Celtic business. 'Blackpool want to give us ten thousand pounds for you,' was Maley's blunt opening gambit once Buchan was before him, and when Maley decided a player was to move, and there was money at stake, the player had little option but to comply. 'I didn't want to leave Celtic, no,' Buchan said. 'I had never even considered moving but I never got a chance to say anything about it.' A £250 cut of the transfer fee afforded Buchan the opportunity to purchase a brand new Ford 10 but deprived Celtic of a key component in lubricating their smooth-moving forward line.

'I can't actually remember him smiling,' Buchan said in recollection of Maley. 'He was very stern, like a major in the Army, and he used to make the younger players tremble. His heart and soul was in Celtic – I wouldn't grudge him that – but you never actually saw Maley unless you were going in to discuss wages or something like that. Jimmy McMenemy took the training. When it came to the team selection, you more or less got it off the papers! So you did! Before a match we wouldn't get any instructions as such from Willie Maley. You just went out and played your game. You knew your position; do you know what I mean? He would say to you, "Just go out there and play your own game."'

Even if the team had played well, Maley never actually congratulated them, as such. Buchan recalled as a particular example a match with Motherwell – a Scottish Cup quarter-final at Celtic Park on St Patrick's

Day 1937 – when Celtic were getting beaten 4-1 and drew 4-4. Even after that game no congratulations were given out to players by Maley. He simply stood there, as Buchan remembered, 'like a statue in the changing room after the match.' It was Maley who introduced the practice of Celtic using the Seamill Hydro as a seaside getaway during the season; he had no more to do with the players there than he did when they were at Celtic Park, but keeping the players there for a week's training enabled him to ensure they were also being kept out of public houses, something that some of them perhaps failed to do in the hours and days after the momentous Cup final victory over Aberdeen. An interesting coda to that Cup-winning season was the club record 8-0 defeat to Motherwell in Celtic's final League fixture, which came six days after the final and in which an identical line-up was fielded to the one that had faced the Dons.

Visitors to the Bank Restaurant would witness Maley, after home matches, carrying bags full of coins and notes into his establishment; the receipts from the turnstiles. Prospective youngsters whom Maley wished to sign for Celtic at some point in the future would visit the appropriately named Bank on a regular basis to receive an under-the-counter brown envelope containing cash as an incentive to commit themselves to the club when the time was right for them to join. A passage from the front section of the restaurant led to a private rear area that would be cordoned off for the Celtic players. Other VIPs, including boxers such as Benny Lynch and stars of the stage, would also be allowed access, to mingle with the footballers. The players would sometimes meet there before matches, and, as they awaited the team bus, Johnny Crum would pick out a tune on the piano, while other players could be seen filling out betting slips to put bets on matches, an illegal practice. If first-team players were in at Celtic Park for training both morning and afternoon, they would retire to the Bank for their midday meal, and the reserve team – reinstated at Celtic in 1930 – would also repair to the Bank on a Thursday for lunch, after training, before participating in their match on a Thursday afternoon. Additionally, all post-match celebrations involving the Celtic players would be held there.

'He must have made millions – and I mean millions – out of the Bank Restaurant,' Willie Buchan said of Maley. 'You got good meals in there; he made sure of that, and I suppose he would charge Celtic for it too. It was a goldmine. The money he was collecting and the number of people he was getting into it meant that you would damn near need a season ticket to get in.'

Jackie Watters, an inside-forward who made his Celtic debut in late 1938, says of Maley, 'He was a very imposing man. When he spoke you would listen to him. He was Mr Celtic, that's for certain. He was a big man, well over six feet, although when I was a youngster he was an old manager. He was always immaculately dressed, always with a soft hat on, a big, powerful man. As soon as he walked into the dressing room there would be silence. He didn't need to ask for it – he got it automatically.

'He was aloof. You never saw him. When I was in the first team he would come in but there were no team talks, nothing like that. He might pass through the dressing room before a game, but his input to the first team was simply picking them. The team was picked on a Thursday and in the *Daily Record* on a Friday. That was how I knew that I was in the team for my debut. I saw it in the paper. Willie Maley said nothing to me. There was no taking you into the office and telling you.'

Those methods brought Maley two great concluding triumphs. Buchan's departure in November 1937 made way for the 'Terrible Trio' – Malky MacDonald, John Divers and Johnny Crum – to whisk Celtic towards the 1937–38 League title, finishing three points ahead of Hearts in a season that saw a record crowd of 92,000 roll up at Celtic Park on New Year's Day 1938 for the match with Rangers. Crum, the centre-forward, MacDonald and Divers, the inside-forwards, scored fifty-six of Celtic's 114 League goals, Buchan had notched thirteen before he left, and Frank Murphy and Jimmy Delaney, the wingers, pitched in with a respectable seventeen goals between them. Joe Carruth, who played in any position in the forward line when the call came, scored sixteen of those goals.

One feature of the play of MacDonald, Divers and Crum was their ability to interchange position at speed while an attack was flowing, a serious innovation for the time, and an early form of total football that caused havoc in opposition defences used to marking forwards who stuck to their positions. This facility for mid-match flexibility brought acclaim to the three players at its heart, a fact that did not go unnoticed by Maley, and the man who never talked tactics or offered a team talk decided that, even so, he ought to get some of the credit for the players' invention. 'I can remember old Maley got up in the Bank restaurant,' Johnnie Wilson, a reserve-team player of the time, says, 'and told all the press that he was the instigator of the Terrible Trio, and the three players said he was a liar! They didn't say that to Maley, of course, or they would have been out the door. MacDonald, Crum and Divers said it was rubbish. They had worked out all that interchanging themselves. He never egged them on, he never suggested what they should do.'

Maley turned seventy that spring of 1938, just as Celtic were clinching their nineteenth title and celebrating their golden jubilee. Chance and coincidence conspired to allow the team to mark that milestone with a display of football that would encapsulate the best qualities of a club that had brought much colour and light to Scottish football since its inception. An Empire Exhibition was being held at Bellahouston Park on Glasgow's south side, and as part of it a tournament for an Empire Exhibition trophy was to take place at Ibrox Park, featuring clubs from the top flight of British football: Brentford, Chelsea, Everton and Sunderland from England together with Aberdeen, Celtic, Hearts and Rangers from Scotland. Victories over Sunderland and Hearts took Celtic into a final with Everton, who featured Tommy Lawton, the centre-forward, and Joe Mercer, the midfield player, both illustrious talents, plus Willie Cook, the right-back and a former Celt, and Torry Gillick and Alec Stevenson, former Rangers players. A crowd of 82,000 was drawn to the contest, which produced much skilful football but which remained at 0-0 after ninety minutes.

'What a game that was!' Jackie Watters, an eighteen-year-old on the fringes of the Celtic first team at the time, recalls. 'After ninety minutes there was no score, and then in extra-time Johnny Crum, who was the centre-forward, nutmegged the centre-half and scored a goal. Every one of those players were great: Kennaway, Hogg, Morrison, Geatons, Lyon, Paterson, Delaney, MacDonald, Crum, Divers and Murphy.

'So we won the game and then we went to the Bank Restaurant. I was one of four or five reserves who had travelled to that match with the team, another of whom was Joe Carruth, who was a very nice man and a great friend of mine as well. I always remember the tables were all set, and at our table was Johnny Crum and the goalkeeper Joe Kennaway, who was a Canadian. On the table there were two bottles of champagne. So we sat down, and after about ten minutes Johnny Crum says, "Well boys," referring to Carruth and I, "you're too young. So I'm taking that home for Mrs Crum, OK?" So then he took the champagne away off the table. Then Kennaway said exactly the same thing. "I'm taking that home for Mrs Kennaway – OK?" So we didn't get any champagne to celebrate the victory!'

Days after the 1-0 victory over Everton, at the Grosvenor restaurant on Gordon Street, Celtic held their fiftieth anniversary dinner, on 16 June 1938. Sir John T. Cargill, honorary president of Rangers FC, made the toast to Celtic, describing it as a 'wonderful club' and wishing Celtic 'continued success for an unlimited number of years'. He concluded by suggesting that so long as association football was played, 'Celtic would be in the van'. Tom White, the Celtic chairman since 1914, then presented Maley with an honorarium of 2,500 guineas, stating that fifty of Maley's seventy years had been spent in service of the club, and that it would be unmindful of the directors not to mark the occasion by making him some sort of presentation. 'The triumphs of the Celtic club were the triumphs of Mr Maley,' White said. 'In these fifty years he has carried out his duties in a wonderful manner.'

Behind the bonhomie, the directors were less than enchanted with Maley and the grip that he held on so many aspects relating to the internal mechanics at Celtic. The board at Celtic was now constructed of businessmen; the team-mates turned directors on whom Maley could rely in his early days of management had all passed away. The new faces disliked his insistence on having sole control of the team and his brusque way of dealing with them. His profitable use of the Bank Restaurant for so much club business also rankled with them. Desmond White, the chairman's son, wanted the position of club secretary, but Maley was still secretary-manager. So when Maley stated that he did not wish to pay tax on the 2,500 guineas that he had received at the Jubilee dinner and insisted that Celtic should do so, the board refused to budge. The row rumbled on for eighteen months until, only a few days before Christmas 1939, Maley was forced into resignation. Maley had eased a host of players out of Celtic by using money as a lever and now the same thing had happened to him. The flawed genius who had moulded Celtic into one of the world's greatest clubs was now part of the history that he had done so much to make so great.

11

THE PRINCE OF GOALKEEPERS

Those who saw a particular young man posing for a picture on the deck of the SS *Caledonia* in May 1931 would have been struck by his confident gaze and assured self-possession. They might have taken him for an heir to a great fortune who was making his way home to the United States of America from the customary rich young man's tour of Europe. Or he could have been a thrusting writer returning from a first sojourn in Paris or an ambitious young businessman. Style, cool and certainty of purpose exuded from him as he looked squarely at the camera, hair brushed neatly upwards, his expression one of calm self-confidence, backed up by his smart garb: checked plus fours, long tartan socks that stretched up to the hem of the trousers and a pair of well-polished brogues. The left hand sat lightly in the left pocket of the trousers, the other played host to a cigarette, which rested, as smartly as any cigarette can, between the index and middle finger. The overall impression was one of lordly elegance, unruffled steadiness. This was the twenty-two-year-old John Thomson, on his way to North America with his Celtic team-mates for their close-season tour in 1931.

That elegance and cool was not reserved for Thomson's off-field persona. Between the sticks, the goalkeeper exerted control and calm in carrying out his work. He was seemingly able to twist and turn to change direction dramatically in the air to reach shots that had been steered or deflected in an unexpected direction. 'A most likeable lad,' as Willie Maley described him, 'modest and unassuming, he was popular wherever he went. His merit as a goalkeeper shone superbly in his play. Never was there a 'keeper who caught and held the fastest shots with such grace and ease. In all he did there was balance and beauty of movement wonderful to watch.'

That beauty, that ease and grace, was to be snuffed out terribly on the afternoon of 5 September 1931 when, with fifty minutes gone of a dour match between Celtic and Rangers at Ibrox Park, Thomson dived low to his left in an attempt to reach a through ball but Sam English, the Glasgow Rangers centre-forward, got there first, sending the ball goalwards with his right foot. Thomson's forward momentum meant that his skull collided with the attacker's left knee, and Thomson's head was thrown back violently, jerking through 120 degrees. Blood began spurting from his wound, and he was removed from the pitch on a stretcher with his head heavily bandaged, surrounded by a shoal of ambulancemen. Thomson had suffered a depressed fracture of the skull, and he was swiftly whisked across the south side in a 1928 Austin ambulance to the Victoria Infirmary at Battlefield. His parents were rushed to Glasgow from their native Fife, in a car arranged by Bill Struth, the Rangers manager, and arrived at the hospital shortly before John Thomson passed away at 9.25 p.m. that Saturday evening.

'I can remember my father coming home on the night Johnny Thomson was killed,' Rolando Ugolini, a Celtic goalkeeper of the 1940s, says. 'He was crying, and I couldn't believe a man like that would cry and I'll never forget that. Everybody loved Johnny Thomson; he was a great, great 'keeper.'

A special train carrying mourners and with two carriages full of floral tributes, left Glasgow's Queen Street station the following Wednesday for John Thomson's funeral in his home town of Cardenden in Fife. Others walked the 55 miles from Glasgow to Cardenden and would travel back in the same manner just to be present on the day. The mourners lined the route six deep as a pipe band ushered Thomson's coffin along the route to Bowhill cemetery.

Thomson's tragedy would have been awful under any circumstances, but it was particularly poignant that he had enormous potential as a goalkeeper and that that had been snuffed out so dramatically. Sixteen months previously, Thomson had made his debut for Scotland, in Paris, and had kept the French at bay in a 2-0 victory, going on to win three further caps in the 1930–31 season and conceding only one goal in establishing himself as Scotland's number one choice. Five months prior to his death, he had won a Scottish Cup medal with Celtic. Herbert Chapman, the Arsenal manager, had watched him and was rumoured to have described Thomson as the best goalkeeper in the world and a man he wished to take to Highbury. He had been the indisputable number one for Celtic since making his debut against Dundee in February 1927, shortly after his eighteenth birthday, a protégé of Steve Callaghan, Celtic's wily talent-spotter and scout in Fife.

If there was a flaw in Thomson's game it was that he could, in his eagerness to perform at his best, be rash and reckless when diving at forwards' feet, and prior to the tragedy at Ibrox there had been precedents of him being injured in just this way. During a match with Airdrieonians in February 1930 he had sustained a broken jaw and rib, a fractured collar bone and lost, into the bargain, two teeth, necessitating hospitalisation and, consequently, an absence from the team of almost two months.

Sam English, who was blameless in the incident that caused Thomson's death, sat with head in hands and weeping into a handkerchief during a memorial service held for Thomson at Trinity Church, Glasgow, on the same day as the goalkeeper's funeral in Fife. One week later, Sam, together with Davie Meiklejohn, the Rangers captain, and Bill Struth, the manager, travelled to Fife to visit the Thomson family and express in person their condolences. The Thomsons expressed their own sympathy for English, whom they could see was suffering greatly, and wished him success in his subsequent career. Unfortunately, English, a fine player and person, never got over the legacy of that day and was a haunted figure for the remainder of his life. Despite scoring a record forty-four goals for Rangers over that 1931–32 season he was soon forced to leave Scotland and join Liverpool due to the jibes that came his way from football supporters. England proved no more welcoming for the same reason, and he quit football when only twenty-eight years of age, later succumbing to motor neurone disease aged fifty-eight in 1967.

Another who felt the loss particularly keenly was Margaret Finlay, John Thomson's fiancée. Margaret had attended Celtic matches in the directors' box thanks to her father, John, general manager of United Collieries. The Celtic directors had courted Finlay to bring his business experience to bear on Celtic by joining the board, but, although he was a Celtic supporter, he had many friends on the board at Rangers and so decided to continue to follow Celtic purely as a supporter, albeit a most distinguished one. The Celtic team bus would, en route to matches on the east coast of Scotland, make a detour to Bedlormie House, close to the village of Blackridge, to collect Finlay and Margaret and Sybol, his daughters. The attraction between John Thomson and Margaret Finlay, three years his junior, was instant and potent. She had been at his bedside when he died and soon afterwards left for London. During the Second World War, she served with MI6 and the Special Operations Executive in Cairo before marrying in 1945 and living in Germany, Singapore and Kenya, later emigrating to Canada – an adventurous spirit whose appetite for life mirrored that of the man whom she had so tragically lost.

'They never die who live in the hearts of those they leave behind,' Willie Maley memorably stated in his tribute to John Thomson. Almost eight decades later that sentiment rings true. A banner dedicated to Celtic's 'Prince of Goalkeepers' is a welcome feature at matches at Celtic Park.

On the eve of that fateful match in September 1931, an *Evening Times* cartoon featured an illustration of a Celtic and Rangers player challenging for the ball in the air, with the slogan 'National Crisis' across the top of the cartoon in reference to how much greater importance was being placed on the Old Firm game than on the national crisis – the Labour government had buckled and collapsed under economic strain, and a national government consisting of Labour, Conservative and Liberal representatives had just been formed to deal with the emergency. It was an understandable comment on the over-emphasis placed on football by so many people even in such straitened times. Sadly, the events at Ibrox the following day had shown that football could be as deadly serious as any other aspect of life.

12
STRANGE DAYS

The chaos and confusion that had marked life during wartime lingered at Celtic long after the Second World War had concluded in 1945. Three years after the war's end, the club almost paid for their ongoing lack of direction throughout the 1940s when they found themselves teetering on the brink of relegation: a prospect that had never previously troubled Celtic and that has never done so again in the six decades since the turbulent events of 1948.

It has since been suggested that the possibility of Celtic being relegated was a phantom threat; the argument being that too many other results involving the other teams at the foot of the table would have had also to go against Celtic for them to take the drop. For the players, however, the prospect was all too real, and not theoretical in the slightest, especially when they travelled to Dens Park for their final match, requiring two points to rid themselves of the threat. 'There is no question that the feeling among the players was that, if we didn't win that match, we would have gone down,' Johnny Paton says. He featured as a winger in the team that met Dundee that afternoon, when a crowd of 31,000, the bulk of them from Glasgow, turned out. 'No question at all that if we didn't get a result we were down,' adds Paton with real conviction. 'It was a fateful day. It was life or death – absolutely! I think we struggled on the day. Pat McAuley got injured, and Celtic discovered a great wing-half that day through injury:

they moved Bobby Evans to that position from inside-forward, and he never went back.'

Another Celtic hero was established that day: Jock Weir, a centre-forward converted to a winger, scored a hat-trick at Dundee and won himself a celebrity in Glasgow that this flamboyant ladies' man and lover of nightlife enjoyed to the full. 'Jock Weir was an amazing fellow,' Paton says. 'He was the best-dressed footballer at Celtic Park – he used to come in with a new suit every month. He liked spending his money on dress wear. He was fast – faster than me – on the wing and a great boy, the life and soul of the party. If our football had been as big as our personalities we would have won the League every year.' Despite the characters populating the playing staff, Alec Boden, the centre-half, recalls those days towards the end of that season as dispiriting and depressing ones. 'When it goes like that,' he says, 'there's no enthusiasm. Nobody is having a wee carry-on in the dressing room or in the bath; it's dull.' Rolando Ugolini, the goalkeeper, also recalls that conclusion to the 1947–48 season with something less than affection. 'It was serious, very serious,' he says. 'I can remember there was a sort of dampness over Parkhead at the time because they didn't want to go down. It affects everybody – everybody talks about it and it gets worse and worse.'

It would have been hard for Celtic to live with the disfigurement of relegation but it might have had a purging, re-energising effect at a club that now lacked the energy and drive for forward momentum. Jimmy McGrory, the manager who had muddled Celtic into relegation trouble, had been ready to resign if relegation had happened and he might have been accompanied in that by Robert Kelly, the club's new chairman, who, whatever his faults in that role, was always guided by his own particular sense of propriety. McGrory had been appointed manager in the summer of 1945, replacing Jimmy McStay, the manager who had toiled through the war after he himself had replaced Willie Maley in the wake of the secretary-manager having been deposed in late 1939. Celtic had failed to match the efforts of other Scottish clubs in maintaining standards during wartime – unlike Hibernian and Rangers and others they opted not to use the widely adopted system of playing high-calibre international footballers from the Football League who were relocated to Scotland while serving with the armed forces. Morton fielded top-notch England internationals such as Tommy Lawton and Stanley Matthews. Celtic did no such thing.

'His appointment came in time of war,' Robert Kelly would say of Jimmy McStay, 'when football was at sixes and sevens and Celtic were having a doleful period. In any case, we had already earmarked the man who we hoped would become the Celtic manager. He was Jimmy McGrory.' McStay read of his dismissal in a newspaper while on his summer holiday in Ayr. The appointment of McGrory in July 1945, just two months after VE Day, suggests that the board saw this as time to get down to business again, with the man they had long espoused as manager being put in charge of the reconstruction of the club for the postwar years.

'It wasn't very good in wartime,' Johnny Paton, a zippy Celtic winger, signed in 1942, says. 'Players like myself went into the forces and were only available now and then. At Celtic, you did your own training. It was left to you to do your own training – a dozen sprints round the park then into the gym for a game of five-a-side football. Alex Dowdells was the trainer and he would look out now and then to see what you were doing, but most of his work was in dealing with injured players. Nobody would supervise training at Celtic Park. There were no coaches at Celtic; no organised training. You never saw the chairman or the manager.'

'I got absolutely no help from Celtic in developing as a player!' Paton states with emphasis. 'You were told to go out and enjoy your game and do your own thing, and that's not a bad idea to a certain extent because they're supposed to have spotted your talent, but I don't advise it – I'd advise coaching, although good coaching, not bad coaching. I never saw Jimmy McGrory out on the pitch once. Spike Milligan never organised anything because that way, he said, nothing could go wrong. He'd have felt at home at Celtic.' For a professional football club, though, as opposed to an anarchic comedian, such an approach is ill advised.

Paton was almost a classic Celtic signing of the first half of the twentieth century: spotted while playing for Dennistoun Waverley, a Junior club, in 1942, at the age of nineteen, he was the possessor of schoolboy and Junior caps for Scotland and had a Celtic lineage in that his father had been on Celtic's books while his grandfather, the owner of a cake and sweetshop near St Mary's Hall, had supplied biscuits and sweets for early Celtic committee meetings and was the proud possessor of Celtic season ticket number two. It suggested that Paton had the potential to be both a skilful asset to Celtic and one committed to the cause – a player with the right pedigree, and one, surely, to be groomed for the future. Instead, with Celtic having no reserve team during the war and being short of wingers, he found himself donning a first-team jersey straight away. 'Jimmy McStay, the manager, signed me,' Paton says. 'I signed forms for him, and he played me straight away, on the Saturday. I was an outside-left – my father had suggested that football clubs were always short of left-wingers, and as I was two-footed I could play on either wing. I signed on the same day as John McPhail so McStay didn't make some bad signings.

'We weren't just unsuccessful after the war – we actually won nothing at all! Other clubs used guest players during the war, but we were inexperienced – Celtic believed in maturing their own young players. That was because of Celtic's youth policy: Celtic in the war years had concentrated on a youth development scheme – they dropped Crum and Divers from that great 1930s team because they were over thirty and put young players in their place. Every time we played Rangers they had seven internationals in their team – they could field the Scottish [international team's] defence. If you concentrate too much on youth, you'll win nothing – there's only one team that's ever countered that and that was Matt Busby's team but that was a freak of nature; that and Honved, who supplied seven of the Hungary team at Wembley and they all came from the same youth club. This only happens every twenty to twenty-five years in football.'

'In the war Celtic didn't use guest players, but Celtic players did appear for other clubs: I joined the RAF and was first of all stationed at St Andrews and joined East Fife as a guest, then appeared for Crystal Palace then Arsenal, then Manchester City, then Leeds. You just contacted the local club to ask to play for them. You got a shilling a day's pay in the forces, and the match fee for a guest player was two pounds ten shillings per game, so it was well paid. Gerry McAloon, an inside-left, is the only player I can remember who guest transferred to Celtic. They later transferred him back to Brentford.' There is a sense, in scrutinising Celtic's actions during this period, that they were marking time, awaiting the end of hostilities when League and Cup football would be restored on an official basis. 'We saw some fair rubbish from Celtic teams in those days,' Brian Quinn, a childhood spectator at Celtic, recalls of the 1940s.

Celtic had been offered the services of guest players such as Frank Swift, the England and Manchester City goalkeeper, one of the greatest of all international goalkeepers, but there was feeling at directorial level that, rather than strengthening the team on a temporary basis, they wished to field players with a Celtic mindset, even if those players were young and inexperienced. Matt Busby, a Liverpool player at war's outbreak, offered his services to the club but was politely told to sling his hook. Busby, recalled James Farrell, a Celtic director from the 1960s to the 1990s, would then, at the end of the war, reject an informal approach from Celtic – made through Desmond White, the club secretary – for him to join the coaching staff, instead becoming Manchester United manager and making glorious football history for the following quarter-century.

During the war, a host of Celtic players had been scattered to the winds; players such as Jackie Watters, who spent six and a half years in the Royal Navy. Alec Boden, a combative centre-half with great ability to read the game and anticipate play, in 1943 opted to sign for Celtic rather than Wolverhampton Wanderers; three months later, Boden was whisked away to join the forces. 'When I went up to Fort George, east of Inverness, there was eleven inches of snow, and I was in the Army for three years.' Contact between players serving their country and Celtic Football Club was minimal throughout the war – Watters and Boden cannot remember any real contact at all – so when they were demobbed and had returned home, they turned up at Celtic Park to ascertain whether or not they might be able to pick up where they had left off with the club.

The appointment of Jimmy McGrory as manager failed to perk up the club. McGrory was a perfect gentleman and had been a terrific player but he lacked the firmness and ruthlessness that every manager requires and was soon supplanted in footballing matters by Robert Kelly, who had become chairman in 1947, following the death of Tom White. Little resistance was offered by McGrory as Kelly imposed his own authority on the club; most notoriously in the matter of team selection, which Kelly would see as his prerogative for the bulk of the following two decades. It soon became an open secret inside Celtic Park that it was the chairman and not the manager who was picking the Celtic first eleven. 'I guarantee you,' Boden, who played until the mid-1950s, says, 'that when McGrory left the house on a Saturday to go up to Parkhead he wouldn't know one player that was playing that afternoon. It was Bob Kelly that was selecting the team, and Kelly would tell Alex Dowdells, the trainer, the team well in advance of the match so that Alex could get each player's boots out and attend to anyone who needed to have an ankle strapped up or any other preparations before taking the field.

'All the time I was there, Jimmy McGrory never had a tracksuit on or came and said anything to you in terms of encouragement or tactically.

He used to come in on a Saturday for the game and stand up at the massage table in the middle of the floor. He had this wee smoker's cough because he was always smoking, although he didn't smoke in the dressing room. He would say, "Come on then, lads. Are we all ready now? Now we've got to win here today! Let's go then! Come on, boys!" McGrory would then give each player a pat on the back as they left the dressing room to take the field. 'Honestly,' Boden says, 'it was diabolical.'

For Rolando Ugolini, the goalkeeper, during the postwar years, 'at Parkhead it was wonderful. I couldn't get a game for Willie Miller – he was the first-team goalkeeper, Scotland's goalkeeper, and I only got five or six games and then only when he was playing with Scotland. He was never injured; they used to call him "the wire man" he was so strong. He was fearless, he went in where the boots were and he was strong as a horse even though there wasn't a lot of him. He was slim and strong. He wasn't scared of anything. But I was always on first-team wages at Parkhead and I'll tell you what we got then: two pounds ten shillings. That was all you could have – two pounds fifty – but . . . we all got ten pounds each. We used to get a package, with "expenses" written on it and that's how they paid us. It was great.

'They organised boxing at one stage to keep us fit. They had a ring and sparring. It was organised by Jimmy Mallan [a full-back] because Jimmy was a good boxer. Alex Dowdells put me in with big John McPhail. I had boxed in Armadale for five years. Alex said, "OK, lads, no hitting in the face. Just bodywork . . ." We had to keep our arms up, but John smacked me hard in the face two or three times. Before the third round, Jimmy said, to me, "Right, sort him out. Give it to him." He never ate for two weeks – his mouth was that sore . . . John was the type who would suggest something, and you had to do it. He wasn't a ruffian, but if you were arguing he was like [Brian] Clough, whom I played with at Middlesbrough. He wanted the last word.'

The early years following the war had seen Celtic maintain their tried-and-tested policy of recruiting players almost exclusively from non-senior clubs: for the 1946–47 season patrons of the stand, who had paid forty shillings for their season-tickets, saw a set of players among whom only Tommy Kiernan, from Albion Rovers, and Tommy Bogan, from Hibernian, had joined from fellow Scottish League clubs, making them the exceptions in the Celtic first-team squad. It was a policy that could still bear much fruit, but when Jimmy Delaney, the great winger who had done much to sustain the club through the war years, was allowed to quit Celtic for Manchester United after a dispute over wages in early 1946, for a fee of £4,000, it seemed worryingly clear that asset-stripping would feature as prominently at Celtic after the war as it had done in the years before 1939. Delaney would prove the kingpin in Matt Busby's first great Manchester United team, winning the FA Cup in glorious style in 1948, the same year in which Celtic were combating the danger of a first-ever demotion from the top flight. Delaney had been thirty-one when eased out of the door at Celtic – too elderly for a Celtic directorate that were eagerly stressing their youth policy.

'I don't know enough about Jimmy Delaney's argument with the club,' Johnny Paton says, 'whether he should have got the extra money or if it was his own fault or what but I will say that bonuses at Celtic were very good. If you won, there was no restriction on bonuses. A normal bonus was two pounds for a win, but it was not uncommon for Celtic to triple that for important games. The working man at the time was on five pounds a week, which was adequate for you just to pay the bills. As a Celtic player you were walking about like a star with a couple of extra pounds in your pocket – but you still couldn't afford a taxi!

'We called our football contract a slave contract because, if you signed for a club, you signed from July through until May, and, although then your contract expired, if you didn't re-sign they wouldn't pay you, and because you were still contracted to the club you couldn't move. I went without wages for six weeks in dispute with the club, but you couldn't join another club if they didn't want to transfer you – I thought it was extremely unfair and still do.'

The flirtation with relegation may have staved off the possibility of resignation for the club's two figureheads but it did force the board to act, and in the summer of 1948, they enlisted the services of Jimmy Hogan, a well-travelled Lancastrian, who, after a modest playing career, had gone abroad to coach in several European countries, which, in the early twentieth century, had been trying to catch up with the British game. Hogan had been most notably effective in Austria, where, with Hugo Meisl, he laid the foundations for the great Austria 'wunderteam' that were unfortunate in losing in controversial circumstances to Italy, the eventual winners, in the semi-finals of the 1934 World Cup. Moving on to Hungary, Hogan had helped to shape the team that would dominate international football in the early 1950s.

Hogan, a gentleman of Irish background, had been fascinated by the exquisite passing skills of the Scottish professionals when a player at Fulham in the early twentieth century, and to some extent his recruitment by the club must have seemed to him initially a bit like taking coals to Newcastle. Alec Boden, while impressed by Hogan's knowledge of the game, recalls that Hogan cut a somewhat eccentric figure at Celtic Park. A deeply religious Roman Catholic, whose father had wanted him to take the priesthood, Hogan, prior to matches, could be found surreptitiously making the sign of the cross over a player's head or sprinkling holy water over the players: his zealous application of this would see Willie Miller, the goalkeeper, running into the shower area to evade a dousing. Hogan, who had picked up a bit of excess weight on his travels, and who was now sixty-six, would also exercise with a gentle jog around the park at super-slow pace, puffing and moving his arms up and down, much like a steam train slowly leaving a station before gradually picking up speed.

With Hogan exerting his influence at the club, he was instrumental in authorising the signings of Charlie Tully from Belfast Celtic, Bobby Collins from Pollok Juniors and Bertie Peacock from Glentoran. All would, in their differing ways, provide excellent service to Celtic over the next decade. Celtic even showed an interest in signing Wilf Mannion, a key player in the great England forward line of the 1940s, when, at the beginning of the 1948–49 season, he was in dispute with Middlesbrough and pictured working on the roads. That would have been a sensation, but even if Middlesbrough had been prepared to let the player go – and they were not – the fee would have most likely been a British record; something in the region of £25,000. That alone would have ruled out Celtic bringing the player to Glasgow, but their interest in him at least showed that the club was not entirely bereft of imagination; Hogan's arrival had in itself sparked some expansive thinking.

'With Jimmy Hogan,' Alec Boden says, 'now you're talking about a guy! By God, did Jimmy Hogan know the game and he knew the exercises and the training regimes and all that. He was over sixty but he was out there every day, and neither McGrory nor McStay were ever out in a tracksuit. McGrory would occasionally stand out at the end of the players' tunnel with his hands in his pockets, smoking, just watching us training, but he wouldn't watch the whole session. McGrory never held coaching meetings or took players aside. Even if something had gone wrong on a Saturday and a player had made an obvious mistake, McGrory would never come across and speak to the guy through the week. We never got an ounce of coaching from either McStay or McGrory.'

There was a considerable contrast with the arrival of Hogan. As a successful manager of Aston Villa in the late 1930s, a role cut short only by the outbreak of war, Hogan, radicalised by his quarter-century of coaching on the continent, had been a pioneering tracksuit manager, the man who was hands-on both on and off the training pitch, and he continued this practice at Celtic. 'He would gather us on the pitch during training,' Alec Boden recalls, 'and insert wee bits of poetry into his speech, and he had great sayings and bits of advice for you to remember. He used to say things like, "See if you're inside the eighteen-yard box and you've nobody to give the ball to, just stick it in the net." Or he would say, "Keep the high balls low," or "Get the ball on the deck – it won't hurt the grass if we move it about on the deck."' Hogan was evangelical about the merits of a quick-passing approach and made the players think hard about the game, introducing elements of coaching such as making runs on the blind side of the opposition defence, trapping the ball on the run, how to head the ball properly and controlling the ball on the outside or inside of the foot. No one could deny McGrory's magnificence as a player or that Hogan had been little more than a journeyman in the Football League, but their contrasting styles on the managerial and coaching side of the game simply proved that a great player does not a great manager make.

Hogan's thoughtfulness about the game was complemented by the practical skills of Alex Dowdells, the trainer, whose all-encompassing role incorporated fitness training, physiotherapy, treatment of injuries, assembly and maintenance of players' kit, as well as being a general help and confidant to the players. It was Dowdells who would inoculate the team before the 1951 tour of North America and who, on the first Tuesday of every month, gave out a bottle of cascara sagrada to the players to get their bowels moving, who presented them with a gift box on the arrival of a new child and who would welcome those who required extra treatment into his home, where he had installed physiotherapy equipment. Yet despite the best efforts of such men, Robert Kelly still had the greatest influence on Celtic in that he could decide who would and who would not be in the side on a Saturday afternoon. He had high standards as to what was required of a Celtic man in representing the club, and that meant that any young player with a louche reputation around town, anyone who liked the bright lights, smart clothes and fast women, might, whatever his ability, find himself subject to Kelly's displeasure and be drummed out of the team and, if Kelly felt it necessary, the club itself. The same would go for any player whom Kelly deemed over-aggressive in his conduct on the field.

The introduction of Hogan met with receptivity on the part of some Celtic players. Johnny Paton, a non-drinking, non-smoking professional who took the tram home to his family immediately after training and matches, became a good friend of Hogan, continuing the friendship after both men had returned to English football, but Paton still sees Hogan's appointment as coach as something of a flawed experiment. 'Jimmy, unfortunately, was sixty-seven years of age,' Paton says, 'and his great days were way behind him. I was one of the few players at Celtic who were interested in coaching, as was Tommy Docherty. He and I went to demonstrations with the ball on stage [in local halls], and Jimmy up with the microphone talking football. We even went to Barlinnie once.'

Hogan would spend half an hour at a time with the players to concentrate solely on developing a minute aspect of the game; going over and over it again and again, and this bored the players. Johnny Paton despaired of their lack of openness to new methods. 'Jimmy would say things such as, "We don't need a gardener here at Celtic Park – our football will cut the grass with the ball. We will cut the grass by keeping it on the ground." The problem was the players didn't have the discipline to take it in – not because of him but because the players didn't take it too seriously. Scottish players, to me, need an iron fist round them. There are too many Jack-the-Lads. The attitude to Jimmy was: "You're going to teach me how to play? I can play this game!" But could they? Their attitude was ignorant. If he'd been twenty years younger . . .'

Hogan remained at Celtic for two years, and then it was back to basics. Jimmy Walsh, a regular first-team player during the 1950s, offers a flavour of the rudimentary nature of the facilities and equipment being used at Celtic. 'They were average for that particular time, after the war. Alex Dowdells was the trainer, and during the war I think Alex must have bought a lot of football boots in, thinking the war was going to last longer than it did, because it took six months to break those boots in – they had a steel toe cap and leather up to the ankle but you got used to them. He was a very good trainer, pretty good with injuries. You got no real coaching – the other players helped you – [Charlie] Tully and [John] McPhail.

'Even then, everyone knew that Kelly was picking the team, but it was

Jimmy McGrory that you dealt with in terms of money. You had to argue about it with McGrory. You got eight pounds in the summer, ten pounds if you were not in the first team during the season and twelve pounds if you were in the first team. Bonuses were where you scored: fifty pounds or a hundred pounds. Celtic did pay well if you'd won a cup or something like that. I also think they had the agreement between the two clubs [Celtic and Rangers]. They were thick as thieves to avoid having not to pay big bonuses for winning an Old Firm game. They had it tied up.'

When Celtic faced Motherwell in the final of the 1951 Scottish Cup, they were seeking their first triumph in a national competition for thirteen years, Celtic's longest stretch without such a trophy. With twelve minutes gone, John McPhail, the centre-forward, squeezed the ball between two defenders and, as he advanced on the goalkeeper, controlled it quickly before scooping it into the net. The image of McPhail powering through for that goal would be imprinted on the minds of many Celtic supporters of that era – the sight of a Celtic player scoring the winning goal in a final, which was what that strike turned out to be, was such a rare one. 'If John had played in England,' Jimmy Walsh says of McPhail, a player with a tendency to put on excess weight, 'he'd have been one of the best centre-forwards ever because he'd have needed to buckle down at training. It was possible to get by in Scottish football without training too hard. I found the difference when I came down to England and I think it would have been good for John too.'

Celtic in the early 1950s was a club listing and pitching without any sense of direction, but the club's course for the future was set fair when Jimmy Gribben, a member of the training staff, suggested the recruitment of a little-known centre-half who had spent eight years as a part-time player with Albion Rovers, who had decamped to Llanelli, in the Welsh League, in 1950 and who was, by late 1951, hankering after a return to Scotland. The player's name was Jock Stein, and when he joined Celtic that December it was, as he put it, 'to patch', to provide cover in the event of injuries to regular first-team players. Instead, a surfeit of absent individuals meant that Stein made his Celtic debut a mere four days after his return from Wales. 'He seemed to make a big difference, so much so it was unbelievable,' Jimmy Walsh says of how the Stein effect worked on the Celtic team in the subsequent weeks, months and years. 'He was nearly managing the side tactics-wise; he was on the ball. We hadn't experienced that before.

'I remember we played Aberdeen, and [Paddy] Buckley was playing with Aberdeen, and he gave big Jock a bit of a roasting. We played them back again and Jock said before the match, "I won't get a roasting today." Buckley never got a kick of the ball. Jock never got any trouble at all from him. The way he spoke to you after games he was very impressive, a very likeable chap who knew his football. I don't think I've met anyone since who knew as much as he did about the game. We had been on the verge of doing things, with Tully, McPhail, Willie Fernie, and when Jock Stein arrived he made a big difference to the defence.'

Stein's presence and captaincy stabilised Celtic – although as with any playing success that Celtic were going to have whilst the club was commandeered by Robert Kelly, it was the next best thing to a fluke that a man brought in as no more than a squad player should prove to have such an enormous influence on everyone around him. It helped that Celtic, despite regularly finishing mid-table and not once coming close to challenging for the League title in the eight years after the war, still possessed a surprising number of players who undoubtedly had that elusive quality of being of 'Celtic class': players such as Tully, Bertie Peacock, Bobby Evans, Bobby Collins and McPhail.

Eighteen months after Stein's arrival at the club, Celtic were one of eight leading British clubs to contest the Coronation Cup, a tournament held in Glasgow over a week in May 1953 to celebrate the coronation of Queen Elizabeth II, which had taken place the previous year. When the players received the news that the club was to participate in the competition, Alec Boden, the club's trade union representative, got their agreement that they would inform Celtic that they would not play unless it agreed to make appropriate payments and bonuses to reflect the players' contribution to a tournament that was expected to draw near-capacity crowds to Hampden Park.

'I was an executive on the players' union, and we had a meeting, and the players' union decided not to play,' Boden recalls. 'Rangers and Celtic players decided that. Kelly heard about it, and he came in on a Friday morning and got us individually into the boardroom. "So you're not going to play?" "No, Mr Kelly, we don't think it's right to get lower wages playing in the close season." "That's all right," Kelly said. He had a foolscap file in his hand and pointing at it he said, "I've got enough players here and I'm telling you now, there will be a Celtic team on the field in the Coronation Cup."

'When I got up and went out I knew then that some of the players had changed their minds. I was dropped entirely for the Coronation Cup and I think I only got five or six games in the Celtic first team that following season and I had been in the team before then. He dropped me and only played me when there was dire need. We weren't getting paid for the Coronation Cup – and we were professional players!'

Drawing power alone had earned Celtic their place in the tournament: the club had finished eighth – only four points above relegated Motherwell – in Scotland's top division that 1952–53 season. Hampden Park had to be filled, so Celtic joined Aberdeen, Arsenal, Glasgow Rangers, Hibernian, Manchester United, Newcastle United and Tottenham Hotspur in a knockout tournament that created huge exotic excitement in Glasgow during an era in which competitive European football had yet to get underway. A Bobby Collins goal, direct from a corner, earned Celtic their 1-0 victory over Arsenal, the Football League champions, in the quarter-finals; then, with 73,000 watching at Hampden, Bertie Peacock and Neilly Mochan got the goals that eliminated Manchester United in the semi-finals, setting up a final with Hibernian, the outstanding Scottish side of the postwar era: League champions in 1951 and 1952 and who had lost the 1953 League title only on goal average to Rangers a few weeks previously. To the 117,060 watching and witnessing Hibernian fielding their Famous Five forward line of Gordon Smith, Bobby Johnstone, Lawrie Reilly, Eddie Turnbull and Willie Ormond, who had frequently trumped Celtic in previous seasons, Celtic were very much the underdogs, but with Stein steady at the back and the players powered by the momentum of having defeated England's two major clubs, Celtic would be no pushovers.

'I can remember the first goal,' Jimmy Walsh, the inside-right in that Celtic team, says. 'Neilly Mochan hit it from about thirty-five yards, and I was in front of him and if I hadn't got out of the road my head would have come off – I've never seen anybody hit the ball so hard.' That goal, after twenty-eight minutes, prodded Hibs into a serious display of style, but despite their magnificent build-up play they could rarely get past Stein and his fellow defenders – and when they did, Johnny Bonnar, the goalkeeper, handled everything they could throw at him. With three minutes remaining, Walsh sealed one of Celtic's landmark victories. 'It wasn't brilliant,' he says of his goal. 'Willie Fernie used to run with the ball a lot, and he was coming in along the bye-line and he hit the ball too far in front of him, so I hit it, and Younger, the goalkeeper, blocked it with his foot, and I hit the rebound into the net. That silenced them.'

The momentum from that triumph was maintained into the subsequent season, and, although Celtic were seven points behind Heart of Midlothian at the end of February 1954, they clinched the Scottish title by winning their final nine fixtures, scoring thirty-two goals and conceding only four in that surge; a gargantuan effort that left them five points clear of Hearts at the end of the season. Stein, the team's rock, Mike Haughney, the right-back, and Peacock and Bobby Evans, the metronomic midfield players, made the most appearances over that League season and did much to provide the type of consistency and sturdiness that had been missing from Celtic teams in previous postwar years.

After the war, the theatres, cinemas and football grounds were full, and packed stadiums had seen Celtic become Scottish football's hot ticket once again. To top off that season, there were 130,000 inside Hampden Park to see Celtic face Aberdeen in the 1954 Scottish Cup final. An own goal, Mochan's cross diverted over the line by a flailing Aberdeen boot, sent Celtic into the lead shortly after half-time, but Paddy Buckley equalised within a minute. As in the Coronation Cup final a year before, a driving run from Willie Fernie set up the second goal for Celtic, when, on sixty-three minutes, he glided down the wing before whisking the ball into the heart of the penalty area, where Sean Fallon, a full-back temporarily converted into a centre-forward, prodded the ball into the net for what proved to be the winning goal. It was Celtic's first double for exactly forty years, but when Stein suffered a career-ending injury in 1955, that glorious sunburst of mid-1950s success would soon be obscured again by scudding, grey clouds as Celtic reverted to type under Kelly's 'guidance'.

When Bertie Auld joined Celtic from Maryhill Harp, a Junior club, at the age of seventeen in 1955, no fewer than four other lads from his successful side joined Celtic at the same time, all procured by Willie Cowan, a Celtic scout, and all of those players would have been right to cherish genuine hopes of achieving success at Celtic Park. Auld says, 'My father told me, "The Celtic reserve team today is the first team tomorrow."' On arrival at Celtic, Auld discovered that training at the top level was far from being an alien experience. 'When I got there it was something similar to what I had experienced at Maryhill. There were no floodlights at the ground – just one light at the tunnel. Training was from six to seven-thirty; two of the all-time Celtic greats, George Paterson and Jimmy McStay, were the trainers and would start you off on the running, round the track – it was all heart and lung stuff – then the senior players would take over from them, and we would go in once the experienced guys felt we had done enough.' Journeyman footballers from Queen of the South and other far-flung Scottish clubs would also be part of the cavalcade of players pounding their way round the running track at Celtic Park with Auld and the other youngsters – provisional and part-time Celts together – on a Tuesday and Thursday evening. Jimmy Gribben, the kit man, well loved and respected by the players, took the reserves on match-days, combining that with his job of repairing boots and providing rub-downs with olive oil.

'In the team, you would be playing with an experienced player who had played at international level and played with you in the reserves, and that was who did the coaching,' Auld adds. 'If you hit a bad pass, they would tell you how to correct it the next time. There wasn't such a thing as being "coached", but if you were in the first team and kept making mistakes, the senior players would bring it to your attention and tell you what you should be looking for; it was during the actual game itself that you learned the game and it couldn't have been any better . . .' This form of apprenticeship, of learning on the job, meant that young players were toughened into shape by the hard realities of the game. Those who had stepped up from Junior football found it a more physical environment, and, with bonuses at stake, senior players would be unsparing in their criticism and advice if a younger, more inexperienced man was proving too much of a liability to the team. For young players who needed to be given experience at senior level away from Celtic, there was no loan system in place; Auld, at nineteen, was instead transferred to Dumbarton in the autumn of 1956, then transferred back to Celtic the following summer after receiving invaluable lessons in first-team football at Second Division level. Jim 'Peem' Docherty, a contemporary of Auld, was trans-ferred to Alloa Athletic around the same time but did not make it back to Celtic.

On his return to Celtic, in mid-1957, Auld discovered a radically different system now in operation at reserve-team level, where Jock Stein, recently retired as a player through an ankle injury, was now in charge of the second team. 'Jock introduced team talks – the likes of which you had never heard before,' Auld says. 'It was a bit more exciting. You were desperate to get to the ground because it was new to you. You could see things happen on the park when you played on a Saturday that you had been practising in training during the week.'

It was also still well understood among the players that it was Robert Kelly who was selecting the first team. 'Jimmy McGrory, the boss, went into town in a taxi on a Tuesday,' Auld recalls, 'and collected the wages from the bank in the city centre then returned by taxi, and that's when you saw him – on a Tuesday – but I didn't see a lot of him on matchdays. Everybody gave him respect because he was such a lovely man. I played in every round of the League Cup in 1957 but got dropped for the 7-1 game [the League Cup final victory over Rangers], and no explanation was given. The team sheet would come up on a Friday, and if your name was in, it was in. There was never any explanation at all, and you never questioned it. You didn't know if it was the boss or the chairman who had decided to leave you out of the team.'

Despite occasional fluctuations in Celtic's fortunes, such as that triumph over Rangers in the League Cup, a new national postwar tournament, which Celtic had also won in 1956 by beating Partick Thistle in the final, sustained success was impossible for Celtic while Robert Kelly was pulling the strings. As the 1950s drew to a close, though, there was no sign of Kelly, a man with only a rudimentary knowledge of football, being prepared to relinquish his iron grip on the playing side at Celtic.

13
WHAT A DIFFERENCE A DECADE MAKES

The pronouncement, 'They think it's all over – it is now' ensured that lasting fame would be attached to the velvety-voiced Kenneth Wolstenholme, BBC Television's chief football commentator in the 1960s. That phrase had captured the moment when Geoff Hurst had sealed England's 1966 World Cup victory, and Wolstenholme was duly dispatched to Lisbon to cover British football's next momentous match: the 1967 European Cup final. With only forty-five minutes played in that match and Internazionale of Milan 1-0 up on Celtic, the Englishman clearly felt that that particular game was also all over. Match hospitality had not yet been invented for football's dignitaries, so at half-time Wolstenholme left the commentary box to stretch his legs and bumped into Bob Kelly, the Celtic chairman, doing the same thing. 'Still, not to worry . . .' Wolstenholme said. 'It's no disgrace to reach a European Cup final and lose to a team such as Inter Milan.' Kelly tipped his glasses on to the bridge of his nose, looked over them at Wolstenholme, as was the chairman's wont when upbraiding someone for a comment to which he objected, and responded, 'Lose? Mr Wolstenholme – we are here to win the European Cup!'

Robert Kelly's conviction on that occasion was admirable, but his contribution to Celtic's great successes of the second half of the 1960s was haphazard – he is best described as the accidental architect of that great victory. A host of young players featured in the Celtic team of the early

1960s, giving the side the nickname the 'Kelly Kids' after Manchester United's 'Busby Babes', but this was a similarity in name only: Matt Busby and Jimmy Murphy, at Old Trafford, tutored young players on the training ground, but there was no equivalent system at Celtic in the late 1950s or early 1960s. Young players were plunged into the first team and left to sink or swim. 'It wasn't organised at all,' Charlie Gallagher, a young player in that era, says. 'It was complete and utter pandemonium. We went up there to train, and the training strips were manky. The part-timers would all be there on Tuesday and Thursday nights, and the training in those days was just running round and round the park. Nobody was there to look after you. There would be one light on at either corner of the main stand, and that was it, and we used to see players jumping away up into the terracing and sitting there for a wee while for a wee smoke. We were young boys up there, at fifteen, sixteen years of age. After training, before you would go in for a shower, there was a wee gym up at Celtic Park, and we used to kick a medicine ball about, and if we managed to get hold of a normal football we used to have five-a-sides and kick hell out of one another. There was no organisation whatsoever. At Kilmarnock amateurs we used to have clean training kit every night we went there and we would train with the Kilmarnock first team. At Celtic you would be wearing someone else's shorts and socks and shirt.

'You don't know if Bob Kelly had a masterplan – he might have had a masterplan but he had nobody running it for him because the training was non-existent. You got no help whatsoever even when you went full-time. We [full-time players] used to get a ball occasionally in training and we had to go out into the car park – we weren't allowed on the park. That's true. My first game for Celtic was in August 1959, and in those days there was a dressing room for the first team and a dressing room for the reserve team, and you couldn't walk into the first-team dressing room. You had to knock the door even to ask for something. So you didn't really know any of them. You'd done no training with them, nobody said anything to you about how to play. The manager – and he was the nicest man in the world, Mr McGrory – came in before the start of the game and said, "We're Glasgow Celtic. We expect to win. We know how to play."'

During the early 1960s, crowds duly dipped as Celtic struggled to attain success, and those supporters who did attend would huddle together inside the Jungle or at the Celtic End, and, while boisterous in support of the team when it was doing well, some inhabitants of the Jungle could also be highly critical of their own players: the teenagers who were trying to force their way into the team in the late 1950s and early 1960s were often lashed by ferocious and foul-mouthed abuse. This induced in some players a tendency not to want the ball, to 'hide'. Celtic players would also, on facing English sides in friendlies at that time, feel inferior; not only were they usually physically smaller but they would feel they were from a smaller club.

'You hardly played in the same position from one week to the next,' Bobby Carroll, a winger at Celtic in the late 1950s and early 1960s, says. 'I would be outside-right, then centre, then outside-left, then inside-right. Stevie Chalmers was the same – in fact everybody was getting switched about. It wasn't very professional, to be quite truthful, at the time.'

The League table reflected the lack of leadership at Celtic: over the first five seasons of the 1960s, Celtic's best showing was in coming third – in 1962 and 1964 – eight points behind Dundee, the champions, in the first instance, and eight behind Glasgow Rangers on the second of those occasions. The team did reach Scottish Cup finals but lost 2-0 to Dunfermline Athletic in a replay in 1961 and 3-0 to Rangers, in the 1963 replay, when the despondent Celtic supporters had melted away from the terracing long before the conclusion of the defeat.

There was a lackadaisical air about Celtic with moments of gloom blending with moments of amateurish fun. Against Airdrieonians in a 1963 League match, Celtic were 9-0 ahead when the referee awarded Celtic a penalty. Almost to a man, the 13,000 crowd at Celtic Park chanted for Frank Haffey, the goalkeeper, to take the kick. He duly obliged, giving it everything, and when Roddie McKenzie in the Airdrie goal saved it, Haffey stood and applauded him. A converted penalty and one more goal would have equalled Celtic's record victory, but that casually missed opportunity was typical of Celtic at the time.

'Jimmy McGrory would chat to the boys,' Tommy Gemmell recalls of the first Celtic manager under whom he played, 'puff on his pipe, pat you on the back and say, "You're doing well, son." He stayed in the background. There would be little discussion of tactics. If you were a full-back your job was to get the ball from back to front: you were expected to boot the ball down the park in the direction of the winger. If you could mark your opponent, get the ball off him and hump it sixty or seventy yards, from back to front, you were termed a good player. We were taught nothing about teamwork. No one tried to knit us together as a team.

'Rangers were winning everything. I don't half remember that season, 1963–64, when Rangers won five games out of five against us and scored eleven goals to our one. They were a tremendous side, and it wasn't a disgrace to be beaten by them, but it was galling for the supporters that they got all the kudos and we won nothing.' There appeared no prospect of Rangers being usurped as the dominant club in Scotland; the Ibrox club won the League title three times in the first half of the 1960s, the Scottish Cup four times and the League Cup four times. They were also good enough to reach the semi-finals of the European Cup and the final of the European Cup-Winners' Cup. 'In some games against Rangers,' John Clark recalls of that time, 'you'd say, "We really gave them a doing," but you'd finished up on the losing side.'

Down at Old Trafford, as Matt Busby rebuilt his Manchester United side in the early 1960s, he could not decide whether to try to sign Jim Baxter of Rangers or Pat Crerand of Celtic, as his new playmaker. The internal strife at Celtic made his decision for him. On New Year's Day 1963, at half-time in the traditional Ne'erday derby, with Celtic 1-0 down, Crerand had a volatile argument with Sean Fallon, who had insisted on long-ball tactics for the second half. Crerand had argued that, with light-weight inside-forwards Charlie Gallagher and Bobby Murdoch up against giant Rangers defenders Harold Davis, an ex-Korean War officer, and Ron McKinnon, a passing game would be better, especially on a frozen surface. There was no future for Crerand at Celtic after that, and he was sold to Manchester United in February 1963. Fallon was being groomed by Kelly for the manager's job in succession to McGrory, and, with Fallon's influence growing at the club, Kelly would not tolerate any dissent against him.

Players who had been spotted and signed by Celtic were achieving great successes during the first half of the 1960s; but they were doing so elsewhere. Talents such as Bertie Auld and Bobby Collins, inner-city Glasgow boys, had skills laced with a fiercely combative approach – often the hallmark of the great Scottish ball-player – but that had been too much for Robert Kelly to take. He had moved them south. Collins had gone to Everton in 1958 then on to Leeds United in 1962, where he was credited with nurturing the Leeds team that would go on to dominate English football from the mid-1960s to the mid-1970s and where, in 1965, he would become the first Scotsman to be named Footballer of the Year in England. Auld had gone to Birmingham City in 1961 and had been a member of their League Cup-winning side and part of the team that had lost, narrowly, a Fairs Cup final to Roma. 'Celtic had actually been wanting me to go to Everton in a double transfer with Bobby Collins,' Auld recalls, 'and I didn't want to leave because I was a homebird; no way was I going just whenever they clapped their hands, but when Collins was leaving I was disappointed because he was one you looked up to and learned from.'

Auld, an extrovert individual, had been settled in Birmingham when he got the call to return to Celtic at the beginning of 1965, at the prompting of Jock Stein, then the Hibernian manager. 'One of his friends phoned me,' Auld says, 'and asked if I wanted to come back. He told me Jock was coming back as manager. I had a nice lifestyle in Birmingham, and Birmingham wanted me to stay, and I wouldn't have come back to anybody else but Celtic.' Auld took a pay cut of five pounds a week in rejoining Celtic; no small amount during an era in which his father, a builder's labourer, was earning only eight pounds a week. He knew success would follow with Stein and speaks with emotion of the unique feeling of pulling on the hooped shirt.

Two goals from Auld, both equalisers, made the score 2-2 in the 1965 Scottish Cup final with Dunfermline Athletic, a match in which, with Stein in the dugout, the club was pursuing its first trophy in eight years. A soaring header from Billy McNeill, nine minutes from time, proved to be the winner. Charlie Gallagher took the corner for McNeill to head the ball netward that afternoon and says, 'Big Billy had a knack for a good run, and he was very good in the air, so I just tried to aim for the spot where Billy wanted the ball. If he gets there and heads it, that's it.'

Although this was a great, symbolic victory, a sign that Celtic, at last, were back, the football on display bore little resemblance to the smooth, assured stuff that would be characteristic of Celtic once Stein had settled himself properly into the manager's chair. The 1965 final was actually a bit of a scrap, with both teams struggling to string passes together, with the ball frequently miscontrolled, panicked players whacking the ball away in any direction; and of overhit, misjudged crosses. A strong, swirling wind did not, admittedly, help. Stevie Chalmers, Bobby Lennox and Charlie Gallagher were among the few to manage to show some style. At Dunfermline's second goal, the Celtic defensive wall had fallen apart like a rotten fence assaulted by a sudden gale, simply by the Dunfermline tactic of changing the angle of the shot on goal by one player nudging the kick a few yards sideways for John McLaughlin, the Dunfermline striker, to hit a crisp twenty-yard shot that slithered into John Fallon's net.

'The '65 Cup final was the most vital one for us,' Bobby Lennox suggests. 'Our team was new for Jock Stein. He was new for us and we've come back from behind to win the Cup. He might have thought, if we'd got beaten, that we were a team of losers. So for him and us we went from strength to strength after that.'

Money was made available to Stein that summer when he was author-ised to pay a club record transfer fee of £22,500 to sign Joe McBride from Motherwell. Celtic had been in four times previously for McBride, but Robert Kelly had refused to pay the fee even after a transfer had been lined up, and the deal had always fallen through at the last minute. McBride, a Celtic supporter, was keen to move to Celtic Park but at the very last moment this time, George Farm, the Dunfermline Athletic manager, offered a higher fee to Motherwell, who began pushing McBride to move to East End Park. Farm even arranged to visit McBride at home, and the player, who was desperately keen to move to Celtic, spoke to Stein on the telephone to ask for advice on how to repel this flattering but unwanted interest. The Celtic manager told McBride to demand a signing fee of £5,000, a sum large enough to enable the player to buy a couple of houses, cash down. That, he suggested, would end Dunfermline's interest.

Farm, on hearing this request from McBride, telephoned his chairman from the player's home and got immediate agreement to pay McBride the astronomical signing-on fee. The player, stalling, asked for time to think it over, and Farm had barely left his house before an agitated Stein was on the phone again, asking to know how the meeting had gone. When McBride told him that Dunfermline had acceded to his request, the silence on the other end of the phone was such that McBride thought he must have lost the connection. 'Hello – anybody there?' he said down the line, rousing a clearly shocked Stein. 'What would you do?' McBride asked. 'I would take it . . .' said Stein, still in a state of bemusement at the news, before hastily backtracking, 'No, no, no . . .' and then going on to sell to McBride the benefits of joining Celtic as opposed to going for immediate financial gain. It did not need much of a sales pitch, and he had got his man, who went on to score a majestic forty-three goals in League, League Cup and Scottish Cup in his debut, 1965–66, season. 'I just had a knack of being there at the right time,' McBride says, 'and I did have an eye for the ball but I could play as well. Jimmy McGrory said I was the best goalscorer he had ever seen. I said, "Did you never see yourself on film, Mr McGrory?"'

The changes under Stein could be subtle but stunning. The first home League match of Celtic's first full season with Jock Stein as manager saw them face Clyde, then their most local of rivals, in early September 1965. With seventy-two minutes gone and the score still 0-0, a foul was committed on a Celtic player just outside the penalty area, and the referee pointed to the penalty spot. One Celtic player in that team was agog with astonishment. 'This must be what it is like to play for Rangers,' he thought to himself. During the first half of the 1960s, Celtic players had found themselves denied blatant penalties – clear handballs and highly visible and deliberate hacks – in matches against Rangers. Now, though, as that player notes, Celtic had Jock Stein standing, glowering on the touchline, an intimidating presence for any referee.

'The defence got more steady,' Charlie Gallagher says of life under Stein, 'and, although he liked to play football, if the ball was in the penalty box it was, "Hoof it!" For us in the middle of the park, it was, "Get the ball to the wingers! Get it to the wingers!" Just wee minor things like that he was good at telling us.'

Stein's methods worked magnificently and when Celtic defeated Rangers 2-1 in the League Cup final of October 1965, Stein knew a barrier had been broken. Defeating their arch-rivals in a major Cup final, after eight years interspersed only by reversals, took his team on to a new level. Both of Celtic's goals had come within the first half hour, and both were from penalties by John Hughes. 'I always put my penalties in the same place: to the goalkeeper's right,' he says, 'but Greig spoke to Ritchie [the Rangers goalkeeper] before the first penalty, I could see him speaking to him, so I changed it. It wasn't a particularly good penalty. It wasn't in the corner, it was about two feet from the corner, and Ritchie half got to it, but it went in, and that made it a good one. The second one I hit where I normally put them, and he got his hand to it, but he didn't stop it. I'm proud of scoring those goals because you're under a lot of pressure taking a penalty, especially against the Rangers. I was quite chuffed with myself after that.'

Celtic powered on relentlessly from that point, and they had scored 105 goals in thirty-three League matches – including a 5-1 New Year's Day defeat of Rangers at Celtic Park – when they travelled to Motherwell for the final match of the 1965–66 season, needing only to prevent a four-goal defeat to be certain of clinching their first League title for a dozen years. The more fanatical among the Rangers support were no doubt hanging on for the favour of a surprise trouncing from the Fir Park side, but two days prior to the fixture John Wilson, the vice-chairman of Glasgow Rangers, had sent a telegram to Celtic Park that read, 'The chase is over. This proves that the "Old Firm" are not infirm. Congratulations on winning the Scottish League. Best of luck in Europe next year.'

It is not known how well those emotions sat with Scot Symon, manager of Glasgow Rangers. A 1-0 victory over Motherwell clinched the title, and Celtic's place in the European Cup and Stein's team followed that with a domestic treble in the 1966–67 season, playing sweet, flowing football and, glaringly at Rangers' expense, winning a second successive League Cup final, 1-0 this time, and clinching the title with a 2-2 draw at Ibrox in early May 1967 before defeating Aberdeen 2-0 in the Scottish Cup final. It could easily have been a second successive treble: in the Scottish Cup final replay of 1966, Kai Johansen had burst through to score a late winner for Rangers, freed to do so because John Hughes, his marker, had a dead leg that prevented him tracking back. During the first match, Celtic had comprehensively outplayed Rangers but had failed to put the ball in the net.

These were Celtic's first League titles since 1954, and Stein's arrival had shattered Rangers' belief that they were, by right, given the occasional inevitable hiccup, the dominant football club in Scotland. Since the appointment of Bill Struth as the Rangers manager in 1920, a culture of discipline, together with an all-Protestant eleven, had taken Rangers far. Symon, his successor, had continued the tradition since 1954, but Stein's progressive style of management had flipped fortunes Celtic's way, and in the autumn of 1967 Symon paid the ultimate managerial price. John Lawrence, the Rangers chairman, had, with a sense of timing that would embarrass the clumsiest of Junior full-backs, stated prior to Rangers' European Cup-Winners' Cup final in May 1967 that Symon's effectiveness as a manager would be measured next to that of Stein. There could only be one winner in that contest: Symon was following Struth's blueprint rather than, as Stein did, placing the emphasis on coaching, flexible tactics and being a tracksuited manager.

While Celtic were in South America to face Racing Club in the World Club Cup in November 1967, Symon was stabbed in the back and sacked by a board who chose an intermediary, Alex McBain, a Glasgow accountant, to deliver the news rather than telling Symon face to face. An even greater measure of the impact Stein had made was that, at that time, Rangers were three points clear of Celtic in the League, albeit with a game more played, although Celtic had already dispatched them from the League Cup. Celtic went on to win that tournament by defeating Dundee 5-3 in the final, a few days prior to Symon's dismissal. A series of Rangers managers would now try – and fail – to wrest power from Stein, with Davie White, Symon's successor, the next to flounder.

A tour of North America in the early summer of 1966 had proved to be the most important such excursion ever undertaken by the Celtic Football Club. During a five-week period, they played eleven matches, in Bermuda, Canada and the United States of America. They won twice against Tottenham Hotspur, drew with Tottenham again and with Bayern Munich and Bologna, won against Atlas, the Mexican club, and sent goals raining past various goalkeepers representing local clubs. More important than the results was the spirit instilled in the players through getting to know each other better. 'Being away for five weeks,' Tommy Gemmell says, 'we got to know each other very, very well, and that increased the team spirit. Being born within thirty miles of Glasgow, we all had the same sense of humour and we were always creating laughs and doing wind-ups on each other. Jock was trying to make us one big family, and he succeeded. We were also hungry for success. We'd never had success so we wanted to win things, and once you start winning things it becomes a habit, and you don't want to stop winning.'

Living out of each other's suitcases during that tour could have an amusing effect. One evening in Canada, the players were attending a party, and after quite a few drinks had been consumed a strawberry from the buffet somehow landed on John Hughes' shoe. Yogi was known for his low tolerance level and immediately sought a perpetrator and, as Tommy Gemmell was nearest to him, blamed the full-back for the connection of strawberry with shoe. Hughes grabbed the back of the shirt Gemmell was wearing and ripped it in two until the collar was the only part of it remaining. 'How do you like your shirt now, Gemmell, eh?' he said. Tommy replied, 'My shirt's fine; it's in the wash – this is one I borrowed from Bertie.'

Such moments would help bind together a group of naturally bois- terous players. 'I was from a family of seven children – four boys and three lassies,' Bertie Auld says, 'and it was like being part of a big family on that tour with Celtic. In a family, you would go to work and then come home and talk about what had happened during the day; with Celtic it was the same – we played and trained and then chatted at night. If somebody in our team got kicked it was like someone kicking a member of the family.'

The triumph in the European Cup final, plus the domestic treble, in 1967 further boosted the Celtic players' belief in their abilities. 'We had players who could play in a variety of positions,' Auld says, 'players who got bums on seats and then got them off them by making supporters stand and applaud.' Stein's creation not only took opposing players by surprise but left the followers of Celtic astonished too.

'They were playing in a way that you thought, "Where the hell did that come from?"' recalls Tony Roper, who watched in amazement as Celtic evolved from losers into gold-standard winners within months in the mid-1960s. 'I can remember Billy McNeill going up for headers. Centre-halfs didn't do that. Tommy Gemmell, Jim Craig, attacking up the flanks; when that first happened, people used to say, "What are you doing?" They were a phenomenal team, astonishing. I remember watching Bobby Lennox and being totally impressed because he might not have beaten the guy and got the cross in, but every time we would get a thrown-in or a corner so there was always the benefit of it. They were a very fast team individually, harriers. Stevie Chalmers attacked the full-backs and harried them when they had the ball. That's what modern forwards should do. There was not one weakness in that team. There was not one guy in that team where you could go, "I'll tell you who'd be better than him ..." No, and I'm talking about the whole of Britain – there wasn't one guy you'd swop from any other team, bar none. That's how good they were.'

The Celtic players of the 1960s performed with excellence all over the world, but their rewards for doing so were materially modest. 'The money in football now is just mind-blowing at times,' John Clark, the sweeper, says. 'When people look at what people are earning now, never in your wildest dreams when you were way back playing, then, would you have ever thought that people would have been paid thousands of pounds with Celtic to play football. Back then, it would just give you a living. I started on a fiver a week, then I got seven pounds a week, then it went to ten, then to fourteen, then to eighteen – the highest wage I got was about sixty pounds a week – and you got bonuses as well. Other people in other jobs could earn the same as us, maybe through working a lot of hours with a lot more effort. It gave us a good enough living back then, but you weren't making enough money to put away plenty for the future – no way could you do that. I wouldn't change my life – in my time I was happy and I enjoyed playing and we got a lot of success, a lot of honours, won everything that was going in football and I got capped by my country. What more could you ask for? You've got to feel honoured and proud about that.

'Equipment, kit, hotels where you stayed were always A1, top level. We were never taken away anywhere cheapskate; it was always top bracket.' There was also an improvement in players' standards of living, albeit a very gradual and incremental one. 'That was the noticeable thing in the sixties,' Bobby Lennox says. 'From going up in the train and the tram when there would be two or three cars there at Celtic Park, there would then be half a dozen cars, and then all the boys would get cars. That was through the sixties.' Gemmell, the most extrovert of that team, went so far as to indulge himself by purchasing a white S-type Jaguar. 'I went on an ego trip when I got that,' he says. 'My head had swollen with our success at Celtic, and I felt that the S-type would fit right in with my image as a flair player. It was great fun to drive up to Celtic Park in that gleaming S-type with the punters all giving you the thumbs-up as you motored past them. Better than riding up to the ground on a bicycle, isn't it?'

The influence of the team was felt far and wide. Coaches from Ajax of Amsterdam visited Glasgow after the 1967 European Cup win to observe Stein's training methods and broke it down systematically and turned it into a programme that would help their own club lift the European Cup in 1971, 1972 and 1973. In 1967–68, a stinging Rangers gave Stein's European champions the tightest chase for the title he would experience in all his years at Celtic, even though his team scored 106 goals and conceded only twenty-four over the League season. As Jim Craig, the full-back, points out, not many teams can do that: score freely while maintaining security at the back. Despite that, Rangers were abreast of Celtic, who topped the table only on goal difference as the season neared its end. Victory looked to be essential in the final two matches, but at Celtic Park in the first of those two fixtures, Morton were holding Celtic 1-1 with seconds remaining. The ball was pitched into the Morton goal-mouth in one desperate final effort to score, and Bobby Lennox got his foot to it to edge the ball into goal. 'I was concerned there might be shades of offside about it,' he says, 'so I looked neither right nor left and was back at the halfway line before the linesman could even think about raising his flag. The goal was given, so we were still in front with a game to go.' When Rangers lost at home to Aberdeen the following Saturday, Celtic were champions again, creating a new club record by scoring more than 100 League goals for a third successive season.

Rangers were burned off efficiently early in the 1968–69 season, and the two Cup finals in the spring of 1969 – a 6-2 League Cup win over a useful Hibernian side and a 4-0 defeat of Rangers – emphasised Celtic's precise passing, speed of action and finishing power. 'There was a real sense of competition,' Jim Craig says of matches with Rangers around that time. 'They had three great players [in the late 1960s]: Willie Henderson was a great outside-right; Willie Johnston was the best outside-left I ever faced; and Colin Stein [the striker] was a right good player as well. The reason we won more of those games than we lost was that Gemmell, myself and McNeill tended to handle the opposition most of the time. We were a better all-round team. We were quicker and faster and had more stamina.

'Jock's instructions were to kick them, in the '69 final. At half-time, with us 3-0 up it was a really enjoyable dressing room – but Jock was saying, "Make sure you keep tight on them. They can still get back into it." We were thinking, "Aye, right." On that day, everyone rose to the occasion and dominated our immediate opponent. It really was a great feeling. It doesn't always work that way – by the law of averages you can play as well as you can, but half the team doesn't. That was an important final because Rangers were just beginning to hint that they could come back, and we had put them back in their place again.'

Celtic in the 1960s was an uncomplicated club; far removed from the white-hot heat of technology. Physiotherapy for a player with, for example, an injured ankle would consist of them plunging the affected joint into a basin of boiling water, withdrawing it, being hosed down by a cold shower, returning the ankle to the hot water again. Training would take place on muddy, rutted Barrowfield. 'We went to Italy a couple of times,' Bobby Lennox says, 'for European ties, to their swanky training grounds, and thought, "This is great." But we went back to Celtic Park and we were quite happy.' The facilities for the players were less than luxurious: two WCs, one shower, a large players' bath and an ordinary bath – the players' bath would be filled with hot water at the interval in a match and by full-time it would have cooled to the requisite temperature. Sean Connery, on the rise as an actor thanks to his role as James Bond, visited the dressing room a couple of times during those years, but this was not a club used to glamour. Still, those basic, oily mechanics behind the scenes had serviced perfectly a set of Celtic players who had motored smoothly and sleekly through the second half of the sixties in a style unimaginable to anyone who had witnessed the wheezing, spluttering Celtic charabanc that had been crawling along in the slow lane at the decade's beginning.

14

THE LIONS ROAR

Detractors were ready to pounce with leonine tenacity when the fortieth anniversary of the Lisbon Lions' feat arrived in the late spring of 2007. Cheap jibes abounded from some followers of other Scottish clubs about the continuing celebration by Celtic supporters of a group of players whose European Cup victory in the Portuguese capital happened before many of the current support were either born or, if alive, fully aware of the nuances of the victory. Anyone who remembered with clarity that win over Internazionale of Milan would have had to have been, by then, well into their fifties and so, went the argument, the Celtic supporters were overdoing it with all their fuss and focus on events of all those years ago. Even in 2003, when the Lions were finally given a testimonial by Celtic, it had been suggested that the whole thing had become a bit overcooked.

There may have been a chink of logic in all those suggestions, and yet there is also a sense in which the achievement of the Lisbon Lions is not celebrated enough; that it would not be over-celebrated even if it were to be marked daily for the next four decades and that even if it is still being celebrated with extreme vigour in 2067, as one comic critic has suggested it will be, and it surely will, there will be every justification for it. The achievement of that group of players would have been great enough in itself if they had merely won the European Cup, but when all of the circumstances surrounding their victory are taken into account their win in Lisbon is unique and unparalleled.

'It is up to us,' Jock Stein said as he prepared to lead his team into the European Cup that season, 'to everyone at Celtic Park now, to build up our own legends. We don't want to live with history, to be compared with legends of the past. We must make new legends, and our League Championship win is the first step towards doing that, but the greatness of a club in modern football will be judged on performances in Europe. It is only in the major European tournaments that you can really get a chance to rate yourself against the great teams.' This sounded like a man either making himself a hostage to fortune or one supremely confident in the talents of his players.

Celtic had never participated in the European Champions' Cup when, on 28 September 1966, the players stepped out at Celtic Park for the first leg of their tie with FC Zurich. The Swiss adopted stiflingly negative tactics, a kicking game that seemed odd given that they were managed by Ladislav Kubala, a great attacking player for Hungary and Barcelona in the 1950s. They held out, for sixty-four minutes, before John Clark stroked a pass into the path of Tommy Gemmell, playing at right-back, thirty yards from goal. With the Swiss expecting the powerful defender to build up play, he instead whacked the ball high into the net guarded by Othmar Iten, Switzerland's goalkeeper of the year. Five minutes later, Joe McBride got Celtic's second to make it a steady 2-0 victory.

'At that point we had no thought of winning the European Cup,' Bobby Lennox says. 'In fact it was just a big thrill for us to go to Zurich for the second leg of that tie, because we had never been there before.' Shocks were in store for the Celtic party on arrival in that neat, rich central European city. Venturing out of the Dolder Grand, their gilded hotel – 'a seven-star job' according to Gemmell – and taking a stroll to the local café, they discovered that even Coca-Colas were an extortionate price, and their finances could only stretch to one each. Then, in a small room inside the hotel, Stein gathered the players together for a team meeting on the day of the match and surprised the players when he told them their tactics for the second leg were to be the same as for the first: to press the Swiss hard and unpick their defence by taking the initiative and using the type of quick, flowing, one-touch and two-touch football they had practised in games in training.

Some players were unsettled by this suggestion, believing that it would leave them open to counter-attacks from Zurich, whom they felt would play their own expansive game now that they were at home. They expressed their doubts to Stein, who responded, 'They haven't got the players to have a go at us. We will beat them here tonight.' Kubala, now thirty-nine, took the field for the return, and the man who was once described by Helenio Herrera, one of Europe's top managers, as 'the greatest player ever' impressed the Celtic players with his strength and ability. It would be his last game at the top level – and Zurich's last in that season's European Cup. Gemmell, after twenty-two minutes, opened the scoring in identical fashion to the manner in which he had done in Scotland. 'I hit the ball from almost exactly the same spot and angle as I had done in the first leg,' he says. 'You would have thought the goalkeeper would have learned from the first one at Celtic Park, but obviously he did not.' A Stevie Chalmers goal shortly before the interval and a Gemmell penalty shortly after it provided Celtic with a comfortable 3-0 win and vindicated Stein's pre-match assessment, adding further to his players' faith in his knowledge of the game.

A greater threat awaited Celtic in the next round, in which Nantes of France started like a whirlwind in their home tie, taking a 1-0 lead through Francis Magny after fourteen minutes. Joe McBride equalised ten minutes later, justifying pre-match reports in the French sporting press that had raved about his scoring exploits and evening things up with his manager after an unfortunate pre-match incident when he opened his kit bag in the dressing room to discover he had only one boot. 'Jock said to me to get a taxi back to the hotel,' McBride says, 'and it was lying on the floor of the hotel, so I got the boot, came back, and Jock was still prancing up and down the dressing room. "Professional footballer, eh?" he kept saying. My head was down, so when I scored, I turned and looked at him and he shouted, "Aye, all right, all right . . ." It was "You're forgiven" sort of thing, but before the match I thought he was going to strangle me.

'In that match, wee Jimmy had hardly kicked a ball in the first half. Jock laid into him at half-time, and you've never seen a performance like his in the second half. He wasn't letting anybody else touch the ball; us as well. He was going off across the park, beating one, two, three, four of them. It wasn't great football, we weren't getting goals from it but we were in front by then, so he would just take the ball for a run and hold them off that way. He was something else.' Further goals, from Lennox and Chalmers, sealed a 3-1 victory, and now the French press were raving about Johnstone, memorably dubbing him 'The Flying Flea'.

'Continental clubs do not expect to be put under pressure at home in European ties,' Tommy Gemmell says. 'They expect to run the show and for the away team to defend. We were of the belief that we could play only one way and that was to attack – so that surprised them.' A 3-1 scoreline at Celtic Park in the second leg the following week mirrored the result in Nantes, and Celtic were in the quarter-finals.

'We must be just as good as anyone,' Stein said. 'I feel we can beat the big shots.' Jimmy Johnstone would recall how Stein was only saying publicly what he was drumming into the players in private. 'That year, Jock used to say, "Do you know something? You could be the greatest team in the world." In Europe he would say that regularly because I think somehow, somewhere, the big man thought it was going to happen for us. We started to believe in ourselves but we never, ever thought we were going to win the European Cup.'

The grey town of Novi Sad, in Serbia, then part of Yugoslavia, a postwar eastern European communist state, welcomed Celtic wanly for the first leg of their quarter-final with Vojvodina. The glamour of the European Cup appeared to have all been used up in this round by the quarter-final tie between Internazionale and Real Madrid. The Celtic players always found visits behind the Iron Curtain to be a grind, with poor food and accommodation, and this was no different, with them billeted in what Gemmell describes as a 'well-worn B&B'. On that opening day of March, Celtic performed in front of a crowd muffled up against deep winter and less than noisy in support of their team. The only colourful thing about the entire place was the Vojvodina team itself, who impressed with their slick, intricate passing and strong defence.

With twenty minutes to go, Celtic were content to be holding such opponents to a 0-0 draw when an error by Tommy Gemmell, who was short with a pass back to Ronnie Simpson, the goalkeeper, allowed Vojvodina to steal a goal. As the Celtic players left the pitch, they were arguing furiously among themselves about how they had lost such a crucial goal. 'If you make a mistake like that,' Gemmell says, 'the only thing to do is to get over it as quickly as possible and do your best to make sure it does not happen again. I was not one for having a hang-up about such things: once it's done it's done and there is nothing you can do about it.'

Stein's words prior to the second leg were inspirational. 'I feel we have the players fit to wear the mantle of champions of Europe,' he said. 'I have told them so. Now it's up to them. I believe our boys and style are good enough to win this match and win the European Cup, with which nothing else compares.' The contest on the field proved just as tight and dramatic as in the first leg. On the hour Ilija Pantelic, the Vojvodina goal-keeper, proved unable to hold a cross from Gemmell, and Chalmers prodded in the equaliser, but as the match reached its dying seconds, Vojvodina and Celtic looked destined for a play-off in Rotterdam. Then Charlie Gallagher took a corner from the right, and Billy McNeill leaped to reach the ball before Pantelic and head the winning goal. 'It was utter pandemonium when that goal went in,' Gallagher says. 'Everybody I meet nowadays was standing behind me . . .'

The jubilation on the terraces was heightened by having had to wait so long for the winner against opposition of exceptional quality. 'The game Celtic played against Vojvodina and won by a header by Billy McNeill; that game I remember with great, great joy,' Billy Connolly says. 'When we won that night, we knew we were going to win the European Cup. Everybody knew then that we could beat anybody because we'd done extremely well to beat Vojvodina. There was something about Vojvodina. There was an explosion that said, "Not only are you going to the final but you are going to beat these people, you are going to be legendary."'

The momentum from the match helped push Celtic through the first leg of their semi-final with Dukla Prague. Bertie Auld pinged a pass deep into the Dukla penalty area after twenty-seven minutes, and Jimmy Johnstone bravely went for the ball as Ivo Viktor, the giant Czech goal-keeper, came rushing from his line. Johnstone got there first to nick it into the net, but a cleverly worked equaliser, scored by Stanislav Strunc, gave Dukla an equaliser and made it 1-1 at half-time. Stein at the interval demanded of his players that they exert even more pressure on Dukla, and they duly obliged. On the hour, Gemmell's pass from the halfway line sat up perfectly for Willie Wallace, signed from Heart of Midlothian for £30,000 the previous December, and the striker cleverly volleyed a first-time shot past Viktor. Five minutes later, Auld, at a free-kick, leaned over the ball and craftily made as if to adjust its position, but instead nudged a free-kick into the path of Wallace, who clipped a low, twenty-yard shot past Viktor to make it 3-1. 'That was Willie's transfer fee paid already,' Gemmell says.

It looked a healthy lead for the Celtic players to work with as they ambled along from the International Hotel in central Prague to the nearby Juliska Stadium on the day of the return match. Instead, it would prove a nerve-racking ninety minutes in a bizarre setting. Brown-uniformed militia crammed into the stadium in support of Dukla, the Army team, generally unpopular but financed by the state in communist Czechoslovakia. They were less than hearty 'supporters'. The largest side of the ground was under construction and was dotted with recently hewn tree stumps; and with no floodlights at the Juliska, the game was played in daylight, at four o'clock in the afternoon.

Some players who featured that day suggest that Stein set Celtic up to play defensively; others that that mode of play was forced upon them by Dukla pushing them back incessantly. Regardless of the reason why, most Celtic players, including Johnstone and Lennox, the wingers, spent the match deep in their own half with Chalmers on his own up front chasing down defenders as they began to build up yet another Dukla attack. 'It was one of the toughest games I ever experienced,' Lennox says. 'The longer it went without them scoring the more comfortable I felt, although you are always aware that a team needs only one small break to score a goal and that if Dukla did so it would lift them enormously. It was an experience that pinched the nerves.' Lennox recalls being driven deep into defence and being in a state of some anxiety on hearing a scoring effort from a Dukla player ping against a stanchion, but it was outside and not inside the net, and he and his team-mates could breathe again. It was a match like that throughout.

It ended 0-0, and the pressure was off Celtic after that – they had, after all, in reaching the final of the European Cup, achieved something no British club had done previously and in facing Inter, champions of Europe in 1964 and 1965, the wealthiest club in Europe, they would go in as underdogs, with few outside of Glasgow expecting them to win. The final, in the heat of Lisbon on 25 May, would be closer to the type of conditions that would suit the Italians, whose slow-slow-quick catenaccio style, built on lazily drawing in the opposition and then hitting them cruelly and mercilessly on the break, was custom-built for such energy-sapping conditions and against more gung-ho northern European opposition as Celtic.

It was a new trophy for which the clubs were playing in 1967. The original European Cup, which resembled a Greek urn, had been kept by Real Madrid after they had won the tournament for the sixth time, in 1966, with their victory over Partizan Belgrade in Brussels. Hans Bangerter, UEFA's general secretary, had commissioned Hans and Jörg Stadelmann, a Bernese father and son, to design a new one. 'We put the design together like a jigsaw puzzle,' Jörg Stadelmann says of an artefact that took 340 hours to create, that is 62 cm in height and weighs 7.5 kilograms. 'It was a "bastardised" design, yet I like it, and I think everybody in football likes it as well.' His creation, with a long, streamlined, convex body and wide, elongated handles, would, for all his playing down of its design, become the iconic symbol of excellence in European football's premier competition.

The European Cup tournament, instituted in 1955, had until that point been won by only four clubs – Benfica, Internazionale, AC Milan and Real Madrid. The nuances of high-level European football, with the emphasis on the technical and tactical aspects of the game, had seemed beyond the scope of the frequently less sophisticated British approach, which seemed appropriate, as it had been a combination of English arrogance and French haughtiness that had resulted in the creation of the tournament. Gabriel Hanot, the editor of *L'Equipe*, the French sports newspaper, had bridled at braying press claims issuing from England in the early 1950s that Wolverhampton Wanderers were the champions of Europe because they had defeated major continental clubs who had visited the Midlands for a series of prestigious friendly matches. Hanot had decided that for a club to claim such a title they would need to attain it on a more organised, better-regulated basis, and he had put forward the proposal for the institution of a formalised tournament to decide Europe's best. Hanot's hunch that the English were blowing their own trumpet too hard appeared to have been proven correct.

'Glasgow was like a desert that night,' Billy Connolly says of the evening of the final. 'It must be the strangest night in Glasgow's history.' A flotilla of cars and aeroplanes had ferried approximately 12,000 Celtic supporters to Lisbon to witness their home-grown side have a tilt at the trophy, and the venue was the most quaint that Celtic had encountered in criss-crossing Europe that season. Rather than playing at the home of Benfica or Sporting, the final would be at the National Stadium, set in woodland six miles west of Lisbon, with one side of the pitch lined by neat hedges that made way for a temporary stand, either end of which sat level with the edge of the eighteen-yard box. Accommodating spectators six deep, this was a type of construction more suited to a Highland Games than a European Cup final. A greater level of grandeur could be found in the rows and rows of marbled benches, without individual seats, that towered over it on the other three sides of the stadium and from which the majority of the 56,000 present would watch the match.

Simpson, Craig, Gemmell, Murdoch, McNeill, Clark, Johnstone, Wallace, Chalmers, Auld and Lennox: the names of the Lisbon Lions are now so familiar to Celtic supporters that it can seem as though this was a settled side that played together for years. This was not the case. This team had only started five matches together after their first outing, a 4-0 victory away to St Johnstone on 14 January 1967, although three of those games had been among the most important fixtures of the season: the 2-2 draw at Ibrox with Rangers that had clinched the League title, the victorious Scottish Cup final against Aberdeen, and the second leg against Dukla. It was an eleven that came together almost by chance; fluctuation in individual careers, form and injuries meant that Stein had decided on his final line-up only weeks before, but, crucially, that eleven had shown their manager they could be trusted to get the right result in major matches. Although that team was a great one, several of its members could reflect that they might not even have still been at Celtic in 1967, far less been selected to appear in the most important fixture in the club's history.

Ronnie Simpson, the goalkeeper, had been at Hibernian for four years when Jock Stein arrived as manager there in 1964, and one of Stein's first initiatives at Easter Road had been to offload Simpson, then almost thirty-three years of age. Simpson had been firmly the number two goalkeeper behind John Fallon at Celtic and when he heard in January 1965 that Stein was en route to Celtic Park Simpson immediately told his wife to expect him to be on the move again. Simpson had instead won over the new manager second time around and had become Celtic's first-choice goalkeeper, but not only was he fortunate in that – few people were given a second chance by Jock Stein – but he could reflect on being lucky to be alive.

Simpson was among several of the Celtic team who, in that era of less advanced dentistry, wore a full set of dentures and, on one occasion, while he was a Newcastle United player in the 1950s, that had almost cost him his life. The procedure for goalkeepers, after catching the ball, at that time was to carry out a two-step: with one step right yourself after catching the ball and with the next kick it clear before the centre-forward could charge at you and knock you over. On one occasion after leaping to clutch a high ball, Ronnie had been just a little too slow in executing the move, and when the forward gave him the dunt, Ronnie's falsers got jammed in his throat. Had it not been for quick thinking on the part of the Newcastle trainer, who extracted them from his trachea, he would have been in mortal danger from choking. After that he would take his false teeth out when playing. Simpson's reduced vocal capacity on the pitch made it easy for defenders to ignore his instructions, as they came out of his mouth in something resembling a gurgle.

Jim Craig, the right-back, had had to endure an agonising wait to stake his place in the side that season. A fixture in the team that had won the championship in 1966, he had found himself under pressure as he combined a first-class football career with his studies in dentistry at the University of Glasgow when due to sit his finals that summer of 1966. Sympathy for the demands being placed on him by football meant that the university allowed him to delay his final examination until September 1966, and Stein, after discussing the matter privately with Jean, his wife, who showed understanding for the dual stresses being placed on the player, told Craig to stay away from the club and maintain his fitness on his own until his examinations were complete; all the while receiving full pay from Celtic. It meant that Craig missed the team-bonding tour of North America in summer 1966, and while his team-mates were elimi-nating FC Zurich in the first round, he was pounding the pavements of Glasgow's south side and the perimeter of Bellahouston Park, building up the stamina that would be needed for his lung-bursting overlaps up and down the right side of the pitch. It would be Christmas 1966 before he would be back in the team.

Gemmell, the left-back, whose overlapping and goals had done so much to take Celtic to the final, had been warned by a coach prior to Stein's arrival that, if he continued to obey his natural instinct and make his way over the halfway line, he would be on his way out of Celtic Park. Bobby Murdoch, the magnificent midfield player, had been struggling at inside-forward before Stein unlocked his potential as a playmaker by moving him to the back of midfield. Billy McNeill, the centre-half, a stal-wart in central defence during the first half of the 1960s, had become so disillusioned by the disorganisation at Celtic prior to Stein that in 1965 he had been on the verge of a transfer, with Manchester United and Tottenham Hotspur among those interested, before being reinvigorated by Stein's arrival.

Jimmy Johnstone had been lingering in the reserves at Celtic when Stein arrived as manager and jolted him into life again. Stevie Chalmers, the centre-forward, had been on the verge of being displaced by the arrival of Willie Wallace from Hearts midway through the 1966–67 season: Stein's plan was for a pairing of Wallace and McBride in attack until a cartilage injury put McBride out of action from Christmas until the end of the season. Bobby Lennox had worried when the new manager's arrival was announced; he had, after several years at Celtic, only just become a regular in the side and was concerned that he might lose his place under the new manager. Bertie Auld had been hustled out of Celtic Park after Robert Kelly had objected to his robust style of play – and few players got the chance to return to Celtic after leaving in such circumstances.

Two years previously, as 'Il Grande Inter' were defeating Benfica to win their second successive European Cup, Celtic had been next to nowhere, emerging from eight years in the shade of not only Rangers but of more successful Scottish clubs such as Dundee, Dunfermline Athletic and Heart of Midlothian. Now they were facing a smooth-running Inter side that showed only three changes – two enforced by injury – from the teams that had beaten Real Madrid and Benfica in the European Cup finals of 1964 and 1965. Celtic had never previously faced an Italian side in a competitive match, but Stein had been the part-time manager of Scotland in November 1965 when the national side had faced Italy in a World Cup qualifying tie at Hampden Park. His instructions to Willie Henderson and John Hughes, his wingers that night, had been to keep moving inside to drag their man-markers out of position. Now, in Lisbon, his instructions to Jimmy Johnstone and Bobby Lennox were identical.

'Jock's team talk in Lisbon was straightforward,' Bertie Auld recalls. 'He told us, "You've made history. You've got to the final. Go out and play to your capabilities." He never mentioned any individual or how they would play. Each and every one of us was confident on the ball, so he trusted us to perform.'

The Celtic players, pre-match, were like everyone else in terms of visualising the outcome. They could not be sure of winning but they were adamant they would not lose without making certain there was, as the Celtic song says, going to be a show. 'There was a confident feeling among us,' John Clark says, 'and we knew we had the ability but we never thought, "We're definitely going to win." Nothing like that ever came into your head. In your own mind, you're wanting to do your best because it's the biggest game in Europe – or the world – a European Cup final.

So everybody's looking in. I don't think we ever gave it a thought that we could get beaten. We felt confident all the time that we were a good team, and this was a stage on which we could prove we were a good team. We knew we were playing the cream; the top team in the world at the time. Their team was loaded with international players from all over the world, wasn't it? They were the team that nobody could beat and they had a style of play that nobody could break down.'

Both sides began brightly. After two minutes, Renato Cappellini flitted down the left wing for Inter, hit the bye-line and crossed for Sandro Mazzola, the striker, to send a flashing, quicksilver header towards goal. Simpson reacted alertly, twisting down to his left to hold the ball. A low shot and a flying header, both from Jimmy Johnstone, made Giuliano Sarti, the Inter goalkeeper, also work hard early in the match, but after seven minutes Inter struck the first blow when they cleared a Celtic corner and broke smoothly and quickly, in quintessential style, and Cappellini, the winger, was sent tumbling by Jim Craig inside the Celtic penalty area. Kurt Tschenscher, the West German referee, pointed to the penalty spot. Tschenscher was swiftly surrounded by a number of jostling Celtic players protesting against his decision, and only when the dust had settled on their dispute with the referee could Mazzola step up to take the kick, stylishly pelting it low and accurately inside Simpson's right-hand post.

'I hold my hands up and admit I ran across him,' Craig says of conceding the penalty, which he still maintains should not have been awarded. 'That night Jock said, "That was rash, Cairney." I said, "Boss, give me a second, there was nothing rash about it." I said, "You put yourself in my position: he's a left-footed outside-left going down the inside channel. What's he going to do?" He said, "He's going to put it on to his good foot." I said, "That's absolutely right. So if he is going to put it on to his good foot, I'm going to run into him. What referee's going to give a penalty kick for that in the seventh minute of a European Cup tie?" I was shocked when he gave a penalty for that.' Craig's justification for his innocence is that he simply angled his body into Cappellini's path rather than outrightly mistackling or fouling the player. It did seem a soft award given in favour of a player running away from goal; although the Italian did his best to embroider the case for a penalty by rolling over several times on the ground. Interestingly Craig was one of the few Celtic players not to protest directly to Tschenscher.

Celtic's response was to pour resources into an attacking game that had Inter pinned deep in their own half for most of the rest of the first half, unable even to muster one of their famed overlaps. It suited the Italian side to face attacking teams such as Celtic, whom they could counter by hitting hard on the break, but such was the degree of what Herrera later described as 'Celtic's force' in pushing down hard on his team that desperate defence was almost all that Inter were able to manage. Despite their incessant attacking, though, Celtic could not score, with Sarti acrobatically keeping out every effort that found its way on target. A Gemmell shot hurtled into the side netting, and one from Auld rapped off the crossbar, but at half-time Inter, ominously, remained 1-0 in the lead.

It was a fuming group of players who tumbled into the Celtic dressing room, furious at the award of the penalty, and Stein had to instruct them to forget about it, although the manager as always was pleased to see passion on the part of his players, believing that it gave them a cause and helped fire them up for whatever action lay ahead. 'At half-time,' Jimmy Johnstone said, 'we knew we would do it simply because of the number of chances we had had, even though we were 1-0 down and even though it was about seventy-five degrees. It would have burned a hole in your head. We were so carried away by the occasion that neither the heat nor anything else mattered.' Johnstone had been apprehensive about facing Inter in the hours before the final; now he was convinced of victory. Tommy Gemmell was less sure of the outcome: Celtic had had so much of the ball without converting their pressure into the hard currency of goals that he wondered whether it was just going to be one of those days.

Gemmell found the solution to his conundrum after sixty-three minutes. Craig advanced up the right wing and drew several defenders to him before rolling the ball into the path of the inrushing Gemmell. 'The guy that was supposed to be on me was Angelo Domenghini,' Gemmell says, 'and he was so lazy. Nobody marked me for the whole game, so when I saw that Jim Craig had been allowed a free run I just set off from my own half. Three times I shouted to Jim to square it to me but he held it . . . and held it . . . and held it . . . Finally he drew another Inter defender to him and decided to cut it back to me diagonally. I was about twenty-two or twenty-three yards out. It was a great pass, right along the deck, and the park was like a bowling green so it was just a case of timing. I hit it with my instep, as hard as I could, confident it was on target.' Armando

Picchi, the sweeper, turned his back on the ball as Gemmell shot, allowing the ball to fly, unfettered, past Sarti. 'When I saw the ball hit their net,' Gemmell says, 'I thought, "That's it. We've got them now." You could see defeat in their faces.'

It is symbolic of Celtic's commitment to all-out attack that it should have been the full-backs who combined for that goal, although Stein's tactic of using overlapping full-backs in the shape of Craig and Gemmell 'was a hard shift', the former of the two says. 'It was an eighty-yard run up and an eighty-yard run back. It's no surprise that the two of us finished our careers early. I had ME and finished at thirty-one, and Gemmell finished in his early thirties as well. I always think the frame packed in eventually, and the overlapping couldn't have helped.' It was vital to Celtic's greatest victory, though. With five minutes remaining, the cavalier Gemmell careered down the left wing, drew defenders to him in the same fashion as Craig and clipped a pass back for Murdoch, who pelted the ball into the penalty area, where Chalmers diverted the ball into the net for the winner. The European Cup was en route to northern Europe, and Glasgow, for the first time. A pitch invasion by Celtic supporters meant the players had to hurriedly make for their dressing rooms and the presence of so many fans prevented the Celtic players being presented with the trophy along with their captain, Billy McNeill; some Celtic players felt less than pleased about being denied such a memorable experience.

Stein said, 'People think we won the match with wingers, but in fact we didn't play Johnstone and Lennox on the wings. I wanted them to take people on in the centre, and leave the sidelines free for Gemmell and Craig to get forward. The wee man put the fear of God into Burgnich. He must have beaten him three or four times in the opening minutes. That can help to lift a team, and it also won over the Portuguese in the crowd. There was not much sympathy for Inter that day. The other thing that helped us was that Corso chose to play very deep on his own left-hand side. That gave Bobby Murdoch so much room, and we just channelled everything through him.'

Giacinto Facchetti, the striker who had been turned into a great over-lapping full-back by Helenio Herrera, the Inter manager, had been trou-bled all afternoon by the pace of Lennox and Johnstone. Inter, in desperation, had mid-match switched Facchetti and Tarcisio Burgnich, the full-backs, to see if it could prove more successful in setting Facchetti free. It did not. 'Many times I tried to get forward in the match,' he said, 'but when I played the ball and ran, I did not get it back. Really we were five men against eleven.' Every time Inter tried to work their way through midfield, they were robbed by an enterprising Celt. Jim Craig, who recovered well from his early setback in conceding the penalty, says, 'I think in terms of performance it would have been hard for any team in the world to play as well as we did in Lisbon.' McNeill suggests that Inter were caught cold by the amount of creativity in the Celtic team, a team that had the ability to vary its play incessantly and attack from any angle. Mazzola admits that Inter did indeed underestimate Celtic's potency and were too casual in their approach to the match, believing that victory was theirs by right. It was not that they dismissed Celtic as such; more that they believed themselves invincible.

It was a 'totally destroyed' set of Inter players that spent an hour and a half in the dressing room afterwards hearing in detail from Herrera how they had been outwitted tactically by a Celtic side whose triumph, the Inter manager said, had been 'a victory for sport'. The Italians, Mazzola says, had been warned categorically by Herrera about Celtic's strengths, and he had specifically stated that 1-0 would not be enough, but habit had led his side to click automatically back into defence once they had their noses in front. They had, the Italian striker says, expected to turn up and defeat a Celtic side among whom they had heard only of Johnstone. 'When they equalised we were running about chasing shadows,' Mazzola says. The Italians were beaten even before the second goal, he suggests.

For Joe McBride it was a day of mixed emotions. He had scored thirty-five goals for Celtic by Christmas 1966 and would have been a near-certainty to take the field in Lisbon had it not been for the crippling cartilage injury that ruled him out of the rest of the season and he had watched the final from high in the National Stadium's stands, sweltering in his blazer, collar and tie and trousers, as part of the official Celtic party. Post-match, Stein displayed a degree of sensitivity towards his players that complemented well his gruff, rough side. 'I'll never forget going into the dressing room after the game,' McBride says. 'By the time we got into the dressing room the boys were jumping about and kissing and cuddling, and I remember I was standing there and delighted for the boys but so upset that I hadn't played that I was nearly in tears. I'll give big Jock his due. He was a hard, big man but he could understand how you were feeling too. I remember him looking over, and he caught my eye, saw me standing there and told me I should, for my own good, get right out of that dressing room. He knew how I was feeling and told me to come back in ten minutes once I had calmed down.

'I asked him for a jersey so he lifted a green and white jersey and gave it to me. So I went out and went to the Inter dressing room and chapped the door, which was shut. Herrera opened the door just enough to look out through a crack and his face was close to mine. 'McBride?' he said softly. 'Mr Herrera, can I change a jersey?' I said. I said I'd like Burgnich's jersey. So he said something in Italian and Burgnich's jersey came flying over, I caught it and I handed him a Celtic jersey. It was hard for me then to find anywhere in and around the stadium that was quiet, but I did and I just had a wee greet to myself.' Burgnich, on the pitch, had exchanged the shirt in which he had played with Lennox; now Celtic players had taken the shirt off his back twice.

'We celebrated all summer, and eventually I had to disappear to Ireland,' Jim Craig says, 'because it was getting to the stage where you couldn't walk along the road. Liz and I went to Donegal, and, although there were people talking to us there as well, there were not as many as in Glasgow. Then we went down to Dublin before coming home again.'

The Lisbon Lions would start together only five more times, and their final outing would, appropriately, be in their first game in defence of the European Cup, when they slipped to a 2-1 defeat at the hands of Dynamo Kiev in the September of 1967. A draw in the second leg led to an unlucky exit for the holders. Stein remained buoyant despite that defeat, looking forward to the World Club Cup: a play-off between the champions of Europe and South America to decide the world club champions. It proved a disquieting episode. Racing Club, Celtic's Argentinian opponents, kicked, spat and gouged their way through the first leg at Hampden Park, which ended in a 1-0 victory for Celtic. Out in Buenos Aires, for the second leg, on 1 November 1967, Simpson was felled by a missile before kick-off and had to be replaced by John Fallon. Argentinian supporters urinated on members of the Celtic party from high above them in the stand and had to be held at bay inside the stadium by 1,000 riot police on horses or with dogs. Racing won 2-1 with the help of a supine referee awarding an offside goal as the Argentinian players again behaved in a wild manner.

Celtic now had to choose between remaining in South America and contesting a play-off in Montevideo, Uruguay, three days later, or returning home. The matches were not FIFA-approved fixtures, so there was no punishment in the offing to prevent a dignified retreat. Instead, Stein and the directors decided to remain in South America for the play-off with fairly predictable results. 'The time for politeness is over,' Stein said in advance of the match. 'We can be hard if necessary and we will not stand the shocking conduct of Racing.' The Celtic players, having kept their discipline under extreme provocation in the first two matches, now cracked. Four were sent off by Rodolfo Osorio, a weak referee from Paraguay: Lennox, Johnstone, John Hughes and Auld, who refused to go and remained on the field for the dying minutes of the match. Alfio Basile and Juan Rulli were sent off from the Racing side, who won 1-0 in a farcical encounter that became so heated that numerous helmeted riot police, batons and swords drawn, had intervened at various stages to attempt to create order. 'Early in the match one of their players sold me a lovely dummy,' Jim Craig recalls, 'and as he went past me I put my foot out and he went over it. Jock had told us to do the same as them when fouling a player, so I said sorry and helped him up and as I did so he spat in my face. Then I heard Jock screaming "Cairney, no, no, no!" Your first reaction when someone does that to you is fury.'

On their return to Scotland, the players were called into a meeting and each fined £250 by Robert Kelly, the chairman, and instead of deducting it from future wages he simply withheld the £250 bonus that had been due to the players for beating Dundee 5-3 in the League Cup final on the day they travelled to Argentina. 'I always thought that was a really despicable punishment,' Jim Craig says of the fine imposed by Kelly, 'because some people had spent the bonus money as soon as it had been obtained. I was quite bitter about that because they [the board of directors] made the decision to play the third game. We shouldn't have played the third game.'

It was a less than harmonious note on which to end the greatest year in the club's history but the positive achievements of that year continue to resonate loudly. Celtic's victory in Lisbon cannot be repeated or even emulated – no one else can be first. It makes that team unique in world football, and the feats of what was in effect a local select, with all of its players drawn from the Glasgow area, ensure that they deserve every word of praise, sentiment and affection that comes their way.

15

THE STEIN SCENE

An almost uncontrollable euphoria seized hold of the Celtic players after they had clinched the most important win in Celtic's history. It meant they were still on a high from that dramatic 1967 European Cup final victory when they heard, shortly after the final, that Celtic had been invited to Madrid to provide the opposition in the testimonial match for Alfredo Di Stefano, the man who had inspired Real Madrid to five successive European Cup victories and who would now be rewarded for his services to the Spanish club by scooping up the takings from a match between Real, the 1966 European champions, and Celtic, their successors. The match would be played just under a fortnight after the Lisbon game at the spectac-ular Bernabeu Stadium in Madrid in front of a capacity crowd of 135,000. 'I can't wait to play in that game,' one prominent contributor to Celtic's triumph in Lisbon said on hearing the news of this fixture, not hiding his puppy-like eagerness and glee at the prospect of such an occasion. Deflation would be his next and instantaneous emotion. 'You're not playing,' Jock Stein growled in the player's direction. 'I pick this team.'

Even in the immediate aftermath of his greatest triumph, Jock Stein felt the need to assert his authority as the manager of Celtic; not for him any relaxation of his grip on power. During the days prior to the game in Lisbon, he had been the players' best pal: having selected his team for the final, he had concentrated on getting his men into the right frame of mind through fun training sessions, games, quizzes and total relaxation during several days at Seamill. Now that they had performed their tasks for him, his cold front had been restored. That controlling obsessiveness, that desire to keep his players on their toes, was an essential element in Stein's nature.

'We were all stripped that night,' Charlie Gallagher, the midfield player, recalls of sitting on the substitutes' bench that evening in Madrid, 'and we were all wanting on, just for five minutes, but he said, "No, no, no." Instead of letting you on for five minutes to say that you had played in the Bernabeu he just said, "No." He was that type – he could be nasty. He'd want to show you he was boss. He had big massive hands, and when you were walking past him he would say "How are you doing?" and bang you around the ear. It would be sore as well. That would be his method of saying, "I'm bigger than you." He was a hard, hard man and nobody would argue with him.'

It is interesting how frequently players who worked under Stein will indulge in doing an impression of him, of his brusque way of dealing with people, through the use of short, sharp, straight-to-the-point bursts of language. 'Word wi' you!', an epithet accompanied by a sour, impatient and almost casually aggressive grimace, is how one former player – through mimicking both Stein's stern facial expression and gruff voice – recalls Stein's no-nonsense way of summoning a player into his office to set them right on some issue or other. As with most strong characters, even his everyday gestures instilled in their observers long and powerful memories.

'He was unpredictable,' Bobby Lennox says. 'He loved to join in a singsong if you had won, and you could leave big Jock on a Monday morning after training on a high, and everybody's happy and chirpy, and the next morning his face would be tripping him and it would be, "Right, everybody, on the track, we're working." That was the man he was.'

Stein's authority at Celtic, from the moment he arrived at the club, made him almost unassailable as manager – he transformed the club and established it as a genuine force in European football. Yet while Celtic owed so much to Stein, he, in turn, owed almost everything to Celtic.

When it came to attracting Stein to Celtic as manager in 1965 and keeping him at Celtic Park for many years after, it helped Celtic that they had not so much resurrected Stein's career as a player as sparked it spectacularly and mesmerically into life just when it had been in danger of fizzling out in obscurity. A rugged centre-half, Stein had spent eight years during the 1940s combining life as a miner with part-time football at tiny Albion Rovers before, in 1950, switching to non-League Llanelli in Wales. With his wife soon hankering for a return to Scotland, Stein, at the age of twenty-nine, in December 1951 found himself dealt a king-sized slice of luck. Celtic needed a centre-half as back-up to their regulars, and Jimmy Gribben, a trainer at Celtic Park, rooting around in his mind for a suitably utilitarian addition to the Celtic staff, came up with the name of Stein and brought him under the Celtic umbrella. Robert Kelly would later suggest that no one at Celtic had actually expected that Stein would ever play a first-team game, but Stein's luck held – owing to injuries, he made his Celtic debut four days after signing, and when his name was announced in the team across the new Celtic Park tannoy system before the match with St Mirren, a ripple of quizzical comment could be heard making its way around the 20,000 crowd. It would be the last time Stein's presence at Celtic would be questioned.

Stein remained in the team for the best part of the next four years, captaining Celtic to a short but glorious slice of League and Cup successes in the mid-1950s before an ankle injury, sustained in a match with Glasgow Rangers in August 1955, forced him to accept a specialist's advice to retire as a player, which he did in January 1957, at the age of thirty-four. It was not footballing ability that had distinguished Stein on the field but his organisational skills – as a limited player, he could not get by on instinct alone and had to manoeuvre his way through a match carefully, watch-fully, thinking closely about what would be likely to happen next. 'Jock Stein was quite a good player,' Alec Boden, a Celtic team-mate, confirms, 'slightly on the slow side and one-footed – left-footed – but good in the air. He gave no impression he would become a manager or become inter-ested in the coaching side. I think it was when he got his very bad ankle injury that that changed his outlook.' Horse racing and attending grey-hound meetings at Shawfield or Blantyre had afforded Stein pleasure in his free time, but it seems significant that he was attracted to hobbies in which there was a powerful element of calculation necessary.

Tactics were becoming a theme of interest to footballers in the 1950s. Up and down Britain, players, constricted by the standard 2-3-5 forma-tion that remained seemingly unalterable, were discussing whether it might be possible to play the game in a different way. Perhaps most famously, a group of West Ham United players, who would fan out to become future managers of the 1960s and 1970s, met after training at Cassettari's Café, around the corner from Upton Park, to create their own school of football theory. Celtic players of the era were not immune to this vogue, and at Ferrari's restaurant on Buchanan Street in Glasgow they would, after lunch, use the salt and pepper pots and cutlery to outline positional variations. Stein was prominent in all this, putting forward revolutionary ideas such as using overlapping full-backs, twin centre-forwards and twin centre-halfs; the 2-3-5 could accommodate only one centre-forward and one centre-half. The younger players listened and learned as Stein expounded, stressing how pace in a player would also to him be an essential component in any team he might field.

Other players would put forward their own ideas on the game, at which Stein would sit back silently and allow them to elaborate on their own theories. It paid for them to have thought out fully their ideas or they could fall victim to Stein's sharpness. One team-mate, after using the props to set out his particular system of playing, came to the end of his spiel to find Stein suddenly sitting forward and scrutinising the table on which the format had been outlined. 'That's fine,' Stein said slowly, eyes still on the table, 'but to play that system you would need twelve men.'

Stein's abilities as a talker, motivator and reader of the game had made up for a certain lack of nimbleness as a player, and Robert Kelly, the Celtic chairman, acted quickly to ensure those talents would not be lost to Celtic once Stein had retired as a player. 'We like the Stein influence at Celtic Park,' he said on learning of the player's decision to quit, 'and have offered Jock a scouting appointment. He will also learn the managerial side of the business from Mr Jimmy McGrory. This will stand him in good stead for the future.'

Within six months, Stein had been appointed reserve-team manager at Celtic, and he was soon leading a talented young team to an 8-2 two-legged Scottish Second Eleven Cup victory over an experienced Rangers side. Stein was different, taking a keen interest in those young players, discussing not only the game of football with them but also their hopes and aspirations, and making representations to ensure such things as the standard of their training kit was improved. He would participate in players' card schools on the lengthy train trip to Aberdeen, in which he had the ability to be simultaneously one of the lads while maintaining a slight distance from them and remaining the boss. He was also a big, hard man, who would test his players on and off the park. One of his favourite pastimes with the young players was a game in which Stein would press his thigh hard up against a bench, with a player on the other side of the bench, also with his thigh flush against its surface. The sport would then begin, with Stein waving a huge, bear-like paw in the air, ready to cuff the youngster, who had to do all he could to avoid the slap. The player could move their head and shoulders and top of their body to try to avoid a whack across the skull from Stein, but if they went so far as to take their thigh back from the bench he would see them as squeamish, cowardly, soft and would not be slow in telling them so in front of their team-mates.

His progress with the reserve team led to him being offered the job of Dunfermline Athletic manager in March 1960, a club then second-bottom of the first division and apparently doomed to relegation. 'We were a wee bit disappointed when he left for Dunfermline,' John Clark, then nineteen, says, 'because he was a kind of father figure.' Stein turned the Dunfermline team around so radically that by the end of the season they were thirteenth, free of relegation cares and only four points below Celtic, whom Dunfermline had defeated 3-2 in Stein's first match as a manager.

One year later, Dunfermline inflicted an even more severe defeat on Celtic, beating them 2-0 in the replayed 1961 Scottish Cup final. It meant that Dunfermline tasted European football before Celtic, and they enjoyed, under Stein, myriad adventures and some stunning successes in the Fairs Cup and the European Cup-Winners' Cup. After four years at East End Park, Stein became manager of Hibernian, almost instantaneously trans-forming them from mid-table meanderers into championship challengers who, in January 1965, were sitting only two points behind Kilmarnock, the Scottish League leaders. It was at that point that Robert Kelly found out from Stein that Wolverhampton Wanderers had asked him if he would be interested in becoming their manager. The two men met and over lunch Kelly offered Stein the job of Celtic manager. 'For me, this is it,' Stein said. 'This is what I have always wanted: a return to Parkhead.'

James Farrell, a newly appointed director of Celtic at the time of Stein's return to the club as manager, recalled, 'Bob Kelly told the board that Jock Stein would accept the job on his conditions and he also told the board that he would worry the life out of us – and he did. Bob Kelly was very fond of Jock Stein. Jock, in turn, was always very, very fond of Celtic, because they had resurrected his career, and Bob Kelly had put Jock Stein to Dunfermline. He wasn't quite so keen on Jock Stein going to the Hibs, because Hibs were a bigger club than Dunfermline, and he didn't want to lose him – but he didn't prevent it. Plus the owner of Hibs at that time was a very wealthy man – [Willie] Harrower, a bookmaker – and he would do everything in his power to keep Jock Stein. He did try – without success.'

The idea that Kelly had sent Stein out to Dunfermline to gain managerial experience and that Kelly had a long-term plan to make Stein the Celtic manager is sometimes seen as a fanciful one, but there may have been an inkling of this in Kelly's mind, as the two men did enjoy a close relationship and understanding. Kelly could be austere and unforgiving towards any player who did not live up to the standards that Kelly decreed were essential in a Celtic player, but when he chose to favour an individual player he could be a most helpful patron and a loyal and long-standing one. Kelly had communicated on a frequent basis with Stein during Stein's spells in Fife and Edinburgh. There would not have been any hard-and-fast arrangement that Stein would return to Celtic as manager – during the early 1960s, after all, Kelly was grooming Sean Fallon to become Jimmy McGrory's successor – but it is not unlikely that there may have been a loose understanding between Kelly and Stein that, if the manager proved himself a success elsewhere in Scottish football, then the post of Celtic manager might just become available at some point. When Stein contacted Kelly to tell him about the Wolves offer, it was the then Hibs manager's way of prompting Kelly into either offering him the Celtic manager's job or losing him, possibly for ever, to English football. It was also to Celtic's advantage that Mrs Jean Stein, after her brief exile in Llanelli, had no desire to leave Scotland again.

'He was fair and he spoke to players,' Alec Boden, who became a Celtic coach during Stein's time as manager, says. Boden also recalls that Stein in the 1950s would partake of the occasional sherry, which conjures up a twee image of this most fearsome of managers, but by the time he was supervising players in the 1960s he had adopted a zero-tolerance attitude towards alcohol. 'Jock had a deep and genuine hatred of drink,' Bobby Lennox says. 'He hated it with real and severe feeling. It would outrage him even to think of one of his players having a pint of beer. He never drank. He thought it was a bad habit.

'I remember one evening on which he did, out of character, actually say to the boys, "Go to the bar and have a drink." They had been there for just a few minutes when he came bowling up and started laying into them. "Look at the state of you standing there drinking." The boys reminded him gently that he had told them that they could have a drink. "Ach, never mind that," he replied. "Look at the state of you there." He more or less told them to get to their rooms, as if they had breached his code of discipline without his permission.'

Players talk of his presence – that rare ability to draw the attention of everyone in a room – and of his bulk. Standing almost six feet in height and with a powerful build, he would seem, when speaking to a player, to grow larger and more imposing with every passing second. 'He filled the whole dressing room when he was angry,' Bobby Lennox says. Bobby Charlton, when he first met Jock Stein, was taken aback by the sheer size of the man. 'Jock Stein knew every player in Scotland,' James Farrell recalled, 'and Jock encouraged arguments – he wanted to know that you were alive.'

The manager's methods could be short and sharp at times, but few players would have questioned his ability to read a game and then use his skills to affect it to Celtic's benefit. 'He was a gruff and rough person,' Charlie Gallagher says, 'and he could be a big bandit at times, but he had a brilliant mind and a great memory. He thought a lot about what he was doing and knew what he wanted, and what he did want when he first started was men behind the ball. A lot of times when we were up the park we would saunter back, but you would hear his big voice: "Get back!" Everyone talked about beautiful, flowing football, but we had a helluva good defence as well, and it all started from the forwards backwards. If you got back it saved a lot of long-ball stuff, but we did play a lot of long-ball stuff as well, because we had speedy forwards up front in Lennox and Chalmers. They had pace, and a lot of goals were scored by using that and playing balls in behind defences.

'I remember playing Rangers in the Glasgow Cup in 1966, and he announced the team at the start of the game, and I was named at outside-left. I never played at outside-left, and big Yogi, who usually played there, looked at me as if to say, "What are you doing playing there?" I just shrugged my shoulders. Stein came up to me and said, "For the first half hour you're not going to get a kick of the ball but you'll be our best man out there." In those days the Rangers full-backs followed their wingers, and after a bit he shouted to me, "Start wandering." I did, and every ball was going out to big Gemmell, and he was just running on to them all, freely up the left wing. We were 1-0 up at half-time, and Jock told us that Rangers would change their set-up for the second half – and they did. They tried to combat Gemmell running riot down the left and they left me and Bobby Murdoch free to hit our forwards, and with them short of cover Bobby Lennox sped in to get a hat-trick, and we won 4-0. It was a clever, clever ploy and it made up for the 4-0 defeat at Ibrox three years previously.

'All this training that you see nowadays, players darting in and out of poles, short sharp sprints and playing with the ball; that was all new to us, and it was introduced by big Jock. We still did a lot of running but we did more running with a ball at our feet, and when you're doing that it doesn't feel like training.'

The strength of Stein's personality and his ability to motivate people and get them to play for him sometimes obscures his exceptional ability as a coach, who understood and exploited the finer points of the game, as Danny McGrain, the full-back, recalls. 'Before one game he told me to play the ball into the centre spot. I thought, "What for?" He said to me, "Well, Bobby Murdoch's going to move from there, and Bertie Auld is going to come in there," and I said, "Yes, OK." The game was going fine, and I looked up to the centre circle, and Bertie Auld moved, and I hit the ball but it didn't reach the centre spot. It happened again, and I hit it too hard. I tried it three times in the second half and I got it the fifth time – we were 3-0 up, so I was maybe more relaxed and more confident – and Bobby Murdoch moved, and up popped Bertie Auld to take the ball. I'd be twenty-one at the time, and that was me learning all about space and being on the same wavelength as someone else. That's when the game became difficult – when you had to think, within milliseconds. It opened my eyes.'

John Divers had been one of Stein's late-1950s reserve-team players and a member of the first-team squad in Stein's first season back at Celtic. He remembers: 'Big Jock had this talent to recognise what you or I are good at, and then to get us to provide that talent on the field to please big Jock. You then gave him 100 per cent. That is a combination that is quite powerful. Why did it work? People wanted to please him – I certainly did. That was his force of character. He had this *je ne sais quoi*.'

From being a team that trotted on to the park almost free of advice or instruction as to how to play the game, Celtic, under Stein, were transformed into one of the most sophisticated sides in world football. 'Jock made us more tactically aware,' John Clark says. 'It was no longer just about going out on to the field and playing. He asked you to think about how you play and how you play your position and explained it all to you on a tactics board. He asked you to try to think for yourself, and you found you developed your game, and your concentration got better. He's the best I've ever seen with a tactical board, and that's no criticism of any other manager. With him, the way he put it out on the tactical board meant that you came out of there with more or less a video inside your head.

'He hated people trying to play above themselves. He would say, "If you've not got that kind of ability, that's not your style, it never will be and you'll never achieve that. Do what you're good at and you'll be able to play and you'll be looked upon as a player." All this backheeling and flicking the ball in the air, you'd never have got away with it in our day unless you were wee Jinky or Willie Henderson or whoever. His training methods were clever as well – just now, when I look to see some of the things that happen here at Celtic, he did that forty years ago. On the field of play, he tried to make us play with our brains rather than our hearts all the time – and we did it.' A creative use of space – using every inch of the playing surface to its full advantage – was one of the character-istics of Stein's teams, and when a player took that extra second to look up and size up a situation before playing a pass, it was almost as if Stein was out there at their side, guiding them to do what he had drummed into them over and over on the training field.

Stein could mistreat and abuse players to get a reaction, and once a player was out of his plans, the individual in question would be blanked completely by Stein, made to train on his own and sometimes not even given a game with the reserves. These could be players who had played vital roles in pivotal moments for Celtic under Stein, but once he had no use for them they would be cast aside the way a child might throw away a once-favourite toy. The hurt would remain with those players for years, decades afterwards.

One who holds no grudges against Jock Stein is Joe McBride, but he, like all Stein's players, was subject to the manager's attention to detail and tight grip on the activities of those in his charge. 'We were in Holland to play Deventer,' McBride says, 'and in the hotel they gave us some lovely soup, a different kind to what we were used to at home. I finished and said to the waitress, "That's beautiful soup – could I have some more?" She was just bringing it over to the table when suddenly I found big Jock at my back, standing behind my chair. He said, "What's happening?" I said, "I'm just having another wee plate of soup." He said, "Oh, are you? Just having another wee plate of soup are you?" Then he motioned to the girl and said, "Take that away." He dropped me for the game that night. Mind you, they scored six.'

A hospital visit from Stein proved less than welcome for Charlie Gallagher, who recalls, 'I got a cartilage injury, and in those days that meant a three-month lay-off through injury. I was lying up in Bon Secours hospital and everyone had been to see me – players and backroom staff. I think he must have got some stick for that, so he came up to visit me and stayed all of five minutes. When he arrived he sat down and said, "I've got some good news for you." I said, "What's that?" He said, "I've signed Tommy Callaghan in your place."' Tommy Gemmell recalls stepping into a lift at Seamill one morning with Stein and the manager saying, casually, 'That's your wee pal away, then . . .' He had just transferred Willie Wallace, a Lisbon Lion, to Crystal Palace, and this was his casual way of breaking the news to Gemmell, one of Wallace's closest friends at the club.

The death of Robert Kelly in 1971 made Stein's relations with the board of directors a slightly less secure one. Desmond White, Kelly's successor, was more inclined to question the manager. 'Oh no,' James Farrell put it, 'Desmond was not quite as close to Jock. Desmond White was not a cipher; he would always speak his mind. There was not quite the same relationship as Kelly and Stein. He just didn't have the bond between him and Jock that Bob Kelly had.' It is not that Stein's position was under any serious threat – he was plum in the middle of winning nine successive League titles and was still taking Celtic regularly to the latter stages of the European Cup – but it was White who held the purse strings at Celtic Park, and, during the 1970s, a series of promising young players would leave Celtic Park due to the tight fiscal policy implemented by the chairman. This, in turn, weakened the manager's team, and it must have been as demoralising for him as it was to the supporters to see his carefully culti- vated youngsters – the Quality Street Gang – slip from his grasp one by one.

Those players found Stein could be sensitive as well as stern. Paul Wilson, a winger, recalls an instance of Stein showing great under- standing and being rewarded immensely by the player. 'My mother had passed away. We buried her on the Friday and had the [1975] Cup final against Airdrie on the Saturday. Big Jock and a lot of the players were at the funeral. I said to Jock afterwards, "Do you mind if I come in and do some training this afternoon? I just want to get away from all this." I went in to Celtic Park and he said, "What about tomorrow? Are you up for it? Do you want to play tomorrow?" I said, "Yes, I do." He said, "You're playing, then." Fair play to him for giving me the chance, and I repaid him by scoring twice and winning the Cup.'

During the summer of 1975, Stein, Jean, his wife, Tony Queen, a book-maker, and his wife, flew into Manchester Airport on their return from a holiday on Menorca. Early in the morning of Saturday 5 July, with Stein at the wheel of his Mercedes, they suffered a collision with another car that was travelling in the wrong direction on the A74 dual carriageway close to Lockerbie. An ambulance whisked Stein to Dumfries Infirmary, where doctors dealing with life-threatening head and chest injuries performed a tracheotomy to enable him to breathe. He remained in hospital for a month and on his release it was agreed, on medical advice, that he would take a year away from Celtic Park to allow him to recuperate fully. Sean Fallon was put in charge of the team, but Stein was soon hovering in the background, attending matches again as early as September 1975, only a month after his release from hospital, and prompting Fallon with pieces of 'advice'.

The desire to be back in charge may still have been there but Stein had changed. On his official return to management in the summer of 1976, players and directors noticed subtle alterations in his character. 'After the car crash in 1975 Jock Stein was never the same man,' is how James Farrell put it. 'He wasn't quite so vital. You see, Jock Stein did everything. Jock Stein, as well as being manager and coach of the players, ran the show. He'd be out in the morning looking at the grass to see if it was growing properly. He was unique. Everything was changed with Jock's accident.' Billy McNeill also noticed the change in Stein. 'The car crash seemed to take his enthusiasm away. It seemed to take his personality away to a degree. He never quite seemed the same big, enthusiastic, outgoing personality that he had been. It probably encouraged him to think of himself and to look after himself more than anything else.' Stein had often participated in training sessions but following his accident he now supervised from the touchline; still a major presence but becoming diminished in all sorts of minor ways.

With Stein officially back at the helm from May 1976, Celtic clinched the 1977 Premier Division title and won the Scottish Cup, but when Kenny Dalglish quit the club for Liverpool in the summer of 1977 it left a vacuum that Stein knew he could not fill. The Dalglish transfer did enable Stein to pull off one final masterstroke, proving that his wiles remained intact even if he had lost some of his energy and fire. Liverpool's initial offer for the player was £300,000, a sum with which the Celtic directors were more than happy, but Stein turned down the offer instantaneously. He was aware that the Anfield club had £500,000 in the bank from their recent transfer of Kevin Keegan to SV Hamburg. Bob Paisley, the Liverpool manager, and John Smith, his chairman, were not unduly concerned. They had agreed between themselves that they would be prepared to increase their initial offer, if necessary, by ten per cent increments up to £400,000. They went to £330,000, and still Stein instructed his directors to turn down the offer; he did so again when Liverpool went to £360,000 and then stretched the fee to £400,000. When Stein still refused to accept this offer, Paisley and Smith began to show signs of twitchiness, but Stein knew that they needed desperately to sign Dalglish before the fast-approaching transfer dead-line for the European Cup and so said, 'I think if you were to suggest another ten per cent we could agree.' Smith and Paisley, now desperate to wind up business, immediately did so, and the £440,000 fee – almost fifty per cent more than their initial bid – became the new record transfer fee for a player moving from one British club to another.

It was a piece of good financial business, but a footballing one that would weaken Celtic and Stein immeasurably. Minus Dalglish, Celtic toiled in that 1977–78 season, finishing fifth, their lowest League posi-tion for thirteen years, and missing out on a place in Europe for the first time since Stein had been manager. It seemed time to go, and Stein himself was as aware of that as anyone else. Not that this was the first time he had considered relinquishing the post of Celtic manager. During the early summer of 1975 he had given the Scottish Football Association the impression that he was on the verge of accepting their offer of the job of national team manager, only to decline at the last minute. A similar scenario had unfolded with the SFA again in the spring of 1977, only for Stein again to withdraw just as he had appeared about to accept the job.

It has become a piece of received folk wisdom that Jock Stein was badly treated by the Celtic directorate when he resigned as manager in May 1978. Yet Jock Stein was never a victim, and in any situation in which wiles and guile were to be employed he could be expected to triumph.

It was Stein himself who had intimated to the board as early as March 1978 that it was time for him to leave the dugout: Celtic were out of European competition, already out of the Scottish Cup and sitting eighth in the ten-team Premier Division after a 2-1 defeat to St Mirren at home. Stein then helpfully assisted the board as the trusted go-between in bringing Billy McNeill to the club as its new manager. He approached McNeill at a function in the MacDonald Hotel, Giffnock, in May 1978 and then, like cold war spies reconnoitring, McNeill followed Stein's car from the hotel to Rouken Glen Park, where, in the shadow of the bandstand, they agreed verbally that McNeill would leave Aberdeen, where he had been manager for a year, to take over at Celtic.

Stein remained associated with Celtic over that summer, playing along with their offer of a directorship, which was to be ratified at the annual general meeting late in 1978, helping persuade a player or two that they should join McNeill at Celtic Park but all the while waiting patiently for his big pay-off: a testimonial match for him with Liverpool, the European champions, on 6 August 1978, which drew a crowd of 60,000 to Celtic Park and brought £80,000 through the turnstiles. Prior to the game he had made sure he would do nothing to loosen his ties with Celtic and potentially lessen the affection for him among the supporters due to roll up with their money at his benefit match, but on the following day, Stein was openly discussing his future with Manny Cussins, the Leeds United chairman, and one week later he was the new manager of Leeds, on a spanking £30,000 annual salary. It is surely no coincidence that these events occurred so swiftly after the match with Liverpool.

'I always felt Jock had a hidden agenda,' Billy McNeill says of those months after Stein had resigned as Celtic manager. 'You know, he said he wanted to retire, but I never, ever believed that. I think he had his career mapped out. He never did anything ad hoc; he never left anything to chance. I think the club handled it badly, but I'm sure he knew he was going to Leeds. I don't think the board would have known that.'

The directors were represented as having insulted Stein by offering him a directorship through which he would be fronting the effort to increase the revenue from the Celtic Pools; the idea is that such a job was not fitting for a man of Stein's stature. 'Oh no – it was Jock Stein who offered himself to the board,' James Farrell insisted. 'You see, Jock Stein ran everything. He ran the club. One of the things Jock was actually very interested in was control of the Pools – he wanted to do your job, my job, his job.'

Later in 1978 with Stein not having formally signed his contract with Leeds United, he returned to Scotland to take up the post of national team manager. After leading Scotland to the finals of the 1982 World Cup, in which the team acquitted itself well, Stein led them into the next World Cup qualifying campaign but this ended in tragedy when, close to the end of a qualifying match in Wales, Stein collapsed on the touchline and within minutes of the final whistle was confirmed as having died of a heart attack.

Greater than any political manoeuvrings is the legacy that Stein left Celtic. More than anything, Stein had a huge belief in Celtic performing with a certain degree of style, and he unerringly put that into effect. 'If the performance hadn't been up to scratch,' Bobby Lennox says, 'he would not be happy, win or lose. We'd troop into the dressing room, and he would lay into us. "That's not the way we play," he would say. "We get it down on the ground and we pass it quicker and we move off it quicker and we defend better and we push up to the halfway line . . ."' Those high standards meant Stein transformed Celtic from strugglers and stragglers into a team that was not only effective but one admired for its style. Stein's broad shoulders and big hands were appropriate appendages in a man who single-handedly established a grip on a club planted firmly in the past before sending it hurtling forward spectacularly into a future that only Stein could have shaped and sculpted.

16
PEAKS AND TROUGHS

There was every reason for Jock Stein to expect the 1970s to yield a series of ongoing successes for Celtic as he stood at the dawn of that decade. A host of young players were jostling for places in the first team, keenly putting pressure on their predecessors and ensuring that the generation who had earned themselves the collective epithet of the Lisbon Lions could not live off their reputations. Players such as George Connelly, Kenny Dalglish, Victor Davidson, David Hay, Danny McGrain, Lou Macari and Paul Wilson were prominent among a group of reserves who won for themselves the nickname the Quality Street Gang. Even in the late 1960s Stein had tinkered with his team selections to allow some of these teenagers to dip their toes in the water in terms of first-team action. He would only field one or two at a time, give them a game or two and then return them to the reserves but what he saw must have encouraged him.

'My first game was at Tannadice,' Danny McGrain recalls of his debut against Dundee United in 1970, 'and I came on at half-time for Harry Hood. When the first ball came to me it went under my foot. I could easily have cracked up. But Bobby Murdoch said, "Hey come on, get back in!" If he hadn't shouted that at me I might just have gone up like a puff of smoke and floated away somewhere. Big Billy McNeill encouraged me too. I never got any abuse. Nobody shouted badly at me. With my next touch I just booted the ball up the park – I wasn't taking any chances. I then felt quite at home, but the first five minutes were very hard. I owe a lot to Bobby Murdoch and Billy McNeill for not giving me stick.

'We just learned from what they did. I learned from watching Tommy Gemmell and Jim Craig and Jimmy Johnstone and Bobby Murdoch. You couldn't help but be amazed by the energy that came from the Lisbon Lions; the fun that they had. We blossomed, and Mr Stein and the Lisbon Lions, I think, had a great deal to do with that because they were just teaching us without us knowing. You weren't aware of how much you had learned from them until ten or twenty years down the road.'

Alec Boden, then a Celtic coach, says of that new generation of Celts, 'You could see that they were looking at ideas about how the game could be played better, which is good, because it can make you a better player.' Boden had helped to oversee the development of those players on their arrival at the club, instilling in them the levels of discipline and fitness demanded by Stein and helping to make them their manager's players, possessed of the qualities he liked to see. They knew no other methods than those undertaken by Stein – unlike their predecessors, some of whom had been subject to the haphazard coaching methods of the Jimmy McGrory era a decade before.

'For the young ones coming through, he was different class,' Paul Wilson says of Jock Stein. 'When you came into the team he had set his plan out as to what he was going to do. He had a second team where, if one of the first team went out, one of the second team could pop into his position without it upsetting the rhythm and style of the team. He was superb. I wouldn't have a bad word to say about him. He gave us rollick-ings all the time, but we deserved them. Jock got you into a frame of mind where you never thought you were going to be beaten, which a lot of managers can't do. With Jock, you either did it or you didn't, and if you didn't you were soon on your way.

'Willie Fernie, who helped out with the reserves, would say, "Take them all on yourself – don't give the ball to anybody." That's the kind of thing Willie had done, I think, as a player. The big man didn't like that. He wanted it to be more like you took the man on when it was on and that you took them on as a team. Wee Jimmy [Johnstone] was the exception – you couldn't tell him not to take people on – but I was never in that class. Jock didn't want that from me – he wanted it to be direct: take the man on, and move the ball on to someone else. He didn't want you turning back. He moulded the team to play the way he wanted. If I didn't do as he wanted, he'd be shouting, "You're out there like a fandancer." Or he'd say, "You want to go down the pits and see what hard work's like. This is nothing compared to that."

'He was a very intelligent man – he could change things tactically but he would do so without cramping your individual style or preventing you playing in the manner he had asked of you before the match – but he would maybe pull you back into a certain position. It's not until later on in your career you look back and say, "I understand now what he was doing." We were playing a game against Red Star [in a pre-season tournament in Australia in 1977], and they were tearing us to bits, and he pulled me back into midfield, left one man up front, making it 4-5-1, and Red Star were hopeless. They couldn't play any more – everything was a long ball – but if you let them play in the middle of the park they were just running right through you, and they were a quality team at that time. We didn't have a great team at that time, but to come in and see you've beaten a team like that . . .' Celtic won 2-0.

Wilson was by that stage one of the few survivors of the team that had shown so much promise in the early 1970s but which had been ripped apart – by the very players whom Stein had tutored so carefully in Celtic ways. The first to chafe against the tight bonds that tied them to Celtic was Lou Macari, who, at the very beginning of 1973, demanded a transfer. Tommy Docherty had just been appointed manager of Manchester United and was willing to pay £200,000, a record transfer fee, for Macari and simultaneously quadruple the player's wages. For the money-conscious Macari it was irresistible, and, although Stein did all he could to manipulate the player into going to Liverpool – managed by Bill Shankly, Stein's friend – Macari slipped the leash and went to Old Trafford instead.

The player's timing could have been better – Stein had been in the Victoria Infirmary at the time of his initial transfer request, recovering from heart trouble. Eighteen months later David Hay followed Macari south, this time to Chelsea and again for a large fee – the Stamford Bridge club shelling out £225,000 for a midfield player who had excelled for Scotland at the World Cup of 1974. Hay's discontentment with the pay structure at Celtic Park had been so deep that he had disputed his contract during the 1973–74 season, an action that had, predictably, not gone down well with Stein. 'I felt we weren't getting paid the rate for what we were doing,' Hay says. 'I didn't want to leave but I felt I merited more money, and there was no freedom of contract, no Bosman, at that time so I was out on a limb.' Hay wanted his basic pay increased from £65 per week to £100 per week, and, after going head to head with Stein on the matter, he found himself dealing with Desmond White, the chairman. White told Hay that if he gave him £100 per week he would have to do the same for every player. Hay suggested that that would be a good idea. When the offer from Chelsea came in, shortly after the World Cup, Stein suggested to the player it was time for him to leave, even though Hay had by then decided he would be content to remain in Scotland and augment his earnings in other ways. 'He may have had a directive from above to take the dough,' Hay says.

George Connelly, Hay's great friend, and a shy individual who had trouble coping with the demands of professional football, had already begun to show signs of instability before Hay's transfer. One team-mate recalls lapping the track with the rest of the first-team squad one day in the early 1970s, when Connelly simply ran down the tunnel and left the ground. A Scotland team-mate recalls the bemusement among the squad when, with the international squad about to depart from Glasgow Airport for a match in Switzerland in mid-1973, Connelly simply disappeared. After a string of absences and disappearances, Connelly finally quit Celtic in 1975, a talent that would never be fulfilled. Victor Davidson left that year too, one member of the Quality Street Gang who had failed to establish himself fully as a first-team footballer.

The most talented of all those players, Kenny Dalglish, first submitted a transfer request in the summer of 1975 but agreed to withdraw it out of respect for Stein and the club: the manager that summer had suffered the near-fatal car crash that almost ended his life. Two years later, Dalglish had become determined to leave, and despite Stein doing all in his power to talk him out of it, the player was soon on the move to Liverpool, the European champions. McGrain remained, but even then Stein was deprived of the full-back's world-class talent after the player suffered a serious ankle injury in a match with Hibernian in October 1977, an injury that would put him out of action for eighteen months.

Money was at the root of much of the unrest that had torn Stein's team apart. Wages in England were rocketing during the 1970s, and Celtic failed either to keep pace or to create a good Scottish approximation of the pay on offer down south; one whereby the pull of home surroundings and of the club itself might just have made up for the shortfall. The difference was instead a drastic one – players could also expect a cut of around five per cent of a transfer fee. Not that Celtic, with Desmond White at the helm as chairman during this period, were terribly resistant to the prospect of receiving sizeable transfer monies from the sales of their better players.

The insistence of so many players on leaving Celtic, players whom Stein had nurtured paternally since boyhood, affected him adversely, and the 1970s also saw him suffer a series of blows of a type that had not been present for him in the 1960s: grief at witnessing the aftermath of the Ibrox Disaster of 1971, in which sixty-six people lost their lives; heart trouble in 1972; Atletico Madrid torpedoing his European Cup hopes and ideals with severe bad grace in 1974; his car crash in 1975; and then the loss of Dalglish, a player who offered some hope for the future as long as he remained at Celtic. His departure tore the heart out of Stein's team.

'You can't blame anybody for moving for the money,' Danny McGrain says. 'They went for big transfer fees, good money, but how can you fill in the space that Kenny has left or Davie Hay has left? Davie scored some great goals and would run through a wall for you and win tackles he shouldn't have won. A lot of players then came and went who weren't Celtic class, and we maybe weren't quite as good a team as we had been before. Nothing stays the same. Other teams were getting stronger, and we weren't filling the gaps left by players such as Macari, Hay, Dalglish. Mr Stein must have found it so difficult to have won the European Cup and then ten years later finding the quality of player wasn't there, because he was a manager who so badly wanted to win.'

The absence of McGrain and a career-ending injury to Pat Stanton, his experienced sweeper, meant that Stein was just about down to the bare bones as the 1977–78 season began rolling along in earnest, a season in which memories of his salad days jousting with the cream of conti-nental coaches became ever more torn and frayed. Celtic suffered four defeats in their opening five League matches, and five successive League defeats post-Christmas meant that by February 1978 they sat eighth in the ten-team Premier Division, kept out of the two relegation spots only by goal difference. They did rally to finish fifth, but by then Stein had agreed with the board of directors that it was time to quit. During the 1970s he had won five Scottish Cups, one League Cup and six League titles, including a 6-1 defeat of Hibernian in 1972 that equalled the record scoreline for a Scottish Cup final. It brought his total of trophies with Celtic up to an exceptional twenty-five: a success rate of almost two national trophies per season. He would be a hard act to follow.

It was Stein who had engineered Billy McNeill's move to Aberdeen as manager in 1977 and, with his former captain having done well in his first season at Pittodrie, finishing as runners-up to Rangers in the League and in the Scottish Cup, Stein was again involved in acting as the go-between to lure McNeill back to Celtic Park. The new manager breathed life back into a club in which standards had slackened and where Stein had signed a series of players in his final days as manager who were not up to scratch. One of those players, on being sent out to warm up at Ibrox, when a substitute in a match there, had veered off to loosen up on the track in front of the Rangers support rather than the Celtic supporters. On returning to the bench, Stein asked the player why he had done so. 'I get less stick from them than I do from our own supporters,' was the response.

There would be no slack under McNeill. 'When big Billy came he changed a lot of things,' Paul Wilson says. 'He was going into these diets and taking your pulse and all sorts of different things. We would be running up and down the terraces and then we'd come back and he would be taking your pulse.' As McNeill's revitalisation programme continued in the autumn of 1978 he signed Davie Provan, a winger, from Kilmarnock and Murdo MacLeod, a midfield player, from Dumbarton and inculcated in his team an honest, straightforward, direct approach to the game, with dynamic players such as MacLeod, Provan, Roy Aitken, Tommy Burns and McGrain driving forward in a robust 4-4-2 formation, a team imbued with McNeill's confidence and one designed to attack. Fuelled by McNeill's spirited desire to win matches and trophies, they won the 1978–79 League title in dramatic style. Facing Rangers in an all-or-nothing midweek fixture on 21 May 1979, at Celtic Park, in Celtic's final match of the season, they knew that a win would make them champions, with a draw or a defeat presenting the title to their opponents.

With Celtic 1-0 down, ten minutes after half-time Johnny Doyle, the winger, was dismissed for kicking Alex MacDonald, the Rangers midfield player, when he was on the ground. Goals from Aitken and George McCluskey, the striker, revived Celtic hopes of victory but despair followed when Bobby Russell, the Rangers midfield player, made it 2-2 with fourteen minutes remaining. A stunning own goal from Colin Jackson, the Rangers centre-back, put Celtic ahead again with five minutes to go, before MacLeod administered the *coup de grâce* with a twenty-yard shot in the final seconds that zoomed high past Peter McCloy in the Rangers goal. It had been a night of ups and downs and thunderous emotions, one entirely in character with McNeill and his team, which seemed custom-built for such occasions.

'That was a good team of the eighties,' Danny McGrain says of the McNeill side that pushed on into the following decade and used that League victory as a springboard to the European Cup quarter-finals and a match against Real Madrid in March 1980. 'We all got on great together. We had a good mould of player who all appreciated each other and were pals. We let ourselves down when we got beaten by Real Madrid. That is one of my biggest disappointments – not that I have many – to have been 2-0 up against Real Madrid and you lose 3-0.' Goals from George McCluskey and Johnny Doyle, in the second half of a hectic first leg at Celtic Park, had given Celtic a good lead to take to the Bernabeu. They were even fairly comfortable on Spanish soil despite being under pressure during the first half of the match in Madrid and then, seconds before half-time, Carlos Santillana, the striker, made his way through the mêlée at a corner to prod the ball into the Celtic net after a sly tug on Peter Latchford's jersey had led to the Celtic goalkeeper being pulled down after catching the ball, forcing him to spill it. Uli Stielike got a second for Real, and Juanito put Real ahead on aggregate. Late in the match, Stielike, the West German international sweeper, handled the ball inside his own penalty area, but Karoly Palotai, the Hungarian referee, whose decisions had favoured Real all night, did not want to know and allowed play to continue.

'To get to the semi-final and be captain would have been great,' McGrain says, 'two games away from the final, which would have been phenom-enal. We lost it at half-time when that goal went in. Real Madrid weren't a great team at that time – as big name as they are, they weren't over-flowing with great players. I thought we had a chance. The fact we had beaten them 2-0 at Celtic Park showed us they weren't invincible. After something like that, you feel so bad inside that to generate enthusiasm for your next League game is so, so hard. Supporters feel let down, but the fact that we did beat Real Madrid put us up a notch. It's in the history books [so it is, right here]. We did well for a team of, basically, Scottish players.'

Celtic, prior to the tie with Real, had been top of the Scottish Premier Division; eight points clear of Morton and St Mirren and ten ahead of both Aberdeen and Rangers, even if Aberdeen did have two games in hand.

As McGrain suggests, the defeat in the European Cup sparked a collapse that saw Aberdeen come through from that position to take the League title on the final day of the season, finishing a point clear of Celtic. 'That makes you stronger as a player,' McGrain says, 'because it doesn't feel nice and you don't want it to happen again.'

Another final-day flurry, to win the Scottish Cup in 1980, after a riveting final with Rangers, saw victory sealed when McGrain's hopeful shot, veering slightly wide of goal, was eagerly diverted by the left shin of McCluskey, who had his back to goal, and into the Rangers net. All the good things about the game, though, were obscured by a notorious Old Firm riot quite different in nature from the one that had disfigured the 1909 final. Some young Celtic supporters, in celebration of the victory, leaped over the perimeter fence at their end of Hampden, and their Rangers equivalents, in frustration, copied them. Soon the field was swarming with thousands of supporters confronting each other, lobbing bricks and bottles, exchanging blows and charging and retreating in turn. There was only the thinnest number of police inside the ground; most of those on duty had been deployed outside the stadium after the final whistle to deal with potential trouble in the surrounding streets. Eventually, officers on horseback, long batons drawn for the first time in Glasgow since the 1926 General Strike, arrived on the pitch to disperse the trouble-makers; galloping into the supporters, one female mounted officer on a white horse with white baton became particularly noticeable. This would be the abiding image of that final, which resulted in 210 arrests and, significantly, the Criminal Justice Act (1980) that forbade football spectators to enter a ground in possession of alcohol or when in a drunken state. It remains with us and has had a transformative effect on the condition and conduct of football supporters in modern times.

Two more League titles, in 1981 and 1982, the second won dramatically on the last day of the season with a 3-0 win over St Mirren at Celtic Park, plus victory over Rangers in the League Cup final of December 1982, meant that McNeill had the useful record of having won a trophy in each of his five seasons as Celtic manager, but all was not well behind the scenes. McNeill had rapidly come to the conclusion that he had left Aberdeen too soon after having been unable to resist the chance to become Celtic manager, which he felt might not have come for him again. Dick Donald, the Aberdeen chairman, had told him, as he left Pittodrie, 'You'll not enjoy working with that board as much as you enjoyed working with us.' Those words proved prophetic. 'Desmond White wasn't interested in investing,' McNeill says. 'Everything was done on the cheap – it was murder. I felt when I went to Celtic that what had happened in the past was good enough for them. It frustrated me. I found great difficulty in establishing any relationship with Desmond White, I really did.'

McNeill, in addition to making good signings, had also brought into the first-team Paul McStay and Charlie Nicholas, bright young talents, the former a clever midfield player, the latter a light, audacious striker who scored forty-eight goals in the 1982–83 season, the highest individual tally by a Celtic player since Jimmy McGrory in the 1930s. It would be the transfer of Nicholas in the summer of 1983 that would finally help ease McNeill out of a job he had cherished.

The sale of Charlie Nicholas became something of a pantomime. The player was hawked around Arsenal, Liverpool and Manchester United, the three wealthiest clubs in England at the time, in the weeks after the conclusion of the 1982–83 domestic season. His leather trousers, supposed liking for champagne and floppy New Romantic haircut saw him cut a distinctive figure, and it seemed as though he was enjoying every moment of the English clubs' very public courtship. Nor did it appear as though it would end there; on radio that summer, Charlie talked of interest from Italy in him and of the suitability to him of what he called 'the lifestyle' in that country. Eventually it would be Arsenal who would win him, but their purchase of this supremely self-confident individual would soon go flat. Nicholas' appearance for Scotland at Wembley in the 2-0 defeat to England during the early summer of 1983 must have had a lot of southern onlookers wondering what all the fuss was about; in an outsize Scotland shirt and with a large gold neckchain ostentatiously displayed, Nicholas looked, that rare thing for him, lost. It was an ominous indication that Nicholas, then twenty-one, could be out of his depth in the swirling southern waters.

Arsenal's seizure of the signature of this eighties stylist and the most exciting player in Britain was tinged with some classic old-fashioned boardroom wheeling and dealing that said much about how Celtic was being run in the 1980s. Ken Friar, the Arsenal secretary, flew to Glasgow, where he was met by Kevin Kelly, a director of Celtic. As they chatted on their way into the city, Friar indicated how much Arsenal were prepared to offer for the player, and Kelly informed him that it was approximately £100,000 short of what Desmond White, the chairman, wished to receive. Friar and Kelly then worked out a way of making up the shortfall.

As Kelly had predicted, Desmond White, on meeting the representative of Arsenal, was unwilling to accept Arsenal's initial offer, telling Friar that if Arsenal failed to match Celtic's valuation of the player, Celtic would get it elsewhere. After some further bluster from White, Friar played his ace. Arsenal would, he said, be prepared to make up the shortfall by travelling to Celtic Park for a friendly match, without demanding an appearance fee and paying all their travelling and accommodation expenses. White liked the sound of that – most particularly the idea of Arsenal paying their own way – and soon Nicholas was on his way to north London for a reported fee of £650,000, although the actual sum may have been closer to £1 million.

Nicholas, when still a Celtic player, had been invited to White's office on West Nile Street in Glasgow at the end of that season. The chairman had told the club's most prized player, 'I'll understand if the challenges are there, and you want to go somewhere else and you want to move on.' It was hardly an exhortation for a star player to remain with the club, and made it easier for Nicholas to move to London, where he was on wages five times higher than at Celtic. McNeill later claimed that the player had been sold 'behind my back' and that White had refused to tell him the transfer fee. It made their relationship, finally, irreparable, and that summer McNeill left Celtic and followed Nicholas south, to become manager of Manchester City.

There appeared a greater chance of harmony inside the club with Celtic's next appointment as manager: David Hay. Back in 1974, when Hay had been seeking a greatly improved contract and had been in prolonged discussion with the club on the matter, he had found that he got on relatively well with Desmond White, and that good relationship must have been in the chairman's mind when making the appointment. Hay had not been involved in football when approached by Celtic – he had been out of the game for a year after having led Motherwell to promotion in 1982 at the end of his first season as a club manager. He had then resigned from Motherwell, planning to emigrate to the USA, but visa difficulties meant he had remained in Scotland, opening a pub in Paisley in early 1983, shortly before being appointed Celtic manager.

'I was thirty-five, and that is too young for someone to become Celtic manager,' Hay admits. 'But at the time, through youthful exuberance, I probably thought that experience meant absolutely nothing.' He made few alterations to the team's style of play but, although a seemingly easy-going type of person, he emphasised to his players that he wished to see them tackle hard and get physically close to opponents, to close them down aggressively. His inexperience did show when he immediately made a rod for his own back by declaring that if the team won nothing in his first season, he would resign. When Celtic did complete the 1983–84 season trophyless, losing the Scottish Cup final to Aberdeen, he was immediately asked by the press if he was going to quit. The laconic Hay responded by stating that Celtic had won a trophy – the BP Youth Cup.

A second successive Scottish Cup final loomed in 1985, with Hay needing his team to win to save the season. Aberdeen had become dominant in Scotland under Alex Ferguson and had notched a second successive Scottish League title, and they and Dundee United, Celtic's opponents in the 1985 final, were becoming known as the New Firm in Scottish football, such was the east coast success in wresting power away from Glasgow. It looked less than promising, then, when Stuart Beedie put United 1-0 ahead ten minutes after half-time, but Hay pushed Aitken into midfield from central defence and added an extra forward by substituting Tommy Burns, the midfield player, with Brian McClair, a striker signed from Motherwell in one of McNeill's final acts as Celtic manager. It worked beautifully in tilting the match in Celtic's favour. With fifteen minutes remaining, Eamon Bannon fouled MacLeod outside the Dundee United penalty area, and Provan sent a terrific free-kick curling high into the United net. Five minutes from time, Aitken, powering down the right, curved a cross into the penalty area, and Frank McGarvey bent his body in mid-air to meet the ball and head it past Hamish McAlpine, the Dundee United goalkeeper, for a most spectacular winner.

The death of Desmond White on holiday in Greece that summer of 1985 led to changes in the boardroom that Hay felt weakened his position as manager. Tom Devlin became chairman for a year until his own death in 1986, when he was replaced by Jack McGinn, and, although Hay won the League title in incredible circumstances in the spring of 1986, time was running out for him. Celtic visited St Mirren on 3 May that year requiring fortune to fall firmly on their side. They had trailed Heart of Midlothian at the top of the table for much of the season but had drawn closer and closer to the Edinburgh side during the final weeks of the season, and, going into the St Mirren game, they had won eight successive matches. They were, though, still two points behind Hearts whom they needed to lose at Dundee, even if Celtic could beat St Mirren by enough goals to overhaul Hearts' goal difference, which was superior to that of Celtic on the morning of that final day of the season.

On the afternoon, Celtic pulverised St Mirren by playing some outstanding football, defence linking with midfield, and midfield linking with attack, all quite seamlessly, to record a 5-0 victory. Dundee, meanwhile and most particularly Albert Kidd, their striker, were doing their bit by defeating Hearts 2-0 at Dens Park, with Kidd notching both goals. The title belonged to Celtic. It was one of the biggest turnarounds in the club's tale but an even bigger turnaround, on and off the field, was in the offing.

17

A SLICE OF PARADISE

It is a curious coincidence that at both Celtic Park and Ibrox Park it is an old-fashioned schoolyard that doubles up as a matchday car park for directors and other boardroom dignitaries. At Ibrox the school sits on the other side of Edmiston Drive from the stadium, diagonally opposite the main stand, and the distance to the main door constitutes a walk that should last only a minute or two. On matchdays, though, that road is the near-exclusive province of Glasgow Rangers supporters, and for Celtic directors the journey can feel as long as any they have ever made. On an Old Firm afternoon in the early 1990s, Kevin Kelly, the Celtic chairman, made that walk, but on this occasion he found it to be an enriching experience. Celtic were in serious financial trouble at the time, and as Kelly picked his way stealthily from car to stadium Rangers supporters tossed coins in his direction. Kelly took the joke in good part, making a show of stooping to collect the proffered financial assistance. 'Did you have any trouble out there, Kevin, on your way in?' David Murray, the Rangers chairman, said as he greeted Kelly inside the directors' lounge. Murray had been watching the events outside from his eyrie high above the milling crowds. 'All I can say, Mr Murray, is that your supporters are very generous,' a grinning Kelly responded.

The financial difficulties that Kelly and his board were then experiencing were close to insurmountable because they were inextricably bound to the Celtic Park ground – and its reconstruction. What would clearly be a costly undertaking had become a pressing and unavoidable issue by the early 1990s and one on which Celtic Football Club would either stand or fall.

Celtic Park had been constructed on its present site in 1892 and was contemporaneously described in *Athletic News* as the finest football ground in Great Britain. One hundred years later, few would have been rushing to apply that description to a stadium that was on the verge of becoming defunct. The Taylor Report of January 1990, commissioned by the UK government after the Hillsborough Disaster in April 1989, where during an FA Cup semi-final 96 Liverpool supporters were crushed to death at the Leppings Lane end of the ground, had advised that all-seater stadiums were safer for spectators, and the government had subsequently stipulated that all top-flight grounds in England and in the Scottish Premier Division had to become all-seater by August 1994. This sweeping requirement hit Celtic particularly hard. Celtic Park, with a capacity of 60,800, at that time had only 8,700 seats, all of them being in the south stand, which was surrounded by three vast terraces. The problem of converting their ground to meet the measures set out in the Taylor Report left the Celtic board struggling not only for their own survival as directors but seemed to make questionable the very survival of the club itself.

It was indicative of how little Celtic had developed the ground that even in the early 1990s it would have been fairly recognisable to those who had seen the second Celtic Park open in 1892. This ground had been constructed through the manual labour of supporters and sympathisers, as, four years previously, had the original Celtic Park, a hop, skip and jump away, on the other side of Janefield Street. 'In the very early days of this club,' Willie Maley, a member of Celtic's first eleven in 1888, recounted, 'when money was very scarce, one cannot tell how much it owed to the hard work of the men who voluntarily built the old ground, and later the new ground to which we moved after our practical eviction ... every penny was required to keep the club's head above water and to disappoint the many unfriends we had in those days who wished to see the club a failure like the other few efforts of previous years, when attempts had been made to form a Glasgow Hibernian club on the lines of the then great Edinburgh club.'

The site of the original Celtic Park, built in 1888, was situated adjacent to Janefield Cemetery – the cemetery wall marked one side of the ground's boundary. It had been rented at a cost of £50 per year and was built by volunteers, largely from the immigrant Irish-Catholic community. Only one week after the meeting of 6 November 1887, at St Mary's in Calton, at which Brother Walfrid's proposal to form a football club had been accepted, the six acres of vacant ground had been leased. Getting their hands dirty in the construction of the ground did much to accentuate the feeling among Celtic's followers that the club belonged to them; they had, after all, lent a hand to build it. Not only was it most unusual for a football ground to be built by the efforts of its own followers but it was unprecedented for a football club to construct a ground before starting to play its fixtures – in the game's early days, footballers would form a team, find themselves becoming a watchable attraction in a local park and then enclose a ground to maximise revenue from the enterprise. Celtic turned the norm on its head. By May of 1888, four months after the club had pleaded for financial assistance for the new enterprise, the ground was opened, even though that financial assistance, as Maley testified, 'came along but not in the amount that was desired'.

The new ground had a modest stand, with dressing rooms for both teams, shower-baths, a small office, a referee's room and a trainer's room and store. Its readiness for business was announced in the *Glasgow Herald* that spring of 1888: 'Opening of the Celtic Football And Athletic Park, Dalmarnock Street, Parkhead, Grand Opening Match Hibernians [sic] (Edinburgh) v Cowlairs (To-day Exhibition Day May 8th) Kick-off at 6pm prompt. Admission 6d. Ladies free. Grand Stand 6d extra each Person. N.B. The Park is two minutes' walk from the Parkhead and London Road Tramcar and Railway Stations.'

A healthy crowd of around 5,000 turned up for that opening match between two of the leading Scottish clubs of the time – and twenty days later Celtic took to the field for the first time by hosting a match against Rangers in front of a 2,000 crowd – but it would be untrue to suggest that things went smoothly from there. The ground's owner quickly voiced complaint at the way his land had been transformed into a football ground and threatened Celtic that he would take them to court. The Celtic committee, in the confrontational fashion that was the norm at a club that was always prepared, by its very nature, for external threats to its existence, responded by stating that they would do the same to him. An uneasy peace reigned for three years until, as Maley put it, 'an old affliction to Irishmen, "The Landlord", forced the club to move. Rack-renting brought about a change of field. A rent raised after three short years' occupancy from fifty pounds to 500 pounds a year proved the mettle of the new Celtic.'

Railing against the grossly inflated increase, the Celtic directors opted to move home rather than give in to extortion. A switch to Possilpark or Springburn, in the north of the city, was considered, but Celtic's friendly relations with Cowlairs, the fellow Glaswegian club that had inaugurated the first Celtic Park, persuaded them not to encroach on that club's territory. Maley was one who saw this gentlemanly decision as an opportunity wasted, in that there was a growing population in that part of Glasgow and cheap land available where Celtic could have built an even more expansive stadium than the one that they constructed by flitting across Janefield Street to the site of the present Celtic Park. At that time, it was a disused quarry; a 'seemingly impossible site,' according to Maley, 'converted quickly into a palatial enclosure . . . as one smart chap said, "like leaving the graveyard to enter Paradise". That title, seized on by a pressman, clung to the present ground for many years.' It still does. The site had been flooded when first inspected by the Celtic committee, and the largely voluntary labourers had, with a near-miraculous effort, shifted an estimated 100,000 cartloads of earth to create the new ground. Michael Davitt, the Irish land reformer and the club's honorary patron, laid the first sod of turf on the centre spot, freshly hewn from Donegal, but this was quickly removed by a thief, much to the chagrin of Celtic's sympathisers.

The new stadium was estimated to hold 70,000 but even at that, Celtic Park would, as football grew greatly in popularity during the early twentieth century, hold considerably smaller numbers than Hampden Park and Ibrox Park. Had the club moved to the north of the city, it might have been able to build a ground closer in size to the two other major Glasgow stadiums. Even on the same site, Celtic might have built a ground to compete with those other mammoths. They had the opportunity to obtain additional land all the way down to London Road and could have laid the pitch north to south, providing space for monstrous terraces along the lines of those at Hampden and Ibrox, but, according to Maley, the expense that would have been incurred in constructing the necessary type of wooden terracing persuaded the Celtic committee to think not-so-big.

Still, it was a splendid new home, proudly displaying a tidy pavilion that, as with its counterpart at the original Celtic Park, housed dressing rooms, offices and rooms for dispensing hospitality. This pavilion was situated just behind the corner flag at what would later become known as the 'Celtic End' of the ground. A neat building, constructed along similar lines to the quaint, surviving pavilion at Fulham's Craven Cottage, it consisted of two tiers and had a balcony from which matches could be viewed by VIPs. The stand, to its left, backed on to Janefield Street and was 320 feet long with fifteen tiers of seats and provided room for more than 3,500 spectators. The rest of the stadium consisted of terracing. A distinctive feature of the ground, although one fairly common in the numerous football grounds springing up across Britain in the late Victorian era, was the cycling and athletics tracks that separated the playing surface from the stand and terraces. The existence of that cycling track would have repercussions for the club that would linger long after cycling races had been abandoned at Celtic Park.

Sports days that included cycling contests were profitable and popular for Celtic, and in 1895 the Scottish Cyclists' Union offered Celtic the hefty sum of £500 to hire Celtic Park for their modestly titled World Cycling Championship. It was a complicated offer, though, as the championship in question would not take place until 1897, and if Celtic were to host it, it was estimated that the club would have to spend £900 upgrading their cycling track to meet the modifications required by the Scottish Cyclists' Union. The long-term benefit would be that the club would then be able to count on receiving the bounty from high-grade cycling meetings long into the future.

This provided fuel for the leading lights on the Celtic committee, such as John Glass and John McLaughlin, founder members of the club, to bring to fruition their long-nursed plan to turn Celtic into a limited liability company, geared towards making profits. It was felt by them that this had been becoming more and more of a necessity since the official authorisation of professionalism in football in Scotland in 1893, although they wished not only to raise funds for players' pay but also to remunerate club officials. Players had always been paid, of course, under the counter, but with professionalism legitimised, the costs involved in running a club had increased, and Glass and others had authorised Celtic becoming overdrawn with the Clydesdale Bank; at one stage in the early 1890s the debt had reached more than £2,000. Seeing the expensive upgrade of the cycling track as an opportunity to exert leverage, in 1896 the agitators for change issued an ultimatum to the membership that either the club become a limited company, one that could efficiently raise capital for improvements or close down altogether. It was an attempt to force the issue and finally silence the rumblings of those within the committee who, for years, had virulently opposed the wholehearted embracing of professionalism at a club that had been founded for charitable purposes and who were becoming concerned that Celtic by the mid-1890s was driven more by the self-interest of its finance-conscious committee members.

The vote was carried, and on 4 March 1897 Celtic became the Celtic Football & Athletic Company Limited. Its first share issue saw Glass granted 200 one-pound shares 'in recognition of his early work for the club', according to Maley, while 800 other one-pound shares were issued in Celtic. Glass was also on the first, seven-man, board of directors of the new limited company, a streamlined version of the previous twenty-man committee. Brother Walfrid was now no longer involved with the club – he had been posted to London by the Marists during the early 1890s – but Willie Maley was well rewarded for energetically backing the move to a limited liability company. Having been match secretary following his retirement as a player, he now became, on 3 April 1897, secretary-manager, in effect the first manager of Celtic.

Debate still raged among the membership as to whether the club was following the right direction, but the club's new standing as a limited liability company did, as the proponents of change had promised, enable it to borrow substantial sums of money, and in December 1897 Celtic paid Lord Newlands £10,000 to own outright Celtic Park, becoming, in the process, the first Scottish club to own its own ground; finally putting to bed any fears of rapacious landlords. And the world cycling championships had indeed taken place in Celtic Park in 1897.

During the following year a second stand was constructed, known as the Grant stand on the London Road side of Celtic Park. Its construction was financed privately by James Grant, one of the seven newly created directors of the club. This edifice was built on stilts, and was a new departure for the club, providing luxurious conditions in which to watch football, with padded seats for patrons and glass windows from behind which the match could be viewed, protecting the well-heeled from the elements – all in all a prototype executive box. It was a flawed experiment: the windows would steam up with condensation from the breaths of the hearties inside, hampering the view of the game, and habituees of the stand objected to the four steep flights of stairs that they were required to climb before they reached their exclusive enclave. The dignitaries also disliked being on the other side of the field from the pavilion, the hub of the club. It proved to be a commercial failure, and Grant suffered financial wounding at its hands. Christmas Day 1893 had seen another failed experiment – a first attempt at floodlighting the ground through hanging lights on a rope around the perimeter; the light afforded was dim and the ball would frequently hit the illuminations.

A packed Celtic Park in late Victorian/early Edwardian days looked tremendous: Grant's south stand, for all its flaws, rose up magnificently above the rest of the ground like the grand folly that it was; the pavilion and the north stand opposite looked ultra-smart in their scrubbed-up infancy; and spectators not only crammed the terraces behind the goals but also planted themselves on the cycling and athletics tracks that circumvented the playing surface as if to symbolise the growing encroachment of football on the other athletic activities for which the stadium had originally been designed.

After that burst of ground construction and modification during the club's first decade, change would be only sporadic during the subsequent ninety years. The most significant and far-reaching alteration would create the most renowned section of Celtic Park – the Jungle – but it was, as with many of the interesting developments in Celtic's history, a change that came about by accident rather than being part of a grandiloquent plan. Indeed it was an enemy of the club who sparked it all off: a fire, very possibly started maliciously, on 9 May 1904 destroyed the original wooden-seated stand on the Janefield Street side of the ground, and once the embers had died, with the damage being costed at around £6,000, the Celtic directors reached a compromise solution to deal with the situation. They decided not to reinstall seating in the north enclosure, instead keeping that part of the ground as terracing, while Grant gladly handed over his loss-making stand to the club, which, with its windows removed, now became the only seated section inside Celtic Park.

Unwittingly, the directors had created a part of the ground that would become inspirational to Celtic teams for decades to come and that would do much to solidify Celtic Park's reputation as an earthy arena and one intimidating for visiting teams. It was not, though, until after the Second World War that the Janefield Street terracing – the old pavilion had been destroyed by fire in 1929 – would be christened 'the Jungle'. One theory for this part of the ground being given that particular nickname in the postwar era is that some Celtic supporters, newly demobbed after seeing action in the jungles of the Far East, compared the conditions found on that terracing to the harsh, unforgiving terrain where they had been sent into combat. Such was the Jungle's state of dilapidation by the 1940s that weeds grew on its terraces, and its corrugated iron roof leaked badly on rainy days, channelling streams of water on to the spectators below, while, on dry days, the same roof sent motes of rust floating on to their heads. Through the 1950s and 1960s the holes in the roof grew larger in size and never seemed to be repaired, but these material drawbacks did little to dampen the enthusiasm of the boisterous individuals below who gave the Jungle its lively reputation. On a bright day, with the fans packed in, and with the gold and the green and the white of their favours reflecting brightly from within its confines, it shimmered with colour like an opened pirate's treasure chest.

'I would stand in the Celtic End,' Billy Connolly recalls of watching Celtic in the 1950s and 1960s, 'that was where I liked to go; not the Jungle. I was never scared to go into the Jungle, but it seemed like a club, and one to which I didn't belong, and although it would have been easy to go into the Jungle I always felt as though they could spot strangers; your father had to put your name down for the Jungle before you were born . . .'

If conditions on the terraces were basic, the Celtic players of the time found themselves far from being pampered and cosseted when they came to work. 'Facilities were a bit tacky,' Alec Boden, a centre-half in the 1940s and 1950s, says. 'The gymnasium was diabolical, terrible. There were medicine balls, skipping ropes and a couple of old rugs, and that was it. The cash takers at the turnstile stalls used the gym for cashing in their ticket money, so you would go in, and there would be tables all over the place, and it was dusty. If it was terribly wet or snowing, we'd get Alex Dowdells [the trainer] to open the doors in the upper stand, and that's where we would do our running and training; in the long corridor at the back of the stand, which, of course, had openings at intervals for stairs. Then we'd come down into this tiny gym.'

The primitive standards maintained in the Jungle and in the gym were matched by those elsewhere inside the ground. 'It wasn't very good,' Billy Connolly says of the spectating facilities that he discovered as a young supporter, when the conditions cramped his always individualistic dress style, 'and it was the same at every Scottish ground at the time. It was especially noticeable to me in my late teens and early twenties, when I would wear light-coloured clothes such as yellow pants, and that ash that they had on the terraces would stain my clothes, and the toilet was nothing more than a brick wall, and the pies were never hot, and the Bovril was like lava. I always struggled with that dichotomy: I thought, "Why don't you put the pies where you put the Bovril?"'

The conditions inside the stadium during the 1950s and early 1960s may have been basic but, as with all varieties of urban squalor, they did help to foster a certain closeness among those subjected to them. 'I always went to the Celtic End, when it was terracing, when I was a boy,' Tony Roper says of those times. 'There was a bus picked us up from the pub, the University Bar, a mixed pub, Celtic and Rangers, and apart from maybe matchdays when it was Celtic and Rangers playing each other, there was always good banter. Depending on who won that game, you might not go to the pub that night after it finished.

'It was the same crowd that went every week – there were about twelve of us and we all stood together, and there were always two guys that never, ever saw it. They were always pissed. If they weren't pissed before they got in, they were certainly pissed during the game, because you could take lager and bottles in with you. There was one guy – I won't name him – and he was pissed at every game. I don't think he ever saw a game the whole way through. He would just slink down the crush barrier and the reason we stood there was so that he could hang on to it. Eventually he would wind up sleeping against your leg. He would then argue about the game later on; after he had come to! "That was never offside!" and that sort of thing. That was a great thing, a fantastic thing, the camaraderie of it.

'They had a toilet, but very few people used it because you couldn't get into it. For 30,000 fans, a toilet that could accommodate fifty or sixty was no use. I never used it. I just pissed where I was. That's what most people did. Think of the logistics. You've been in a pub all day, you're drinking, you're drinking, you're drinking. You're going to the game. You didn't have reruns [on television or on a big screen], so if you missed a goal, you missed it. You weren't going to do that, so what you did was you took a bottle with you and pissed into the bottle, unless you were really flaked out and then you just pissed ... more than once, somebody just pissed against my leg. It was just part of it – this was why it was more of a man's thing to go to football, because there were no facilities there for women either.

'Then if you wanted a pie there was a wee stall with one person heating up pies for 20,000 people. When you went for a pie, you couldn't see the game. It was down a wee hill. The facilities were of their time, shall we say. There was no roof on the Celtic End, but that didn't matter because most of the guys that went to the game had bunnets on, and most of them had the bunnets they wore in the shipyards, and they were waterproof, because they had had engine oil spilled on them. You could see these guys standing there with their bunnets on and water just bouncing off the top. It was like the precursor of Gore-Tex but it worked a lot better, because nothing got through. At my age, you wouldn't wear a hat because your hair was all-important to you. You just got soaked and that was it. That was called Paradise because it was a long way from what it had been before – but it was a long way from Paradise.'

It seemed symbolic of the radically changing times at Celtic in the mid-1960s that with, finally, a bright and vibrant team on the park under the tutelage of Jock Stein, the Jungle should finally be renovated, in 1966, after decades of neglect. The ash and timber steps were replaced with concrete and a smart new roof, although one still low enough to amplify and channel outwards, on to the park, the noise created by the supporters underneath it. Only one year earlier, on Bertie Auld's return to Celtic in January 1965, the Jungle had been thick with rumour that the club was on the verge of bankruptcy and possibly the subject of a takeover. It was the one part of the ground that would remain packed even when the ground held its thinnest attendances, and, as well as being a source of inspiration to the team, it was a treasure trove of basic humour.

'Without question my funniest memory of Celtic was the testimonial for Jimmy Johnstone and Bobby Lennox,' Billy Connolly says, thinking back to the spring of 1976. 'Before Celtic played Manchester United, they had a game involving former Manchester United and Celtic players, an exhibition game, and Jock Stein asked me would I be the referee? I was sitting with Joe Beltrami, the lawyer, in the stand, and Jock Stein insisted I wore a Rangers scarf and hat and a blue tracksuit and rubber boots – wellies. When Jock Stein asked you to do something, you did as you were told. So I led the teams on to the park, and the booing from the Jungle as I walked towards them . . . because in those days you were facing the Jungle. Where I got the courage from I'll never know, but I had the ball under my arm, and the booing was deafening as I walked towards them, so I sent them off – I raised my arm to signal it – and the mayhem that broke out!' As one man, they sang out to Connolly exactly where he could stick his wellies. 'What a rammy it was!' he says. 'I will never forget it as long as I live! They can speak about the Kop but they will never live with that Jungle.'

The terraces gave rise to much rough and ready wit, but once Glasgow Rangers began to redevelop Ibrox Park in the late 1970s into a spanking new all-seated arena, questions began to be asked among the Celtic support about the basic nature of their own ground. When Desmond White, the Celtic chairman from 1971 to 1985, reacted to this poser by stating that the supporters of Celtic liked to stand, he came in for much flak, delivered almost reflexively from some supporters – a risk that figures of authority at Celtic always run when making any sort of public state-ment – but there was also more than a grain of truth in his argument. Yet while a number of fans did like to stand, it was the lack of improve-ment to their conditions that really grated, such as the poor view of the action from behind each goal – not only were the terraces at the two ends of the ground extremely shallow, but the terrace was also sepa-rated from the pitch by an extensive patch of grass behind the goals, supplemented by the running track, and this made viewing the action at the opposite end of the field of play well-nigh impossible to follow in any sort of detail.

This contrasted with the stand, the section to the south of the ground, off London Road, which, from 1904, had been the only part of Celtic Park to be seated and where matches were watched by White and his contem-poraries and predecessors on the Celtic board of directors, other well-heeled individuals and those willing to extend their cash to treat themselves to a better, more elevated view of the game. The Grant stand had been replaced in 1929 by a new south stand, designed by Duncan & Kerr, the Glasgow architects, and which featured 4,800 wooden seats, with a terraced enclosure to the front and new dressing rooms inside. 'It was a much more upright stand than those of today,' Brian Quinn recalls. He was first taken to Celtic Park as a boy, during that decade. 'In the old stand of the forties the seats were wooden, tip-up seats and not as wide as those of today. Wealthy people went to the stand; the people who went to the stand had a drink in Rogano's [the smart art-deco fish restaurant in Glasgow city centre] at lunchtime; the people who went to the terracing went to the pub on a Saturday evening; and in my part of Glasgow that would be the Govan Arms or the old Harmony Bar.'

That Duncan & Kerr-designed stand was in turn, when it became run-down and outmoded, replaced in the summer of 1971, at the very start of White's chairmanship of the club, with an ultra-modern edifice that surpassed, for style and comfort, anything that had previously been erected at a Scottish football ground. A streamlined, cantilevered construction, free of the posts and pillars that had previously blighted the view from the seats, it featured 8,700 plastic seats, in lurid, space-age orange, with a pressbox dangling in the air, suspended centrally over the heads of spectators. Roofing had by then been added above the west and east terracing, in 1957 and 1967 respectively, giving Celtic Park more cover than any ground in Britain, other than Wembley Stadium.

That, until the early 1990s, was just about that in terms of extensive change to the stadium. Other clubs, such as Glasgow Rangers, Manchester United and Aberdeen, embraced greater levels of seating for spectators – Pittodrie in 1978 became Britain's first all-seated football ground – but Celtic determinedly stuck to their guns, the touchstone of tradition maintaining their commitment to terracing. The only radical change to the ground occurred in the centenary year of 1988, and again it was the elite who benefited from it. Two million pounds was spent on upgrading the facilities inside the south stand, including the creation of a stylish new façade, executive suites, the Walfrid restaurant, the club's first on-site eating establishment, a players' lounge and a gymnasium. No wonder rumblings began to be heard from the unreconstructed terraces over the following few years.

It was a sign of desperate times when, in 1993, with the implications of the Taylor Report hanging over them, Celtic took the drastic step of revamping the Jungle, when, after almost ninety years of terracing in that part of the ground, it was colonised by seating; the new design being similar to some degree to the one that had originally been in place in 1892 when the Janefield Street section of the ground had been the only seated section at Celtic Park. It had been into the Jungle that Jimmy Johnstone had chosen to throw his boots at the conclusion of his joint-testimonial with Bobby Lennox in 1976; Paul McStay threw his shirt into the Jungle when seemingly on the verge of leaving the club in 1992; and Tommy Burns threw his boots in there on his final appearance for Celtic, in a 1989 friendly match with Ajax. Now, instead of being part of a swaying, baying crowd, denizens of the Jungle were serried into tip-up seats, and the change in atmosphere was instant.

After such a bitty, insubstantial attempt at modernisation it was, without exaggeration, quite amazing to witness, only twelve months later, the manner in which Fergus McCann set about establishing the greatest trans-formation in Celtic Park for more than a century. With the tenacious little Scots-Canadian in charge, there was no room or time for sentiment: the terraces were razed to the ground in the summer of 1994, together with the new, all-seated Jungle, and, with Celtic spending the 1994-95 season as tenants of Queen's Park at Hampden, work began in December 1994 on a new two-tier north stand. As in the 1890s, the new stadium for Celtic was built by the supporters, not, as in the Victorian era, through muscle, sweat and hard labour, but through a share issue that was fantastically oversubscribed, showing that McCann's plans had caught fire with the Celtic support. A steel framework was quickly erected in place of the Jungle, and by mid-1995, with £18 million already having been spent on stadium reconstruction, the 26,000-seater stand was ready to open on 5 August, for a friendly match with Newcastle United, in front of a crowd of 34,000; the maximum that could be held by the north and south stands combined.

The intrigue surrounding the new stadium created a demand that meant 29,500 season tickets were snapped up immediately for the 1995–96 season, and, in December 1995, work began on the new east stand, which, at a cost of £6 million, would bring the capacity up to 50,000 for the begin-ning of the 1996–97 season. All three stands would be sold out for that season, providing Celtic, over the course of that campaign, with its highest ever average crowds. This was a phenomenal transformation at a club operating within the confines of Scottish football – only the most compet-itive matches, in domestic competition or in Europe, had previously drawn such crowds to the ground. Now, supporters were committed months in advance, through their season tickets, to attendance at all fixtures, large and small.

McCann, correctly, receives praise for overseeing the reconstruction of Celtic Park and for having the vision to believe that tens of thou-sands of seats could be filled over a season for home matches; yet after those two new stands had been built, leaving only the west stand to be completed to bring Celtic Park up to a capacity of 60,000, Brian Quinn witnessed McCann hesitate over whether it would be wise to proceed with completion of the third new stand or whether to leave Celtic Park as a three-sided ground. He had even, Quinn recalls, at one point, early in his time as managing director at Celtic, pondered whether to leave Celtic Park two-sided.

'Fergus knew the size of the Celtic support and that there was a great untapped Celtic support,' Brian Quinn, a director appointed in the mid-1990s, says. 'Celtic Park was built in stages. There was a design for 60,000, but there wasn't a commitment to build a 60,000-seater stadium. The commitment was to build the north stand, which we did. The east stand and the west stand were separate investment projects, so when we built the north stand and that was in place, Fergus was actually a bit doubtful, especially about the west stand. The east stand was put in place first of all, and the idea was to rent out quite a lot of the stand underneath the seating to commercial activities, and that was slow, that wasn't happening, so Fergus was not persuaded that there was a case for building the west stand.

'So we sat down and did investment projects, cost-benefit analysis, and worked it out. I would say that the further west we went the more faith was involved; so when we got to considering whether to build the west stand, we said, "Look, the fans love the way the ground has been rebuilt up to this point, they think it's their stadium, they've put in quite a lot of the money; let's complete it." The cliché in American sport is, "If you build it they will come." That was true, but to fill it we had to win football matches, win trophies, had to raise the profile of Celtic on the football field, and then the 60,000 would come. It wasn't, "Here's a design for 60,000, let's do it." The plans were there, but they would only be put in place if the conditions were met; you had to satisfy yourself that the conditions were going to be met.'

Eventually, on 8 August 1998, four years after the reconstruction of Celtic Park had begun, the Lisbon Lions and Lady Jean Stein opened the Jock Stein stand at the west end of the ground prior to a friendly match with Liverpool, and the new Celtic Park was complete. 'I think everybody who is interested in football has to know about Celtic,' Lubo Moravick, who signed for Celtic later that year, says, 'but when I came and saw for the first time the stadium, I said, "I heard about Celtic, but I didn't imagine how big." I knew on seeing the stadium I couldn't play badly.'

The camaraderie that Tony Roper enjoyed through travelling by supporters' bus and returning to the same spot on the Celtic End terracing during the 1950s no longer exists for him and has been replaced by a modern-day match experience that seems radically different but in which he detects similar qualities. 'I've lost that sort of thing,' he says of standing with a set of friends in the same spot for game after game, 'because I sit in the executive club now. I drive and I park but I still sit at the same table with all my pals. We don't go there together but we meet up so we still have that same thing of being together with a group of guys. People who don't sit in the executive club probably think it's a bunch of fat cats, and we're all loaded and have got luxury beyond belief. It's not, it's just a bunch of ordinary guys; some have got their own business, some haven't. I've never met anybody posh in the executive club – they are people who have probably done what I've done and got a couple of quid; not vast, excessive sums of money. The fee is 2,300 quid. Some say it's too much. I don't pay that because I turned into a pensioner and I get mine for 1,650 pounds; forty short of the dreaded 1,690. All you get for that is a pie and a cup of tea at the interval. We actually fork out quite a lot of money just to support the team.

'The people in there are still Celtic fans, and I'm sure that's the same all round the ground in all the corporate sections that have been set up, which the club now has to do to pay the money because we don't get it any longer from Sky. All the money in football in Scotland comes from the fans. They pay it just for the love of the club. The players come and go; the club's the thing.'

The most recent piece of construction has been away from Celtic Park; the new training ground at Lennoxtown, East Dunbartonshire, which was opened in October 2007. Barrowfield, a set of training pitches a few hundred yards on the other side of London Road from Celtic Park, had been used since the late 1950s, and the players of the Lisbon Lions era and beyond would jog the few hundred yards west along the road to Barrowfield for their daily session. By the twenty-first century, and the era of sports science and advanced fitness, physiotherapy and medical methods and of monitoring of players' nutrition, it made sense to switch to a purpose-built facility; the major English clubs had long had their own training centres, usually situated in peaceful, countryside areas. Now players can train in the morning, have lunch and then return for training in the afternoon.

Martin O'Neill, as Celtic manager, had initially stated that, if Barrowfield had been good enough for Jock Stein, it was good enough for him but after two years as Celtic manager, he had begun to chafe against its restrictions, particularly a lack of undersoil heating that meant that in the depths of winter training sometimes could not take place there. O'Neill described what was being offered by Barrowfield as 'facilities that would be laughed at by most clubs in the SPL, never mind Europe'. More lightly, O'Neill would joke that when signing a new player from outside Scotland, he would wait until it was dark before taking them to see the training ground.

'We'd known for years that Barrowfield isn't what it should be,' Brian Quinn, the former chairman, says, 'but it's extremely difficult to get permission to build on land in the Glasgow area, and we had many discussions with Glasgow City Council. We looked at several potential venues, but none were suitable, and then we became aware that the site of the disused Lennoxtown Hospital was available and so we began to negotiate that, and I was very, very keen to carry that forward, because I had seen a lot of to-ing and fro-ing and upping and downing so I said we've got to carry this forward or we'll be discussing and negotiating for ever. It's got to happen. We've got to raise the money for it and Dermot [Desmond] absolutely agreed, so the purpose of the last share issue [in late 2005, which raised £15 million] was to raise the money for Lennoxtown. We went to the fans with a share issue that Dermot underwrote in part, raised the money and got it done.'

The new facilities are noticeably more compact than those of, say, Arsenal at London Colney and Manchester United at Carrington, consisting of a squat, glass-fronted building with pitches to the front and to the side, but, as Quinn explains, there is scope for development. 'We think it's absolutely right for our needs – we wanted ours to be a functional training ground; we didn't want anything that was lavish or in excess of the needs that we could see for ourselves. We did want a piece of ground that was capable of being developed so this is phase one; phase two we will expand the areas available for training and we will build accommodation for the academy, so the young players will live up there. We've got three full-sized grass pitches all to the same dimensions as Celtic Park; we've got the artificial pitch, the indoor facility, the goalkeepers' training ground and the gymnasium, everything we need. It's rather like building the new Celtic Park: we're doing it in phases.'

18

A SWITCH IN TIME

It is inconceivable that a club that is at the centre of the existence of so many might itself go out of existence, but that potential fate appeared to hover over Celtic during the first half of the 1990s. This was a club whose stadium had suddenly become a millstone around its neck; a club whose directors appeared consumed with a level of intense infighting that was seemingly matched in inverse proportion only by their lack of imagination and business nous; a club spiralling into ever greater levels of debt whilst seeing ever fewer numbers of supporters attending its matches.

The root causes of Celtic's troubles during the first half of the 1990s can be found in the latter half of the previous decade. Glasgow Rangers had, after the arrival of Graeme Souness as player-manager in April 1986, begun spending large sums of money in transfer fees and wages, to entice to Ibrox players from England, a number of whom were internationals. Rangers, in addition to good money, could offer to players such as Terry Butcher, the England captain, and Chris Woods, the England international goalkeeper, the prospect of European football, from which English clubs had been banned by UEFA after the 1985 Heysel Disaster. At that European Cup final between Juventus and Liverpool, thirty-nine people were killed when a wall collapsed, crushing the victims.

The new influx of strength from England revived a Rangers side that had stuttered through the 1980s until that point, and it blew apart the cosy cartel whereby Celtic and Rangers had paid wages well below the going rate at the top level in England, relying on the loyalty of local players to bolster their teams' efforts. The new buying power afforded to Souness, who would not have returned to Scotland from club football in Italy without the assurances of such funding, left Celtic in Rangers' slipstream. David Hay's side had been nine points clear of Rangers in mid-season, but after a New Year's Day defeat in the Old Firm derby the remainder of Celtic's season was dotted with defeats, while Rangers bore forward to finish six points clear in spring 1987.

The need to strengthen his defence had been a priority for Hay that season, but money was not forthcoming from the directors. 'If Davie's going to buy a couple of players, the money will have to come out of his own pocket,' Jack McGinn, the chairman, said. This would later be dismissed by him as a jokey remark, but it emphasised the gulf between the attitude at Rangers and that at Celtic. Bizarrely, after the end of the 1986–87 season, Hay was finally allowed to sign the type of defender he had craved during it, making Mick McCarthy, the Manchester City centre-half, the highest-paid player at Celtic, on a groundbreaking £1,000 per week. Even more bizarrely, it proved to be Hay's final important action as Celtic manager – one week later he was dismissed by the Celtic board.

Hay believes that the decision to replace him was made speedily by the Celtic directors after they had spoken to Billy McNeill at a function to celebrate the twentieth anniversary of the European Cup win. McNeill had, that May of 1987, been let go by Aston Villa and was free to take over at Celtic. He was given funding to bring in players such as Frank McAvennie, Joe Miller, Chris Morris, Andy Walker and Billy Stark, and his buccaneering team won the League and Cup double in the memorable 1987–88 centenary season, driven on by the irrepressible McNeill, delighted to be back at Celtic after a testing time in England. Enormous crowds at Celtic Park willed Celtic on to exciting victories that season, and by its conclusion they were ten points clear of Hearts at the top of the Premier Division. An explosive Scottish Cup final in the sun against Dundee United saw Celtic go behind to a goal from Kevin Gallacher before rousing themselves for a stunning finish to the match. A headed equaliser from McAvennie made it 1-1 and then, in the final minute, Miller's corner-kick veered towards Stark, inside the Dundee United penalty area, and when he knocked the ball goalward, it clipped off the shin of David Narey, the United centre-back, and into the path of McAvennie, who, from the edge of the six-yard box, speared the ball into the net.

That victory was not atypical of Celtic that season. On numerous occasions they rallied to score goals late in matches, driven on by the desire of McNeill, the ultimate supporter-manager, to meet the sentiment generated by the centenary of Celtic's foundation by winning silverware. The team had clicked from the start of the season, and their attacking formation allowed pacy full-backs Morris and Anton Rogan to supplement attacks – almost like prototype wing-backs – and Celtic to adopt a pressing game, with McStay peerless in midfield and McAvennie and Walker snapping up chances consistently. McNeill described his team's play in the first Old Firm match as possibly the best he had ever seen in such a fixture. Through visiting numerous supporters' functions that year, the players became aware of the importance of the anniversary.

It was a happy year, but the memories and emotions it generated would have to be stoked by Celtic supporters to warm themselves for a considerable number of years afterwards. McAvennie, McNeill's leading goalscorer, left for West Ham United in March 1989. The manager began to feel even more frustration with his board of directors than he had done first time round, in the early 1980s; frustration at a lack of proper investment in training facilities, youth development and signings to match those of Rangers.

Joe Miller, a winger, was switched to striker for the 1989 Scottish Cup final with Rangers following McAvennie's departure and saved the day, and the season, by scoring the only goal of the game, latching on to a Gary Stevens pass-back and steering the ball beyond Chris Woods, the goalkeeper. It was Celtic's only trophy of the 1988-89 season but that would look like rich pickings in comparison with the first half of the 1990s. When Maurice Johnston, an exciting potential replacement for McAvennie, pledged to sign for Celtic in summer 1989 and then slipped through the club's hands to Rangers, it was another serious blow.

The all-seater stadium ruling, following the Hillsborough Disaster, would also have a severe effect on Celtic during this period, with the pressure on to construct an almost entirely new set of spectating facilities at Celtic Park. It was a difficulty that would have taxed even the most able board of directors, but the incumbents at Celtic appeared both ill-prepared and ill-equipped to deal with it, not least because they were desperately short of cash. Rangers, in contrast, already had in place a 45,000-capacity, all-seater stadium – one that they had been filling since Souness' arrival.

The Ibrox Disaster of 1971 had made safety a priority with the Rangers directors and had made them progressive champions of all-seater accommodation, giving them a headstart on Celtic and most other British clubs.

The first step that the Celtic board took to cope with this situation turned out to contain the seeds of their eventual demise. Brian Dempsey, a property developer, was brought on to the Celtic board, pending full approval by the other directors, in May 1990. With his knowledge of the construction industry, Dempsey could, it seemed, be a handy adviser with regard to stadium reconstruction. His appointment had to be ratified at the annual general meeting in October of that year, but by then relations between Dempsey and two of the other directors, Michael Kelly, who had joined the board at the same time as Dempsey, and Christopher White, had deteriorated badly.

An impatience to get ahead with the business of building a new stadium on Dempsey's part was at the root of the dispute. He had insisted that Parkhead was not a viable site for the construction of the type of stadium demanded by the Taylor Report. Instead, he suggested strongly that the club should relocate to Robroyston in the north east of Glasgow, close to Bishopbriggs. Dempsey had barely taken his seat on the board before he had begun arguing vehemently that the club should agree immediately to his plan. His persistence convinced some directors to back his argument, but Christopher White and Michael Kelly were suspicious of his desire to hurry the board along and took the opposite view to their fellow directors, opposing Dempsey's plan to move. There was also unease in the boardroom that for Dempsey, the property developer, there might potentially be a conflict of interest in the proposed move to a new site. Michael Kelly and White's opposition was deadly to Dempsey – White and Kelly held the greatest proportion of shares in the club and, thus, the balance of power on the board. They opposed, successfully, the ratification of his appointment to the board, easing him out at the AGM in October 1990. Over those five months in 1990, between Dempsey joining the board and being ejected from it, a great deal of personal animosity had developed between him and his nemeses, leading to open, no-holds-barred arguments.

'Brian Dempsey rushed his fences; he should have gone in calmly, but Brian Dempsey was excitable,' is how James Farrell, another member of the board at the time, put it. This brief episode made Dempsey a sworn enemy of the board. A bombastic son of a Lanarkshire member of parliament, with a fondness for turning up at Celtic Park in green suits, Dempsey would now do all he could to rally support behind those who were becoming increasingly impatient with a board that appeared to be floundering not only with respect to creating a new stadium but also, more immediately and more relevantly for most supporters, struggling to match Rangers. Two days after the board meeting that resulted in Dempsey's exit, Celtic capitulated to Rangers in the League Cup final, and at the end of the 1990–91 season, Rangers landed their third successive League title. Demonstrations against the board had started to take place that season. Dempsey would soon be rallying disaffected supporters, through addressing protest organisations such as Save Our Celts, to make a stand against the board. Other groups, such as Celts For Change, provided a focal point to demand the directors' resignations.

With the addition of Michael Kelly to the board, the Celtic directors had hoped to benefit from his expertise in public relations: a former Lord Provost of Glasgow, Michael Kelly Associates, his PR company, had engineered the 'Glasgow's Miles Better' campaign of the 1980s, with Mr Happy as its symbol. The campaign was designed to get across the message that the city had engineered a transformation away from its mean, dark, violent industrial past to a new, lively, re-energised present. It had been a major success, persuading not only outsiders but Glaswegians themselves of its validity. Yet as one of the most prominent members of the Celtic board in the early 1990s, Michael Kelly would signally fail to push the right buttons with the supporters.

The board's next move was another one that looked positive but which would, once again, backfire badly. They appointed Terry Cassidy as the club's first chief executive in January 1991. His first significant action was to instruct the Bank of Scotland not to increase the club's overdraft. Cassidy had been informed on joining that Celtic did not have a business plan and therefore no strategy to repay the overdraft, so he informed the bank of this and suggested the overdraft should be curtailed. This fairly sensible suggestion immediately drove a wedge between him and the board. Cassidy also expressed publicly his displeasure at not having been asked to become a director and, close to the conclusion of the 1990–91 season, a memo from him outlining the best means to dismiss Billy McNeill as Celtic manager was leaked harmfully to the press just as McNeill was trying desperately to salvage a UEFA Cup place from a second successive trophyless season.

'If the board felt I wasn't doing it, they could have sat down and talked reasonably about it,' McNeill says. 'I think there is a way you can treat people who have served you well and I think I served Celtic very well. You can treat people properly; you don't treat them like a bit of dirt that's attached to your shoe. It took me a long time to lose my bitterness towards that board of directors.'

When McNeill was replaced in the summer of 1991 by Liam Brady, tensions between Cassidy and the new manager sprang up almost immediately. Given an assurance on his appointment as manager that he would have the chance to speak to all players who were out of contract, in particular Paul Elliott, the centre-back, Brady returned to London only to discover that a source within Celtic had leaked to the press that Elliott would definitely be leaving the club. Furious, Brady felt he had been undermined even before a ball had been kicked with him as the new manager.

With the board under pressure, Tom Grant and James Farrell, two of the directors, appeared to be prepared to back a potential takeover by Dempsey in early 1992, but Grant backtracked to create a ten-year agreement with Kevin Kelly, who took over the chairmanship from Jack McGinn in 1991, Michael Kelly, Christopher White and David Smith, a financial analyst and a new addition to the board. Under this agreement, if one of the directors who had signed up to it opted to sell his shares, he had to give first refusal to the others involved in the pact, solidifying those directors' hold on the club – they owned, in total, approximately 60 per cent of the shares. This self-defence mechanism was put in place even as the directors came under ever-increasing pressure from supporters who were frustrated by what they saw as indecision and lack of zest; by early 1992, Rangers were en route to a fourth successive championship title, and Celtic had gone without a trophy of any sort for three years.

The Celtic board had released money to Brady to allow him to compete with Rangers' multi-million-pound signings. Tony Cascarino, in the summer of 1991, subsequently became Celtic's record signing, for a fee of £1.1 million from Aston Villa, plus wages of £3,000 per week. But the striker proved a disastrous addition to the Celtic squad and, despite earning sums that greatly outweighed his goalscoring productivity, was unhappy in Glasgow and shipped out to Chelsea in February 1992 having scored just four times in thirty matches. Gary Gillespie, a Scottish international centre-back but now thirty-one years old, was signed from Liverpool for a fee close to £1 million and was also on the type of hefty wages to which he had become used in England's top-flight, but injury limited him to only two appearances in the 1991–92 season. Stuart Slater, a twenty-three-year-old midfield player, arrived from West Ham United in the summer of 1992 for a record fee of £1.7 million but flopped at Celtic; Brady later admitted that the move had probably torpedoed the player's career. With pieces of business such as this and crowds at Celtic Park plummeting, sometimes as low as 12,000–15,000, Celtic's debt was rising almost uncontrollably.

Farrell, a lawyer and a director of Celtic since 1964, and the longest-serving member of the board, could sometimes be found attending meetings of supporters dedicated to affecting regime change at Celtic Park, a most curious position for a serving director, and an indication of the severity of those times. 'I felt that something had to happen,' Farrell said. 'It wasn't going very well. I knew my fellow board members were not the right people to be leading Celtic and I said so in board meetings.' It helped Farrell, in maintaining such an independent position, that he did not have a major shareholding in Celtic, unlike Michael Kelly and Christopher White.

The board's biggest attempt to stem the flow of criticism of them came in April 1992, when Cassidy presented a blueprint for a new stadium and entertainment complex at Cambuslang in south-east Glasgow; Kevin Kelly smilingly posed for snappers with a picture of the proposed ground, a 32,000-seater stadium which would also encompass a 200-bedroom hotel, an eight-screen cinema complex and restaurants. Phase one of this bold project would, the directors announced, be complete by late 1994, but two years later work on it had yet to begin. Smith and Kevin Kelly, in late February 1994, said that £20 million of underwriting had been obtained from a backer to finance the new stadium, but when it became clear that they were nowhere near signing off on a concrete agreement, the board were living on borrowed time.

'David Smith, Chris White, who was not the same man as his father, and Michael Kelly were not the right people to be leading Celtic,' James Farrell suggested. 'Tom Grant and Kevin Kelly felt very insecure; Kevin Kelly had only a few shares in the club. At this time, you were talking about divisions between Michael Kelly, David Smith and Chris White and the rest. We had to go to the bank and have several meetings, and from what I can recall Michael Kelly said, "You can't do this" [that they could close Celtic] and the bank was saying, "Oh yes, we can."'

The board's unpopularity with the supporters had been emphasised during the 1994 New Year's Day match when, with Celtic 3-0 down to

Rangers at half-time, Mars Bars, scarves, coins and pie foils had been launched in the direction of the directors' box. Demonstrations against the board outside the ground on matchdays now became ever more vocal and populous. Security men had to guide them through the throng and into the relative safety of the stadium.

Fergus McCann was a Scot who had emigrated to Canada as a young man, an accountant who had made his fortune in North America by marketing custom-built golfing trips to Europe. He had long been a thorn in the board's side and, rather cheekily, in the summer of 1993, had asked for permission to take measurements of the stadium in preparation for the day when he would be supervising, as club owner, its reconstruction. His somewhat abrasive, confrontational style did not endear him to Michael Kelly and friends.

The arrival of Lou Macari as manager in October 1993, a move described by McCann as 'a publicity stunt', as the successor to Brady, saw Macari use his knowledge of English football's lower divisions to bring a number of workmanlike professionals to Celtic for modest fees; a reflection of the club's plight. Willie Falconer, a midfield player signed from Sheffield United in the second week of February 1994 and once of Watford, Middlesbrough and Aberdeen, was no exception to this rule. 'I don't expect Willie to set the world on fire,' Macari said of his new arrival. The circumstances surrounding Falconer's signing, though, did make him special and turned Celtic's world upside down. When Sheffield United demanded the first instalment of the £350,000 transfer fee that they had been promised for Falconer, the Bank of Scotland refused to release the money. It was clear that time was running out for that board as custodians of Celtic.

The board's farrago of folly and unfulfilled promises finally came to a head on 3 March 1994, when the Bank of Scotland told the board that the level of debt had risen so high that the bank was now ready to call in the receivers. This would have meant the bank taking over all of Celtic's assets. With White and Michael Kelly now finding the club on the brink of bankruptcy, they finally decided to sell their shares, not to McCann but to Gerald Weisfeld, a Glasgow entrepreneur. Grant and Kevin Kelly, though, were not prepared to sell to Weisfeld, and under the terms of the 1992 directors' pact, stymied that particular deal. They preferred the proposal put forward by Fergus McCann's Investor Group; McCann would not only invest millions of pounds of his own money in the club but also had a strong business plan that he wished to put in place, and was intending to offer the supporters the chance to invest in Celtic through a public issue of shares. Grant, Kevin Kelly, Jack McGinn and Farrell informed the bank that they favoured McCann and as they formed a majority of the directors, the bank had to accede to their wishes. McCann, on 4 March 1994, assumed control of Celtic Football Club.

Farrell, who had known McCann as a boy in central Scotland, was aware of just how determined he would be in transforming Celtic. 'As a boy he was a very cheeky upstart,' Farrell said, 'a cheeky, cheeky boy. I didn't like him. His father was a headmaster in Stirling and his father used to come to our house in Falkirk to get guidance from my father. So I always knew he [Fergus McCann] was a very strong-willed character, very much so. He is a most unusual man. He was full of ability but he was also full of habits I would not agree with; just in his way of dealing with people.'

When Fergus McCann stood on the steps of Celtic Park on 4 March 1994, the decades of control by the Kelly and White families was at an end. The two families had passed the chairmanship of Celtic between them, almost baton-like, down the decades. James Kelly, the centre-half in the first Celtic team, had been chairman from 1909 to 1914, succeeded by Tom White, who, on his death in 1947, was succeeded by Robert Kelly, in turn replaced by Desmond White, until 1985. After a brief interim period – during which Tom Devlin and Jack McGinn had the chairmanship, Kevin Kelly took the reins in 1991 and when McCann took control of the club in 1994, his cousin Michael was a board member, as was Christopher White, son of Desmond.

'We have new people,' McCann said, 'a new plan, a new vision and the strength to go forward. We have every intention of reaching the objective that you want, which is Celtic at the very top.' Dempsey, who had consistently agitated against the board in the preceding years, volubly stated, 'The rebels have won!' It was, strangely enough, to be Dempsey's last stand. He would play no part in the new regime at Celtic. As Dempsey faded into the background, all eyes would be on McCann, who had promised to remain at Celtic for a five-year period. It would be a time unlike any other that the club had experienced.

19

McCANN THE MAN

It was clear that there was something decidedly different about Fergus McCann from the moment he first flew into Glasgow to try to do a deal with Celtic. With a bunnet, glasses, a slight physique and an unprepossessing gait, he was a less than imposing figure but as a businessman he was all muscle. His stewardship of Celtic, after pipping Gerald Weisfeld to win ownership of the club, was crammed with interesting moments as McCann attempted to apply hard business sense to the often fanciful, whimsical world of football, in which money could be thrown about in cavalier fashion, something that was never his style. It is greatly to McCann's credit that he was consistent in his desire to run the club in a manner that would not see him squander the money invested by supporters through Celtic's successful share issue of 1995, but one of the ironies of that period is that a number of those very supporters voiced severe discontent at those methods. Almost a decade after his departure from the club and with him back in North America after fulfilling his promise to be at the helm of Celtic for five years flat, McCann is relaxed and conversational as he discusses his involvement with a club with which he has had a near-lifelong association.

'I saw my first game at Celtic Park as a teenager – I believe the opposition was East Fife – along with my father and since that time I have been a keen supporter of the club. In 1962 I attended every game – home and away – and in September 1963 even managed to get to Basle when I was earning only £4.50 a week. When I emigrated to Canada in 1963, I still kept up to date with results from Scotland; I would get the *Montreal Star* Saturday final edition with the British football results, for example. This was in the 1960s, when communications were not what they are today. At the time of Lisbon in 1967, I was at a seminar in the Laurentians, north of Montreal, and working for the Marconi Company. I had a Grundig short wave radio and was sitting at the back of the room listening to the BBC broadcast of the game from Lisbon. Nobody knew why it was so important and what I was talking about.

'The first time I had a connection with the club was in 1972 when I put on, in Toronto, a closed-circuit transmission of a repeat of that European final against Inter Milan, this time in the European Cup semi-final, from Celtic Park. The club was very helpful and supportive; Desmond White charged me a very low fee to show this match in Toronto. It was a very expensive and loss-making operation. The BBC had let me down regarding use of facilities, and I had to set up my own broadcasting unit; at the same time the game went on for 152 minutes of satellite use at $10,000 per hour. [That match not only went to extra time but also saw Celtic's first involvement in the extended drama of a penalty shoot-out.] Although 7,000 fans – mostly Scottish – appeared to watch the game in Maple Leaf Gardens, the turnout of Italian fans – who were expecting a defeat – was low so revenues were not as high as I'd counted on.

'Although I lost my shirt doing this, I certainly learned a lot in a short time, and, as I say, Celtic was very supportive. At the same time, unfortunately, STV took advantage of the situation and used my equipment in Scotland to broadcast the game live without my consent. They only had permission to use the video for late-night highlights. Instead, they got a huge audience and made a lot of money from commercial revenue and paid me nothing. They stole the show, literally. However, it was a good example of learning at the "school of hard knocks", which is probably the best place to get a business education. You do not forget the lessons.

'In the late 1980s Celtic went into decline after they had reached the centennial year in 1988, when they won the League Championship. The next several years brought hard times for the club. I could see that Celtic was very much out of touch with modern sports marketing and I made contacts with them around 1990. By that time, I had substantial resources, having sold a successful business a few years earlier, and I met with

Jack McGinn and later some other directors, with proposals to try to improve things at Celtic Park.

'At that time I had no interest whatsoever in taking control of the club but I learned very quickly that the club was very short of marketing abilities and capital. Management abilities also appeared to be lacking. I asked Jack McGinn what the club needed, and he said "Money!" At that time, Celtic shareholders had only invested a total of £15,000 in 102 years; this was the entire capital of the club. The stadium was completely out of date and needed vast improving, if not destruction and rebuilding.

'My proposal to the club at that time was to build 15,000 seats on the north side and convert the stadium into 24,000 seats and 48,000 standing, which would have made it much more effective as a means of producing revenue to support the high costs of a major club. I offered loan capital to do this at half the bank rate in return for a small commission on increased ticket revenue, mainly from season tickets. I had no plans or interest in ownership or control or even moving to Scotland. At that time the club had only 7,000 season ticket holders, and the view of the board was that a larger number would cause problems and demands by supporters for benefits such as away tickets and so forth.

'My visits to Celtic over the next two years were completely unproductive, and it became clear that a complete refinancing, takeover and new management of the club was essential. In 1992 I went to Scotland and met four investors who said they would support a plan I would put into action. These men were Brian Dempsey, John Keane, Gerald Weisfeld, and Tony Gallagher. They would put up £1 million each and I would provide £7.2 million, in capital of a new company, Celtic's Future plc. This company would also offer shares to the supporters and then ask the club to make a rights issue to take in this new funding for new shares. This would ensure new management at the club, with my group in control, and sufficient funds to deal with the challenges facing Celtic.

'The next two years featured opposition by the Celtic board, much publicity, boycotts by supporters, share proxy fights, and shareholders' meetings – along with publicity for the plan for Celtic's future. Meantime the club's financial condition was deteriorating. The proposal to move to Cambuslang cost it even more money with little prospect of success. Eventually the club faced bankruptcy in March 1994, at which time I was able to take over the loan from the bank, remove the opposing directors and secure support for new capital and change in shareholder ownership.

I did not want the club to go bankrupt, although that would have been a less costly option, with the former shareholders receiving no money and the overall cost of refinancing being reduced.

'The initial capital I paid in to Celtic was in the form of a loan which paid off the bank. This was replaced by new share capital in respect of £1 million invested each by John Keane and Albert Friedberg and £500,000 each from Michael McDonald (stepson of Gerald Weisfeld) and Willie Haughey. The fourth million, which at one stage was perhaps going to come from Brian Dempsey, I replaced with a further sum so that my total amount invested came to just over £9.2 million, about two-thirds of all I had.

'At that time, the next part of the financing required a heavy investment by the supporters, and this was eventually accomplished in January 1995. Dermot Desmond invested £4 million, and the share issue to supporters, which had a target of a minimum of £5.4 million, actually raised £10 million. This was the most successful share issue by a football club, indeed the only one by which substantial funds were obtained by investment from the fans at large.

'As part of the overall plan, continued bank financing was an important element. The Bank of Scotland, having been completely taken off the hook for £5.25 million – unrecoverable in 1994 – was given the opportunity to be the banking partner. Instead they offered only a £2.5 million loan, *fully secured*, which was not much more than an insult. The club had no difficulty going to another bank; in this case it was the Co-op bank, a comparatively small bank in Manchester, which provided a £10 million line of credit, unsecured, at a very reasonable rate of interest.

'I stated that I would hold a 51 per cent ownership position in the club for five years and leave after that time, but there was much to be done in the meantime. I had to put in a new management team to run the operations of the club and expand them greatly in areas of ticket revenues, sponsorship, commercial operations, merchandising and so on. Secondly, the playing side had to be strengthened and improved. Thirdly, and equally importantly, Celtic Park had to be rebuilt as a modern stadium to provide the key revenues to support a large club. I decided on an objective of a 60,000-seat covered stadium, which was well in excess of the club's apparent needs in 1994, when attendance averaged 28,000. But I felt strongly that, with the proper management and running of the club and good marketing, we would have had a team, and a venue, to which the support would respond in big numbers.

'Having my investor partners at the outset – and the support of 10,000 shareholding fans – meant we were able to attract some top-quality individuals as board directors, such as Brian Quinn, Sir Pat Sheehy and Dermot Desmond. I think some fans underestimated their value to the club in providing benefits not available to our competitors. I was also fortunate in working with an excellent team of executives and staff which together set the quality of the operations of the club – not just football – ahead of other major British football clubs.

'A year at Hampden Park – 1994–95 – was a very difficult year, spent trying to make the best of the relocation while the project to rebuild Celtic Park began. The cost was high, Queen's Park was most uncooperative, the stadium was inadequate, and there were many difficulties. However, the year passed, and we returned to Celtic Park in August 1995 with a new north stand providing 27,000 excellent seats, the first phase of the new stadium. Meantime 18,000 seats had been sold as season tickets at Hampden with the right to return to Celtic Park with first refusal and choice of seats in the new stadium. This programme continued while the east and west stands were completed in the next two seasons, and finally the club had the support of 53,000 season ticket holders.

'Meantime, on the field, things were improving, and a new manager, Tommy Burns, was in charge for the first three years, followed by Wim Jansen for one year. New players were brought in, some very expensive in relation to Celtic's income at that time, but many of them delivered improved performance on the field. There were a few setbacks, notably the loss of important Cup ties to Raith Rovers and Falkirk, but eventually Celtic recaptured the League Championship in 1997–98. By that time the new stadium was complete, the club showed a record profit of £7.5 million, and a good organisation was in place to expand the operations and financial base of Celtic plc as it went forward.

'The 1998–99 season turned out to be a difficult year on the field, principally from the effect of the World Cup in France in the summer of 1998. Celtic had ten players at the event, more than any club in the world, other than Barcelona. When it was over, with our players having been used – and at pre-event matches in the US, as well as the loss of 'downtime' that the close season can provide – it also resulted in Celtic having to start the season two players short. Absent were Marc Reiper – who never returned – and Morten Wieghorst, who suffered cruciate damage in a pre-season testimonial. And the others had had a tiring summer.

'Memories: a rainy Friday evening in January 1995, looking out my office window at the crowd standing in the car park, in a queue to buy shares in Celtic – many with borrowed money. Several newspapers had claimed the share issue would not be successful. But by the next day, when the offer closed, £10 million had been raised from 10,000 supporters. I remember feeling a very heavy burden of responsibility. I could not let these people down.

'Of a visit to Queens Park's solicitor, to sign an agreement to rent Hampden Park for 1994–95, who said, "It's been made quite clear to me by certain parties that this clause is a deal-breaker." [The clause in the agreement that forbade Celtic from flying any 'foreign' – i.e. Irish – flag at matches to be played at Hampden.]

'Of Tommy Burns asking me in 1995, "Would you pay £3.5 million for a defender [Alan Stubbs]?"

'Of Tommy Burns saying to me in 1996, "It would be great to get both [Jorge] Cadete and [Paolo] Di Canio, but if you could only get one, I would prefer Di Canio." (We got both.)

'Of Jock Brown telling me in 1997, "[Henrik] Larsson has a transfer clause in his contract, but Feyenoord refuse to let him go. It will go to an [Dutch] Association hearing, but I think I can still get him." (Larsson was bought for £650,000.)

'Of the SFA blocking efforts by Celtic to get more than the basic £2 million (new grandstand) grant from the Football Trust. While Sunderland got £5 million, for example. Instead, £10 million went to the completely unnecessary and inferior Hampden project; the total of £64 million of taxpayers' funds could have instead revitalised Scottish football with needed training centres. I regret not trying to join with David Murray in making the SFA "an offer they couldn't refuse" [not to rebuild Hampden Park and for the Scottish Cup final use Celtic Park and Ibrox at no charge in alternate years, Hampden Park for a football academy and move the national side around the country, with smaller games at the smaller grounds and the big games at Celtic Park and Ibrox].'

'The rebuilt Celtic Park project turned out even better than we had hoped. Although it was a big financial risk, I felt such a stadium was an essential asset to have for the Club in order to benefit from its huge support, and pay the bills. But it turned out to be more than that. It is a symbol; it makes a statement of where Celtic has come to, over a century after its humble beginnings. It is a source of pride to the support as it dominates the skyline of the East End of Glasgow. To me, I like to think that when any team visits a full Celtic Park they will see it as a fortress, a place where they will feel they are taking on a daunting task.

'Overall, I felt my time at Celtic was rewarding in different ways. Yes, it turned out to be personally profitable – more so than I expected – although I was a hostage to a five-year departure date when a low share price could have meant a huge loss.

'It was also a great privilege – and a heavy responsibility - to run this great institution that is Celtic FC. I made some mistakes and no doubt rubbed a few people up the wrong way. But much had to be done in a short time in an environment that was often not ready for change – or to be changed. I learned a lot and had to make some difficult decisions. In the end, however, I feel that I helped Celtic, and as a supporter I get a lot of personal satisfaction from that.'

20

A NEW LEASE OF LIFE

There had been only six team managers in Celtic's history by the time the 1990s got underway but by the conclusion of that decade a further six individuals would have been at the helm. This doubling of the managerial roll in such a short space of time is one indication of how much Celtic changed during that decade, although the rapid turnover was not an altogether unhealthy matter. It produced, for the first time since the 1970s and the era of Kenny Dalglish and Danny McGrain, a Celtic side containing a duo of world-class performers: Henrik Larsson and Lubomir Moravcik, who were first brought together in late 1998. Wim Jansen, a Dutchman, appointed head coach in 1997, brought Larsson to Celtic from Feyenoord, the Swede having become discontented with his progress at the Rotterdam side. Doctor Jozef Venglos, the Slovakian who became Jansen's successor in the summer of 1998, soon brought to Glasgow Moravcik, a fellow Slovakian who, in common with Larsson, was unhappy with his lot at another continental club, MSV Duisburg in the Bundesliga. Both players would prove to be magnificent successes at Celtic Park.

It could be suggested at that time, and not at all facetiously, that the policy of changing manager – or head coach – every summer, as Celtic did every year from 1997 to 2000, was one that could in itself bring enormous benefits to the club. Each new and experienced continental coach could be relied upon to have, on their travels, come to know of a Larsson or a Moravcik; a player who could plump up their own individual fortunes and those of Celtic by coming to Glasgow. On Venglos' departure, in 1999, the club appointed John Barnes, in contrast, a deeply inexperienced individual who had never held such a position before, with Kenny Dalglish as Director of Football. Even during their relatively unsuccessful period at Celtic, they brought to the club Stilian Petrov, a driving midfield player from CSKA Sofia, and the Bulgarian, who combined muscularity and physicality with the deftest of touches, proved to be another useful asset to the team.

This rapid succession of helmsmen owed much to Fergus McCann, the man who had saved Celtic from the prospect of the scrapheap in early 1994 and who was the club's majority shareholder for the next five years. A sharp and direct businessman, McCann found repulsive the British managerial merry-go-round, whereby managers could fail in a job, receive hefty sums of compensation to buy up their contract and then swiftly find themselves another well-paying post. He had appointed Tommy Burns as manager in 1994, but when Burns' time drew to an end in 1997, after three seasons in which Celtic had won only one trophy, McCann was insistent that the next man to take charge of the team would be titled 'head coach' and not manager and that he would report to a director of football.

This system, hugely familiar in continental European football but alien to the game in Britain, would free the team selector to focus on football and coaching while the wages and transfers would be dealt with by the director of football. Early on in the Burns era, the transfer of Phil O'Donnell, a midfield player from Motherwell, had created friction between the manager and the club's new owner. Burns had dealt directly with Motherwell, agreeing a then record fee for Celtic of £1.75 million; when McCann got in touch with John Chapman, the Motherwell chairman, it was to discover that the terms of the transfer had been agreed without him and that he was expected to provide the rubber-stamp. McCann had either to go along with the deal or risk a confrontation with his new manager and chose the former course.

McCann's deep dislike of the traditional system of British team management, whereby the manager would have a say in how the money was spent, on transfers, wages and such like, and the type of wastage that he believed it produced, stemmed to a large degree from his desire, and from a deep sense of responsibility, to see the supporters' money spent wisely, prudently and well.

'Fergus is one of the few men who have left a football club having made a profit,' Tony Roper says of McCann, who stuck solidly to the five-year term he had set himself to remain in control of Celtic, 'so hats off to him for that. One thing he did was make the supporters shareholders, which we now know means nothing, but everybody thought they were going to have a say in what Celtic were about. You're not. It didn't matter how you voted – he still had the controlling rights. Shares went up, up, up, up. My shares at one point were worth a lot of money [shares in Celtic were sold at 62p each in 1995 and soared in value in subsequent years]. Now they're worth about twenty-four pence or something like that. The older board could have done that, but they didn't have that business acumen that Fergus did, whatever you say about him. He had that in spades and he also had a ruthlessness.'

When McCann did leave Glasgow in the spring of 1999, it was with a massive profit on his initial investment in the club, thanks to another successful share issue, this time to sell the 51 per cent of the share-holding that he had owned. He had had no guarantee when he arrived in 1994 that the share price would be high when he left, but football shares across the spectrum turned out to be buoyant in the late 1990s, and Celtic was in a healthy condition – by the 2000s, as Roper points out colour-fully, football shares would drop dramatically [in mid-2008 Celtic shares were trading at around 50p each]. McCann took the risk and the resultant spoils. When, in the early 1990s, he had seen the weakness in the Celtic board, he would have been as happy to remain in Canada – albeit as a more moderate investor in Celtic – if someone of a similar ilk to himself had come along to turn the club around.

Brian Quinn, who joined the board of directors shortly after the 1995 share issue, says, 'There had been a lot of jockeying to see who would win control. People were scrabbling to get control of the club, and Fergus had to be very tough to see them off. He loved the club – he didn't love it the way I love it, but so what? If you take the mixture between emotional commitment and financial success, the mix was different in his case. He wanted financial success because he was an investor. He had paid off the debt through his own resources and put money into the club – it was very important to him to recover those funds and make a bit of money.'

A manager had been *in situ* when McCann had taken charge at Celtic: Lou Macari had arrived at Celtic Park in late October 1993, shortly after Liam Brady had resigned, with Celtic sitting seventh in the Premier Division.

'The club was just too big for a guy who wasn't experienced in football management,' Brady says, 'and going into a situation that was a mine-field really, with what was happening off the field at Celtic Park.' The Irishman had been thirty-five when appointed Celtic manager in the summer of 1991; it was his first managerial post in football, and, by the time of his departure, Celtic, a club in turmoil during the early 1990s, had not won a national trophy for more than four years. Macari, Brady's replacement, had pushed the club into fourth position by the end of the 1993–94 season, but that summer he was dismissed by McCann, who informed him of the decision by telephone after Macari had made a call from the airport as he was about to fly out to the USA to combine a family holiday with watching matches at the 1994 World Cup, held in that country.

Within weeks of taking control of Celtic in March 1994, McCann had written a letter warning Macari, who had joined Celtic from Stoke City, that it was incumbent on the manager to move home to the Glasgow area rather than remain in Stoke-on-Trent. When Macari, who had also railed privately against strict new working practices instilled by McCann, failed to follow that instruction, he found himself dismissed as manager – without the type of compensation managers like to receive in such circumstances. Macari launched an action against Celtic for breach of contract, claiming £400,000 in damages from the club. Three years later, Lady Cosgrove, the presiding judge, heard eight weeks of evidence in the case at the Court of Session in Edinburgh and rejected Macari's claim. It was not the first or last case that McCann would win in relation to his time at Celtic.

'The residence term was important,' Lady Cosgrove summed up, 'and Mr Macari's breach of the clause was no technicality but was contributing to an unsatisfactory situation where he was absent from Celtic Park for much of the week.' Macari, she said, had been guilty 'of a wilful and continuing act of disobedience of a legitimate and reason-able order of the employer'. On that basis alone, McCann had been entitled to dismiss him as manager, although the Celtic owner did not escape her censure. He was, she said, 'a rather devious individual' and 'an uncompromising and somewhat arrogant employer who expected unquestioning compliance'.

Early on in Tommy Burns' time as manager it became clear that he and McCann were at odds. Burns, in his office at Celtic Park, would fulmi-nate frustratedly about what he saw as McCann's lack of passion for foot-ball. McCann, upstairs, was working hard to deal with the chaos left behind by the previous board and was determined to balance the demands of creating a fine new team on the field of play and the expensive construction of a 60,000-seater stadium.

A Celtic victory over Airdrieonians in the 1995 Scottish Cup final, with a Pierre van Hooijdonk header in the ninth minute the only goal of the game, provided Burns with a trophy at the end of his first season and ended a six-year barren period for Celtic. It was a gritty, undistinguished game, and that afternoon at Hampden belonged to the grafters in the Celtic side, such as Rudi Vata, the Albanian centre-half, Peter Grant, the hard-working, hard-tackling, midfield player, and Willie Falconer, a willing forward. 'The game was ninety minutes long, but for me the game lasted as long as my five years as captain and our six years without a trophy,' was Paul McStay's Cup final experience that afternoon.

The win over Airdrie also did much to make up for the defeat to Raith Rovers in the League Cup final six months earlier. The Kirkcaldy side were fourth in the First Division at the time of that final and when Charlie Nicholas, brought back to Celtic in 1990 by Billy McNeill and now thirty-three years old, put Celtic 2-1 ahead with six minutes remaining, Burns looked set to clinch the first trophy available to him as Celtic manager. Three minutes later, Gordon Marshall, the Celtic goalkeeper, failed to hold on to a shot from Jason Dair and Gordon Dalziel worked the ball over the Celtic line – using his nose. The subsequent penalty shootout saw the first five players from each team score all of their penalties, sending that section of the match into sudden-death. Jason Rowbotham, the Raith left-back, scored with the first kick, but Paul McStay saw his penalty saved by Scott Thomson, their goalkeeper.

A more substantial Celtic side, now featuring Andreas Thom, the German striker, Jackie McNamara, a promising young full-back signed from Dunfermline Athletic, and John Hughes, a rumbustious and experienced centre-back, pushed Rangers all the way for the 1995–96 League title, losing only once but drawing eleven times, cripplingly, and finishing four points behind the Ibrox side. Significantly, Celtic had failed to defeat all season a powerful Rangers team constructed by Walter Smith to play punishingly and powerfully on the counter-attack. The trend continued in the 1996–97 season, Celtic losing all four League fixtures to Rangers, and although Celtic did finally defeat Rangers when the two clubs met in a Scottish Cup quarter-final at Celtic Park, an exit to Falkirk, a First Division side, followed in a semi-final replay in April 1997. The three-year contract Burns had signed in 1994 would not be extended. For years afterwards, Burns, a passionate and emotional man, would feel anger at behind-the-scenes manoeuvrings that he felt had had an undermining effect on him and that had more than once left him on the point of resignation. McCann, meanwhile, had decided that Burns was not the type of manager he required at Celtic. 'I probably did about fifteen or twenty years as a manager in those three years,' Burns would later say.

A very different individual would replace Burns: Wim Jansen, appointed as head coach in the summer of 1997, cut an eccentric figure, with a mop of curls on his head that looked strange on a 50-year-old man. A World Cup finalist as a midfield player with Holland in 1974 and 1978 and a pal of Johan Cruyff, Jansen had worked as manager of Feyenoord in the early 1990s but in 1997 he was coming off a three-year stint as coach to Sanfrecce Hiroshima and was next to unknown among the Scottish public. McCann had expressly made it a matter of internal policy that the new man in charge of the playing side at Celtic must be non-British; an individual designed to operate within a system whereby they would coach the first team and pick the side for matches but leave all financial dealings to a director of football. The person selected for this task was Jock Brown, a Lanarkshire lawyer who specialised in sports law and negotiation at a law practice in Glasgow, but best known as a football commentator for the BBC.

'Wim was a very knowledgeable person about world football,' John Clark, appointed Celtic's kit man in summer 1997, says. 'If you asked him about a player, he'd know that player. To this day he is still the same. He was a right down-to-earth football guy; just concentrated on the first team at Celtic Park. His first priority was to strengthen that and get it right; what was underneath didn't bother him too much; he was a focused person. Wim wouldn't bawl a player out although he would point the finger at them.'

It was a more disciplined, tactically aware Celtic that the supporters saw that 1997–98 season. The defence and the midfield stuck closely to their positions, and on the training pitch Jansen drilled the players thoroughly, painstakingly, to play his way. Initially, the players found his detailed training ground methods to be severely demanding but gradually they began to see the results and his efforts on the practice pitch began to bear fruit in competition. Hysteria had been building among the Celtic support for some years about the possibility of Rangers superseding

Celtic's achievement of ten titles in a row during the Jock Stein era. It had been tough to take when Rangers had equalled that achievement in 1997 – statistically if not in style – and the pressure of stopping it had been well understood by Burns, who felt hampered to a degree in his efforts to rebuild the team painstakingly by the demands of the supporters to stop Rangers at all costs. Those fans now dreaded seeing Rangers go one better in 1998. Jansen's Dutch detachment meant that he was immune to much of this. Celtic recovered from two defeats in their opening two games to go top of the Premier Division in late February 1998 but faltered near the end of the season, drawing matches at home to Hibernian and away to Dunfermline Athletic that could have been fatal to their championship chances if Rangers had not lost their second-last fixture, at home to Kilmarnock. Instead, a beautifully curved shot from Larsson put Celtic 1-0 ahead against St Johnstone at Celtic Park on the final day of the season, in front of a 50,000 crowd ready to pop from their seats like champagne corks to celebrate a first championship in a decade. When Harald Brattbakk scored after seventy-two minutes the championship was sealed.

It had been the signing of Brattbakk that, as McCann recalls, inadvertently ended the career of Wim Jansen at Celtic. Shortly before Christmas 1997, with Celtic interested in purchasing a player who had scored close to a goal a game for Rosenborg Trondheim in the Norwegian League, Jansen was asked to go to Norway to watch the player in action but refused. Celtic were prepared to pay a fee of £2.2 million for Brattbakk and had a policy that with any player being bought for a fee greater than £1.5 million, the manager had to go and see him play. Jansen responded that while that may have been Celtic's policy it was not his policy. It had cost £7,000 for Celtic to hire a private jet for Jansen to go and watch Brattbakk in Norway. For McCann, that was the last straw with regard to another manager with whom he found it difficult to deal. At that point, Jansen had erased himself from Celtic's future despite going on to haul in the League title and the League Cup that 1997–98 season. Although he had signed a three-year contract, there was a clause therein that allowed either side to terminate the arrangement after one year. Jansen resigned whilst in Lisbon for a friendly match two days after clinching the title, although McCann stated that, if the head coach had not quit, he would have been dismissed. Accusations and counter-accusations flew from each side in the wake of his departure. 'That's football,' is how Wim

Jansen, in characteristically understated style, would later sum up the strange conclusion to his year in charge of Celtic. Funnily enough, a decade later, Brattbakk could be found working as an aeroplane pilot in the USA.

A huge hoo-haa surrounded Jansen's departure. Jock Brown was unpopular among the press for what they portrayed as a high-handed style, and when McCann emerged to unveil the championship flag at the beginning of the 1998–99 season, he was roundly booed by a large number of the 60,000 inside the ground, where the Jock Stein stand, completed that summer, had increased Celtic Park's capacity to make it the largest of any ground in Britain in the late 1990s. Jozef Venglos, the new Celtic head coach, had been unaware of the political difficulties inside Celtic when he arrived at the club to replace Jansen in the summer of 1998, and amidst his puzzlement at this reception for the club's owner, he had a tough start to his tenure. Post-World Cup tiredness and injuries hampered the team at the beginning of the 1998–99 season.

When Venglos, disgracefully and unjustifiably portrayed as an out-of-touch bumbler by the less scrupulous elements of the Scottish media, signed Moravcik for a fee reported as £350,000 in November 1998, he was scorned for bringing a cut-price thirty-three-year-old to Celtic Park. 'I was trying to be professional in my work, but some people in the press were not,' Venglos says. 'I didn't always read these things. I would read the press that produced constructive criticism. Every coach and every player needs that. When Lubo came, they did not behave nicely. They said I was his uncle and so on. It's a pity that they didn't know a player who had played in the World Cup and in his national team many times. They also started to speak about my English. It wasn't fair play.'

The loudest retort that the subtle Venglos could provide was success on the field of play, and by early 1999, with Moravcik in outstanding form, Celtic were on a run that looked good enough to bring them a second successive championship. Following Moravcik's arrival and his inspirational role in beating Rangers 5-1 in November 1998, Celtic dropped only nine points from a possible forty-five. 'If you are missing top players,' Venglos says, 'and that season we were missing many top players, it's difficult to maintain the balance within the team because you are giving a chance to young players. After two or three months the players were responding to me with a beautiful passing game that was attractive to the supporters.' Then, at Fir Park on 21 February 1999, during a 7-1 victory over Motherwell, Moravcik pulled a hamstring, keeping him out of action for a three-month period during which he would miss the concluding League fixtures and the Scottish Cup final.

A turbulent 3-0 defeat at home to Rangers on a rainy Sunday evening in May saw the Ibrox side win a League championship title at Celtic Park for the first time. Stephane Mahé was dismissed, it seemed harshly, and Vidar Riseth followed him down the tunnel. One Celtic supporter became so carried away that he fell from the top tier of the Jock Stein stand but survived to tell his own peculiar tale. Hugh Dallas, the referee, received a cut to the head from a coin thrown from that end of the stadium, and more than sixty people were arrested. Those events ended weekend evening kick-offs in Old Firm games and led to the police asking the Scottish Premier League to do all they could to avoid, in future, a Celtic–Rangers fixture being a championship decider. A 1-0 defeat in the Scottish Cup final, with both Celtic and Rangers performing in mediocre fashion, left Dr Venglos trophyless at the conclusion of his sole season in charge of Celtic. He had performed the inimitable trick of getting on well with McCann but had only ever been due to remain at Celtic for one year, and with McCann having left for North America that spring of 1999, further change was on the way at Celtic. 'With things not easy for him at the beginning,' Moravcik says, 'we lost contact with Rangers, but after that we played very well and we performed really well in some games. We played nice football, attacking football, players were confident and playing well.'

A chief executive, Allan MacDonald, was running the club's operations by mid-1999, following McCann's departure, and he opted to appoint Kenny Dalglish as director of football – Jock Brown having left in November 1998 – with John Barnes as head coach. It would prove an unforgettable experience for the Celtic followers. Barnes, as with Brady, an inexperienced coach appointed at the age of thirty-five, had been winding down a top-class football career at Charlton Athletic the previous season and now would be in charge of a squad of players close to his own age. It proved a costly experiment both for Celtic and for the Jamaica-born former England international, who remained gentlemanly to a tee throughout his testing time at Celtic Park.

On arrival in Glasgow, Barnes could immediately sense a degree of opposition towards him. 'I felt that a lot of people thought I shouldn't have been there,' he says. 'When I was dealing with the press you could feel the hostility.' Even after Celtic had won nine of their opening eleven

League matches he was still being questioned intensely and unforgivingly by the press, so when they lost the twelfth of those games, an Old Firm match at Ibrox, to go seven points behind Rangers, the press really opened fire. When Henrik Larsson then sustained a broken leg in the away leg of a UEFA Cup tie with Olympique Lyonnais, Barnes knew he was in serious trouble. 'I said that we still had a chance [of winning the title] and that we had players good enough to compete, but obviously we didn't. So that was that.'

Celtic rallied briefly in December, but a series of catastrophic signings told against Barnes. Eyal Berkovic, an Israeli international and a £5.75 million Scottish-record purchase, from West Ham United, proved less than effective. Rafael Scheidt, a Brazilian centre-back purchased from Gremio, cost £5 million, a fee Barnes was happy to pay, even though he had only seen the player on ESPN 'two or three times'. Ian Wright, then thirty-five years old and starting out on his television career, was brought in as a temporary replacement for Larsson but flopped dreadfully. It was as if all the painstaking work McCann had carried out in terms of husbanding Celtic's resources thriftily was being laid waste by careless heirs.

During a training break in Portugal in the month of January 2000, players, confined together, began to grumble and groan about the Barnes-Dalglish regime, and matters finally came to a head on a fateful night at Celtic Park on 8 February 2000 when, with Celtic out of contention for the League title, they faced Inverness Caledonian Thistle of the First Division in a third-round Scottish Cup tie. Three days previously, the match had been called off close to kick-off when high winds had dislodged a piece of roofing and, on safety grounds, the match was postponed. When the game was played, the roof really did fall in on Barnes.

Injuries forced Barnes to play a lightweight midfield, and, with his team 2-1 down after twenty-five minutes, the prospect was, he says, already very real to him of Celtic being eliminated. Eric Black, Barnes' assistant, at half-time chivvied the players fierily, and, as tempers rose, he recalls, Jonathan Gould, the goalkeeper, rounded on Berkovic to demand greater effort from the midfield player. Mark Viduka, the striker, then took exception to some of Black's comments, and the burly Australian advanced menacingly towards the coach, being restrained before matters really got out of hand. Viduka threw off his boots and refused to take the field for the second half. With Celtic in disarray, they lost a further goal, while

Inverness motored through the remainder of the match. 'It was just an accident waiting to happen,' Barnes says. His short stint as head coach of Celtic ended the following day, Black departing along with him. Dalglish took over as caretaker manager and lifted the League Cup in March with a victory over Aberdeen, after having brought Burns back as coach, but, as the Celtic players and staff walked round the track at the end of the match, it was the name of Burns, not Dalglish, that the supporters chanted.

The short-termism and uncertainty of the preceding years was of immeasurable help to Martin O'Neill when he arrived as Celtic manager at the beginning of June 2000. Press and supporters alike were now primed for a period of stability, and that was what O'Neill provided. He was deeply demanding of the players – if someone didn't give it, tough luck, they were out. 'One thing I will guarantee is they will give 100 per cent, whether they are winning or losing,' O'Neill said. 'The day they don't give 100 per cent, I'm not doing my job. We may win, we might lose; that's a different story.' Fortune also favoured him in that Larsson was fresh and raring to go at the start of that 2000–01 season, desperate to make up for the time lost in spending most of the previous season injured. 'One of my jobs at the start,' O'Neill also quipped, 'was trying to find out why we had spent some of our money on Rafael Scheidt.' The Brazilian had made just three appearances for Celtic.

This time it was Dermot Desmond who had selected the manager, just as MacDonald had been on the verge of appointing Guus Hiddink. 'There was only one simple reason for hiring Martin O'Neill,' Desmond says. 'He will win trophies and he would help the performance of Celtic. It wasn't about raising the profile or anything else. It was purely about getting the best manager that we could find to create stability at Celtic, because we'd gone through a lot of managers, gone through a lot of uncertainty. We wanted to find somebody that we believed, one, had the capability of developing a strong Celtic side and, two, could play the type of football that we wanted to play at Celtic and that we continue to aspire to play at Celtic and, three, would bring some consistency to the whole club.'

One of O'Neill's first acts was to ask the players why they hadn't won anything the previous season. A few players said bits and pieces and aired certain grievances – one of which was that their wives and girlfriends had not been able to sit together and had had to sit separated in the directors' box. O'Neill stated that from that moment on, all the wives would sit in the one place, and that there would be a crèche for the children. He didn't say he would talk to the directors and come back to the players with a yes or a no – he just said he would make the change immediately. That had been a major grouse among the players, and now it had been sorted, raising morale instantly. From that day, players say, they began respecting O'Neill. Whatever they wanted got done; no messing about – as long as they did what he required of them on the field of play.

The extra seating for the Celtic WAGs was provided by moving high-paying executive club members two rows further back, which led to them grumbling among themselves about this, and when their next scheduled meeting with the manager was on the horizon they discussed among themselves that they would complain directly to O'Neill about it. O'Neill bowled in to their meeting and said, 'Sorry guys, thanks very much for you moving two rows back. I very much appreciate you doing it for me.' After that, not a word was raised in complaint.

Nor was anybody among the wider support complaining when Celtic powered to a stunning 6-2 victory over Rangers in late August 2000, a flagship victory in O'Neill's period as Celtic manager. Moravcik was the common factor in all three opening goals, which had them 3-0 ahead and Rangers visibly wilting in the intense, late-summer midday heat. Indeed Celtic could have had a fourth prior to half-time when a sublime over-head kick from the Slovakian set Larsson free only for the Swede to fluff his shot and allow Stefan Klos to make the save. Three further goals in the second half, with hitting the Rangers net now becoming a matter of routine, made up for that.

With serious finance at his disposal, O'Neill wasted little time in making the team his own; framing the players in a 3-5-2 formation that had worked well for him at Leicester City, his previous club. Gould was replaced mid-season by Rab Douglas, a powerfully built former building site labourer who was recruited from Dundee. Joos Valgaeren, a £3.8 million Belgian international signed from Roda JC Kerkrade, joined Johan Mjallby, the enthusiastic and vigorous Swedish international, and Ramon Vega, a Swiss international, in forming a formidably hefty back three. Others bought that season to play the O'Neill way included Neil Lennon and Alan Thompson, the midfield players, from Leicester City and Aston Villa respectively, and Didier Agathe, a wing-back, snatched from Hibernian, who had signed him only on a short-term contract at the beginning of the 2000–01 season. Petrov and Bobby Petta, Barnes signings both, were revived by the new manager's drive, enthusiasm and will to win, as was Paul Lambert, a holding midfield player who had been brought to the club by Jansen in late 1997. Chris Sutton, who had been languishing at Chelsea after a close-to-disastrous season there, joined Larsson in attack.

Those players would form the basis of O'Neill's teams for the following seasons, and after that period of non-stop recruitment, in that first year, players such as Thompson, Agathe, Douglas, Petrov, Sutton, Valgaeren and Lennon would still be at the heart of O'Neill's Celtic when they defeated Dundee United in the 2005 Scottish Cup final, his final match as manager of Celtic. During the 2000–01 season they proved unstoppable, storming to the treble in sumptuous style. A Larsson hat-trick saw off Kilmarnock in the League Cup final in March; during April the title was tied up with six fixtures remaining; and in May a goal from Jackie McNamara and two from Larsson – his fifty-second and fifty-third of the season – clinched the Scottish Cup in a 3-1 victory over Hibernian.

Weeks before Christmas 2001 it was clear Celtic were about to seize a second title in succession, and with all the major components now in place, O'Neill's side simply charged to the title once again, losing just one League match, at Aberdeen on 22 December, and drawing only four, to accumulate a Scottish-record total of 103 points. Celtic now had 53,000 season ticket holders, and O'Neill's policy of bringing in experienced players delivered the type of results that that captive audience required.

A first tilt at the UEFA Champions League ended in frustration for O'Neill, although a stirring 4-3 victory over Juventus in their sixth and final group stage match in October 2001 kept their hopes kindled until the final minute of that match; those hopes extinguished only with the news that Porto had beaten Rosenborg Trondheim to pip Celtic to qualification by one point. An earlier exit from the UEFA Champions League in the summer of 2002, in the third qualifying round, paved the way for the thrilling run to the final of the 2003 UEFA Cup, and, although Celtic lost the League title on the final day of that 2002–03 season, on goal difference to Rangers, that was offset entirely by the thrill for supporters of experiencing a European final.

During that season, though, O'Neill had met Peter Ridsdale, the Leeds United chairman, and signed a document with Ridsdale to say that he would go to Leeds as manager, subject to certain conditions. With only six months remaining on his initial three-year contract as Celtic manager, O'Neill, as of January 2003, was free to discuss his future with other clubs. Brian Quinn recalls that episode well: 'We knew, because he told us that Leeds United were courting him and that Ridsdale had made a very attractive offer, so he did tell us that. He told Dermot, and Dermot told me, and I said to Martin, "You would be mad to go to Leeds United – they have overstretched themselves, they're going to be in trouble." So he did tell us, but I did not know that he had signed a letter. I had no idea, and when I saw that I was a bit taken aback that he had gone to that length.'

O'Neill said of the matter, in 2007, 'I'd signed a three-year contract at Celtic, and into the last few months of that contract, when there had been no discussions about a new deal, I assumed Celtic wanted me to see my time through. So I was within my rights to speak to somebody and went to meet Peter. I signed a statement of intent which included quite a number of conditions. One was that Peter told me Terry [Venables], the [Leeds United] manager at the time, wanted to leave. It was not a contract. Peter was pleading that he needed a signature indicating a serious intent, and, of course, there had to be, because I had to see if I had the potential to be working after 30 June 2003. When I realised that what Peter had said to me had not stacked up, when I spoke to Dermot and realised Celtic didn't actually want me to leave and that the conditions were not being adhered to, I wrote to Peter and left it there.'

The matter was resolved when O'Neill signed a one-year rolling contract in January 2003 and he pushed Celtic to another convincing title win, losing only four League matches in the 2003–04 season and scooping up the Scottish Cup with a 3-1 victory against Dunfermline Athletic in the final. That match would prove to be Larsson's final competitive appearance for Celtic, the Swede exiting in style, with two fine goals, before leaving for Barcelona. In attempting to replace Larsson, O'Neill brought in on loan Henri Camara, a Senegalese World Cup striker who had failed to turn up for training at Wolverhampton Wanderers after that club had been relegated from England's top flight. The loan involved Celtic paying a fee of £1.5 million to Wolves to facilitate the deal. Camara, at his best, was an explosively powerful and accurate finisher, but he was only sporadically at his best with Celtic and returned south in January 2005.

Juninho Paulista, a Brazilian who had done well at Middlesbrough and had been part of the 2002 World Cup-winning squad, also arrived that summer, on a free transfer – Celtic's first World Cup-medal winner. 'We'll fit him in somewhere,' said O'Neill insouciantly on signing the player, but Juninho soon exasperated the manager and after only nine starts in the

League he too was on his way out of Celtic, to Palmeiras in his home country in early 2005. The frustration of being starved of the type of resources to which he had previously been used was beginning to tell on O'Neill, who stated in September 2004, 'Celtic and Rangers are fantastic football clubs, great clubs, who stand still in their environment because of money.' Craig Bellamy, a Welshman, arrived on loan from Newcastle United in January 2005 after a dispute with Graeme Souness, the manager, and proved a success as a pacy, exciting goalscorer, but even he could not prevent Celtic losing a League title that seemed firmly in their grasp on the final day of the 2004–05 season.

With five minutes remaining at Motherwell's Fir Park, Celtic were leading 1-0 through a goal scored by Chris Sutton on the half hour. A win would leave them one point clear of Rangers if the Ibrox club were to win their game at Easter Road, against Hibernian. Three minutes from time, Scott McDonald, the Motherwell striker, scored to make it 1-1, which was no good to Celtic, who would be weighed down by a disadvantageous goal difference if finishing level on points with Rangers. That became academic in the final minute, when McDonald pounced again to score the winning goal and deprive Celtic of a title in the most dramatic fashion. The champagne that Celtic had taken down to Fir Park with them they generously offloaded to the Motherwell players, and although a Thompson goal was enough to defeat Dundee United in the final of the Scottish Cup at Hampden six days later, after which O'Neill walked round the track and waved farewell to the supporters, the drastic loss of the title made the resultant celebrations far from bubbly.

21
IMPORTANT IMPORTS

It was not long after Johannes Edvaldsson had arrived in Glasgow that a supporter decided he would help make him feel at ease in his new surroundings. Taking a seat beside the Icelandic centre-back, who had signed for the club in the summer of 1975, the fan, slowly and deliberately, in loud, clear English, mouthed the words, 'How ... are ... you ... settling ... in ... Glasgow?' Edvaldsson, impassively, responded, in the smoothest and crispest diction, 'Very well indeed, thank you.'

Such unfamiliarity with the mores of foreign players was understandable. Non-British footballers were notable only for their scarcity at Celtic during the club's initial century. For most of its history this has been a homogeneous club, with its players drawn largely from Scotland, so much so that it was a matter of some note when any type of non-Scot featured in the first team, such as Edvaldsson or Peter Latchford, the English goalkeeper of the 1970s. That the greatest Celtic team of all, the Lisbon Lions, were the most locally drawn team ever to lift the European Cup was entirely consistent with the club's history. Englishmen, Irishmen and Welshmen do dot the very earliest Celtic teams, but once Willie Maley had opened the twentieth century by instituting his policy of recruitment of young players from local Scottish clubs, the club became even less cosmopolitan.

The first notable player from outside Britain and Ireland to become established at Celtic was Joe Kennaway, a Canadian goalkeeper, who had represented Fall River against Celtic during the tour of North America in the summer of 1931. Maley described him then and there as the equal of John Thomson, and after Thomson's tragic death had robbed football of his talents in September 1931, Maley sent for Kennaway the following month. Sterling service followed from the confident, handsome Canadian for the remainder of the 1930s, and he became unique in Celtic's history when, in 1938, he was capped by Scotland, making him the only Celtic player to have represented three different countries at international level: Canada, Scotland and the United States of America. An even more exotic contemporary of Kennaway was Mohammed Abdul-Salim Bachi Khan, an Indian international and a thirty-two-year-old midfield player, who arrived in 1936 from the Mohammedan Sporting Club in his native country. One of the first Asian players to join a European club, on his feet he wore puttees rather than boots, and although he failed to feature for the first team, he did appear on two occasions in the reserves, impressing with his ball control and crossing and scoring with a penalty in a 5-1 victory over Hamilton Academical's reserve side.

The outbreak of the Second World War saw Kennaway return home and the arrival of another goalkeeper, Rolando Ugolini, at Celtic, in 1944, shortly after the surrender of Italy, whose participation in the war had been less than favourable to him. 'I was born in Lucca in Italy,' Ugolini says, 'although my father and my Uncle Orlando had come over to Scotland after the First World War, in 1920, and my father had settled in Armadale and my uncle in Uphall. For me, what happened was that, when my mother was expecting me [in 1924], she wasn't well, the pregnancy was a bit dodgy. The doctor said they should send her back to Italy for a wee holiday because the weather would do her good and to be with her mother in familiar surroundings. Anyway, she had me over there, and my father brought me back when I was six months old, and I was in Armadale all my life after that.

'When I was sixteen my father was interned – but only for a month because he was well in with the police, and the police got him out. My sister, my mother and myself were sent to Cambuslang, which was a non-protected area. That's where all the bombing was. Every night we were in the shelter with shrapnel hitting off the shelter. And where was my brother? He had been born in Armadale, so he was in the Black Watch, while we were in that situation!

'My father was very well liked in Armadale – he had a great fish and chip shop and he was known all over and he was on the committee of the Cooperative and he was a bookie and he used to give them money for the Gala Day and things like that. He was very kind. My sister was queen of the Gala Day, which was a great thing. Hearts, Motherwell and Falkirk had all wanted to sign me, but my father said, "You're not signing for anybody. You're signing for Celtic if they come." When I signed for Celtic from Armadale Thistle [in March 1944] my father was so proud, because I was Italian and Italy had been against Britain, and for an Italian to sign at that time was tremendous. I regard myself as half Scottish, half Italian. When Scotland meet Italy I'm just hoping the best team wins.'

The postwar years also saw Konrad Kapler, an outside-left, and a Pole who had arrived in Scotland with the Polish Army, make a series of sporadic appearances for Celtic during a two-year spell. Johnny Paton, whom he understudied, says, 'Konrad Kapler was a very good player. I had to be careful and watch myself or I'd have been out of the team.' Even more notably, Gilbert Heron, a Jamaican, joined in August 1951 and was Celtic's first black first-team player. Another player who had impressed Celtic while they were on a North American tour, in his case while playing for Detroit Corinthians, Heron made just five first-team appearances but is notable for being the father of Gil Scott-Heron, the musician who attained world-wide prominence in the 1970s with meaningful songs such as 'The Revolution Will Not Be Televised' and 'The Bottle'. There were signs of artistic leanings in his father, while he was at Celtic. 'I thought he was a cameraman,' Jimmy Walsh says of Heron, 'because he was always taking pictures – always doing things away from football.' His approach to life was as much bohemian as sportsman. A lover of what Glasgow had to offer in terms of nightlife, Heron found his way into the affections of a number of Scottish women. He remained at Celtic Park for only the 1951–52 season before moving on to Third Lanark, again for a year, and then returning to Detroit Corinthians and establishing a post-football career as a poet.

Although Jock Stein was the man who fielded the famous 1967 West of Scotland eleven, he was not averse to the idea of bringing foreign players on board. Two months after his arrival at Celtic he was in Dublin to watch two players in the Spain team that faced the Republic of Ireland. 'We don't ignore any information we get on players of this class,' Stein said. 'We can't afford to do that. We have to know how much the player is likely to cost, how much he would be wanting and whether he would like the Scottish climate.' Despite discussions with the players' agent, there were no Spanish ayes for Celtic that year. Within weeks, an even more imaginative move was made by Stein. Four Brazilian players – Ayrton Inacio, Marco Di Sousa, Fernando Consul and Jorge Fara – arrived at Celtic from South America in August 1965 for a one-month trial. 'If your teams intend to be successful in Europe,' Juan Ramos, the Brazilians' agent, said, 'then they must be ready to bring top-class players from other countries. Celtic, I now know, want that European success, and I think they will achieve it.' The Brazilians did little to impress the Celtic players, and potential problems in obtaining work permits for them plus their agent's too-high valuation of the worth of their talents saw the players return to Brazil, but even to consider such a move in the mid-1960s was revolutionary.

Once Stein's all-Scottish teams began to click and whirr unerringly towards repeated successes, he decided not to change a winning formula and he replenished his team with home-grown players. He would make only a very occasional foray into the market for foreign footballers, bringing in Bent Martin, from Denmark, in the mid-1960s, and Edvaldsson a decade later. Stein's attention to detail was quite exceptional as Martin, a young goalkeeper, found out. Jock had signed Bent, a tall, slim Dane given to a serious expression, after he had played well for Aarhus against Celtic in a European Cup-Winners' Cup tie in late 1965. Celtic had won 3-0 on aggregate, but Martin had played exceptionally well in both legs of the tie. 'The thing was,' says Tommy Gemmell, 'as Jock discovered when he got Bent to Celtic Park, that the young Dane did not like to be challenged physically inside his own six-yard box. On the continent, that simply wasn't done, but it was part of the game in Scotland. So in training, for fifteen to twenty minutes daily, for around a month, Jock had a session whereby corner-kicks would be played into the six-yard box, and Billy McNeill and I were to put Bent under pressure. 'Just hit him,' Jock would growl under his breath in our direction, as he supervised those sessions, and we needed no second invitation. By the end of that month, Bent was much better at dealing with balls into the six-yard box. That was one example of one of the thousands of small actions that Jock knitted together to make Celtic a great modern-day club.' It may also have embedded in Stein's mind an aversion to signing continentals; even those who appear outstanding under close scrutiny in one or two games. Martin failed signally to establish himself at Celtic, did not make a first-team appearance and was soon moved on to Dunfermline Athletic, where he fared much better.

It was not until the 1990s that foreign footballers would predominate at Celtic, but too many of those who landed at Celtic Park flattered to deceive: such as Dariusz Dziekanowski, who arrived from still-communist Poland in 1989 and swiftly peaked with four goals against Partizan Belgrade in a European Cup-Winners' Cup tie before slumping spectacularly after relishing too greatly, as Billy McNeill memorably suggested, the new-found freedoms of the West. Rudi Vata, an Albanian, and Dariusz Wdowcyck, another Pole, were, as with Edvaldsson before them, competent defenders but not players to get the pulse racing, although, when he put his mind to it, Wdowcyck could hit a mean free-kick.

Perhaps the most unusual entrance made by any foreign football player to Celtic was that of Andreas Thom, a skilled forward who arrived in the summer of 1995 from Bayer Leverkusen. Thom was so highly regarded inside German football that he had been the first East German to move to the West after the reunification, a process that had begun in November 1989 and which saw the player switch to Leverkusen from Dynamo Berlin, a club backed in communist times by the Stasi and Erich Mielke, that organisation's boss. Thom had an impressive list of honours to his name: winner, with Dynamo, of five successive East German League titles in the 1980s, East Germany's footballer of the year and top goalscorer in 1988 and holder of fifty-one caps for East Germany and ten for Germany post-reunification; he had been a member of the Germany side that lost to Denmark in the final of the 1992 European Championship in Sweden. Celtic had never previously signed a player with such a pedigree. Even so, Thom must have been surprised at the near-hysterical scenes that greeted him when he arrived at the club, with fans mobbing him and pressing in on his car when he turned up at the stadium.

That wild reception was less to do with Thom himself than with the frustration that had been building that summer among the Celtic supporters, who, in the wake of the successful share issue of January 1995, reckoned that the club was now swimming in cash and wanted to see some of it splashed out on top-class signings – and the trend in British football in the mid-1990s was to garland teams with foreigners. Players such as Jürgen Klinsmann, the German international striker, at Tottenham Hotspur, and Eric Cantona, the Frenchman, at Manchester United had added a different dimension to English football. Celtic supporters, having pumped money into the club, were no longer prepared to watch and wait for home-produced players to establish themselves at Celtic. They wanted their own foreign talismen.

Barely a day had gone by that summer of 1995 without the club being linked with a different exotic international footballer; David Ginola, the French forward, had actually been at the club, but opted instead to join Newcastle United. With the 1995–96 season imminent and still no signings having been made, the supporters linked the lack of action with Fergus McCann's determination to run a tight financial ship – and with each passing day the pressure on the managing director was increased, a factor that Thom's agent, eyes lighting up, observed with the reception given to his player and that he used, once inside Celtic Park, to negotiate a vastly superior financial deal for his player than Celtic had been planning to agree. Those inside Celtic vowed never to be held hostage in such a manner again.

Once Thom's signature had been secured for a £2.2 million fee and the initial excitement had died down, it proved a signing of mixed success; as might be expected of such a rushed job, Celtic seemed to have purchased a player who, at twenty-nine years of age, was perhaps just past his best. His most memorable moment was a stunning twenty-yard shot that opened the scoring against Glasgow Rangers in an enervating 3-3 draw at Ibrox in November 1995; that same month, though, Kenny Dalglish, seated in the directors' box at Celtic Park, was seen to wince as Thom, having done the hard work in wriggling into the Paris Saint-Germain penalty box, then miskicked horribly in front of goal. That summed up Thom's three-year sojourn at Celtic: a mixture of craft and haplessness.

The subsequent few years would bring recurring examples of this theme. Paolo Di Canio, Jorge Cadete and Pierre van Hooijdonk were well received by the club's supporters, but to those able to stand back from the hysteria surrounding them, they always seemed to fall somewhat short of what one would have desired of a really top-notch foreign player. Much was made of Di Canio having been signed from Milan, but at that club he had not been a first-team regular, and he was a player who possessed a fiery temperament that tended to get in the way of his talents. Celtic got a skilled but erratic player who pledged loyalty to the club but who, after one year, turned his back on them, pleading illness to remain in Italy rather than attend pre-season training, before negotiating a move south to Sheffield Wednesday.

Cadete was notable for one of Fergus McCann's most formidable triumphs. At McCann's behest, an independent commission examined the circumstances behind the transfer of Cadete's registration from Sporting Lisbon to Celtic in the spring of 1996. James Farry, the chief executive of the Scottish Football Association, was found by the commission, in 1999, to have deliberately delayed Cadete's registration to prevent him playing against Glasgow Rangers in the Scottish Cup semi-final that year; a match that Celtic lost. Farry was promptly dismissed by the SFA for gross misconduct. As with Di Canio, Cadete remained with Celtic for one season before refusing to return from Portugal in the summer of 1997 and engineering a move to Celta Vigo. His arrival in spring 1996 had created its own problems. 'That produced another ego thing,' Tommy Burns, the then manager, said when looking back on that time, 'because [Pierre] Van Hooijdonk and Thom had become the fans' big favourites. Cadete coming seemed to take a wee bit of the glory away from them and definitely created a wee bit of friction there.'

Van Hooijdonk had been the first prominent foreigner to arrive in the McCann era; a twenty-five-year-old striker, known as the 'geldwolf', the money wolf, in Holland, he was signed for £1.3 million from NAC Breda and, although a player with a sometimes clumsy style, he was useful in the air, as he showed in scoring the only goal of the 1995 Scottish Cup final with Airdrieonians, and proficient at free-kicks. Forty-four goals in sixty-nine games was a good return for his money, but Van Hooijdonk was not happy with the gold he was getting in return and demanded that his contract be reviewed. McCann, acknowledging the progress the player had made at Celtic in his first two years, presented Van Hooijdonk with a decent counter-proposal in early 1997, but the player responded by stating crassly on radio, 'Seven thousand pounds may be good for a homeless person, but seven thousand pounds a week is not good enough for a top-class forward.'

'Things were too far gone by then,' Burns said, 'because Van Hooijdonk had started to mess us about a bit. He was doing things like coming back late from internationals, taking another day. The club needed those players. They lifted the team, and people enjoyed watching them. If anything, the problem they caused me was trying to play the four of them in the one team. It was defensively where they caused us a problem. I remember playing Hamburg [in a 1996 UEFA Cup tie] and playing the four of them [Cadete, Di Canio, Thom and Van Hooijdonk]. I realised five minutes into the game that that was a mistake, because we were already a goal down, and Hamburg were causing us all sorts of problems. When they attacked we were four players down. The Van Hooijdonk thing became a problem, but we addressed the problem very quickly – we just moved him on to Forest for £4 million – £3 million more than we paid for him. So that was very good business.'

It was only once these players had left – lauded and loved as they were – in mid-1997 that Celtic, through tight-knit teamwork, finally wrested away a League title from Rangers and prevented the dreaded ten in a row. It was strange to see Di Canio and Van Hooijdonk besieged for autographs on subsequent visits to Celtic Park, especially as it was only after their departure that Celtic supporters saw the real and sustained quality and commitment that imported players can offer.

Henrik Larsson, a vital component of the 1997–98 title-winning team and a man who not only liberally displayed his skills but also worked hard for his team-mates, was joined in November 1998 by Lubomir Moravick, the Slovakian, a wonderfully cerebral player, a former university student in Czechoslovakia, and with the mark of a world-class player in that every touch of the ball, every movement, however subtle and understated or deceptively indirect, was done with the clear purpose of creation, either of a goal for himself or of disorientating a defence to present an opportunity for a team-mate. A beautifully balanced player, he would also display his humour on the field of play. During the early 2000s, Steve Walford would take the players through a pre-match warm-up in which they would gather in a circle, and each player would demonstrate a routine for the others to follow before progressing to the next player's choice of routine. Most players would undertake only a predictable stretching, jumping or jogging exercise; on Lubo's turn he would have them all following a routine of eastern-European-type dancing; with arms folded and legs criss-crossing while bobbing up and down. On another occasion, in a match against Heart of Midlothian, Moravcik, finding himself in space on the left wing, timed the bounce of the ball to use his backside to trap it perfectly.

A classic number ten, a playmaker in the mould of Michel Platini, his hero, Moravcik had featured at the 1990 World Cup for Czechoslovakia, who reached the quarter-finals, and soon afterwards he switched from FC Nitra to St Etienne in France. His displays for Les Verts attracted Olympique Marseille, then building the team that would go on to win the European Cup in 1993, and it was at that point that Celtic's luck held. Rather than transferring to Marseille and surely, inevitably, attracting the attention of the great Italian clubs, dominant in Europe at the time, Moravcik opted to remain at St Etienne. Thereafter, following short stints with Bastia and with MSV Duisburg, where he was made miserable at being used as a holding midfield player, Moravcik, at thirty-three, found himself on the verge of quitting the game. It was then that Dr Jozef Venglos, previously his manager with Czechoslovakia and, on independence, Slovakia, stepped in to bring him to Celtic Park. 'Mostly, he's a skilful player,' Dr Venglos said, in the understatement of the year, when introducing Moravick that November day in 1998. A genuine genius, Moravcik made the spectacular look routine, habitually knocking in shots and free-kicks from twenty-five to thirty yards.

A home match with Dundee saw Lubo ease his way into the side, using the outside of his right boot to serve up a delicious cross for Henrik Larsson to head a goal in a 6-1 victory. Two weeks later, Celtic faced a Rangers side resurgent under Dick Advocaat, a former manager of the Holland national team. With twelve minutes gone, Simon Donnelly advanced down the left wing. His zippy, low cross was cleverly dummied, on the move, by Larsson, and when the ball came to Moravcik, twenty yards from goal, he met it with a curling, low, left-footed shot that whirred pleasingly into the corner of the Rangers net. Moravcik stated that prior to that Old Firm match he had been in a state of nervousness similar to that when he had made his debut for Czechoslovakia a decade earlier, but it only helped him – a second goal from him, a strong header, did much to push Celtic on to a 5-1 victory. With the lively Larsson pushed up against the Rangers defence and Moravcik floating behind in a withdrawn role, Rangers could not even get a slippery grip on the Celtic attacking players.

Moravcik possessed two of the best feet ever seen in world football and was described by Zinedine Zidane as the best attacking midfield player he had ever seen. With him combining superbly with Larsson in the late 1990s and early 2000s, Celtic supporters were treated to some of the finest football ever put on display by the club.

A flood of foreign players have whirred through the doors of Celtic Park since the mid-1990s and are now an established facet of Celtic; of the team that started the championship-clinching match against Dundee United in May 2008, five had been born outside the British Isles. The most intriguing member of that team and the standard bearer for excellence from abroad is Shunsuke Nakamura, the Japanese, who was one of Gordon

Strachan's first signings for Celtic in summer 2005 and who, in common with Larsson and Moravcik, inspires supporters to expect the unexpected. Perhaps the highest tribute that can be paid to Nakamura is that after 120 years he is a type of player unlike any ever seen before at the club, and it is the desire to see the new and innovative that spurs on supporters. A player with mesmeric ball control, and with a beautifully balanced, light, willowy frame, his neat lay-offs, his spins and turns and sharp passing are as enjoyable to watch as his stunningly spectacular goals.

The novelty of the club's first Japanese player, and one with such an array of eyecatching skills, ensures that the corner of Celtic's superstore that vends 'Naka' memorabilia has become highly popular, whilst the presence of the player at Celtic has also increased awareness of the club in his native land, at a time when clubs in the West are seeking new markets in the Far East.

'It was in mind,' Peter Lawwell says in relation to commercial concerns being of interest to the Celtic directors when signing Nakamura. 'The world won't come to Scotland – we need to go to the world – and the one way of doing that was to identify players in growing markets. We spoke about Asian players pre-Gordon, actually, with Martin. Gordon was looking for a playmaker, a guy who could pass, and Nakamura's name came up. The priority was, "Can he play?" And that was undoubted, and that neatly fitted in with what we were trying to do. The other side was Du Wei, where we went for a Chinese guy for commercial reasons, and he came here for a trial, which was fine, and it didn't work, so the football was the priority. It wasn't done just for the market. If you've got a guy who meets your commercial targets and another who doesn't – and they're equally good – then you go for a Nakamura. Commercially, he has not been a transformer for the club, but he has opened up the Far East for Celtic. It would be an objective to continue that connection – it has been a great experience in terms of his attitude and professionalism.

'We've got an Australian, a New Zealander, a Pole; the hoops are iconic. We beat AC Milan in the hoops with Nakamura and with Artur Boruc, so that's a powerful package, and the foundation is being created – we're on the map globally.'

There are nuances in each country across the globe that mean that converting the locals into support for Celtic will have varying results. 'The Japanese people are very strange,' Nakamura says. 'They wouldn't support Celtic for life or something like that. Not many people in Japan would do that. We also have baseball and different kinds of sports in Japan. Football is not really the main sport in Japan, but I suppose many people watch Champions League matches and they do talk to me about them a bit when I go home.'

The move to Scotland has been a most successful one, football-wise, for Nakamura, but life off the grass on the other side of the world is, he says, 'really difficult, very different. You'll know if you go to Japan . . . I was in Italy and that was quite a hard environment for me too – it was easier to adjust here than it was in Italy. At Reggina, the club was in the countryside, and there was nothing around.'

There was little difficulty in attracting Nakamura to Celtic Park, Strachan says. 'He was at Reggina at the time and he was in and out of the team so we've given him, instead of Reggina and in and out of the team, Champions League and playing in front of 60,000 people. I don't think he knew how successful he was going to be. I don't think he could have dreamed of being this successful; I don't think any of us could. We knew we had a good player there and we didn't show him any place other than Celtic Park.'

If it is easy to attract foreign footballers to ply their trade on the smooth, lush surface at Celtic Park, once they have signed for the club, visits to some of the smaller grounds in Scotland can be less appealing. 'If we want to enjoy it, we can enjoy it,' Andreas Hinkel says of such outings. 'It's our choice if we go to the pitch and say, "Let's have fun, let's play good football." It's a mental thing.'

With a stream of foreign players moving in and out of the club, it has been essential for Celtic to provide help in settling them into life in Scotland. Stilian Petrov, the Bulgarian who arrived from Sofia in 1999, would later complain that he had been dropped into Glasgow by Celtic and, with a poor standard of English, left very much to fend for himself in a foreign city. Soon a stack of utility bills, meaningless to the Bulgarian, were piling up ominously on his mantelpiece. His complaints about finding himself in that situation sparked the club to do more for a later batch of new arrivals, with the appointment of Elaine Hamilton as player liaison officer in January 2006.

'I have to tell them things they shouldn't do,' Hamilton says. 'Artur Boruc is a perfect example. He and his girlfriend would walk home after a match at Celtic Park, through Bridgeton, where it is not advisable for anybody to walk through in a Celtic shirt, never mind a player who likes to have his moments, shall we say, with the Rangers supporters. Artur had started at Celtic six months before I started doing what I am doing, so nobody had said to him, "I wouldn't advise that." But if you talk to most of the players, they'll say that they've never had any hassle from Rangers supporters or anybody, because people are just fascinated by footballers.

'People think football is very glamorous, but they only get one day off a week and they never know when that day is going to be so if they are here on their own that means they don't know when they can go back and visit their family. The biggest thing I've noticed is how much more technically advanced the foreign players are in terms of using the internet and corresponding with their families back home by e-mail. The local players do everything by mobile phone. Most of them [the foreign players] have got a big collection of DVDs, and golf is a big thing, at places like Gleneagles and Turnberry; great for the family and great for golf. They like Glasgow, they like the feel of Glasgow, they like the buzz of Glasgow. If they are coming from Germany or France or Holland there is enough that's the same that they don't have any issues. For the players from Poland or the Czech Republic, the culture is quite different.

'Shunsuke and Koki Mizuno live next door to each other in the same block and come into work together. They are so far removed from home. Koki is a lot younger than Naka, and Naka has really taken him under his wing, probably because it was such a cultural adjustment for him.

'Everything is dictated by the football. I've yet to come across some-body who says they hate it here, that they're leaving because they can't stand it here. They may get frustrated at not playing, or their agent may have a better deal on the table. Players are constantly surprised by Glasgow, although I advise that they don't go out on the night of Old Firm games and things like that. I think they are surprised by the architecture and how beautiful some of the buildings are, and they are always talking about great new restaurants that they have discovered. The weather, I have got to say, is a big issue. A lot of them really moan about it, and that's why it can be really difficult for them not knowing when they are going to get time off, because a lot of the guys want to go home for a few days to get guaranteed good weather. They just hate the rain, the dreich weather, they get really fed up with it. They can't go home and sit in the sun.' With that sentiment, if nothing more, Celtic's foreign contin-gent has something in common with the locals.

22
CONTINENTAL JAUNTS

The contrast between the brilliantly lit green of the football field and the darkness elsewhere in the arena means there is an almost theatrical drama about European nights at Celtic Park. These are matches imbued with intense meaning – a stage on which Celtic are able to stretch their limbs freely and see how far they can go in competition with names large and small from across the continent; an opportunity to be measured against institutions of a similar size and weight and to leave behind for a while the sometimes cramped confines of the Scottish League. There is an anticipation at seeing something special – even a pleasure in the rare sight of Celtic occasionally going into a home game as the seemingly inferior side – and the unusual nature of such occasions makes them memorable.

European football has wrung out almost every emotion from the club's supporters: admiration and applause for expert practitioners of the game on their own and on opposing sides; anger and frustration at underhand and sometimes vicious gamesmanship alien to Scottish shores; and boundless exuberance at the exploits of Celtic on being pushed to the limit and emerging triumphant from a great contest of skill, nerve and decisiveness.

Enormous importance is now attached to European football by Celtic and their supporters, but the club was one of the game's late developers in such competition. The beginnings of organised, Europe-wide competition in the mid-1950s coincided with the start of the slump that saw Celtic snoozing into the 1960s. The club did install floodlights at Celtic Park in 1959, specifically for use in European matches, but it would be another three years before they would qualify to compete on the continent; third place in the 1961–62 season providing them with a slot in the Fairs Cup, a competition so named because it had, on its institution in 1955, been open to clubs from cities that held trade fairs. That rule had been relaxed by the early 1960s to allow entry to those clubs who had finished behind the champions of their country, and who had not won their national Cup competition, but as European football began to settle down and become organised, the tournament still had its quirks. Valencia, Celtic's opponents that September of 1962, had won the previous season's tournament only a fortnight earlier; their two-legged final with Barcelona having been held over until both clubs saw fit to play it.

A party of forty – comprising twenty-one players, three directors, three backroom boys plus some newspaper men and a handful of well-heeled supporters – landed in Valencia in the early hours of the day before the match; a thunderstorm was raging as they stepped off the plane but the air was still hot, and the rain from the storm heightened the musky air scented by the nearby orange groves. 'We hadn't known what to expect,' Mike Jackson, an inside-forward, says, 'and going abroad was new then, so we were excited.' At the Hotel Recati, on the coast twelve miles out of Valencia, the players slept three to a room, some on bunk beds, while the directors were allocated individual chalets. One reporter, billeted at the same hotel as the players, became so incapacitated through drink that he fell asleep while pouring a bath and flooded his floor of the hotel. Later on the trip, he was again so drunk that Celtic players phoned through his post-match report to his office in Glasgow. Crazy golf and mucking about in the hotel pool took up much of the players' time on the day before the match. More seriously, that Tuesday afternoon, two young Swiss boys, larking around in an inflatable dinghy, began to be carried out to sea. Their father came running up from the beach seeking help, and Sean Fallon, the assistant manager, formerly a lifeguard in his native Sligo, dived into the water and swam 300 yards out to bring them back.

It was against this colourful background that Celtic were launched into European competition against a powerful Valencia side at 10.30 p.m. on Wednesday 26 September 1962. 'We had never seen a stadium like theirs before,' Bobby Carroll says. The Mestalla stands and terraces veered sharply upwards, in contrast to the more gentle inclines found at Scottish stadiums. 'The supporters were so close to the park that they seemed to be towering above you,' Charlie Gallagher concurs. 'It was a big, round bullring type of stadium, and the crowd were right on top of you, shouting at you. It was bulls to matadors sort of thing.'

It was a young Celtic team that was pitched in against the Fairs Cup holders that sultry Spanish evening. Carroll, a winger, found himself fielded at centre-forward, in one of the random changes that Robert Kelly, the team-picking chairman, would frequently foist on the players. 'They were a bit harder than we had experienced,' Carroll says of Valencia, 'and they were fast; stronger than us. They were big, bulky guys; the defenders were anyway. They were a large, fit, strong team but a sporting team. I seemed to get more room against them, more time on the ball.'

Nine minutes had passed when Luis Coll, the Valencia outside-left, at a corner, gave his side the lead, and with just under half an hour gone, the same player struck again. Nervousness, dehydration from the stifling heat and competing with a physically imposing team seemed to be taking its toll on Celtic but in the thirtieth minute Carroll notched the first goal for Celtic in European competition.

'Some reporters said it was an own goal,' Carroll remembers, 'but what I remember of it would suggest it wasn't. The ball came across from Mike Jackson, and I hit it. I beat the goalkeeper, who was just off his line. A defender, behind him, tried to stop it with his foot, but he couldn't, and it went in. He was in the middle of the goal – it wasn't as if the ball was going wide – and he sent it into the net.' Manolo Mestre, the left-back, was the Valencia man who had, in vain, attempted to prevent the goal, and he would later often be credited as having scored an own goal in that instant. This was the first cross-cultural misunderstanding of Celtic's ongoing European odyssey. The Spanish tradition is that whoever gets the final touch on the ball is credited with the goal; the British way is to decide whether attacker or defender played the decisive part in the goal being scored before naming the scorer.

Only another two minutes had passed before Vicente Guillot restored the Spanish side's two-goal lead, and two minutes after the interval he made it 4-1 to the home side. It looked for a while as though Celtic might capitulate, but a second goal from Carroll, after Celtic had rallied, ended the scoring, and a 4-2 defeat was a highly respectable result against a side that featured Spanish internationals and Brazilians. 'They had hit us like a whirlwind at the start,' Jackson says. 'They were quick, and it was hot, and they had a couple of big Brazilians playing for them, and they played one-touch football, and their passing and movement was superb. It was great to watch, and in the first half we watched a lot of it! They were playing a different game from us. Once we settled down I thought we did well and in the second half I thought we played very well. It was a great experience.'

Jackson had laid on both goals for Carroll to score, but for the following Saturday's fixture with Raith Rovers they were the only two players dropped from the team that had played in Valencia. 'Nobody said anything to you,' Carroll says. 'You were simply dropped. For us to be axed when the defence let in four was a wee bit disappointing.' Carroll was restored to the Celtic team for the next three Scottish League games, scoring two of Celtic's four goals in those outings but on the day of the return, Bobby Craig, a Blackburn Rovers player, was rushed to Glasgow and signed for £15,000. Carroll was instantaneously sidelined and would never play for Celtic again. Jackson, who had made one appearance since the Valencia game, would also not feature in the return, which ended 1-1 – a result that eliminated Celtic from the Fairs Cup. Jackson too would never again play for Celtic.

The crazy ways of Robert Kelly still held sway at Celtic as they ventured into Europe again the following season; this time plunging into the European Cup-Winners' Cup for the first time, courtesy of their status as losing Scottish Cup finalists in 1963 to Rangers, the champions and qualifiers for the European Cup. Numerous changes had been made in the side, and now a number of young players, such as Tommy Gemmell, Jimmy Johnstone and Bobby Murdoch had injected new life into Celtic. It took them all the way to the semi-finals of the tournament, where they faced MTK Budapest, and a goal from Johnstone plus two from Chalmers saw the first leg, at Celtic Park, conclude 3-0 to Celtic. The players emerged from the dressing room, some in stocking soles, to complete a lap of honour; a rarity at the time. The tie looked to have been tied up, even with ninety minutes to come in Hungary.

A heatwave awaited them when they arrived in central Europe that April of 1964, but there was no possibility of the players being allowed to lie low and tick over gently prior to the return match. On the morning of the day before the game, they were given a guided tour of Budapest by the British ambassador, then the Celtic party went shopping before Antol Bakas, the wily MTK manager, insisted on having the Celtic squad out to the Nep Stadium, where he gave them a guided tour of the 100,000 capacity bowl, with the sun beating down and the weary Celtic players, in blazers and ties, becoming irritated at all these distractions from their work. Not only would they get little rest that day but they would not partake of any training. The MTK players, meanwhile, were in complete seclusion at their training base sixteen miles out of the city and would not leave it until two hours before kick-off. As they partook of a light meal on that evening before the match, the Celtic players were at a reception at the British Embassy.

Desmond White, the club secretary, appeared to believe that Celtic were as good as in the final. He stated that he was planning to contact UEFA to suggest a change of plan for the final, which was scheduled for Brussels. He wished to have it played either on a home and away basis or, alternatively, for the toss of a coin to provide for one finalist or the other to be given home advantage in a one-off final. White had also told John Divers, who had been injured and unavailable for the first leg, not to travel to Budapest for the return but to concentrate instead on getting fit for the final. As the players awaited the start of the game in an unusually luxurious dressing room, one crammed with beautifully upholstered armchairs and sofas, Kelly was among them to deliver his pep talk. 'Ach, we beat them over in Glasgow,' rapped the chairman, slapping his glove into his hand, 'and we can beat them here as well. Just go out and play.'

It was not long before thoughts of the final were being put firmly on hold. Karoly Sandor, a Hungarian international who had been missing through injury for five months and had not been in Glasgow, zipped away from Tommy Gemmell, and Istvan Kuti got to his cross before John Fallon, the Celtic goalkeeper, and jabbed the ball into the net. Eleven minutes had passed. Shortly before half-time Gemmell handled on the line to deflect a goalbound shot over the bar and Mihaly Vasas made it 2-0 with the penalty. Sandor, after sixty minutes, went gliding through the thick of the Celtic defence before flicking the ball over John Fallon to level the tie on aggregate. With twenty minutes remaining, Kuti made it 4-0, and MTK were in the final.

'Sandor was the trickiest type of outside-right,' Gemmell says, 'with a style similar to that of wee Jinky and nearly as good. I couldn't even catch him to kick him. I had a terrible game but I was not our worst performer on the night. I don't think there was anyone in our team who played well. You would think the management would tell us to keep things nice and tight and make the opposition chase the game and work for everything they were to get. No, Sean Fallon, who was in charge of team affairs by this time, wanted us to hump the ball fifty and sixty yards. You just don't do that sort of thing. We didn't deserve to get anything from the game while they deserved to beat us by 4-0 and maybe more.'

John Clark says in relation to the 1964 European Cup-Winners' Cup semi-final, 'We were so naïve in general, the whole club. We should have closed ranks at 3-0 up.' Instead, under Kelly's and Fallon's instructions, Celtic had not adjusted their normal game to deal with the circumstances.

It was a very different Celtic that reached their second European semi-final, again in the Cup-Winners' Cup, in 1966. Now gunned into professionalism by the vitality of Jock Stein, they faced Liverpool in the first leg and, in front of 80,000, a record attendance for a midweek match at Celtic Park, Celtic rolled over the English side but managed just the one goal, Bobby Lennox squeezing the ball over the line at the near post after Bobby Murdoch had nattily eluded flailing Liverpool defenders to dodge to the goal line and cut the ball into Lennox's path. 'It was 1-0 going on four or five,' Tommy Gemmell recalls. 'We gave them a real doing and just couldn't put the ball in the pokey hat.' Lennox agrees. 'We should have put the tie beyond them and didn't. It was a nice night in Glasgow, the pitch was nice and hard, quite firm. Down there it was the complete opposite – the pitch was heavy, and they probably played better against us.' A Tommy Smith free-kick after an hour of the second leg took a nasty deflection off Celtic's defensive wall on its way into the net, and a header five minutes later from Geoff Strong had Liverpool 2-0 ahead. Then came a moment that all associated with Celtic at the time continue to resent.

With minutes remaining, Lennox flitted swiftly on to the ball, ran clear of the Liverpool cover and nicked the ball into the net. At 2-2 on aggregate the tie, as was the custom in the mid-1960s, would have gone to a play-off at a neutral venue but that did not happen. Josef Hannet, the Belgian referee, signalled for offside. On seeing television replays, he later admitted he had got it wrong. He was not the first or last referee to be deceived by Lennox's speed. 'We were all raging,' Lennox says. It made the matter worse that the final was to be at Hampden Park, and, with the stadium packed with Celtic supporters, that would have been the next best thing to a home match. 'I headed the ball onwards past the big centre-half to Bobby Lennox, who was running from behind me to go past me,' Joe McBride says. 'It wasn't offside. In the final at Hampden, Liverpool got beaten by Borussia Dortmund, but we would have beaten the Germans. I have no doubt in my mind about that. So that was a big disappointment.'

Four years later, Celtic left no margin for error, refereeing or other-wise, when they pulverised another English side, Leeds United, over two legs of their semi-final in the European Cup. The English media had touted Leeds, managed by Don Revie, and powered by Scots such as Billy Bremner and Eddie Gray, as European champions elect, and Stein had used their over-confident press columns as a huge motivating factor for his players, slapping a pile of English newspapers down in front of them at breakfast time before the first leg. 'Look at them, eh?' he said. Celtic duly defeated Leeds 1-0 at Elland Road in the first leg and then 2-1 at Hampden Park in front of 136,505 on 15 April 1970. That remains the record attendance for any match in European competition.

'Winning was fine,' Billy Connolly recalls of the great Celtic sides of the late 1960s and early 1970s, 'but the style with which players such as Tommy Gemmell and Billy McNeill conducted themselves meant that Celtic were, like, different from all the other Scottish football clubs. Celtic were competing at the top end of footballing competition in Europe, among the prestigious clubs, and Celtic looked as though they belonged there. They looked the part. There was an athleticism about us. We looked serious. We didn't come shuffling on like some wee team from out of town; you couldn't confuse us with a team such as that. We looked like a top European club. Madrid and teams like that – they looked amazing – even their hair was good, shiny and trendy. Celtic had that aura too.'

En route to that meeting with Leeds, Celtic had eliminated a Benfica side featuring Eusebio and Fiorentina, the Italian champions. 'Tonight San Siro is our goal,' Stein wrote in the match programme for the semi with Leeds, 'San Siro and a second European Cup victory for tonight the victors must indeed be favourites for that honour.' The other semi-final featured a contest between Feyenoord of Holland and Legia Warsaw of Poland. That seeming dismissal or underestimation of the opponents in the 1970 final in Milan – Feyenoord as it transpired – may have been understand-able in that the champions of Poland and Holland lacked the rich European pedigree of Celtic's previous opponents that year. Dutch football was at that point only just beginning to emerge from obscurity. Professional football had not been introduced in that country until the mid-1950s, and although Ajax had reached the European Cup final the previous year they had been well beaten by Milan, while the Dutch national side had not reached the World Cup finals since the 1930s. Stein, on arrival in Italy for the final, was anxious to stress the threat from the Dutch side, who had, after all, eliminated Milan, the holders, in the second round.

'Feyenoord are more or less in the same position as we were in 1967,' Stein said at Celtic's hotel in Varese, two days prior to the final. 'We were the underdogs then, with nothing to lose. I cannot agree with the current impression that Celtic cannot be beaten. As far as I am concerned it is a problem and certainly not an attitude I fancy at all. Our team won't be professionals if they are caught out by all this talk at this stage, and I will be driving the point home to them in our discussions after training tomorrow.'

It did not take long for Feyenoord to assert their right to be taken seriously once the final was underway. 'I had a save in the first few minutes up in the top right-hand corner from [Wim] Van Hanegem,' Evan Williams, the Celtic goalkeeper that night, says. 'They played it about, and he volleyed it from about twenty-five yards, and the ball was going at quite a speed from the moment that he hit it. I caught the ball, but it had me saying to myself, "By God, this team's not here to mess about."'

There was a lack of verve about Celtic on the night, but after half an hour, Bobby Murdoch edged a free-kick into the path of Tommy Gemmell, and the full-back pelted on to it to fire a shot goalwards from outside the penalty area. Concetto Lo Bello, the showy Italian referee, conveniently ran across the eyeline of Eddy Pieters Graafland, distracting the Feyenoord goalkeeper, as the ball whistled towards the target, and Celtic were 1-0 ahead. 'He certainly impeded the goalkeeper by running across his line of vision,' Gemmell says, 'but I wasn't worrying too much about that at the time.' It took Feyenoord just three minutes to equalise, through a Rinus Israel header. 'One of our players headed it back when it was going out,' Williams says, 'and the Feyenoord guy headed it back across me where I had come out at the near post.'

Feyenoord grabbed a grip of the game, passing the ball slickly and smoothly, moving into space for each other and closing Celtic down quickly when the Scots took possession. 'In the last twenty-five minutes they gave us a turning over,' Williams says. 'I think at one point I had four or five saves within ten seconds; I think I blocked three or four shots one after another. The European Cup final was my best game for Celtic because of the number of saves I had in the match.' Williams' heroics kept the score level and pushed the match into extra-time, but there was no respite for Celtic. 'In extra-time I think Feyenoord came into it even more,' Williams says. Despite that, a matchwinning opportunity fell to John Hughes when he intercepted a pass close to the Dutch side's penalty area and went through on Pieters Graafland only to knock the ball against the goalkeeper. With three minutes remaining, Ove Kindvall, Feyenoord's Swedish striker, sped into the penalty area in anticipation of meeting a long, high ball from midfield. Billy McNeill, falling backwards, handled the ball, but that only had the effect of making it drop nicely for Kindvall to loop it over Williams' head and into the net for the winner.

'I just missed getting to it and no more, and Kindvall got there before me,' Williams says. 'I think with Billy handling it, it slowed the pace of the ball down; if you look at it, it may have been going out for a goal-kick. Kindvall just got his toe to the ball and toed it over the top of me. I stopped for the split second before he scored because I thought the referee was going to give a penalty. Then I realised that the whistle had not gone and that he was playing the advantage.' On such moments are European Cups won and lost.

It is difficult to understand why Lo Bello played the advantage rule. After all, what could have been more advantageous to Feyenoord than a penalty, and if Kindvall had failed to find the net with his lob, the referee would then have been in the difficult position of possibly awarding a penalty when he had already allowed the game to continue. The most simple explanation would seem that Lo Bello, a flamboyant but erratic referee, had, close to the end of an arduous 120 minutes, been caught out by the sheer speed of events unfolding in front of him.

In the years since, explanations have abounded for Celtic's poor performance. Some players have suggested that Stein lulled them into a false sense of security by underestimating Feyenoord's strengths in his pre-match instructions. There have also been insinuations that the players were distracted by discussions over commercial arrangements with an agent. Other suggestions are that Stein's preparations were too slack. The most practical analysis, and perhaps the one that may have accuracy at its heart, is that Stein omitted George Connelly, a prime performer in previous rounds and especially against Leeds, from his midfield and went for a 4-2-4 against Feyenoord's 4-3-3. Stein appeared convinced that, if Celtic poured resources into attack, Feyenoord would have no answer to it – but they most certainly did.

'The game against Feyenoord, we weren't up for it; I don't know why,' Jim Craig, a substitute for that final, says. 'You hear all sorts of theories, but I've never been very convinced by any of them because I know some of them to be nonsense. Those meetings we had for money were just to give us a chance to make a few bob, which we never got the first time out. Our generation does complain about money because we feel we weren't that well paid, but it would never have interfered with you on the day. They were better on the day.'

Evan Williams recalls that, 'There was just this deadly silence on the bus going back to our hotel. It was as if the whole world had collapsed. You could sense how disappointed all the boys felt. Nobody spoke. I think that they were the better team on the night, and that happens in football.'

Five years after Celtic had bested Internazionale in the European Cup final in Lisbon the two clubs were drawn together at the semi-final stage of the same tournament. Much praise had been given to Celtic for dismantling Inter's catenaccio system through incessant attacking in that wonderful match, but for the two-legged semi Stein, the arch-pragmatist, adopted a different approach, going 4-5-1 in Milan, with Lou Macari, the Scots-Italian of whom the locals had made a huge fuss, the lone striker. Inter, despite being at home, matched Celtic's caution. 'They didn't really create many chances as such,' Evan Williams says. 'We played well and I think we thought we were through when it ended up 0-0.' Mogadon and valium were distributed to the players on the evening before European matches away from home in the 1970s to help the players sleep more easily, and while it has now been established that it can take days for the effects of such palliatives to wear off, against Inter there was no sign of any adverse effect as the players exerted maximum concentration on the task in hand.

The return at Celtic Park drew a crowd in the region of 80,000, as did all the major European matches of the late 1960s and early 1970s, but it proved to be a sorry spectacle. Inter sat tight in defence throughout the ninety minutes of normal time and then into extra-time. This was not even catenaccio, the system of the 1960s whereby Italian sides would place the accent on defending efficiently and hitting hard and fast on the break. Inter had no ambition even to make the occasional breakaway, and all eleven of their players simply camped in and around their own penalty area, breaking the flow of Celtic's play through the unnatural number of players billeted in that part of the pitch. 'They were so boring,' Williams says of that Inter side. 'I don't think they had a shot on our goal all night. We just couldn't prise them open. We attacked them, but they seemed to win everything; I don't think they lost a ball in the air all night from our crosses into the box. Once Celtic got a few passes together and got the thing flowing, the Inter players stopped it by giving away a free-kick.'

A meeting of UEFA on the day of Celtic's 1970 European Cup final with Feyenoord had seen the introduction of the rule that penalty kicks would be used to settle any European tie that had ended in stalemate. The Celtic supporters had expected their side, so strong at home, to have settled the affair long before the end of regulation time, but now they were witnessing Celtic's first penalty shootout and watched in a state of some bafflement as a conclusion then entirely foreign to the Scottish game took place.

'Big Jock put a coat around me while we were waiting for the penalty kicks to start,' Williams recalls, 'but what I actually wanted was to be given a ball for a quick warm-up because I was cold – I had had nothing to do all night. I remember saying, "Boss, can I get a ball and do a wee bit of diving around?" He said, "No, no, wait here until we tell you who is going to do what." He actually said where the penalty kicks were going to go and, to be fair to him, he was right.'

Stein's advice meant that Williams almost reached the first Italian penalty kick, from Sandro Mazzola, the goalkeeper diving low to his right, but the ball evaded him narrowly and slithered over the line to put Inter one ahead. Dixie Deans, the Celtic striker, stepped up next and, changing his mind at the last second, aimed for the top corner and sent the ball high over the bar. Giacinto Facchetti, another survivor of 1967, then stepped up to take his penalty, shooting close to the centre of goal where Williams, again anticipating well, managed to get a touch on the ball this time. 'I dived and just put my hand up,' he says, 'and I actually thought I had saved it. It hit the bar, went behind the line and bounced out.' When Inter scored their next three penalties – even though Celtic scored their remaining four – the Milanese were in the final with Ajax. 'For the game to end like that made it so frustrating,' Bobby Lennox says. 'To me, that was like getting put out on a technicality.' Jock Stein went further, describing the shootout, then a novelty, as 'a circus act'.

The bonus for beating Internazionale in that 1972 semi-final would have been the same as it had been for conquering Dukla Prague at the same stage in 1967: £750 per player. 'The bonuses were always the same while I was there,' Jim Craig says. '£125 for the first round, £250 for the second round, £375 for the quarter-final, £750 for winning a semi-final and £1,500 for winning the final; we only got that once . . . but we should have won the European Cup four times in my opinion. In '69 we drew 0-0 with Milan in Italy and if you go to the San Siro and don't concede and then lose one goal to AC Milan over a hundred and eighty minutes, defensively you've done your job.' This was a quarter-final of the European Cup in which Celtic played exceptionally well to hold out for a 0-0 draw in the first leg in Italy only to lose an early goal through a defensive slip in the return at Celtic Park, allowing Milan to settle into defence and see out a 1-0 aggregate victory. The Italian side progressed to win the trophy that year and Gianni Rivera, their midfield player, later stated that he knew the trophy was within their grasp once they had managed to get over the huge hurdle presented by Celtic. Had the Milanese not won that quarter-final, Celtic would have been the most formidable club left in the competition and the way would have been clear for them to lift the European Cup for a second time. Jim Craig adds, 'In 1972 we went to the San Siro with Inter and again over a hundred and eighty minutes we didn't lose any goals but couldn't get the one goal that we needed. So we should have won both those games and the 1970 final.'

There is merit in Craig's suggestion: Inter's approach to the match at Celtic Park showed how much they feared the Glasgow team's attacking power, and although Milan in 1969 and Feyenoord in 1970 were excellent sides, Craig, as a sportsman and a winner, is correct in believing that Celtic were at least on a par with them and could have edged the encounters with those sides if the ball had run the right way for them.

The anticipation of seeing something different enthused and energised everyone who attended Celtic Park for major European matches, especially in the days before satellite television, when the first that most people would see of an opposing continental team would be when they trotted on to the turf at Celtic Park to begin the match. There was certainly something surprisingly different about the Atletico Madrid side that Celtic faced in the semi-finals of the European Cup in 1974. At the conclusion of the first leg at Celtic Park, Dogan Babacan, the harassed Turkish referee, had dismissed three Atletico players and issued nine bookings to players in the Spanish team. Far from this being a matter of dismay for the Atletico players, they celebrated enthusiastically at the final whistle. They had achieved a 0-0 draw by any means possible against a Celtic side renowned for their attacking ability at home.

The evening's violence did not conclude there. As the players moved towards the tunnel, Jimmy Johnstone, who had been belted black and blue all evening, was kicked in the back and punched on the head, and twenty policemen piled in as a brawl got underway outside the dressing rooms. 'That was some game,' John Clark, a Celtic coach in 1974, says. 'It was fights from the dugouts right through to the dressing room. I've never seen so many people in my life swinging punches. The Spaniards had lost their heads, and security and police were trying to separate people. You thought it would go on for ever, but a couple of minutes later it had calmed down. At the time it was a bit of a stramash; there were that many people in the corridor and the tunnel; the whole thing was congested.'

Atletico were managed by Juan Carlos Lorenzo, who had been manager of Argentina when they had met England in a controversial, and violent, World Cup quarter-final at Wembley in 1966, and the Spanish side's persistent, niggly fouling had disrupted the flow of play to make it a 'non-game', as David Hay describes it. Their lack of interest in making a match of it was underlined by Miguel Reina, the goalkeeper, who, when he got the ball in his hands, would deliberately belt it straight into the 'Jungle' rather than aim for one of his team-mates. 'We all got kicked that night,' Hay says, 'even me, and I was normally associated with kicking other people. They were just doing everybody. It became farcical. They wouldn't come out of their box.'

One of the Atletico players who had been dismissed was arrested and put in the back of a van by police, after an incident in the players' tunnel, and word of that got back to Madrid, where the press worked the locals into a frenzy with tales of police brutality. Celtic had hoped for strong action from UEFA – possibly through switching the venue for the return leg to a neutral country – but European football's governing body merely issued a wan warning to Atletico as to their future conduct. This was an irrelevance – Lorenzo had, on purpose, fielded a team of hatchet men for the first leg, and, although six were suspended for the game in Madrid, that did not disrupt his plan to field ball-players in the return. Desmond White, the Celtic chairman stated that the club found UEFA's inaction 'illogical and unjust' and stated that Celtic would play the return 'under protest'.

The visit to Madrid was a less than pleasant experience for Celtic. Jimmy Johnstone was in bed at 1 a.m. at the Hotel Monte Royal, where the Celtic party was heavily guarded by armed police, when the telephone rang. 'I was half-sleeping,' Johnstone recalled. 'The voice on the other end said, "You're dead." Then they put the phone down. I thought it was some crank. On the morning after I got that call, big Jock took me aside and said, "Look, we've had a death threat. They're going to shoot me and you." I said, "What? I'm going home." He said to me, "Listen, what chance have they got of hitting you when you get out there and you start jinking and jiving? I can't move. I'm sitting in that dugout."' For all Stein's clever psychology, it was still a subdued Johnstone on the pitch at the Vicente Calderon stadium that evening.

'It was a nightmare in Madrid from when we got off the plane until we left,' Johnstone said. 'At the airport we had the police and the Army to protect us and they escorted us back and forward to training sessions.' Water cannon, tear gas, police dogs and hundreds of police officers from the mounted division were in place to protect Celtic, but the ferocity of the crowd was still such that the Celtic players were forced to cut short their pre-match warm-up for their own safety. 'The ground was a cauldron,' Johnstone says. 'I had never seen as much hatred in my life.'

Stein had been outraged by Atletico's approach to the first leg. 'We have never wanted to win a game more,' he said prior to the return. 'It's not so much that we want to reach another European Cup final but because we dearly want to deprive Atletico of any chance of winning it – a Cup they have dishonoured, a tournament of which they have made a farce.' After all the pre-match aggro, the game, when it began, finally flowed freely. Celtic held their own until late in the match, when, after severe pressure from Atletico, José Eulogio Gárate opened the scoring. With four minutes remaining, Gárate eased the ball into Adelardo's path, and the midfield player swished it into the Celtic net to subvert the old saying and prove that cheats do sometimes win.

'Atletico were disgraceful,' Bobby Lennox says. 'I am convinced that, if we had beaten them in Glasgow, we would have gone through to the final. We could have beaten Bayern, who won it that year.' That was the last glimpse of European glory under Stein, and for the next decade Celtic spluttered and stuttered in European competition.

When Rapid Vienna, a name redolent with footballing history, came to Glasgow for the second leg of a Cup-Winners' Cup tie in 1984, their antics offered a variation on those used by Atletico to negotiate a tricky tie at Celtic Park. Rapid were 3-1 up from what had been a turbulent first leg and would have been confident of progressing to the next round, but goals from Brian McClair and Murdo MacLeod gave Celtic the upper hand in the second leg as half-time arrived. There was no prospect of Celtic easing off and being cagey despite now being ahead on the away goals rule: a packed Parkhead and the demands of David Hay, the manager, to harry and harass their opponents meant Celtic continued to play impressively and at full throttle.

Midway through the second half, Karl Ehn, the Rapid goalkeeper, dived low to his left to try to gather a ball that looked sure to be his. The ball slipped slightly from his grasp as Tommy Burns, the Celtic midfield player, slid towards him, studs up, making contact with the ball and prodding it away from Ehn. Burns was then the quicker of the two players to react, rising from the ground to turn and poke the ball into the Rapid net. Furious Rapid players protested long and hard to Kjell Johansson, the Swedish referee, but he ruled that the goal would stand. Two minutes later, and with twenty minutes remaining of the match, Rapid rapidly began to lose the plot, when an angry Reinhard Kienast, the Rapid midfield player, punched Burns on the back of the head. Kienast was dismissed by the referee. Ehn was next to exact retribution on Burns, kicking the player inside the penalty area and conceding a spot-kick.

Riled Rapid players again protested long and hard against the decision, persuading Johansson to consult with his linesman on the touchline in front of the Jungle. With the officials surrounded by Rapid players, a bottle and coins flew from the terracing, and Rudi Weinhofer, the Rapid substitute, collapsed to the ground. As ambulancemen attended to the prone player, Hans Krankl, the Rapid captain, motioned to his players to leave the field of play, and half a dozen trotted after him as he headed for the mouth of the players' tunnel. He was intercepted by the Rapid vice-president, who told him to keep the players on the field, where Rapid would play out the remainder of the match under protest. Celtic players maintain that the bottle thrown from the Jungle landed twenty yards away from Weinhofer; Krankl insists that the bottle landed on the player's head, opening up a wound. It remains true that if no objects had been thrown on to the field, Rapid would have had no case at all for their post-match moves. Following a delay of ten to fifteen minutes, Peter Grant, Celtic's nineteen-year-old penalty taker, sent the spot-kick wide of Ehn's post, although Grant insists his miss had nothing to do with nervousness caused by the overall situation. The match ended 3-0 to Celtic, and they looked to have won through to the quarter-finals, albeit in unusual circumstances. 'I remember Paul McStay saying to Krankl, in very clear English, so that he would be sure to understand, "You are a cheat!"' recalls Grant. 'It was almost as if they planned for it,' David Hay, the Celtic manager, concurs.

Rapid sent a telex to UEFA the following day to protest against having to conclude the match with nine men, following the supposed head injury to Weinhofer. It seemed in Celtic's favour when Dr Hubert Claesen, the official UEFA observer, stated that the bottle had not struck Weinhofer. Nine days after the match at Celtic Park, UEFA's disciplinary committee, after studying the television evidence, censured Rapid for making their claims. Kienast was banned for four European matches, and Baric, who had thrown his own bottle on to the field of play, for three. Celtic were fined £4,000 for the unruly behaviour of the offending supporters; Rapid £5,000 for the behaviour of their employees.

It looked like the end of the affair, but Rapid were not finished. They appealed against this decision and now changed their story, alleging that Weinhofer had been struck by a coin, not a bottle. UEFA's appeals committee doubled Rapid's fine but wrongfooted Celtic by declaring that the second leg had been 'irregular' and that it would have to be replayed a minimum of 100 kilometres from Glasgow.

'Rapid prepared very well,' James Farrell, a Celtic director, said, looking back on that episode. 'The other side engaged a barrister and two lawyers and they were very much better-prepared than we were. That was how they swayed UEFA. It wasn't one of our best efforts. I think they had been over the course before us. We were very annoyed, but there wasn't much we could do about it.'

The venue chosen by the Celtic directors for the third game – Old Trafford – was unpopular in Vienna, who believed that this would be too much like a home game for Celtic. It was, but it backfired on the Glasgow club. The supporters were overheated in their desire for revenge against the Viennese, and Tommy Burns remembered 'venom on their faces' as the team bus rolled into Old Trafford, with the Celtic supporters banging the bus aggressively as they demanded their team get stuck into the Austrians. Amidst it all, Rapid kept their cool, outplaying Celtic and, after little more than quarter of an hour, hitting them on the break. Roy Aitken had struck the post with a shot, and when the ball was whipped out of the Austrians' penalty area, Rapid whisked it forward at speed, and Peter Pacult, the striker, clipped it into the Celtic net to send Rapid through. Two Rapid players were assaulted by Celtic supporters who managed to get on to the pitch that night, and as a result Celtic were forced to play their next European home tie – ironically against Atletico Madrid – behind closed doors.

Having been in the quarter-finals, then kept out of them by a whimsical UEFA, it would be nearly twenty years before Celtic would again reach that stage of European competition, but they made up for that long time on the shelf by going two steps further and reaching the final of the 2003 UEFA Cup in Seville. 'I don't believe 50,000 Celtic fans will travel to Seville,' Rafael Carmona, security chief at the final, stated as the south of Spain awaited the final. 'That is madness. It is an exaggeration. I think a fair number will be around 4,000. We are talking about a final to be played on a Wednesday, a day when people normally work.' That 50,000 figure would turn out to be at the low end of estimates for the number of Celtic supporters who turned up in Andalucia that May midweek – more extreme estimates put the figure at 80,000. Three-quarters of the Stadio Olimpico was crammed by Celtic supporters that humid night, and almost all were in replica shirts; with Porto's fans taking up only one end of the stadium.

A series of seriously challenging clubs had been defeated by Celtic en route to the final: Blackburn Rovers, Celta Vigo, VfB Stuttgart and Liverpool among them but it was clear from the start of this match that Porto, whose manager, José Mourinho, had provided each of his players with a DVD of their immediate opponent, would be the most formidable opposition of all. With only three minutes gone, and Porto looking hungry and eager, Maniche, their midfeld player, cracked in a shot that whistled past half a dozen Celtic defenders and that Rab Douglas, the goalkeeper, restored to the side after a month's absence through injury, saved low to his left. Porto were in control of the midfield through Deco, Dmitri Alenitchev and Nuno Capucho and Celtic did well to prevent a goal during a first half in which Porto dominated. Then, in the first minute of time added on for stoppages, Deco and Derlei, the striker, combined to open up some space inside the Celtic penalty area that allowed the clever Alenitchev the freedom to race in and shoot for goal. Douglas blocked, but Derlei sent the rebound into the net.

Ten goals from Henrik Larsson had been the main ingredient in Celtic's

← Kenny Dalglish hurdles Willie Miller and Bobby Clark, the grounded Aberdeen players, to celebrate a goal with Bobby Lennox.

← Celtic captain Kenny Dalglish celebrates a 1–0 Scottish Cup final win over Rangers in May 1977.

↙ A notable Celtic midfield player of the 1970s and 1980s, Tommy Burns later became manager in the 1990s, head of youth development and then first-team coach in the 2000s.

↓ Danny McGrain, a full-back who had brought much flair and creativity to his defensive role, takes possession of the ball against Aberdeen, watched by Drew Jarvie.

COLORSPORT

⬆ Lubomir Moravcik clips a beautifully judged shot past Rangers' Antti Niemi for his first Celtic goal. Moravcik's two goals in Celtic's 5 –1 victory in November 1998 immediately endeared the new signing to the supporters and their appreciation of his talents remained undimmed until he was given a standing ovation on his final appearance for the club in the spring of 2002.

→ Shunsuke Nakamura lets fly to score one of the most outstanding goals ever seen at Celtic Park: a stunning, swirling shot from 30 yards that curls away from Allan McGregor in the Rangers goal and sends Celtic firmly on the way to a 2–1 victory, a win that was essential to clinching the 2007–08 League title.

↘ Nakamura's shot streaks into the back of McGregor's net. A 90th minute goal from Jan Vennegoor of Hesselink gave Celtic a 2-1 win.

↓ Ne'er the twain shall meet? A tightly stewarded dividing line separates the supporters of Celtic and Glasgow Rangers in the Lisbon Lions Stand for an Old Firm match in the 2000s.

GETTY IMAGES

PA PHOTOS

↑ In 15 years as a first-team player, Paul McStay produced a pleasingly consistent level of skilful and stylish passing, but he was never more effective than in the 1987–88 season, when Celtic celebrated the centenary of the club's formation.

← The £650,000 that Celtic paid Feyenoord in 1997 for Henrik Larsson brought to Glasgow a player who, during the subsequent seven seasons, made the exceptional look routine.

COLORSPORT

→ Initially signed on loan from Legia Warsaw by Gordon Strachan in the summer of 2005, Artur Boruc's impressive shot-stopping has since earned him two lengthy contract extensions and his displays in the Champions League and the 2008 European Championship finals have placed him among the most highly regarded goalkeepers in the world.

➤ Henrik Larsson rises above Ricardo Costa of Porto to meet Didier Agathe's cross for a header that the Swede curled to perfection over Vitor Baia, the Porto goalkeeper.

➤ Henrik Larsson and Alan Thompson celebrate after Larsson's second equaliser against Porto. Larsson scored a record 12 European goals for Celtic that 2002–03 season and hit 35 overall in Europe during his time with the club.

⬆ Scott McDonald celebrates after prodding a close-range shot past Dida in the Milan goal in the final minute of the Champions League game in October 2007. It was the first time Celtic have defeated a team that is the reigning European champions in a competitive match. McDonald scored 31 times in his debut season with the club.

⬆ Shunsuke Nakamura scoops a glorious free-kick over a leaping Manchester United defensive wall for the only goal of the Champions League group game in November 2006.

⬇ Jan Vennegoor of Hesselink, Celtic's Holland international striker, gets in front of Gabi Milito, the Barcelona defender, to smooth a header past Victor Valdes and put Celtic 1–0 ahead in the Champions League tie at Celtic Park in February 2008.

➡ Barry Robson celebrates gleefully after his wonderful headed goal put Celtic 2–1 ahead against Barcelona in the same match.

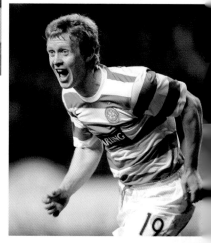

Brian Quinn (left), the Celtic chairman, Dermot Desmond (centre), Celtic's major shareholder, and Sir Patrick Sheehy, a Celtic director, emerge from Celtic Park in May 2000.

Fergus McCann acknowledges with a smile the applause of supporters as he attends his final match as Celtic's managing director.

↓ Martin O'Neill punches the air and springs high off the ground to celebrate a goal against Aberdeen at Celtic Park.

↓ Gordon Strachan lifts the Scottish Premier League trophy after Celtic's 1–0 win over Dundee United at Tannadice on 22 May 2008.

COLORSPORT

COLORSPORT

← Celtic supporters sport the colours for the 1969 Scottish Cup final. Collar and tie predominate but one fan is a lot less formal in attire and attitude.

← The long hair and tammy, de rigueur for young men in the early 1970s, are now optional, although the wearir of rosettes to matches is long defunct.

↓ Modern Celtic supporters, young and old, happily get behind their team.

run to the final, and he did not avoid his responsibilities once there. By far Celtic's most successful performer on the night, when he was not menacing the opposition in the heart of their penalty area, he was back in midfield, doing all he could to prompt team-mates to match Porto's swirl of inspiration in that part of the pitch. Two minutes after the break, Didier Agathe's high cross to the back post found Larsson, who timed his climb into the air with aplomb to guide a cushioned header back across the face of goal and into the far side of the net, providing Vito Baia, the goalkeeper, with no chance of saving. It was a fitting way for Larsson to score his 200th goal for Celtic. Seven minutes later, the Celtic defence was carved open again, and this time Alenitchev, with a similarly incisive run to the one that had produced Porto's first goal, finished the chance himself to restore Porto's lead.

A goal celebration lasting one and a half minutes between Porto players and their fans, who were behind the goal at which the Russian had scored, would lead to complaints from Martin O'Neill after the game – as if that had had a severe effect on the match. It had – but only to Porto's detriment. Mourinho's instruction to his players had been to hold possession, but, after scoring that goal, they instead fragmented, and again Celtic equalised only two minutes after Porto had taken the lead. This time it was a high back-post cross from Alan Thompson that Larsson met with another superbly timed header, thumping the ball past Baia for the Swede's forty-fourth goal of the season and turning ecstatic the Celtic following behind the goal.

Now Celtic came into their own, matching Porto move for move, but neither side could prevent the match heading into extra-time, the first half of which saw Bobo Balde dismissed for a wild foul on Derlei when the Brazilian was in a far from threatening position. With Celtic reduced to only ten men in the sapping, thirty-degree heat, five minutes from time Douglas saved from Porto's Marco Ferreira, and when the ball rebounded to Derlei he slammed it into the net. There was no way back for Celtic, whose Paul Lambert said of Porto, 'I thought they were great and deserved everything they got.' That showed commendable professional honesty on his part.

'I still can't believe we got beaten,' Tony Roper says. 'Every time I watch it, I'm still convinced we're going to win. I sit there, saying, "We're going to win this," at 2-2, "We're going to win this."' It was tough for the supporters to take that they had gone so close after such an exciting and varied run to the final, but they did conduct themselves peaceably, doing nothing at all on the night to sully the club's good name and receiving a FIFA Fair Play award for their conduct in Spain from none other than Sepp Blatter, the FIFA general secretary, on a rare visit to Celtic Park for a European tie the following year. It was not what they had gone to Seville to seek, but for a club whose supporters have made them formidable at home in Europe, it made for a momentous away victory.

23
FIRM RIVALS

When Celtic were drawn in the UEFA Champions League group stages with AC Milan in the August of 2007 an overwhelming sense of ennui engulfed those inside the club. This was the Milan of Kaká, the Brazilian about to be named European Footballer of the Year, and of Ronaldo, one of his predecessors, and of Cafu, in common with Ronaldo a three-times World Cup winner, and of Italian 2006 World Cup winners such as Filippo Inzaghi and Andrea Pirlo; this was the Milan that had only three months previously become European champions. Yet Gordon Strachan, the manager, and Aiden McGeady, Celtic's wing artist, were content to go on record in the aftermath of the draw as saying that it seemed a bit samey to be playing Milan yet again as Celtic had faced the Italian side in the previous season in the last sixteen of the same competition and had also faced them in the 2004–05 season UEFA Champions League group stages. Nor were they lone eccentrics in these thoughts: similar sentiments were being expressed by the Celtic support.

The Italians were due at Celtic Park on 3 October 2007, but already some supporters were looking a fortnight beyond that and the first encounter of the 2007–08 season with Glasgow Rangers. No one was suggesting that there was a jaded aspect to that match even though the two major Glasgow sides, since the introduction of the Premier Division in 1975, now faced each other a guaranteed four times every season and, habitually, when progressing in cup competitions, sometimes five or six times. This is a rivalry that, chameleon-like, will always take on a new and alluring hue with each passing year.

That match at Ibrox proved to be a regular, run-of-the-mill Old Firm occasion: with a quite surprising nine Celtic players booked by Mike McCurry, the referee, who saw fit to dole out only two bookings on the Rangers side; a match in which Stephen McManus, the Celtic captain and centre-back, was knocked unconscious by Daniel Cousin's over-enthusiastic mid-air challenge, which gained particular notoriety among Celtic supporters; and a match in which, at its conclusion, Artur Boruc, Celtic's Polish goalkeeper, ensured that further controversy would linger longer when he refused to shake the hands of Rangers players, later stating, 'I don't like this team.' There was enough involved in that encounter to keep the fans talking until the next instalment of this long-running rivalry in the spring of 2008.

Even those who follow Scottish football intensely may often accept that the professional game in their own country, while engrossing to them, is, in wider terms, seen as small beer. Yet it can still boast a fixture billed with some justification as the greatest derby match in the world – an epithet that might once have been seen as a parochial exaggeration but that has been fully endorsed in the twenty-first century by several of the sophisticated, well-travelled continentals recruited by the Old Firm, veterans of such fiery fixtures as Real Madrid–Barcelona or Ajax–Feyenoord, but who could not get enough of the Old Firm match and who unhesitatingly billed it as standing on its own in the world game in terms of the atmosphere that surrounds it. 'In Holland you had Feyenoord–Ajax, Feyenoord–PSV,' Henrik Larsson said, 'but it's so much bigger here – you have the build-up for the week from the press, the media, the fans.' Paulo Di Canio was even more emphatic: 'You could take all the derby matches in the world, add them all together and they still wouldn't equal one-millionth of the Old Firm. There is nothing like it.'

It is a fixture that has traditionally relied on a combustible mixture of the twin Glaswegian passions for football and religious bigotry to give it its inimitable character, and the very nature of the elements that provide it with its special standing mean that it is not to everyone's taste.

'I don't have very good memories of Old Firm games,' Billy Connolly says. 'It seems to bring out the worst in people. There's a darkness in it that I'm very uncomfortable with, and I've rarely seen one that came up to any expectation. It's not my favourite game, and I would actually go miles to avoid it. It brings out bigotry that I loathe and it attracts the kind of person I don't like – and it's their favourite game. It's not just religion but the blind aggression involved. I thought it was a great thing when I was younger, but even then I was always a bit scared of it, scared that if I went along to one of those games I'd get a smack in the mouth.' That fear remains among the more rational supporters, on both sides, despite the enormously sophisticated police operation that swings into action at modern Old Firm matches, whereby, in the vicinity of the stadium, well-coordinated efforts are made to ensure that the supporters of both sides are kept as distant from each other as possible, and the two sets of followers can only gaze at each other from afar, across a no man's land created by the authorities. Charlie Gallagher, a fine Celtic player of the 1960s, has watched only one Old Firm match since leaving the club: the 1973 centenary Scottish Cup final to which he was invited along with other former players. 'I just don't like the atmosphere at them at all,' he says. 'I don't even watch it on television or listen to it on the radio. Yet I loved playing in those games.'

It may seem surprising, then, that the rivalry between the two clubs began not in bitterness but in bonhomie – Rangers were, after all, Celtic's first opponents when, on 28 May 1888, the Ibrox club, then already fifteen years old, sent their second team, the Rangers Swifts, to Celtic Park for a friendly match. Early relations between Celtic and Rangers were exceptionally cordial – after that first match, players and officials attended a reception at St Mary's Hall, at which individuals from the two clubs toasted each other the greatest success. 'The light blues are favourites with the Celtic crowd,' one commentator noted after witnessing another early Celtic–Rangers encounter. It was not such an anomaly as it might superficially seem: it was soon clear that it was in the business and sporting interests of the two clubs to create a special rivalry: no fewer than twenty-one clubs from Glasgow had been registered with the Scottish Football Association in 1888, all jostling for attention as the new game of football enjoyed growing popularity among the public. In the face of such competition, it would prove self-sustaining for Celtic and Rangers to cultivate a rivalry that would draw greater attention to its two partic-ipants than to their rivals and that would enable them to carve up a greater share of the available football-following public. Celtic was already unique in Glasgow in being readily associated in the public mind with

Catholicism and Irishness – and when Rangers, then a non-sectarian organisation, developed into their major footballing rivals, so they tended to attract those native Scots who sought a football club to follow and who might have felt rather uncomfortable, aliens in their own land, inside the bawdy, colourful green-and-white confines of Celtic Park.

It would be two years after their initial friendly encounter before Celtic and Rangers would meet competitively, and that Scottish Cup tie, in September 1890, saw a 16,000 crowd crammed into the cramped confines of the original Celtic Park, with a further 6,000 locked out and having to rely on overhearing the sways and bays of emotion from inside the ground to try to follow the progress of the match, which Celtic won through a goal from Willie Groves. The burgeoning rivalry between Celtic and Rangers would soon cast a shadow over the rest of the Glasgow clubs; like two behemoths dominating the jungle, they would send smaller entities scurrying for their burrows and hedgerows for survival. Clubs such as Pollokshields Athletic, who played in the romantically rarefied surroundings of the Pollok Country Park, on the south side, and Cowlairs would become extinct altogether; others, such as Partick Thistle and Clyde, would carve out a modest niche following, while Queen's Park would find its previously elephantine influence over the game shrink to mouselike proportions once the amateur era ended in 1893, to be replaced by open professionalism.

Celtic and Rangers had, even within a decade of Celtic's birth, already created an identifiable establishment in Scottish football, and although Dumbarton and Heart of Midlothian also won Scottish League titles in the 1890s, they could not match the attendances that could be generated by the two ever-growing, major Glasgow clubs. Until the mid-1890s Celtic's matches with Hearts, Hibernian and Rangers would draw similar-sized attendances – around 15,000 to 25,000 – to the new Celtic Park, but by the end of that decade the League encounters between Celtic and Rangers would draw two or sometimes three times as many spectators as could be generated by meetings with any of the other clubs capable of giving them a good, close match. That is how quickly the rivalry grew.

It all resulted in the joint nickname that has bound Celtic and Rangers together, through thick and thin, to this day. Prior to the 1904 Scottish Cup final, to be contested by the two, a sharp-witted cartoon appeared in the *Scottish Referee*, one of the lively specialist sports papers that had grown in popularity with the snowballing momentum that was building up behind football in the late Victorian and early Edwardian era. The cartoon featured a sandwich-board man, complete with battered top hat, patched trousers, smouldering pipe and worn-out, bleary expression, who was weighed down by a board that read 'Patronise the Old Firm', as if touting some well-known business establishment. At the foot of the cartoon was the punchline, 'Rangers, Celtic Ltd'. Thus the 'Old Firm' was born. The implication of the cartoon was clear: the burgeoning rivalry and the gates it generated between the two clubs was good for business, and the two clubs' interests were intertwined: during the first decade of professionalism, the Scottish League title had gone to Celtic Park four times and to Ibrox four times; the Scottish Cup had been won twice by Celtic and four times by Rangers. Between them they had carved up seventy per cent of the prizes in the country's national football competitions. It was a stranglehold on the Scottish game that has only rarely been relinquished by the big two.

Even the supporters could be bound in common cause, as in 1909, when another Old Firm final concluded in a riot, although with the two sets of supporters not in opposition but joined together to protest long, loud and hard against officialdom. A crowd of 60,000 had turned up at Hampden Park for the replay after the first match had concluded in a 2-2 draw. When the second match also ended level, at 1-1 after the ninety minutes, both sets of supporters remained in place, expectant of extra-time, a process that had been hinted at in the press. Some of the players also remained on the field of play; they too were of the belief that an additional half-hour would be played to establish a winner, but when they were instructed to leave the field, the crowd grew restless.

During those initial decades of football, it was often suspected by supporters, and sometimes correctly, that Cup matches were fixed to end in a draw and thus garner extra revenue from a replay. Fuelled by this suspicion, the supporters at Hampden that April of 1909 began to vent their ire, and some supporters left their places on the terraces and advanced on to the pitch in protest. Soon the turf was swarming with fans of both sides. Elsewhere in the ground, the payboxes at which the fans had surrendered their hard-earned entrance money were set ablaze. Firemen who arrived to try to douse the flames were attacked. Fencing was set alight on the track that separated the Hampden pitch from the terraces. Missiles were thrown at the police: bottles, bricks, parts of the goalposts, bits of metal fencing. The Hampden Riot went on for hours into the evening, and, as a result, the SFA withheld the trophy for the only time in its history. It also ordered the two clubs to pay a joint fine of £300 to Queen's Park Football Club for the necessary repairs to the stadium.

Such conjoining of protest would seem unimaginable in the modern era: the second Hampden riot, in 1980, which also came at the end of an Old Firm Scottish Cup final, saw venom directed by the Celtic and Rangers supporters directly at each other when they invaded the field of play, but in the early 1900s the divisive religious tensions that would scar the rivalry had yet to be established. Certainly, it was clear already that these were two very different football clubs, supported in general by people of distinctly different backgrounds but it was still chiefly a sporting rivalry. When Davie Adams, the Celtic goalkeeper, was unfit for the start of the 1906–07 season, Tom Sinclair, the Rangers goalkeeper, joined Celtic on loan, playing in Celtic's six opening League fixtures, keeping a clean sheet in every game, all victories, and helping Celtic win a third League title in succession.

Willie Maley, Celtic's first manager, was to put a date on the change that would colour the business of the Old Firm for the following century. 'In 1912 the rift in the lute appeared,' he said, 'and the Brake Clubs became in the main the happy hunting ground for that breed termed "gangster" which has become such a disgrace to our city, and religion became the common battlefield for those supposed "sports".' Maley's tracing to 1912 of the source of the serious sectarianism that has scarred the face of the Old Firm ties in with Harland & Wolff, a Belfast ship-building company, establishing a yard on Clydeside and importing largely Protestant workers from the north of Ireland to work there. They brought with them Belfast-hardened religious bigotry and hardline support to Rangers Football Club, the most highly visible bulwark against Celtic, the most successful and vibrant symbol of Catholic and Irish-immigrant success in Scotland.

Religious tensions in Scotland became more highly charged when in 1916 the Easter Rising, organised by the Irish Republican Brotherhood, saw a rebellion in Dublin against British rule and the subsequent establishment of the Irish Free State in 1922, which encompassed the whole of Ireland but from which six counties in the north of Ireland, Protestant-dominated, opted out. When, in 1923, a widely publicised report to the General Assembly of the Church of Scotland spoke of the 'menace of the

Irish race', it sent fat spitting on to the fire. The report suggested control of immigration from the newly created Irish Free State, deportation of Irish people and a suggestion that, in the area of public works, Scots should be given preference of employment, as that area of employment was 'over-gorged' with Irishmen. With unemployment and poverty rife, this message hit home among the followers of both clubs and widened the growing schism between their followers. Rangers became seen as the club of the Scottish Protestant establishment and played on this to help obtain the successes masterminded by Bill Struth in the 1920s and 1930s. Celtic was seen as the club of the immigrant Irish underclass. Rangers now had an unwritten policy not to employ Catholics.

The 1920s and 1930s were the most bitter in terms of the bigotry surrounding the clubs, and although Catholics would continue to face discrimination, both overt and covert, in the years after the Second World War, the heat surrounding the issue would never again be quite so intense. While Rangers continued to operate a discriminatory policy in the 1970s and 1980s, they were widely seen, in those more liberal times, as less a stalwart upholder of Protestant values as a laughable anachronism, with television skits by comedians such as Rikki Fulton poking fun at them and journalists such as Ian Archer penning articles criticising their 'policy'.

It is also the case that, while relations between supporters may have at times been strained, if that's not to put it too lightly, the footballers of Celtic and Rangers have continued to enjoy a relationship that would not have been alien to the players who socialised together after those initial encounters of the 1880s and 1890s.

'We were very friendly,' Jimmy Walsh, a Celtic player of the 1950s, recalls of his relationship with his Rangers counterparts. 'We couldn't believe all the trouble that went on at times. All the players mixed together, so to us what was happening on the terraces was unbelievable. I've been in games between Celtic and Rangers where spectators at the front of the Jungle were running on to the pitch because they were throwing bottles down from behind them. You then had to get past a couple of spectators before you came to a Rangers player – and those supporters were supposed to be on our side! It's funny looking back but it was not funny when it was happening. The ref never stopped the game. He just let it carry on, and the police never seemed to be around. The spectators eventually went back, but when they were on the pitch they were running next to you.'

It was still sweet to score against the greatest rivals of all. 'Against Rangers I scored one of my best goals ever,' Walsh remembers fondly. 'Any goal against Rangers is brilliant, but this one was exceptional. I picked up the ball on the halfway line, went by Ian McColl, then round Sammy Cox, then past Willie Woodburn. You couldn't get better than that, could you? Then, from about twenty-five yards, and George Niven was in goal, I hit it past him. He came from the same place as I did, lived just up the road from me. We had played in the same youth teams together, so I was quite pleased when it went by him.'

Another who tasted the Old Firm atmosphere in the immediate postwar years was Johnny Paton. 'They were something exceptional,' he says of those fixtures. 'I never experienced anything in England like that – the atmosphere is electric. I know there is a religious aspect that gives it venom and I think that's ridiculous; schoolboy stuff. I don't like that kind of thing. I was glad to get away from it; it was great to come to England and to be free of it, but on the other hand I know that it was because of it that it made the atmosphere exceptional in these games. I know that Celtic was formed by Brother Walfrid, but when the game developed in the modern world and by the time I was playing for Celtic money and profit took over from all that.

'Rangers at that time were too developed and experienced for us. They had the Scottish international team's defence, with players such as Bobby Brown in goal, Tiger Shaw, George Young, Willie Woodburn. If you were a nervous type, playing against them in that atmosphere, it would affect you but I would say you should use it to give you adrenaline, and that creates energy. I always saw it that you were in the team because you had the talent to be there, and that this was an opportunity to show it.

'When I played for Celtic in the late forties there were as many Protestants in the teams as Catholics. Big George Young and I had played for Scotland together as schoolboys and so I would go into the Rangers dressing room just to say hello to big George, which was forbidden normally. There was no animosity between the players on the two sides – only between the supporters. I absolutely detested it. A few years ago, in 1995, I sat at Celtic Park and watched the Celtic–Rangers match and I couldn't believe the obscene behaviour: pointing fingers and arms at each other. I think it's got worse. I was appalled by the terrible, vicious attitude of the fans.'

Bertie Auld, who began his Celtic career in the mid-1950s, recalls,

'Rangers games were always difficult because they were demanding. It took quite a bit to play against Geordie Young and Willie Woodburn, big-name players. We always had marvellous individuals, and they were stars but we really never won an awful lot. It's a magnificent feeling walking out with the hoops on, it's very, very special. The jersey never seemed big enough for the Rangers game. The most important thing was the result. If it went against you, you never went out that Saturday night; in fact, you never went out all weekend and you emerged only to go to training on the Monday morning.'

George Niven was again in goal for the sweetest Old Firm victory of all, which took place in October 1957, when Celtic sent seven goals past the Rangers man, who had had the ceiling of his Bearsden home painted blue; following that thumping it must have been spinning sickeningly above him for days. At the end of the game, Dick Beattie, Niven's counterpart in the Celtic goal, turned to the spectators in the Celtic end at Hampden Park and raised seven fingers to acknowledge the victory; perhaps he was concerned that some onlookers, shocked by the repeatedly successful assaults on the Rangers goal, might have lost count. It was an afternoon that immediately slipped into Celtic's iconography. More than three decades later, Tommy Burns, interviewed after being part of a Celtic team on the end of a shocking 5-1 pummelling by Rangers at Ibrox in August 1988, stated that towards the end he had been praying only that his opponents on the day would be unable to reach seven. That 1957 result remains the record score in a Scottish or English top-flight Cup final and the highest margin of victory for either side in an Old Firm game.

It provided the Celtic support with much-needed sustenance into the early 1960s, a period in which Celtic regularly lost to Rangers, but by 1963, when the two clubs met in the Scottish Cup final, the Celtic fans, six years without a trophy, were becoming most frustrated. That final, after a 1-1 draw, saw Rangers coast through a replay to win 3-0 and the special importance of Old Firm occasions was brought home to John Divers, a Celtic forward who missed a key chance in that game, long afterwards.

'This would be about ten years after the '63 Cup final,' he says. 'I had become a student at Strathclyde University and was waiting for a bus to take me to Lanarkshire. I was standing at the bus stop when I saw across the road this young man dressed in a white painter's outfit. I saw him looking at me and thought to myself, "He's going to come over and speak to me." And he did. He came across the road and he said to me, "Are you John Divers?" And I said, "Yes, I am." And he said, "How did you manage to miss that chance against Rangers in the Scottish Cup final in '63?" Now I remember that chance, obviously, missing it; a big point in my life. It was obviously also a big part in his life ten years after the event. I couldn't give him a proper answer.'

Divers' father, also John, had been part of Celtic's Terrible Trio during the late 1930s and had been on hand for his son to remind him of some eternal truths about the Old Firm derby when John junior had been on the verge of making his debut in the fixture during the late 1950s. 'I was eighteen or nineteen and I was very worried and nervous about playing in an Old Firm match,' he says, 'and I spoke to my father about it. He was a man of few words but he said to me, in his own way, "Don't worry about playing in this game. They are actually easy games to play." I said, "I don't see that. I'm really nervous." He said, "Oh no. The support are every bit as nervous as you are, and if you kick the ball away from your own goal towards the opposition's goal, you'll get a cheer because you've kicked the ball away out of the danger zone, and that makes people dead relaxed." I know he was tongue in cheek when he was saying it, but to this day, in Old Firm games, there is a certain amount of truth in it. Kick the ball away from your own goal against the Rangers and it's a relief.'

Meetings between the big two in Glasgow create islands of intensity. 'The tempo of the game would be higher,' John Clark says as he thinks back to encounters between the two sides in the 1960s. 'You'd be quicker to the ball and in parting with the ball; your concentration had to be higher because, if you made a mistake against the Rangers and it cost you a goal, people would be telling you even now how it happened. You'd meet somebody in the street and they'd say, "You made a mistake and it cost us the game."

'The atmosphere was great, especially when you consider the grounds weren't covered. It was a noise – you couldn't distinguish singing or anything – it was just a noise; one big noise. Good games to play in; I used to love them. Anyone will tell you, you are more switched on when it comes to a big game. Celtic and Rangers can maybe struggle against what they think is a lesser team and then go in at half-time, get a blast and in ten minutes they've done the business and the game's over.' Not so in the Old Firm fixture, where almost always tension tears at the heart from first moment to last.

'In most games that you play for Celtic,' Joe McBride, a Celtic striker in the second half of the 1960s, says, 'you get this feeling that you're playing for the best team in the world, and, having been a Celtic fan all my days, every time I pulled that jersey on it gave me a kick, but I must admit the Rangers games always had that wee bit extra. There was that extra bite put into your effort, which shouldn't really be the case. You should have the same bite in every game. You couldn't help it – it was the environment around about you that caused it: 60,000, 70,000, 80,000, 100,000 people shouting – half for one team and half for the other. It was a cauldron.' Enjoyment is the principal feature that McBride recalls from those matches, but there were other ingredients that made this game decidedly different.

'You must remember that for a Catholic brought up in the west of Scotland,' Jim Craig says, 'there was always an edge to it. As a schoolboy I'd go for Scotland trials and stroll through the game and go and see Jimmy Smith [a former Rangers player], who was the Rangers scout, and say, "How was I today, Mr Smith?" He'd say, "Jim, you did very well." I'd say, "Well, I'm ready to sign any time, Mr Smith." He'd say, "Jim, you know how it is." It was disgraceful that you should be deprived of earning a livelihood because they wouldn't sign a player from that particular background. I would never have signed for Rangers – but the principle was wrong.

'So once you started playing against them, there was a wee bit of a kind of cause. I think the ones that went to Catholic schools would have thought, "This is payback time." You were going to make a mark on something – or someone. It's not nice to think of football, as a sport, being played like that but there is no doubt the Scotland of the 1950s was very sectarian. Curiously enough, Ibrox wasn't the worst. The worst was Tynecastle. I got a right going over there: "Fenian" this and "Fenian" that. There were no problems at all between Celtic and Rangers players.' It is worth noting that for Rangers scouts, it was a matter of extreme frustration – on performing their task of spotting good players, that work could be undone simply through them learning of the individual's background.

Bobby Lennox enjoyed the week's build-up to Old Firm matches and took pleasure in the fixture. 'It was the game you looked forward to most when the fixtures came out,' he says. 'I really enjoyed the game because, when you are on the park, you can do something about it. I think you enjoy the game more if you are involved on the field than if you are sitting in the stand, watching. On the park you can change things, make a contribution. I wouldn't say Rangers games were much more physical than other games – they didn't kick you any harder than a Dunfermline player.

'I was never, ever miscalled by a Rangers player. You'd maybe sometimes get a player from another team saying something they shouldn't be saying but the Rangers players always treated you with total respect, I felt. Big Jock loved to beat the Rangers. I think he had a few friends who blew him out when he joined the Celtic, so that was one reason he loved to beat them. He would say publicly that it was only two points that were at stake, as in all the other games, but he felt it was more than that. Everyone was desperate to beat the Rangers. Football is strange – the feeling of elation in beating Rangers wasn't as high as the low, the depression, of getting beaten, especially then, because you wouldn't get back at them for four or five months, as it was in those days.

'I think Celtic have always played with a bit more flair and been a bit more attack-minded than most teams. Before I joined, Rangers had a defence that was called the Iron Curtain, and even when we played they always seemed to have good, big defenders. It was just how they seemed to be. It may just be in people's minds but I'd think if Celtic are playing Rangers, people would expect Celtic will attack and Rangers will counter-attack.'

The Ibrox Disaster of 1971 drew the clubs and supporters together in grief. Bobby Lennox recalls that the players were sitting on their team bus after the game, unaware of the tragedy that had occurred at the very end of the match, on a stairway crammed with departing Rangers supporters from their end of the ground. Jock Stein had remained inside to help with the victims and the team bus departed without him and the Celtic directors. 'It affected Jock severely,' Lennox says. 'He was down for a long while after that. It got to him that people had lost their lives after having come to a football match to be entertained. It hurt him. Jock possessed a hard-faced exterior but he was a deeply emotional man and the events of that day at Ibrox stirred his soul. It was a real tragedy and it cast a pall over football for a long time afterwards.'

Certain players tend to be targeted by supporters of either side during Old Firm matches, for grievances imagined or real, or for deeply offensive ones – Paul Wilson, a winger for Celtic in the 1970s, and who was erroneously regarded by many Glaswegians as a Scots-Asian, was one such victim. 'I loved those games,' he says. 'You got quite an adrenaline rush before those games. The family I married into were all Rangers supporters, so it was nice to beat them.

'The Rangers supporters used to give me terrible stick. My father was half-Scottish, half-Irish; my mother was Dutch-Portuguese. In the summer I used to take a good tan. They [the Rangers supporters] would shout, "Wilson's a darkie," and then the other lot would shout, "I'd rather be a darkie than a Hun." You're talking about 60,000 or 70,000 people, you know? In a lot of those games, I used to score and I never used to turn round and do anything [towards the crowd]. I just got on with it. I think big Jock had a wee soft spot for me because of the stick I took. This was in the days before black players were playing down south. It actually never really bothered me. I got it all the way through school and obviously I must have been doing something right to have them get on to me like that.'

Although relations between Celtic and Rangers players are generally good, the tension present in the match can lead to conflagrations between players on the day of a game, but a competent referee can usually calm tempers within a minute or two. One such incident, in an Old Firm match at Ibrox in October 1987, would have serious repercussions. When Chris Woods, the Rangers goalkeeper, gathered a ball to his chest, he was confronted by Frank McAvennie, the Celtic striker recently signed from West Ham United. Woods objected to McAvennie's close attentions and pushed the Celtic man in the face. Terry Butcher and Graeme Roberts, the Rangers defenders, quickly joined in and Jim Duncan, the referee, stepped in to dismiss McAvennie and Woods. Only 17 minutes had been played. Duncan also sent Butcher from the field after 62 minutes for a foul on Allen McKnight, the Celtic goalkeeper. It had been a lively afternoon for Butcher, whose own goal had put Celtic 2-0 ahead but despite Rangers being restricted to nine men, they recovered to draw 2-2. Roberts had taken over in the Rangers goal and was filmed, later in the match, apparently 'conducting' Rangers supporters as they sang one of their more choice numbers. Following the match, the Procurator Fiscal's office issued charges of breach of the peace to all four players. When the case went to court, McAvennie was found not guilty; the charges against Roberts were not proven; Woods was fined £250 and Butcher £500. It seemed odd for the legal establishment to have selected this incident to remove disciplinary matters from the hands of the football authorities and in the years since, they have generally withdrawn gracefully and left it to the football authorities.

When Rangers did finally break the mould and sign a Catholic, they did so in a manner that piled provocation on top of the routine controversy that was always going to accompany such a move. Maurice Johnston, the Scotland international striker, had been in great form in early 1989, scoring goals that had pushed Scotland to the verge of qualification for the 1990 World Cup. Two years after having left Celtic for Nantes, he appeared an improved player for his continental experience. So when Roy Aitken, the Celtic captain, returned from a Scotland training session to inform Billy McNeill, the Celtic manager, that Johnston was hankering after a return to Celtic, McNeill, with alacrity, arranged a £1.2 million transfer fee with Nantes and personal terms with Johnston. 'I don't want to play anywhere else,' Johnston said when paraded in a Celtic shirt at a press conference at Celtic Park in late May 1989; although at that point Johnston had signed only a letter of intent to join Celtic, rather than a contract.

Shortly afterwards, McNeill began to hear rumours that Rangers had attempted to snatch the player from under Celtic's nose and in July 1989, Johnston duly appeared at Ibrox in a smart, navy blue blazer alongside David Murray and Graeme Souness, the manager. Outside Ibrox, after his signing had been announced, one or two individuals made a show of burning season tickets but these instances were notable only for their rarity. Rumours abounded that the player had been offered a massive signing fee or that Rangers had settled a large outstanding tax bill with the French authorities on his behalf. Whatever the reasoning behind Johnston's switch of allegiance, Rangers had finally signed a prominent Catholic player, but it was a bitter pill for Celtic supporters to swallow because of the manner in which it had happened and the calibre of player that they had thought they were getting – and had now lost for ever. Souness and Murray had severely embarrassed Celtic but they deserved commendation for a move that previous regimes at Ibrox would never have even contemplated. The time was also right: money, television and sponsorship were playing an ever-greater role in professional football and for Rangers to hang on to such an outmoded tradition could have been potentially bad for business. It did have the long-term effect of loosening the barriers that had made it tough for players – of whatever religion – to have played for both major Glasgow clubs and in the early 2000s several players were with Celtic who had previously been on Rangers' books. The Ibrox club, meanwhile, went on to sign several more Catholic players during the 1990s and beyond.

The two clubs' officials have often seen their interests as being intertwined – when Celtic were threatened with closure during their 'great flag flutter' with the SFA during the early 1950s, it was Rangers who stood four-square behind them in support from start to finish. When the Celtic party returned from winning the European Cup in Lisbon, John Lawrence, the owner of Rangers, was at the airport to greet them on their return. When the Scottish Premier League was set up in 1998 and the then ten elite clubs broke away from the Scottish Football League, the cavalcade was driven by David Murray, chairman of Rangers, and Fergus McCann, managing director of Celtic. There have also been many jarring moments of discordancy; when Fergus McCann launched his 'Bhoys Against Bigotry' campaign in the mid-1990s, there was little that came from Ibrox in response. It was only a decade later, and after the threat of punitive action from UEFA with regard to offensive chanting from the Rangers support, that Rangers were sparked into confronting the problem in terms of a coordinated and well-publicised anti-bigotry front that mirrored McCann's initiative of more than a decade before.

The Old Firm rivalry remains a visceral one, evinced most clearly in the utter silence that always descends on the supporters of either side in the few minutes after they have lost a goal in this game. Five or ten minutes afterwards, defiance may have been summoned and aggressive support of their team reinitiated, but in those moments after a goal the contrast between the goalscoring team's following and the terrible hush of their foes is one of the most evocative, unchanging aspects of British football.

'I was great friends with everybody in the pub,' Tony Roper recalls of the University Bar, the 'mixed' hostelry, frequented by Celtic and Rangers supporters, from which he would depart to watch Old Firm matches. 'I don't remember a fight with anybody in it, but during that hour and a half of that game, [when at the match] all of us screamed hate, abuse and bile at one another. Then you'd get back on to the bus, come back into the pub, and I don't remember any of that carrying on, because you knew you'd get barred from the pub. Maybe outside there'd be a couple of scuffles, but only because of the drink really; not because of anything else. In younger men particularly there is that aggression, and that gets it out of the system for an hour and a half without anybody getting hurt so I think it's a fantastically healthy thing, football, in that way. I'm not sure it's healthy to stop all that. Celtic and Rangers can easily afford to lift the religion out of it. It won't affect anything in the slightest bit. You'll still not like them, and they will still not like you. It's ingrained now; that's the two big rivals.'

The conclusion to the 2007–08 season visited upon Scottish football the unprecedented scenario of three Old Firm League matches in the final seven weeks of the season – matches that would go a long way towards deciding who would win the title.

Rangers won the first game, at Ibrox, only for two exceptionally taut, tight team performances from Celtic, in two victories at Celtic Park, to ensure that the race for the League title would now be almost certain to go down to the last day. During the early twenty-first century, Celtic and Rangers were indisputably dominating the Scottish League like never before.

For Dermot Desmond, Celtic's major shareholder, it is essential that Celtic should be striving always to be doing better than their great adversaries. 'It's extremely important,' he says, 'because they're our key opponents, and we don't want to give them any bragging rights because they're pretty good at bragging . . . There's a major rivalry there, and I think that's particularly healthy. It makes Celtic a better club, having a rivalry with other teams, particularly Rangers. Hopefully, we do the same for Rangers. In every match with them, 10-0s, 9-0s, any score like that would be a good score against Rangers as far as I'm concerned.'

It is a rivalry that touches every aspect of the co-existence of these two clubs. It is hard to eschew the memory of driving past Ibrox Park on the final day of the 2002–03 season and seeing Rangers supporters triumphantly strolling towards the ground in the shirts of Porto, who had defeated Celtic in the final of the UEFA Cup four days previously. Every triumph and defeat for one side – in whatever sphere – is seen as a reverse defeat or triumph for the other side.

As an outsider who has only just received an inside look at the Old Firm rivalry, Andreas Hinkel, Celtic's German full-back, offers a concise and perceptive view of the rivalry. 'It is because of games such as the ones against Rangers that a professional football player plays football,' he says. 'There is a special atmosphere, pressure is there, it's a good challenge. Maybe there was something bad in the history, but I think both clubs need each other. I know many supporters hate the other club, but if one club wasn't here it would not be the same. Celtic would say they need Rangers. Rangers would say they need Celtic. Maybe some supporters hate each other but also they love each other because they need the derby. If there is no derby something is missing. I think it's very important for Glasgow, the derby.' For all its unpleasant side-effects, especially in the hours after a particularly significant Old Firm game, it is hard to imagine the city without it.

24

A SPECIAL SUPPORTER

It can be hard to arrange a meeting with the manager of Celtic, but Jack Marshall went a greater distance than most people before enjoying his first encounter with Gordon Strachan. It was in the summer of 2006, and Celtic were in Poland for friendly matches with Legia Warsaw and Wisla Krakow. Jack had taken his seat for one of those matches and was intent on watching the action when the Celtic manager, sitting behind him, won Jack's attention and launched into a conversation that lasted a good fifteen minutes before Strachan finally had to make his way down to the touchline to supervise his players through the action on the field. One reason for the manager's interest, other than Jack being an engaging conversationalist, was that this was him revisiting a land in which he had spent much of the Second World War as a prisoner of Germany.

'I'd be about seven when I first went to see Celtic,' Jack, a vigorous eighty-six-year-old who remains active both in his own business and in supporting Celtic, says. 'I saw Johnny Thomson, you know. I was only a boy. Of that team in the 1930s, I remember Peter Wilson, a great half-back, saying that he never realised how heavy a jersey was until he played for Celtic. Willie Buchan, another gentleman, was the penalty taker. He would put the ball down, take two steps back, shuffle his feet, and the ball would go one way and the 'keeper the other. Malky MacDonald was my favourite player of all – he was at his best at inside-forward but he could play in any position on the park. My favourite Rangers game is the 6-2 game – the one before the war; in 1938, when we beat Rangers 6-2.

'When the war began I joined the Navy, boarding a brand-new destroyer in Dumbarton, where it had been built at Denny's, the boatyard. My Navy number was PGX303416. I had undergone training at Portsmouth and on the Isle of Man and, after a week's leave, had been assigned a ship. After four or five weeks at sea, we were sunk in the Atlantic Ocean by a German submarine. Only a dozen people survived, and the reason I know that is that there was only one naval prisoner of war camp, so anyone who had survived ended up in there alongside me.

'I don't know how I survived it, other than that I could swim quite well. It had been all hands on deck, and we had had to wait for the skipper to say "abandon ship" to get off and save ourselves. As soon as he gave the order, I slid off the fo'c'sle and, I'll never forget it, I had sandshoes on, and I was holding on to bits of wood, anything I could to help me float. When the ship eventually sank, I heard screams all over the place: even if people were a distance away, the suction of the ship going down would mean they got sucked right in and back to the ship again. In those days, in the Navy, in wartime, it was different; it wasn't like nowadays, when you need to be a swimmer.

'It was pitch black, and the sub that had put a torpedo through us surfaced and came right alongside us, and I saw two Germans, and they got me, grabbed me out of the water and started touching my face. It would be some years yet before I started to shave, and they were touching my face and they must have been saying, "This is only a little babba." They gave me a tot of rum – the first drink I had ever had in my life. I could feel it as it went all round my body to heat me up.

'I was transported to Germany and I found myself in the hands of the Gestapo – bad pigs they were – the Nazis and the Youth movement. There were some good Germans – you could chat to them. German was not a bad language to pick up because it was a bit like broad Scots. The Germans liked and admired the Scots – they called the kilted soldiers the "ladies from hell". I spent four and a half years as a prisoner of war, and three of those were spent in a camp in Krakow in Poland – I was Navy prisoner of war 729 – and we would get parcels with thirty cigarettes and three bars of chocolate, but I used all this for business – that's how I became a businessman after the war. I remember I traded a cigarette for an egg and had to keep it in my mouth to hide it from the Germans.

One guard, seeing I couldn't speak freely, said, "*Was machen sie, Kamerad?*" – what's wrong with you? He pushed me, and the egg broke inside my mouth, but I kept it until Harry, my friend, and I could cook it on the stove, and when we did it was like having a three-course meal. The Poles were desperate for cigarettes and I was desperate for carrots, turnips, you name it.

'My parents thought I was dead because it was eight months before they were notified that I was a prisoner of war. Once that happened I was allowed to receive my mail, and my father would send me wee snippets from the *Sunday Mail* to keep me up to date with how Celtic were doing. The Germans would scrutinise it to try to work out what it was all about. Celtic were always at the bottom of the wartime League, always.

'After the war, I went up to see Robert Kelly, who knew I had been a prisoner of war; he knew I had a war injury. He offered me then and there two season tickets for the south stand, which I've had ever since, and I'm not budging from them now.'

 # **Epilogue**

After a weekend of incessant summer rain, the clouds part kindly to provide an interval of sunshine that will last just long enough to accommodate Celtic and St Mirren as they contest the first fixture at Celtic Park in the 2008–09 season.

This August day, the crowd is in early and even though the ground is crammed to its 60,000 capacity, there are few queues to gain entry to Celtic Park, even in the minutes close to kick-off. Spectators are eased swiftly through the recently automated, unmanned turnstiles, with season tickets presented to a computerised reader that bleeps to signal a quarter-turn of the turnstile and the safe entry of the card-holder to the ground – twenty-first-century technology harnessed to ensure the smooth and safe working of one of football's lengthiest traditions. There is no faffing around looking for and receiving change.

The championship flag, a third in succession, is to be raised this day, and few wish to miss seeing it unfurled; another mark by which to measure Celtic having become the pre-eminent club in Scotland during the first decade of the century, having won six of the nine available championships. There is a tinge of sadness to the celebrations: Rosemary Burns, the wife of Tommy, who passed away in May 2008, will bravely step out on to the turf with Doctor John Reid, the club chairman, and Stephen McManus, the club captain, to perform the ceremony.

Burns was a traditional Celtic signing; a boy who grew up within walking distance of Celtic Park and who featured in more than 500 matches for the club. But he also, as the Celtic manager, did much to usher in the future, by becoming the first to sign several continental players. Now, on the pitch before the game, Marc Crosas, a 20-year-old and the club's first signing from Barcelona, emerges in a Celtic shirt and denims to receive an enthusiastic battery of extended applause to welcome him to Glasgow.

In the stands, as the supporters prepare for the action, it is as if a great, informal reunion is taking place. Rosemary Burns performs her role in the flag-raising ceremony, the clapping for the previous season's achievements dies down and the players emerge. Gordon Strachan takes his place in the technical area – another recent innovation that would have baffled previous generations of Celtic followers – and then takes a few paces forward to test, gingerly, the degree of spring in the turf. In the stands, the new fashion for draping banners from the top tier sees several competing for attention with the League championship flag, which is now wheeled off on its temporary dais to fly above the north stand over the coming year. One banner in the Lisbon Lions stand features an ornate reproduction of the club's original badge – Celtic must have some of the most historically aware supporters in the world – while another states straightforwardly '1888–2008: The Story Continues'. It certainly does: Barry Robson completes the first paragraph of the next chapter by putting away a penalty that gives his team all three points and another intriguing phase of Celtic's constantly unfolding tale is underway.

120 Years of Celtic Records

FACTS AND FIGURES 1888–2008

All statistics are correct to the end of the 2007–08 season.

In 1975–76 Scottish League Division One became known as the Scottish Premier Division and in 1998–99 the top teams broke away to form the Scottish Premier League.

The League was suspended during the Second World War only, whereas the Scottish Cup was suspended for both the First and Second World Wars. Games were played during the Second World War but do not count in the official records.

Players' appearances and goals do not include competitions such as the Glasgow Cup and Glasgow Charity Cup although they were important competitions in their day. All records include the League, Scottish Cup, League Cup and Europe (including the World Club Championship).

References to the Scottish League Cup include the Bells League Cup (1979–1981), the Skol Cup (1984–1993), the Coca Cola Cup (1994–1998) and the CIS Insurance Cup (1999–present).

KEY

L = League
SC = Scottish Cup
LC = League Cup
EC = European Cup
CL = Champions League
UEFA = Uefa Cup
CWC = Cup Winners' Cup
FC = Inter-Cities Fairs Cup
WCC = World Club Championship
CLQ = Champions League Qualifier

CL Gp = Champions League Group Stage
Rd = Round
QF = Quarter-Final
SF = Semi-Final
WIN = Winners
RU = Runners Up
R = Replay

og = own goal
aet = after extra time

In lists of appearances, substitute appearances are given after the + symbol or in brackets

In lists of results, Celtic's score is always given first

CELTIC FC 1888–2008

HONOURS

LEAGUE CHAMPIONS (42 times)

1892–93	1893–94	1895–96	1897–98	1904–05	1905–06
1906–07	1907–08	1908–09	1909–10	1913–14	1914–15
1915–16	1916–17	1918–19	1921–22	1925–26	1935–36
1937–38	1953–54	1965–66	1966–67	1967–68	1968–69
1969–70	1970–71	1971–72	1972–73	1973–74	1976–77
1978–79	1980–81	1981–82	1985–86	1987–88	1997–98
2000–01	2001–02	2003–04	2005–06	2006–07	2007–08

SCOTTISH CUP WINNERS (34 times)

1891–92	1898–99	1899–00	1903–04	1906–07	1907–08
1910–11	1911–12	1913–14	1922–23	1924–25	1926–27
1930–31	1932–33	1936–37	1950–51	1953–54	1964–65
1966–67	1968–69	1970–71	1971–72	1973–74	1974–75
1976–77	1979–80	1984–85	1987–88	1988–89	1994–95
2000–01	2003–04	2004–05	2006–07		

LEAGUE CUP WINNERS (13 times)

1956–57	1957–58	1965–66	1966–67	1967–68	1968–69
1969–70	1974–75	1982–83	1997–98	1999–00	2000–01
2005–06					

EUROPEAN CUP WINNERS
1966–67

CORONATION CUP WINNERS
1952–53

EMPIRE EXHIBITION TROPHY WINNERS
1937–38

YOUTH CUP WINNERS (9 times)

1983–84	1986–87	1988–89	1995–96	1996–97	1998–99
2002–03	2004–05	2005–06			

CELTIC PLAYER OF THE YEAR AWARDS

PLAYER OF THE YEAR		YOUNG PLAYER OF THE YEAR		PLAYERS' PLAYER OF THE YEAR	
2003	Bobo Balde	2003	Shaun Maloney	2003	Henrik Larsson
2004	Neil Lennon	2004	Stephen Pearson	2004	Jackie McNamara
2005	Stilian Petrov	2005	Aiden McGeady	2005	Stilian Petrov
2006	Shaun Maloney	2006	Aiden McGeady	2006	Shaun Maloney
2007	Shunsuke Nakamura	2007	Aiden McGeady	2007	Shunsuke Nakamura
2008	Aiden McGeady	2008	Paul Caddis	2008	Aiden McGeady

SPECIAL AWARD		GOAL OF THE SEASON	
2003	Jimmy Johnstone	2003	John Hartson v Liverpool 2-0 (A) UEFA Cup 20 Mar 03
2004	John Clark	2004	Alan Thompson v Rangers 3-0 (H) SPL 3 Jan 04
2005	Paul Lambert	2005	Alan Thompson v Rangers 1-0 (H) SPL 29 Aug 04
2006	Billy McNeill	2006	Shaun Maloney v Rangers 2-0 (H) LC 9 Nov 05
2007	Danny McGrain	2007	Shunsuke Nakamura v Manchester United 1-0 (H) CL 2 Nov 06
2008	Phil O'Donnell	2008	Shunsuke Nakamura v Rangers 2-1 (H) SPL 16 Apr 08

SCOTTISH FOOTBALL WRITERS' ASSOCIATION
FOOTBALLER OF THE YEAR (began 1965)

1965	Billy McNeill
1967	Ronnie Simpson
1969	Bobby Murdoch
1973	George Connelly
1977	Danny McGrain
1983	Charlie Nicholas
1987	Brian McClair
1988	Paul McStay
1998	Craig Burley
1999	Henrik Larsson
2001	Henrik Larsson
2002	Paul Lambert
2004	Jackie McNamara
2005	John Hartson
2007	Shunsuke Nakamura

SCOTTISH PROFESSIONAL FOOTBALLERS' ASSOCIATION
PLAYERS' PLAYER OF THE YEAR (began 1978)

1980	Davie Provan
1983	Charlie Nicholas
1987	Brian McClair
1988	Paul McStay
1991	Paul Elliott
1997	Paulo Di Canio
1998	Jackie McNamara
1999	Henrik Larsson
2000	Mark Viduka
2001	Henrik Larsson
2004	Chris Sutton
2005	John Hartson (joint winner)
2006	Shaun Maloney
2007	Shunsuke Nakamura
2008	Aiden McGeady

SCOTTISH PROFESSIONAL FOOTBALLERS'
ASSOCIATION YOUNG PLAYER OF THE YEAR
(began 1978)

1981	Charlie Nicholas
1983	Paul McStay
1996	Jackie McNamara
2001	Stilian Petrov
2004	Stephen Pearson
2006	Shaun Maloney
2008	Aiden McGeady

SCOTTISH PROFESSIONAL FOOTBALLERS'
MANAGER OF THE YEAR
(began 2007)

2007	Gordon Strachan

SCOTTISH FOOTBALL WRITERS' ASSOCIATION
MANAGER OF THE YEAR (began 1987)

1988	Billy McNeill
1998	Wim Jansen
2001	Martin O'Neill
2002	Martin O'Neill
2004	Martin O'Neill
2006	Gordon Strachan
2007	Gordon Strachan

DECADES	Trophies won				
	League Titles	Scottish Cup	League Cup	Europe	Total
1888–1889	0	0	0	0	0
1890–1899	4	2	0	0	6
1900–1909	5	4	0	0	9
1910–1919	6	3	0	0	9
1920–1929	2	3	0	0	5
1930–1939	2	3	0	0	5
1940–1949	0	0	0	0	0
1950–1959	1	2	2	0	5
1960–1969	4	3	5	1	13
1970–1979	7	5	1	0	13
1980–1989	4	4	1	0	9
1990–1999	1	1	1	0	3
2000–2008	6	4	3	0	13
	42	34	13	1	90

Full Record

Season	Pld	W	D	L	F	A	Pts	Pos	Top League Scorer	Goals	Scottish Cup	League Cup	Europe
1888–89											Runner Up		
1889–90											Round 1		
1890–91**	18	11	3	4	48	21	21	3	Peter Dowds	15	Quarter-Final		
1891–92	22	16	3	3	62	21	35	2	Sandy McMahon	20	Winners		
1882–93	18	14	1	3	54	25	29	1	Sandy McMahon	12*	Runner Up		
1883–94	18	14	1	3	53	32	29	1	Sandy McMahon	18*	Runner Up		
1884–95	18	11	4	3	50	29	26	2	Sandy McMahon	9	Quarter-Final		
1885–96	18	15	0	3	64	25	30	1	Allan Martin	18*	Round 1		
1886–97	18	10	4	4	42	18	24	4	Sandy McMahon	10	Round 1		
1887–98	18	15	3	0	56	13	33	1	George Allan	15	Round 2		
1888–99	18	11	2	5	51	33	24	3	Sandy McMahon	13	Winners		
1899–1900	18	9	7	2	46	27	25	2	Pat Gilhooly	8	Winners		
1900–01	20	13	3	4	49	28	29	2	Sandy McMahon	11	Runner Up		
1901–02	18	11	4	3	38	28	26	2	Johnny Campbell	9	Runner Up		
1902–03	22	8	10	4	36	30	26	5	Johnny Campbell	13	Quarter-Final		
1903–04	26	18	2	6	69	28	38	3	Sam Gilligan	13	Winners		
1904–05	26	18	5	3	68	31	41	1	Jimmy Quinn	19*	Semi-Final		
1905–06	30	24	1	5	76	19	49	1	Jimmy Quinn	20*	Quarter-Final		
1906–07	34	23	9	2	80	30	55	1	Jimmy Quinn	29*	Winners		
1907–08	34	24	7	3	86	27	55	1	Jimmy Quinn	19	Winners		
1908–09	34	23	5	6	71	24	51	1	Jimmy Quinn	22	Final - Cup withheld		
1909–10	34	24	6	4	63	22	54	1	Jimmy Quinn	24*	Semi-Final		
1910–11	34	15	11	8	48	18	41	5	Jimmy Quinn	14	Winners		
1911–12	34	17	11	6	58	33	45	2	Jimmy Quinn/ Willie Nichol	8	Winners		
1912–13	34	22	5	7	53	28	49	2	Jimmy Quinn/ Jimmy McMenemy	10	Quarter-Final		
1913–14	38	30	5	3	81	14	65	1	Patsy Gallacher	21	Winners		
1914–15	38	30	5	3	91	25	65	1	Jimmy McColl	25	Cup Suspended		
1915–16	38	32	3	3	116	23	67	1	Jimmy McColl	34	Cup Suspended		
1916–17	38	27	10	1	79	17	64	1	Jimmy McColl	24	Cup Suspended		
1917–18	34	24	7	3	66	26	55	2	Patsy Gallacher	17	Cup Suspended		
1918–19	34	26	6	2	71	22	58	1	Jimmy McColl	17	Cup Suspended		
1919–20	42	29	10	3	89	31	68	2	Tommy McInally	28	Quarter-Final		
1920–21	42	30	6	6	86	35	66	2	Tommy McInally	28	Quarter-Final		
1921–22	42	27	13	2	83	20	67	1	Joe Cassidy	18	Round 3		
1922–23	38	19	8	11	52	39	46	3	Joe Cassidy	23	Winners		
1923–24	38	17	12	9	56	33	46	3	Joe Cassidy	25	Round 1		
1924–25	38	18	8	12	77	44	44	4	Jimmy McGrory	17	Winners		
1925–26	38	25	8	5	97	40	58	1	Jimmy McGrory	36	Runner Up		
1926–27	38	21	7	10	101	55	49	3	Jimmy McGrory	48*	Winners		
1927–28	38	23	9	6	93	39	55	2	Jimmy McGrory	47*	Runner Up		
1928–29	38	22	7	9	67	44	51	2	Jimmy McGrory	21	Semi-Final		
1929–30	38	22	5	11	88	46	49	4	Jimmy McGrory	31	Round 3		
1930–31	38	24	10	4	101	34	58	2	Jimmy McGrory	36	Winners		
1931–32	38	20	8	10	94	50	48	3	Jimmy McGrory	28	Round 3		
1932–33	38	20	8	10	75	44	48	4	Jimmy McGrory	22	Winners		
1933–34	38	18	11	9	78	53	47	3	Frank O'Donnell	22	Quarter-Final		
1934–35	38	24	4	10	92	45	52	2	Jimmy McGrory	18	Quarter-Final		
1935–36	38	32	2	4	115	33	66	1	Jimmy McGrory	50*	Round 2		
1936–37	38	22	8	8	89	58	52	3	Jimmy McGrory	18	Winners		
1937–38	38	27	7	4	114	42	61	1	John Crum	24	Round 3		
1938–39	38	20	8	10	99	53	48	2	John Divers	17	Quarter-Final		
1939–40***	5	3	0	2	7	7	6	4	John Crum/ John Divers	2	Cup Suspended		
1946–47	30	13	6	11	53	55	32	7	Gerry McAloon	12	Round 1	Group Stage	
1947–48	30	10	5	15	41	56	25	12	Tommy McDonald	7	Semi-Final	Group Stage	
1948–49	30	12	7	11	48	40	31	6	Jackie Gallacher	11	Round 1	Group Stage	
1949–50	30	14	7	9	51	50	35	5	John McPhail	13	Round 3	Group Stage	
1950–51	30	12	5	13	48	46	29	7	Bobby Collins	15	Winners	Quarter-Final	
1951–52	30	10	8	12	52	55	28	9	Bobby Collins	12	Round 1	Semi-Final	
1952–53	30	11	7	12	51	54	29	8	Bertie Peacock	8	Quarter-Final	Group Stage	

Season	Pld	W	D	L	F	A	Pts	Pos	Top League Scorer	Goals	Scottish Cup	League Cup	Europe
1953–54	30	20	3	7	72	29	43	1	Neil Mochan	20	Winners	Group Stage	
1954–55	30	19	8	3	76	37	46	2	Jimmy Walsh	19	Runner Up	Group Stage	
1955–56	34	16	9	9	55	39	41	5	Neil Mochan	15	Runner Up	Group Stage	
1956–57	34	15	8	11	58	43	38	5	Neil Mochan	12	Semi-Final	Winners	
1957–58	34	19	8	7	84	47	46	3	Sammy Wilson	23	Round 3	Winners	
1958–59	34	14	8	12	70	53	36	6	John Colrain	14	Semi-Final	Semi-Final	
1959–60	34	12	9	13	73	59	33	9	Steve Chalmers	14	Semi-Final	Group Stage	
1960–61	34	15	9	10	64	46	39	4	Steve Chalmers	20	Runner Up	Group Stage	
1961–62	34	19	8	7	81	37	46	3	John Divers	19	Semi-Final	Group Stage	
1962–63	34	19	6	9	76	44	44	4	Bobby Craig	13	Runner Up	Group Stage	FC Rd 1
1963–64	34	19	9	6	89	34	47	3	Steve Chalmers	28	Quarter-Final	Group Stage	CWC SF
1964–65	34	16	5	13	76	57	37	8	John Hughes	22	Winners	Runner Up	FC Rd 2
1965–66	34	27	3	4	106	30	57	1	Joe McBride	31*	Runner Up	Winners	CWC SF
1966–67	34	26	6	2	111	33	58	1	Steve Chalmers	23*	Winners	Winners	EC Winners
1967–68	34	30	3	1	106	24	63	1	Bobby Lennox	32*	Round 1	Winners	EC Rd 1
1968–69	34	23	8	3	89	32	54	1	Willie Wallace	18	Winners	Winners	EC QF
1969–70	34	27	3	4	96	33	57	1	Willie Wallace	16	Runner Up	Winners	EC RU
1970–71	34	25	6	3	89	23	56	1	Harry Hood	22*	Winners	Runner Up	EC QF
1971–72	34	28	4	2	96	28	60	1	Dixie Deans	19	Winners	Runner Up	EC SF
1972–73	34	26	5	3	93	28	57	1	Kenny Dalglish	23	Runner Up	Runner Up	EC Rd 2
1973–74	34	23	7	4	82	27	53	1	Dixie Deans	24*	Winners	Runner Up	EC SF
1974–75	34	20	5	9	81	41	45	3	Kenny Dalglish	16	Winners	Winners	EC Rd 1
1975–76****	36	21	6	9	71	42	48	2	Kenny Dalglish	24*	Round 3	Runner Up	CWC QF
1976–77	36	23	9	4	79	39	55	1	Ronnie Glavin	19	Winners	Runner Up	UEFA Rd 1
1977–78	36	15	6	15	63	54	36	5	Johannes Edvaldsson	10	Round 4	Runner Up	UEFA Rd 2
1978–79	36	21	6	9	61	37	48	1	Tom McAdam/ Andy Lynch	7	Quarter-Final	SF	
1979–80	36	18	11	7	61	38	47	2	George McCluskey	10	Winners	Quarter-Final	EC QF
1980–81	36	26	4	6	84	37	56	1	Frank McGarvey	23*	Semi-Final	Semi-Final	CWC Rd 1
1981–82	36	24	7	5	79	33	55	1	George McCluskey	21*	Round 4	Group Stage	EC Rd 1
1982–83	36	25	5	6	90	36	55	2	Charlie Nicholas	29*	Semi-Final	Winners	EC Rd 2
1983–84	36	21	8	7	80	41	50	2	Brian McClair	23*	Runner Up	Runner Up	UEFA Rd 3
1984–85	36	22	8	6	77	30	52	2	Brian McClair	19	Winners	Quarter-Final	CWC Rd 2
1985–86	36	20	10	6	67	38	50	1	Brian McClair	22	Quarter-Final	Quarter-Final	CWC Rd 1
1986–87	44	27	9	8	90	41	63	2	Brian McClair	35*	Round 4	Runner Up	EC Rd 2
1987–88	44	31	10	3	79	23	72	1	Andy Walker	26	Winners	Quarter-Final	UEFA Rd 1
1988–89	36	21	4	11	66	44	46	3	Mark McGhee	16*	Winners	Quarter-Final	EC Rd 2
1989–90	36	10	14	12	37	37	34	5	Dariusz Dziekanowski	8	Runner Up	Semi-Final	CWC Rd1
1990–91	36	17	7	12	52	38	41	3	Tommy Coyne	18*	Semi-Final	Runner Up	
1991–92	44	26	10	8	88	42	62	3	Charlie Nicholas	21	Semi-Final	Quarter-Final	UEFA Rd 2
1992–93	44	24	12	8	68	41	60	3	Andy Payton	13	Round 4	Semi-Final	UEFA Rd 2
1993–94	44	15	20	9	51	38	50	4	Pat McGinlay	10	Round 3	Semi-Final	UEFA Rd 2
1994–95*****	36	11	18	7	39	33	51	4	John Collins	8	Winners	Rr Up	
1995–96	36	24	11	1	74	25	83	2	Pierre van Hooijdonk	26*	Semi-Final	Quarter-Final	CWC Rd 2
1996–97	36	23	6	7	78	32	75	2	Jorge Cadete	25*	Semi-Final	Quarter-Final	UEFA Rd 1
1997–98	36	22	8	6	64	26	74	1	Henrik Larsson	16	Semi-Final	Winners	UEFA Rd 1
1998–99******	36	21	8	7	84	35	71	2	Henrik Larsson	29*	Runner Up	Rd 3	CLQ Rd2/UEFA Rd2
1999–2000	36	21	6	9	90	38	69	2	Mark Viduka	25*	Round 3	Winners	UEFA Rd 2
2000–01	38	31	4	3	90	29	97	1	Henrik Larsson	35*	Winners	Winners	UEFA Rd 2
2001–02	38	33	4	1	94	18	103	1	Henrik Larsson	29*	Runner Up	Semi-Final	CL Gp/UEFA Rd3
2002–03	38	31	4	3	98	26	97	2	Henrik Larsson	28*	Quarter-Final	Runner Up	CLQ Rd3/ UEFA RU
2003–04	38	31	5	2	105	25	98	1	Henrik Larsson	30*	Winners	Quarter-Final	CL Gp/UEFA QF
2004–05	38	30	2	6	85	35	92	2	John Hartson	25*	Winners	Quarter-Final	CL Gp
2005–06	38	28	7	3	93	37	91	1	John Hartson	18	Round 3	Winners	CLQ Rd 2
2006–07	38	26	6	6	65	34	84	1	Jan Vennegoor of Hesselink	13	Winners	Quarter-Final	CL Last 16
2007–08	38	28	5	5	84	26	89	1	Scott McDonald	25*	Quarter-Final	Quarter-Final	CL Last 16

* Top Scorer in League   ** Four points deducted   *** League suspended   **** Premier Division
***** Three points for a win introduced from season 1994–95   ****** SPL

Opponents

	Pld	W	D	L	F	A		Pld	W	D	L	F	A
Rangers	380	137	92	151	518	541	Sporting Lisbon (Por)	4	2	0	2	6	4
Heart of Midlothian	319	171	69	79	595	369	Stenhousemuir	4	3	1	0	6	1
Hibernian	306	175	75	56	642	313	Ujpest Dosza (Hun)	4	2	1	1	5	6
Aberdeen	307	154	70	83	520	345	Valencia (Spa)	4	1	1	2	5	7
Motherwell	281	165	63	53	596	313	FC Zurich (Swi)	4	2	1	1	8	5
Dundee	261	158	51	52	531	270	Arthurlie	3	2	0	1	14	5
St Mirren	255	173	45	37	590	242	Gretna	3	3	0	0	8	1
Kilmarnock	220	143	46	31	517	205	Inter Milan (Ita)	3	1	2	0	2	1
Partick Thistle	214	141	40	33	498	212	Porto (Por)	3	1	0	2	3	6
Dundee United	198	114	45	39	375	204	Racing Club (Arg)	3	1	0	2	2	3
Falkirk	169	112	31	26	376	165	Anderlecht (Bel)	2	1	0	1	3	2
Airdrieonians	164	113	30	21	399	153	Artmedia Bratislava (Svk)	2	1	0	1	4	5
Clyde	163	119	30	14	439	138	B1903 Copenhagen (Den)	2	1	0	1	4	2
Morton	144	100	28	16	327	112	Bayern Munich (Ger)	2	0	1	1	1	2
Third Lanark	144	92	26	26	341	164	Blackburn Rovers (Eng)	2	2	0	0	3	0
Dunfermline	127	94	16	17	328	118	Bordeaux (Fra)	2	0	1	1	2	3
St Johnstone	108	69	18	21	240	103	Carfin Shamrock	2	1	1	0	5	3
Raith Rovers	100	67	18	15	244	89	Celta Vigo (Spa)	2	1	0	1	2	2
Hamilton Accies	97	74	14	9	254	95	FC Cologne (Ger)	2	1	0	1	3	2
Queen's Park	96	73	8	15	249	94	FC Copenhagen (Den)	2	1	0	1	2	3
Ayr United	94	74	8	12	267	89	Croatia Zagreb (Cro)	2	1	0	1	1	3
Dumbarton	56	44	10	2	165	40	Cwmbran Town (Wal)	2	2	0	0	10	0
Queen of the South	52	27	10	15	122	70	Dinamo Batumi (Geo)	2	2	0	0	7	2
East Fife	49	30	8	11	131	68	Dinamo Zagreb (Cro)	2	1	0	1	4	2
Stirling Albion	41	30	5	6	126	36	Diosgyor Miskolc (Hun)	2	1	0	1	7	2
Arbroath	32	29	2	1	112	21	Dukla Prague (Cze)	2	1	1	0	3	1
Albion Rovers	27	22	3	2	91	20	Dundalk (Ire)	2	1	1	0	3	2
Cowdenbeath	27	22	3	2	82	18	Ekeren (Bel)	2	1	1	0	3	1
Livingston	20	19	1	0	60	13	Elgin City	2	2	0	0	9	1
Clydebank (new)	20	17	1	1	66	12	Eyemouth United	2	2	0	0	7	0
St Bernards	19	17	1	1	61	16	Fiorentina (Ita)	2	1	0	1	3	1
Port Glasgow Athletic	17	14	2	1	51	11	Ghent (Bel)	2	1	0	1	3	1
Inverness Caledonian Thistle	16	11	2	3	35	17	Go Ahead (Net)	2	2	0	0	7	0
Clydebank (old)	14	9	3	2	28	10	Guimaraes (Por)	2	2	0	0	4	2
Leith Athletic	13	11	0	2	41	16	Hamburg (Ger)	2	0	0	2	0	4
Alloa Athletic	9	9	0	0	31	7	Hapoel Tel Aviv (Isr)	2	2	0	0	3	0
Montrose	9	8	1	0	39	6	HJK Helsinki (Fin)	2	1	0	1	3	2
Abercorn	8	7	1	0	31	10	Honved (Hun)	2	1	0	1	4	1
AC Milan (Ita)	8	1	3	4	3	7	Hurlford	2	2	0	0	10	0
Barcelona (Spa)	8	1	3	4	6	11	Innsbruck (Aus)	2	1	0	1	2	4
FC Basle (Swi)	8	5	1	2	21	9	Inter CableTel (Wal)	2	2	0	0	8	0
East Stirlingshire	8	8	0	0	26	5	Kaunas (Lith)	2	2	0	0	5	0
Ajax (Net)	6	3	1	2	8	8	KPV Kokkola (Fin)	2	2	0	0	14	0
Benfica (Por)	6	3	0	3	7	7	FC Kosice (Slo)	2	1	1	0	1	0
Dynamo Kiev (Ukr)	6	1	3	2	8	8	Leeds United (Eng)	2	2	0	0	3	1
Forfar Athletic	6	5	1	0	17	4	Leixoes (Por)	2	1	1	0	4	1
Liverpool (Eng)	6	2	3	1	6	5	Lochgelly United	2	2	0	0	6	2
Renton	6	6	0	0	19	5	Manchester United (Eng)	2	1	0	1	3	3
Bo'ness	5	5	0	0	20	4	MTK Budapest (Hun)	2	1	0	1	3	4
Brechin City	5	4	1	0	17	3	MTK Hungaria (Hun)	2	2	0	0	5	0
Stranraer	5	5	0	0	16	4	Nantes (Fra)	2	2	0	0	6	2
Vale of Leven	5	3	1	1	21	7	Neuchatel Xamax (Swi)	2	1	0	1	2	5
Aarhus (Den)	4	4	0	0	8	1	Nottingham Forest (Eng)	2	0	1	1	1	2
Atletico Madrid (Spa)	4	0	2	2	2	5	Olympiakos (Gre)	2	0	1	1	1	3
Berwick Rangers	4	4	0	0	16	0	Paris St Germain (Fra)	2	0	0	2	0	4
Boavista (Por)	4	2	2	0	5	2	Partisan Tirana (Alb)	2	1	0	1	4	2
Borussia Dortmund (Ger)	4	1	0	3	3	6	Partizan Belgrade (Yug)	2	1	0	1	6	6
Cambuslang	4	3	0	1	13	6	Peebles Rovers	2	2	0	0	7	0
Cowlairs	4	4	0	0	19	1	Politehnica Timisoara (Rom)	2	1	0	1	2	2
Jeunesse D'Esch (Lux)	4	4	0	0	22	1	Rapid Vienna (Aus)	2	0	0	2	1	4
Juventus (Ita)	4	2	0	2	7	8	Real Madrid (Spa)	2	1	0	1	2	3
Lyon (Fra)	4	1	0	3	4	5	Real Sociedad (Spa)	2	1	0	1	2	3
Rosenborg (Nor)	4	3	0	1	6	4	Red Star Belgrade (Yug)	2	1	1	0	6	2
Shakhtar Donetsk (Ukr)	4	2	0	2	3	6	Sachsenring Zwickau (Ger)	2	0	1	1	1	1

Opponents (cont.)

	Pld	W	D	L	F	A			Pld	W	D	L	F	A
St Etienne (Fra)	2	1	0	1	4	2		Bathgate	1	1	0	0	3	1
St Patrick's Athletic (Ire)	2	1	1	0	2	0		Burntisland Shipyard	1	1	0	0	8	3
Shamrock Rovers (Ire)	2	2	0	0	3	0		Dalbeattie Star	1	1	0	0	6	0
Sliema Wanderers (Mal)	2	2	0	0	7	1		Dumfries	1	1	0	0	2	1
Slovan Bratislava (Svk)	2	2	0	0	2	0		Duns	1	1	0	0	4	0
Spartak Moscow (Rus)	2	0	2	0	2	2		Feyenoord (Net)	1	0	0	1	1	2
Stuttgart VfB (Ger)	2	1	0	1	5	4		Forres Mechanics	1	1	0	0	5	0
FC Suduva (Lith)	2	2	0	0	10	1		Gala Fairydean	1	1	0	0	6	0
FK Teplice (Cze)	2	1	0	1	3	1		Galston	1	1	0	0	1	0
FC Tirol (Aus)	2	1	0	1	7	5		Keith	1	1	0	0	6	1
TPS Turku (Fin)	2	2	0	0	9	1		Linthouse	1	1	0	0	3	1
Valur (Ice)	2	2	0	0	9	0		Nithsdale Wanderers	1	1	0	0	5	0
Vejle BK (Den)	2	1	1	0	1	0		Our Boys Dundee	1	1	0	0	3	1
Villarreal (Spa)	2	0	1	1	1	3		Ross County	1	1	0	0	2	0
Vojvodina (Yug)	2	1	0	1	2	1		Royal Albert	1	1	0	0	2	0
Waterford (Ire)	2	2	0	0	10	2		Shettleston	1	1	0	0	5	1
Werder Bremen (Ger)	2	0	1	1	0	1		Solway Star	1	1	0	0	2	0
Wisla Krakow (Pol)	2	0	1	1	2	4		Thornliebank	1	1	0	0	3	0
Young Boys Berne (Swi)	2	1	1	0	1	0		Whitehill Welfare	1	1	0	0	3	0
5th KRV Kirkcudbright	1	1	0	0	7	0		Wishaw Thistle	1	1	0	0	6	2
6th GRV Dalbeattie	1	1	0	0	8	1								

A detailed look at the seasons where Celtic either reached a European final or won the treble, or in the case of 1966–67 both.

1966–67

League

Date	Opponent		F	A	
10 Sep 66	Clyde	A	3	0	
17 Sep 66	**Rangers**	H	2	0	
24 Sep 66	Dundee	A	2	1	
1 Oct 66	**St Johnstone**	H	6	1	
8 Oct 66	Hibernian	A	5	3	
15 Oct 66	**Airdrieonians**	H	3	0	
24 Oct 66	**Ayr United**	H	5	1	
2 Nov 66	**Stirling Albion**	H	7	3	
5 Nov 66	**St Mirren**	H	1	1	
12 Nov 66	Falkirk	A	3	0	
19 Nov 66	Dunfermline	A	5	4	
26 Nov 66	**Hearts**	H	3	0	
3 Dec 66	Kilmarnock	A	0	0	
10 Dec 66	**Motherwell**	H	4	2	
17 Dec 66	**Partick Thistle**	H	6	2	
24 Dec 66	Aberdeen	A	1	1	
31 Dec 66	Dundee United	A	2	3	
7 Jan 67	**Dundee**	H	5	1	
11 Jan 67	Clyde	H	5	1	
14 Jan 67	St Johnstone	A	4	0	
21 Jan 67	**Hibernian**	H	2	0	
4 Feb 67	Airdrieonians	A	3	0	
11 Feb 67	Ayr United	A	5	0	
25 Feb 67	Stirling Albion	A	1	1	
4 Mar 67	St Mirren	A	5	0	
18 Mar 67	**Dunfermline**	H	3	2	
20 Mar 67	**Falkirk**	H	5	0	
25 Mar 67	Hearts	A	3	0	
27 Mar 67	Partick Thistle	A	4	1	
8 Apr 67	Motherwell	A	2	0	
19 Apr 67	Aberdeen	H	0	0	
3 May 67	**Dundee United**	H	2	3	
6 May 67	Rangers	A	2	2	Title won
15 May 67	**Kilmarnock**	H	2	0	

	Pld	W	D	L	F	A	Pts
Celtic	34	26	6	2	111	33	58
Rangers	34	24	7	3	92	31	55
Clyde	34	20	6	8	64	48	46
Aberdeen	34	17	8	9	72	38	42
Hibernian	34	19	4	11	72	49	42
Dundee	34	16	9	9	74	51	41
Kilmarnock	34	16	8	10	59	46	40
Dunfermline	34	14	10	10	72	52	38
Dundee United	34	14	9	11	68	62	37
Motherwell	34	10	11	13	59	60	31
Hearts	34	11	8	15	39	48	30
Partick Thistle	34	9	12	13	49	68	30
Airdrieonians	34	11	6	17	41	53	28
Falkirk	34	11	4	19	33	70	26
St Johnstone	34	10	5	19	53	73	25
Stirling Albion	34	5	9	20	31	85	19
St Mirren	34	4	7	23	25	81	15
Ayr United	34	1	7	26	20	86	9

League record	Pld	W	D	L	F	A	Pts
Home	17	14	2	1	61	17	30
Away	17	12	4	1	50	16	28
Away	17	12	4	1	50	16	28
	34	26	6	2	111	33	58

League Cup

Group Stage

13 Aug 66	Hearts	A	2	0
17 Aug 66	**Clyde**	H	6	0
20 Aug 66	**St Mirren**	H	8	2
27 Aug 66	**Hearts**	H	3	0
31 Aug 66	Clyde	A	3	1
3 Sep 66	St Mirren	A	1	0

Quarter-Final

14 Sep 66	**Dunfermline**	H	6	3
21 Sep 66	Dunfermline	A	3	1
		Agg	9	4

Semi-Final

17 Oct 66	Airdrieonians	N	2	0

Final

29 Oct 66	Rangers	N	1	0

	Pld	W	D	L	F	A	Pts
Celtic	6	6	0	0	23	3	12
Hearts	6	3	1	2	10	10	7
Clyde	6	2	0	4	7	16	4
St Mirren	6	0	1	5	3	14	1

League Cup record

	Pld	W	D	L	F	A
Home	4	4	0	0	23	5
Away	4	4	0	0	9	2
Neutral	2	2	0	0	3	0
	10	10	0	0	35	7

Cup Final Line-up

R Simpson
T Gemmell
W O'Neill
B Murdoch
B McNeill
J Clark
J Johnstone
B Lennox
J McBride
B Auld
J Hughes (S Chalmers)

Scorer Lennox (19)

Attendance 94,532

Scottish Cup

Round 1

28 Jan 67	**Arbroath**	H	4	0

Round 2

18 Feb 67	**Elgin City**	H	7	0

Quarter-Final

11 Mar 67	**Queen's Park**	H	5	3

Semi-Final

1 Apr 67	Clyde	N	0	0
5 Apr 67	Replay	N	2	0

Final

29 Apr 67	Aberdeen	N	2	0

Scottish Cup record

	Pld	W	D	L	F	A
Home	3	3	0	0	16	3
Away	0	0	0	0	0	0
Neutral	3	2	1	0	4	0
	6	5	1	0	20	3

Cup Final Line-up

R Simpson
J Craig
T Gemmell
B Murdoch
B McNeill
J Clark
J Johnstone
W Wallace
S Chalmers
B Auld
B Lennox

Scorer Wallace (42,49)

Attendance 126,102

European Cup

Round 1

28 Sep 66	**FC Zurich**	H	2	0
5 Oct 66	FC Zurich	A	3	0
		Agg	5	0

Round 2

30 Nov 66	Nantes	A	3	1
7 Dec	**Nantes**	H	3	1
		Agg	6	2

Quarter-Final

1 Mar 67	Vojvodina	A	0	1
8 Mar 67	**Vojvodina**	H	2	0

Semi-Final

12 Apr 67	**Dukla Prague**	H	3	1
25 Apr 67	Dukla Prague	A	0	0

Final

25 May 67	Inter Milan	N	2	1

European record

	Pld	W	D	L	F	A
Home	4	4	0	0	10	2
Away	4	2	1	1	6	2
Neutral	1	1	0	0	2	1
	9	7	1	1	18	4

Cup Final Line-up

R Simpson
J Craig
T Gemmell
B Murdoch
B McNeill
J Clark
J Johnstone
W Wallace
S Chalmers
B Auld
B Lennox

Scorers

Mazzolla (7pen) Inter
T Gemmell (63)
S Chalmers (85)

Attendance   55,000

Season Total

	Pld	W	D	L	F	A
Home	28	25	2	1	110	27
Away	25	18	5	2	65	20
Neutral	6	5	1	0	9	1
	59	48	8	3	184	48

APPEARANCES

	Lge	LC	SC	Eur	Total
John Clark	34	10	6	9	59
Tommy Gemmell	34	10	6	9	59
Billy McNeill	33	10	6	9	58
Ronnie Simpson	33	10	6	9	58
Bobby Murdoch	31	10	4	9	54
Steve Chalmers	29	10	6	9	55
Jimmy Johnstone	26	10	5	9	50
Bertie Auld	27	9	5	8	49
Bobby Lennox	27	7	5	7	46
John Hughes	19	4	4	5	32
Willie O'Neill	18	10	0	4	32
Willie Wallace	21	0	6	3	30
Jim Craig	17	1	4	5	27
Joe McBride	14	10	0	2	26
Charlie Gallagher	11	1	3	2	17
David Cattenach	0	0	2	0	2
John Cushley	1	0	0	0	1
John Fallon	1	0	0	0	1
Ian Young	1	0	0	0	1
Jim Brogan	1	0	0	0	1

GOALSCORERS

	Lge	LC	SC	Eur	Total
Steve Chalmers	23	5	3	5	36
Joe McBride	18	15	0	2	35
Bobby Lennox	13	5	5	2	25
Willie Wallace	14	0	5	2	21
Tommy Gemmell	9	1	2	4	16
Jimmy Johnstone	13	1	0	2	16
Bertie Auld	7	2	0	3	12
John Hughes	6	1	1	0	8
Bobby Murdoch	4	2	2	0	8
Billy McNeill	0	2	0	1	3
Charlie Gallagher	2	0	0	0	2
Own Goals	2	0	0	0	2

Gross attendance for 58 games *	2,101,162
Ave att	36,227
Ave home att	38,018
* no attendance given for League match away to Hearts	

1969–70

League

			F	A	
30 Aug 69	St Johnstone	H	2	2	
3 Sep 69	Kilmarnock	A	4	2	
6 Sep 69	Dunfermline	A	1	2	
13 Sep 69	Hibernian	H	1	2	
20 Sep 69	Rangers	A	1	0	
27 Sep 69	Clyde	H	2	1	
4 Oct 69	Raith Rovers	H	7	1	
11 Oct 69	Airdrieonians	A	2	0	
29 Oct 69	Aberdeen	A	3	2	
1 Nov 69	Ayr United	A	4	2	
8 Nov 69	Hearts	H	0	2	
15 Nov 69	Motherwell	A	2	1	
29 Nov 69	Morton	A	3	0	
1 Dec 69	St Mirren	H	2	0	
6 Dec 69	Dundee	H	1	0	
13 Dec 69	St Johnstone	A	4	1	
17 Dec 69	Dundee United	H	7	2	
20 Dec 69	Kilmarnock	H	3	1	
27 Dec 69	Partick Thistle	H	8	1	
1 Jan 68	Clyde	A	2	0	
3 Jan 68	Rangers	H	0	0	
17 Jan 68	Hibernian	A	2	1	
31 Jan 68	Dunfermline	H	3	1	
16 Feb 68	Partick Thistle	A	5	1	
25 Feb 68	Raith Rovers	A	2	0	
28 Feb 68	Airdrieonians	H	4	1	
7 Mar 68	Dundee United	A	2	0	
10 Mar 68	Morton	H	4	0	
21 Mar 68	Ayr United	H	3	0	
25 Mar 68	Aberdeen	H	1	2	
28 Mar 68	Hearts	A	0	0	Title won
4 Apr 68	Motherwell	H	6	1	
6 Apr 68	Dundee	A	2	1	
18 Apr 68	St Mirren	A	3	2	

	Pld	W	D	L	F	A	Pts
Celtic	34	27	3	4	96	33	57
Rangers	34	19	7	8	67	40	45
Hibernian	34	19	6	9	65	40	44
Hearts	34	13	12	9	50	36	38
Dundee United	34	16	6	12	62	64	38
Dundee	34	15	6	13	49	44	36
Kilmarnock	34	13	10	11	62	57	36
Aberdeen	34	14	7	13	55	45	35
Morton	34	13	9	12	52	52	35
Dunfermline	34	15	5	14	45	45	35
Motherwell	34	11	10	13	49	51	32
Airdrieonians	34	12	8	14	59	64	32
St Johnstone	34	11	9	14	50	62	31
Ayr United	34	12	6	16	37	52	30
St Mirren	34	8	9	17	39	54	25
Clyde	34	9	7	18	34	56	25
Raith Rovers	34	5	11	18	32	67	21
Partick Thistle	34	5	7	22	41	82	17

League record	Pld	W	D	L	F	A	Pts
Home	17	12	2	3	54	18	26
Away	17	15	1	1	42	15	31
	34	27	3	4	96	33	57

League Cup

Group Stage

			F	A	
9 Aug 69	Airdrieonians	H	6	1	
13 Aug 69	Rangers	A	1	2	
16 Aug 69	Raith Rovers	H	5	0	
20 Aug 69	Rangers	H	1	0	
23 Aug 69	Airdrieonians	A	3	0	
27 Aug 69	Raith Rovers	A	5	2	
Quarter-Final					
10 Sep 69	Aberdeen	A	0	0	
24 Sep 69	Aberdeen	H	2	1	
		agg	2	1	
Semi-Final					
8 Oct 69	Ayr United	N	3	3	
13 Oct 69	Replay	N	2	1	
Final					
25 Oct 69	St Johnstone	N	1	0	

	Pld	W	D	L	F	A	Pts
Celtic	6	5	0	1	21	5	10
Rangers	6	4	1	1	14	7	9
Raith Rovers	6	1	1	4	10	20	3
Airdrieonians	6	1	0	5	5	18	2

League Cup record						
	Pld	W	D	L	F	A
Home	4	4	0	0	14	2
Away	4	2	1	1	9	4
Neutral	3	2	1	0	6	4
	11	8	2	1	29	10

Cup Final Line-up
J Fallon
J Craig
D Hay
B Murdoch
B McNeill
J Brogan
T Callaghan
H Hood
J Hughes
S Chalmers (J Johnstone)
B Auld

Scorer   Auld (2)
Attendance   73,067

Scottish Cup

Round I

24 Jan 70	**Dunfermline**	H	2	I

Round 2

7 Feb 70	**Dundee United**	H	4	0

Quarter-Final

21 Feb 70	**Rangers**	H	3	I

Semi-Final

14 Mar 70	Dundee	N	2	I

Final

11 Apr 70	Aberdeen	N	I	3

Scottish Cup record	Pld	W	D	L	F	A
Home	3	3	0	0	9	2
Away	0	0	0	0	0	0
Neutral	2	1	0	1	3	4
	5	4	0	1	12	6

Cup Final Line-up
E Williams
D Hay
T Gemmell
B Murdoch
B McNeill
J Brogan
J Johnstone
G Connelly
W Wallace
B Lennox
J Hughes (B Auld)

Scorers   J Harper (27pen)   Aber

D McKay (82)   Aber
B Lennox (89)
D McKay (90)   Aber

Attendance   108,434

European Cup

Round I

17 Sep 69	FC Basle	A	0	0
I Oct 69	**FC Basle**	H	2	0
		Agg	2	0

Round 2

12 Nov 69	**Benfica**	H	3	0
26 Nov 69	Benfica	A	0	3
		Agg	3	3 Celtic won on toss of coin

Quarter-Final

4 Mar 70	**Fiorentina**	H	3	0
18 Mar 70	Fiorentina	A	0	I
		Agg	3	I

European record	Pld	W	D	L	F	A
Home	4	4	0	0	10	1
Away	4	1	1	2	1	4
Neutral	1	0	0	1	1	2
	9	5	1	3	12	7

Semi-Final

I Apr 70	Leeds United	A	I	0	
15 Apr 70	**Leeds United**	H	2	I	
		Agg	2	I	

Final

6 May 70	Feyenoord	N	I	2	aet

Cup Final Line-up
E Williams
D Hay
T Gemmell
B Murdoch
B McNeill
J Brogan
J Johnstone
B Lennox
W Wallace
B Auld
J Hughes (G Connelly)

Scorers	Gemmell (30)	
	Israel (32)	Fey
	Kindvall (116)	Fey

Attendance   53,187

Season total

	Pld	W	D	L	F	A
Home	28	23	2	3	87	23
Away	25	18	3	4	52	23
	59	44	6	9	149	56

APPEARANCES

	Lge	LC	SC	Eur	Total
Billy McNeill	31	11	5	9	56
Tommy Gemmell	29	10	5	9	53
Willie Wallace	30	10	5	8	53
Jim Brogan	28	7	5	7	47
Jimmy Johnstone	27	6	4	9	46
Davie Hay	27	6	5	7	45
Bobby Murdoch	26	6	5	7	44
Harry Hood	27	11	3	5	46
John Hughes	21	8	4	6	39
Bobby Lennox	20	8	4	7	39
John Fallon	16	10	0	4	30
Jim Craig	23	6	3	2	34
Evan Williams	16	0	5	5	26
Bertie Auld	18	5	2	7	32
John Clark	9	9	0	3	21
Tommy Callaghan	14	4	1	3	22
George Connelly	7	4	1	5	17
Lou Macari	15	0	2	0	17
Steve Chalmers	5	6	0	2	13
Kenny Dalglish	2	2	0	0	4
Ronnie Simpson	2	1	0	0	3
Vic Davidson	1	0	0	0	1
Jimmy Quinn	1	0	0	0	1
Dave Cattanach	1	0	0	0	1

GOALSCORERS

	Lge	LC	SC	Eur	Total
Willie Wallace	16	5	1	2	24
Bobby Lennox	14	2	3	0	19
John Hughes	10	4	3	1	18
Harry Hood	8	6	1	2	17
Tommy Gemmell	9	3	0	3	15
Jimmy Johnstone	10	0	1	0	11
Lou Macari	7	0	2	0	9
Bertie Auld	4	2	0	1	7
Billy McNeill	5	2	0	0	7
Bobby Murdoch	5	0	0	1	6
Steve Chalmers	2	3	0	0	5
Jim Brogan	1	1	0	0	2
Tommy Callaghan	2	0	0	0	2
George Connelly	0	1	0	1	2
Vic Davidson	1	0	0	0	1
David Hay	0	0	1	0	1
Own goals	2	0	0	1	3

Gross attendance for 59 games 2,439,669
Ave att   41,350
Ave home att   49,173

2002–03

League

3 Aug 02	**Dunfermline**	H	2	1
10 Aug 02	Aberdeen	A	4	0
17 Aug 02	**Dundee United**	H	5	0
24 Aug 02	Partick Thistle	A	1	0
1 Sep 02	**Livingston**	H	2	0
10 Sep 02	Motherwell	A	1	2
14 Sep 02	**Hibernian**	H	1	0
22 Sep 02	Dundee	A	1	0
28 Sep 02	**Kilmarnock**	H	5	0
6 Oct 02	**Rangers**	H	3	3
20 Oct 02	Hearts	A	4	1
27 Oct 02	Dunfermline	A	4	1
3 Nov 02	**Aberdeen**	H	7	0
10 Nov 02	Dundee United	A	2	0
17 Nov 02	**Partick Thistle**	H	4	0
24 Nov 02	Livingston	A	2	0
1 Dec 02	**Motherwell**	H	3	1
4 Dec 02	Hibernian	A	1	0
7 Dec 02	Rangers	A	2	3
15 Dec 02	Kilmarnock	A	1	1
21 Dec 02	**Dundee**	H	2	0
26 Dec 02	**Hearts**	H	4	2
29 Dec 02	**Dunfermline**	H	1	0
2 Jan 03	Aberdeen	A	1	1
29 Jan 03	**Dundee United**	H	2	0
2 Feb 03	Partick Thistle	A	2	0
9 Feb 03	**Livingston**	H	2	1
2 Mar 03	**Hibernian**	H	3	2
8 Mar 03	**Rangers**	H	1	0
6 Apr 03	Dundee	A	1	1
13 Apr 03	**Kilmarnock**	H	2	0
19 Apr 03	Hearts	A	1	2
27 Apr 03	Rangers	A	2	1
3 May 03	Dunfermline	A	4	1
7 May 03	Motherwell	A	4	0
10 May 03	**Hearts**	H	1	0
14 May 03	**Dundee**	H	6	2
25 May 03	Kilmarnock	A	4	0

	Pld	W	D	L	F	A	Pts
Rangers	38	31	4	3	101	28	97
Celtic	38	31	4	3	98	26	97
Hearts	38	18	9	11	57	51	63
Kilmarnock	38	16	9	13	47	56	57
Dunfermline	38	13	7	18	54	71	46
Dundee	38	10	14	14	50	60	44
Hibernian	38	15	6	17	56	64	51
Aberdeen	38	13	10	15	41	54	49
Livingston	38	9	8	21	48	62	35
Partick Thistle	38	8	11	19	37	58	35
Dundee United	38	7	11	20	35	68	32
Motherwell	38	7	7	24	45	71	28

League record

	Pld	W	D	L	F	A	Pts
Home	19	18	1	0	56	12	55
Away	19	13	3	3	42	14	42
	38	31	4	3	98	26	97

League Cup

Round 3

23 Oct 02	**Inverness C T**	H	4	2	
Quarter-Final					
6 Nov 02	**Partick Thistle**	H	1	1	5-4 on pens
Semi-Final					
6 Feb 03	Dundee United	N	3	0	
Final					
16 Mar 03	Rangers	N	1	2	

League Cup record

	Pld	W	D	L	F	A
Home	2	1	1	0	5	3
Away	0	0	0	0	0	0
Neutral	2	1	0	1	4	2
	4	2	1	1	9	5

Cup Final Line-up
R Douglas
J Valgaeren
J Mjallby (S Petrov)
B Balde
A Thompson
N Lennon
P Lambert
C Sutton (S Maloney)
J Smith (M Sylla)
H Larsson
J Hartson

Scorers	C Caniggia (23) Ran
	P Lovenkrands (35) Ran
	H Larsson (57)

Attendance 52,000

Scottish Cup

Round 3						Scottish Cup record					
25 Jan 03	**St Mirren**	H	3	0			Pld	W	D	L	F	A
Round 4						Home	2	2	0	0	6	0
23 Feb 03	**St Johnstone**	H	3	0		Away	1	0	0	1	0	1
Quarter-Final						Neutral	0	0	0	0	0	0
23 Mar 03	Inverness C T	A	0	1			3	2	0	1	6	1

Champions League Qualifier

Round 3				
14 Aug 02	**FC Basle**	H	3	1
28 Aug 02	FC Basle	A	0	2
		Agg	3	3	lost on away goals rule

UEFA Cup

Round 1						European record					
19 Sep 02	**FK Suduva**	H	8	1			Pld	W	D	L	F	A
3 Oct 02	FK Suduva	A	2	0		Home	7	5	2	0	18	5
		Agg	10	1		Away	7	4	0	3	10	7
Round 2						Neutral	1	0	0	1	2	3
31 Oct 02	**Blackburn R**	H	1	0			15	9	2	4	30	15
14 Nov 02	Blackburn R	A	2	0	
		Agg	3	0	
Round 3					
28 Nov 02	**Celta Vigo**	H	1	0	
12 Dec 02	Celta Vigo	A	1	2	
		Agg	2	2		won on away goals rule
Round 4					
20 Feb 03	**VfB Stuttgart**	H	3	1	
27 Feb 03	VfB Stuttgart	A	2	3	
		Agg	5	4	
Quarter-Final					
13 Mar 03	**Liverpool**	H	1	1	
20 Mar 03	Liverpool	A	2	0	
		Agg	3	1	
Semi-Final					
10 Apr 03	**Boavista**	H	1	1	
24 Apr 03	Boavista	A	1	0	
		Agg	2	1	
Final					
21 May 03	Porto	N	2	3		aet

Cup Final Line-up
R Douglas
J Valgaeren (U Laursen)
B Balde
J Mjallby
A Thompson
P Lambert (J McNamara)
N Lennon
S Petrov (S Maloney)
D Agathe
H Larsson
C Sutton

Scorers	Derlei (45,115) Porto
	Larsson (47,57)
	Alenichev (54) Porto

Attendance   52,972

Season total

	Pld	W	D	L	F	A
Home	30	26	4	0	85	20
Away	27	17	3	7	52	22
Neutral	3	1	0	2	6	5
	60	44	7	9	143	47

APPEARANCES

	Lge	LC	SC	Eur	Total
Bobo Balde	36	3	0	14	53
Joos Valgaeren	35	2	2	14	53
Henrik Larsson	35	2	2	12	51
Stilian Petrov	34	2	0	14	50
Neil Lennon	28	3	1	14	46
Chris Sutton	28	2	1	12	43
Paul Lambert	31	3	1	13	48
Alan Thompson	29	3	1	12	45
Robert Douglas	21	3	0	14	38
Didier Agathe	27	2	0	11	40
Ulrik Laursen	22	2	3	9	36
John Hartson	27	4	2	12	45
Johan Mjallby	14	1	2	7	24
Momo Sylla	18	3	2	8	31
Steve Guppy	17	0	2	6	25
Jackie McNamara	19	0	2	7	28
Jamie Smith	13	4	3	5	25
Shaun Maloney	20	3	3	4	30
Magnus Hedman	8	1	1	0	10
Javier Sanchez Broto	8	0	2	0	10
David Fernandez	10	3	3	3	19
Stephen Crainey	12	2	2	2	18
Bobby Petta	2	1	0	2	5
Colin Healy	1	1	2	1	5
Jonathan Gould	2	1	0	1	4
Tom Boyd	0	2	0	0	2
Stanislav Varga	1	0	1	0	2
John Kennedy	0	1	0	1	2
Liam Miller	0	1	0	1	2
Simon Lynch	0	0	0	1	1
David Marshall	0	0	1	0	1
Ross Wallace	0	1	0	0	1

GOALSCORERS

	Lge	LC	SC	Eur	Total
Henrik Larsson	28	2	2	12	44
John Hartson	18	2	3	2	25
Chris Sutton	14	0	0	4	18
Stilian Petrov	12	0	0	2	14
Alan Thompson	8	1	0	3	12
Paul Lambert	3	1	0	2	6
Shaun Maloney	3	1	0	1	5
Bobo Balde	2	2	0	0	4
Momo Sylla	2	0	1	1	4
Joos Valgaeren	2	0	0	1	3
Johan Mjallby	3	0	0	0	3
Jackie McNamara	1	0	0	0	1
Jamie Smith	0	0	1	0	1
David Fernandez	0	0	0	1	1
Own Goals	2	0	0	0	2

Gross attendance for 60 games 2,213,488
Ave att   36,891
Ave home att   53,218

1968–69

League

7 Sep 68	Clyde	A	3	0
14 Sep 68	**Rangers**	H	2	4
21 Sep 68	Dunfermline	A	1	1
28 Sep 68	**Aberdeen**	H	2	1
5 Oct 68	**Dundee United**	H	2	0
12 Oct 68	Hearts	A	1	0
19 Oct 68	**St Johnstone**	H	2	1
26 Oct 68	Morton	A	1	1
2 Nov 68	**Dundee**	H	3	1
9 Nov 68	Arbroath	A	5	0
16 Nov 68	**Raith Rovers**	H	2	0
23 Nov 68	Partick Thistle	A	4	0
30 Nov 68	**Hibernian**	A	5	2
7 Dec 68	**St Mirren**	H	5	0
14 Dec 68	Falkirk	A	0	0
21 Dec 68	**Kilmarnock**	H	1	1
28 Dec 68	Airdrieonians	A	0	0
1 Jan 69	**Clyde**	H	5	0
2 Jan 69	Rangers	A	0	1
4 Jan 69	**Dunfermline**	H	3	1
11 Jan 69	Aberdeen	A	3	1
18 Jan 69	Dundee United	A	3	1
1 Feb 69	**Hearts**	H	5	0
5 Mar 69	**Arbroath**	H	7	1
8 Mar 69	Raith Rovers	A	3	1
15 Mar 69	**Partick Thistle**	H	1	0
24 Mar 69	**Hibernian**	H	1	1
29 Mar 69	St Mirren	A	3	0
1 Apr 69	St Johnstone	A	3	2
9 Apr 69	**Falkirk**	H	5	2
19 Apr 69	**Airdrieonians**	H	2	2
21 Apr 69	Kilmarnock	A	2	2 Title won
28 Apr 69	**Morton**	H	2	4
30 Apr 69	Dundee	A	2	1

	Pld	W	D	L	F	A	Pts
Celtic	34	23	8	3	89	32	54
Rangers	34	21	7	6	81	32	49
Dunfermline	34	19	7	8	63	45	45
Kilmarnock	34	15	14	5	50	32	44
Dundee United	34	17	9	8	61	49	43
St Johnstone	34	16	5	13	66	59	37
Airdrieonians	34	13	11	10	46	44	37
Hearts	34	14	8	12	52	54	36
Dundee	34	10	12	12	47	48	32
Morton	34	12	8	14	58	68	32
St Mirren	34	11	10	13	40	54	32
Hibernian	34	12	7	15	60	59	31
Clyde	34	9	13	12	35	50	31
Partick Thistle	34	9	10	15	39	53	28
Aberdeen	34	9	8	17	50	59	26
Raith Rovers	34	8	5	21	45	67	21
Falkirk	34	5	8	21	33	69	18
Arbroath	34	5	6	23	41	82	16

League record	Pld	W	D	L	F	A	Pts
Home	17	12	3	2	50	19	27
Away	17	11	5	1	39	13	27
	34	23	8	3	89	32	54

League Cup

Group Stage

10 Aug 68	Rangers	A	2	0
14 Aug 68	**Morton**	H	4	1
17 Aug 68	**Partick Thistle**	H	4	0
24 Aug 68	**Rangers**	H	1	0
28 Aug 68	Morton	A	3	0
31 Aug 68	Partick Thistle	A	6	1

Quarter-Final

11 Sep 68	**Hamilton A**	H	10	0
25 Sep 68	Hamilton A	A	4	2
		Agg	14	2

Semi-Final

9 Oct 68	Clyde	N	1	0

Final

5 Apr 69	Hibernian	N	6	2

	Pld	W	D	L	F	A	Pts
Celtic	6	6	0	0	20	2	12
Rangers	6	4	0	2	14	5	8
Partick Thistle	6	2	0	4	8	18	4
Morton	6	0	0	6	2	19	0

League Cup record	Pld	W	D	L	F	A
Home	4	4	0	0	19	1
Away	4	4	0	0	15	3
Neutral	2	2	0	0	7	2
	10	10	0	0	41	6

Cup Final Line-up
J Fallon
J Craig
T Gemmell (J Clark)
B Murdoch
B McNeill
J Brogan
J Johnstone
W Wallace
S Chalmers
B Auld
B Lennox

Scorers   Wallace (23)
                 Auld (30)
                 Lennox (45,58,73)
                 Craig (75)
                 O'Rourke (82) Hibs
                 Stevenson (87) Hibs

Attendance   74,000

Scottish Cup

Round 1				
25 Jan 69	Partick Thistle	A	3	3
29 Jan 69	**Replay**	H	8	1
Round 2				
12 Feb 69	Clyde	A	0	0
24 Feb 69	**Replay**	H	3	0
Quarter-Final				
1 Mar 69	**St Johnstone**	H	3	2
Semi-Final				
22 Mar 69	Morton	N	4	1
Final				
26 Apr 69	Rangers	N	4	0

Scottish Cup record

	Pld	W	D	L	F	A
Home	3	3	0	0	14	3
Away	2	0	2	0	3	3
Neutral	2	2	0	0	8	1
	7	5	2	0	25	7

Cup Final Line-up
J Fallon
J Craig
T Gemmell
B Murdoch
B McNeill
J Brogan (J Clark)
G Connelly
S Chalmers
W Wallace
B Auld
B Lennox

Scorers   McNeill (2)
                 Lennox (44)
                 Connelly (45)
                 Chalmers (76)

Attendance   132,870

European Cup

Round 1

18 Sep 68	St Etienne	A	0	2
2 Oct 68	**St Etienne**	H	4	0
		Agg	4	2

Round 2

13 Nov 68	**Red Star Belgrade**	H	5	1
27 Nov 68	Red Star Belgrade	A	1	1
		Agg	6	2

Quarter-Final

19 Feb 69	AC Milan	A	0	0
12 Mar 69	**AC Milan**	H	0	1
		Agg	0	1

European record	Pld	W	D	L	F	A
Home	3	2	0	1	9	2
Away	3	0	2	1	1	3
	6	2	2	2	10	5

Season Total

	Pld	W	D	L	F	A
Home	27	21	3	3	92	25
Away	26	15	9	2	58	22
Neutral	4	4	0	0	15	3
	57	40	12	5	165	50

APPEARANCES

	Lge	LC	SC	Eur	Total
Billy McNeill	34	9	7	6	56
Tommy Gemmell	31	8	7	5	51
Jim Brogan	30	9	5	6	50
Bobby Murdoch	30	8	7	5	50
Willie Wallace	31	8	7	6	52
Jim Craig	32	5	6	6	49
Jimmy Johnstone	31	8	6	5	50
Bobby Lennox	28	9	6	4	47
John Hughes	27	8	5	6	46
John Fallon	22	3	4	4	33
Steve Chalmers	21	3	6	4	34
Ronnie Simpson	12	6	3	2	23
John Clark	10	4	2	4	20
George Connelly	7	8	1	2	18
Tommy Callaghan	15	0	5	0	20
Bertie Auld	13	2	3	2	20
Willie O'Neill	4	6	1	1	12
Harry Hood	7	0	0	0	7
Joe McBride	7	0	0	0	7
Lou Macari	1	3	0	0	4
David Hay	0	1	1	0	2
Pat McMahon	1	1	0	0	2
David Cattenach	1	0	0	0	1
Charlie Gallagher	1	0	0	0	1
John Gorman	0	1	0	0	1
Jimmy Quinn	0	1	0	0	1
Bobby Wraith	0	1	0	0	1
Kenny Dalglish	0	1	0	0	1

GOALSCORERS

	Lge	LC	SC	Eur	Total
Willie Wallace	18	10	4	2	34
Bobby Lennox	12	14	3	1	30
Steve Chalmers	11	5	4	1	21
John Hughes	10	2	4	0	16
Tommy Gemmell	8	1	0	1	10
Jimmy Johnstone	5	0	2	2	9
Bobby Murdoch	4	1	2	1	8
Billy McNeill	3	0	3	0	6
Tommy Callaghan	3	0	2	0	5
Harry Hood	5	0	0	0	5
Joe McBride	1	2	0	1	4
George Connelly	1	1	1	0	3
Jim Craig	1	1	0	1	3
Bertie Auld	1	1	0	0	2
Jim Brogan	2	0	0	0	2
Pat McMahon	1	1	0	0	2
John Clark	0	1	0	0	1
Lou Macari	1	0	0	0	1
Own goals	2	1	0	0	3

Gross attendance for 55 matches*   2,211,952
Ave att   40,217
Ave home att   42,944

* no attendance given for League matches away to Arbroath and Dundee

2000–01

League

			F	A	
30 Jul 00	Dundee United	A	2	1	
5 Aug 00	**Motherwell**	H	1	0	
13 Aug 00	**Kilmarnock**	H	2	1	
19 Aug 00	Hearts	A	4	2	
27 Aug 00	**Rangers**	H	6	2	
9 Sep 00	**Hibernian**	H	3	0	
18 Sep 00	Dunfermline	A	2	1	
23 Sep 00	**Dundee**	H	1	0	
1 Oct 00	Aberdeen	A	1	1	
14 Oct 00	**St Mirren**	H	2	0	
17 Oct 00	St Johnstone	A	2	0	
21 Oct 00	**Dundee United**	H	2	1	
29 Oct 00	Motherwell	A	3	3	
5 Nov 00	Kilmarnock	A	1	0	
12 Nov 00	**St Johnstone**	H	4	1	
18 Nov 00	**Hearts**	H	6	1	
26 Nov 00	Rangers	A	1	5	
29 Nov 00	Hibernian	A	0	0	
2 Dec 00	**Dunfermline**	H	3	1	
10 Dec 00	Dundee	A	2	1	
16 Dec 00	**Aberdeen**	H	6	0	
23 Dec 00	St Mirren	A	2	0	
26 Dec 00	Dundee United	A	4	0	
2 Jan 01	**Kilmarnock**	H	6	0	
4 Feb 01	Hearts	A	3	0	
11 Feb 01	**Rangers**	H	1	0	
21 Feb 01	**Motherwell**	H	1	0	
25 Feb 01	**Hibernian**	H	1	1	
4 Mar 01	Dunfermline	A	3	0	
14 Mar 01	St Johnstone	A	2	1	
1 Apr 01	Aberdeen	A	1	0	
4 Apr 01	**Dundee**	H	2	1	
7 Apr 01	**St Mirren**	H	1	0	Title won
22 Apr 01	**Hearts**	H	1	0	
29 Apr 01	Rangers	A	3	0	
6 May 01	Hibernian	A	5	2	
13 May 01	**Dundee**	H	0	2	
20 May 01	Kilmarnock	A	0	1	

	Pld	W	D	L	F	A	Pts
Celtic	**38**	**31**	**4**	**3**	**90**	**29**	**97**
Rangers	38	26	4	8	76	36	82
Hibernian	38	18	12	8	57	35	66
Kilmarnock	38	15	9	14	44	53	54
Hearts	38	14	10	14	56	50	52
Dundee	38	13	8	17	51	49	47
Aberdeen	38	11	12	15	45	52	45
Motherwell	38	12	7	19	42	56	43
Dunfermline	38	11	9	18	34	54	42
St Johnstone	38	9	13	16	40	56	40
Dundee United	38	9	8	21	38	63	35
St Mirren	38	8	6	24	32	72	30

League record

	Pld	W	D	L	F	A	Pts
Home	19	17	1	1	49	11	52
Away	19	14	3	2	41	18	45
	38	31	4	3	90	29	97

League Cup

			F	A	
Round 2					
5 Sep 00	**Raith Rovers**	H	4	0	
Quarter-Final					
1 Nov 00	Hearts	A	5	2	aet
Semi-Final					
7 Feb 01	Rangers	N	3	1	
Final					
18 Mar 01	Kilmarnock	N	3	0	

League Cup record

	Pld	W	D	L	F	A
Home	1	1	0	0	4	0
Away	1	1	0	0	5	2
Neutral	2	2	0	0	6	1
	4	4	0	0	15	3

Cup Final Line-up
J Gould
J Mjallby
J Valgaeren
R Vega
L Moravcik (J Smith)
P Lambert
N Lennon
C Healy
B Petta (S Crainey, T Boyd)
C Sutton
H Larsson

Scorer   Larsson (47,74,80)
Attendance   48,830

Scottish Cup

Round 3					
28 Jan 01	Stranraer	A	4	1	
Round 4					
17 Feb 01	Dunfermline	A	2	2	
7 Mar 01	**Replay**	H	4	1	
Quarter-Final					
11 Mar 01	**Hearts**	H	1	0	
Semi-Final					
15 Apr 01	Dundee United	N	3	1	
Final					
26 May 01	Hibernian	N	3	0	

Scottish Cup record	Pld	W	D	L	F	A
Home	2	2	0	0	5	1
Away	2	1	1	0	6	3
Neutral	2	2	0	0	6	1
	6	5	1	0	17	5

Cup Final Line-up
R Douglas
J Valgaeren
J Mjallby
R Vega
L Moravcik (J McNamara)
D Agathe
N Lennon
P Lambert (T Boyd)
A Thompson (T Johnson)
C Sutton
H Larsson

Scorers   McNamara (38)
                Larsson (48,80pen)

Attendance   51,284

UEFA Cup

Qualifier					
10 Aug 00	Jeunesse D'Esch	A	4	0	
24 Aug 00	**Jeunesse D'Esch**	H	7	0	
		Agg	11	0	
Round 1					
14 Sep 00	**HJK Helsinki**	H	2	0	
28 Sep 00	HJK Helsinki	A	1	2	aet
		Agg	3	2	
Round 2					
26 Oct 00	Bordeaux	A	1	1	
9 Nov 00	**Bordeaux**	H	1	2	aet
		Agg	2	3	

European record	Pld	W	D	L	F	A
Home	3	2	0	1	10	2
Away	3	1	1	1	6	3
	6	3	1	2	16	5

Season total

	Pld	W	D	L	F	A
Home	25	22	1	2	68	14
Away	25	17	5	3	58	26
Neutral	4	4	0	0	12	2
	54	43	6	5	138	42

APPEARANCES

	Lge	LC	SC	Eur	Total
Henrik Larsson	37	2	6	5	50
Joos Valgaeren	35	3	6	5	49
Johan Mjallby	35	2	5	6	48
Paul Lambert	27	2	6	5	40
Alan Thompson	30	3	6	0	39
Chris Sutton	24	3	4	4	35
Didier Agathe	27	0	6	2	35
Stilian Petrov	28	2	3	5	38
Tom Boyd	30	4	5	5	44
Bobby Petta	20	4	2	5	31
Jackie McNamara	30	3	4	5	42
Rab Douglas	22	0	6	0	28
Lubo Moravcik	27	3	5	5	40
Ramon Vega	18	2	6	0	26
Neil Lennon	17	2	6	0	25
Jonathan Gould	15	3	0	6	24
Tommy Johnson	16	3	4	2	25
Stephane Mahe	10	1	0	2	13
Colin Healy	12	3	0	6	21
Alan Stubbs	10	1	0	0	11
Eyal Berkovic	4	1	0	4	9
Jamie Smith	7	2	0	0	9
Olivier Tebily	4	1	1	1	7
Vidar Riseth	1	1	0	3	5
Mark Burchill	2	1	0	1	4
Stephen Crainey	2	2	1	0	5
Shaun Maloney	4	0	0	0	4
Rafael Scheidt	0	1	0	2	3
Mark Fotheringham	1	0	0	1	2
Dmitri Kharine	1	0	0	1	2
Stewart Kerr	0	1	0	0	1
Simon Lynch	0	0	0	1	1
Liam Miller	0	0	0	1	1

GOALSCORERS

	Lge	LC	SC	Eur	Total
Henrik Larsson	35	5	9	4	53
Chris Sutton	11	1	1	1	14
Lubo Moravcik	9	1	1	3	14
Stilian Petrov	7	0	0	1	8
Jackie McNamara	3	1	3	0	7
Tommy Johnson	5	2	0	0	7
Joos Valgaeren	3	0	1	0	4
Johan Mjallby	4	0	0	0	4
Alan Thompson	3	1	0	0	4
Ramon Vega	2	0	2	0	4
Mark Burchill	1	0	0	3	4
Didier Agathe	3	0	0	0	3
Eyal Berkovic	0	0	0	2	2
Jamie Smith	1	1	0	0	2
Paul Lambert	1	0	0	0	1
Bobby Petta	0	0	0	1	1
Alan Stubbs	1	0	0	0	1
Neil Lennon	1	0	0	0	1
Colin Healy	0	1	0	0	1
Vidar Riseth	0	0	0	1	1
Stephen Crainey	0	1	0	0	1
Own Goals	0	1	0	0	1

Gross attendance for 54 matches	1,912,450
Ave att	35,416
Ave home att	54,313

50 MATCHES IN A SEASON

Season	Player	Matches
1956–57	Mike Haughney	51*
	John Jack	50
1963–64	Steve Chalmers	52*
1964–65	Ian Young	53
	Bobby Murdoch	51
	Tommy Gemmell	50
1965–66	John Clark	60*
	Tommy Gemmell	60*
	Bobby Murdoch	57
	Jimmy Johnstone	54
	Joe McBride	51
1966–67	John Clark	59*
	Tommy Gemmell	59*
	Billy McNeill	58
	Ronnie Simpson	58
	Bobby Murdoch	54
	Steve Chalmers	53+2
	Jimmy Johnstone	49+1
1967–68	Billy McNeill	50*
1968–69	Billy McNeill	56
	Tommy Gemmell	51
	Jim Brogan	50
	Bobby Murdoch	50
	Willie Wallace	49+3
	Jimmy Johnstone	48+2
1969–70	Billy McNeill	56
	Tommy Gemmell	53
	Willie Wallace	51+2
1970–71	Billy McNeill	54
	Evan Williams	53
	Davie Hay	51+1
	Jimmy Johnstone	51
	Harry Hood	48+4
1971–72	George Connelly	55
	Billy McNeill	55
	Tommy Callaghan	50+2
	Kenny Dalglish	49+1
1972–73	George Connelly	55
	Kenny Dalglish	53
	Danny McGrain	51
	Billy McNeill	51
	Dixie Deans	49+2
1973–74	Steve Murray	57
	Jim Brogan	56
	Kenny Dalglish	54+2
	Billy McNeill	53
	Danny McGrain	50+1
	Harry Hood	48+7

Season	Player	Matches
1974–75	Paul Wilson	48+2
1975–76	Johannes Edvaldsson	52
	Peter Latchford	52
	Kenny Dalglish	51
	Danny McGrain	51
	Andy Lynch	50
	Pat McCluskey	50
1976–77	Danny McGrain	55*
	Kenny Dalglish	53
	Ronnie Glavin	52
	Johnny Doyle	50+1
1977–78	Peter Latchford	51*
	Roddie MacDonald	51*
1979–80	Peter Latchford	54*
	Murdo MacLeod	54*
	Roy Aitken	52
	Danny McGrain	52
	Davie Provan	52
	Tom McAdam	51
1980–81	Pat Bonner	52
	Tom McAdam	52
	Roy Aitken	50
1982–83	Pat Bonner	54
	Murdo MacLeod	54
	Paul McStay	53
	Roy Aitken	51
	Danny McGrain	51
	Davie Provan	51
	Charlie Nicholas	50+2
	Tom McAdam	50
	Frank McGarvey	48+4
1983–84	Pat Bonner	55
	Murdo MacLeod	55
	Danny McGrain	54
	Tommy Burns	53+1
	Paul McStay	53
	Roy Aitken	51
	Frank McGarvey	48+3
	Brian McClair	44+11
1986–87	Brian McClair	56+1
	Pat Bonner	56
	Paul McStay	56
	Roy Aitken	55
	Derek Whyte	54
	Maurice Johnston	52+1
	Murdo MacLeod	50+1
1987–88	Chris Morris	55*
	Roy Aitken	54
	Paul McStay	54
	Andy Walker	51
	Derek Whyte	50

50 MATCHES IN A SEASON (cont.)

Season	Player	Matches
1991–92	Derek Whyte	49+2
1992–93	John Collins	54
	Tom Boyd	53
	Paul McStay	53
2000–01	Henrik Larsson	50
2001–02	Robert Douglas	51
	Johan Mjallby	51
2002–03	Bobo Balde	53
	Joos Valgaeren	53
	Henrik Larsson	51
	Stilian Petrov	47+3
2003–04	Henrik Larsson	57+1
	Stanislav Varga	55
	Stilian Petrov	52+3
	Neil Lennon	52+1
	Bobo Balde	49+1
2006–07	Artur Boruc	51
	Shunsuke Nakamura	49+1
2007–08	Stephen McManus	53
	Gary Caldwell	50+1
	Scott McDonald	49+3

* started every first-team match

THE 300 APPEARANCES CLUB

	Player	Games	Total	League	LC	SC	Europe
1	Billy McNeill	790	790	486	138	94	72
2	Paul McStay	677	671+6	509+6	54	66	42
3	Roy Aitken	672	670+2	483	82+2	55	50
4	Danny McGrain	663	653+10	443+8	105+1	60	55+1
5	Pat Bonner	641	641	483	64	55	39
6	Alec McNair	604	604	548	0	56	0
7	Bobby Lennox	589	508+81	297+50	107+14	46+4	58+13
8	Bobby Evans	535	535	384	87	64	0
9	Jimmy McMenemy	515	515	456	0	59	0
	Jimmy Johnstone	515	498+17	298+10	87+5	47+1	66+1
11	Tommy Burns	508	467+41	325+32	70+1	38+5	34+3
12	Bobby Murdoch	484	480+4	287+4	84	52	57
13	Peter Grant	478	444+34	338+26	40+3	34+4	32+1
14	Jimmy McStay	472	472	409	0	63	0
15	Patsy Gallacher	464	464	432	0	32	0
16	Bertie Peacock	453	453	318	79	56	0
17	Alec Thomson	451	451	392	0	59	0
18	Willie McStay	446	446	399	0	47	0
19	Jimmy McGrory	445	445	378	0	67	0
20	Jim Young	443	443	392	0	51	0
21	Andy McAtee	439	439	407	0	32	0
22	Charlie Shaw	436	436	420	0	16	0
23	Tommy Gemmell	418	418	247	74	43	54
24	Adam McLean	408	408	367	0	41	0
25	Tom Boyd	407	391+16	296+10	31+2	31+3	33+1
26	Steve Chalmers	405	391+14	253+9	57+2	44+2	37+1
27	Peter Wilson	395	395	344	0	51	0
	Murdo MacLeod	395	386+9	274+7	44	36+2	32
29	John Hughes	383	377+6	233+3	62+1	42+1	40+1
30	Joe Dodds	378	378	351	0	27	0
31	Tom McAdam	365	354+11	251+7	45+1	30+2	28+1
32	Jackie McNamara	349	307+42	221+26	17+2	26+5	43+9
33	Jim Brogan	341	332+9	208+5	55+2	37+1	32+1
34	Jimmy Quinn	331	331	273	0	58	0
35	Peter McGonagle	325	325	286	0	39	0
36	Bobby Hogg	322	322	278	10	34	0
37	Bobby Collins	320	320	220	62	38	0
	Kenny Dalglish	320	313+7	200+4	56+3	30	27
39	Charlie Geatons	319	319	286	0	33	0
	Charlie Tully	319	319	216	68	35	0
41	Willie Fernie	317	317	219	59	39	0
42	Henrik Larsson	315	312+3	218+3	11	25	58
43	Stilian Petrov	311	288+23	215+13	9+5	15+3	49+2
44	Harry Hood	310	263+47	161+28	53+9	25+4	24+6
45	Willie Loney	305	305	254	0	41	0
46	John McFarlane	304	304	268	0	36	0
	Neil Lennon	304	300+4	212+2	10+1	26	52+1
48	Davie Provan	303	287+16	192+14	41+1	29	25+1

EVER-PRESENTS

Players who have appeared in every first-team game in a season. Players in bold have appeared in every League game, but not every first-team game.

1890–91	Peter Dowds
1891–92	John Campbell, Dan Doyle, Jerry Reynolds
1893–94	Jimmy Blessington, Joe Cassidy, Joe Cullen, Jerry Reynolds
1897–98	John Campbell, Davie Russell
1899–00	John Bell
1900–01	John Campbell, Sandy McMahon
1902–03	Andrew McPherson
1904–05	Davie Adams, James Hay, Willie Loney
1905–06	Davie Adams, James Hay
1907–08	Davie Adams
1909–10	**Jim Young**
1910–11	Davie Adams, Alec McNair
1911–12	Jim Young
1912–13	Joe Dodds
1913–14	Charlie Shaw
1914–15	John Browning, Andy McAtee, Charlie Shaw, Jim Young
1915–16	John Browning, Joe Dodds, Charlie Shaw
1916–17	Joe Dodds, Charlie Shaw
1917–18	Charlie Shaw
1920–21	Charlie Shaw
1923–24	Charlie Shaw
1924–25	Paddy Connolly, Alec Thomson
1925–26	Jimmy McStay, Peter Wilson
1926–27	Paddy Connolly
1927–28	Paddy Connolly, Jimmy McStay, John Thomson, Peter Wilson
1928–29	Peter McGonagle, Jimmy McStay
1933–34	Bobby Hogg
1934–35	Joe Kennaway
1935–36	Willie Buchan, John Crum, Bobby Hogg, Willie Lyon
1937–38	Bobby Hogg, **John Crum**
1938–39	Bobby Hogg
1948–49	**Charlie Tully**
1950–51	Bertie Peacock
1951–52	Joe Baillie, Sean Fallon, **Bobby Collins**
1952–53	Bobby Evans
1953–54	Bertie Peacock
1954–55	Bobby Evans, Mike Haughney
1956–57	Mike Haughney
1961–62	John Divers
1963–64	Steve Chalmers
1965–66	John Clark, Tommy Gemmell
1966–67	John Clark, Tommy Gemmell
1967–68	Billy McNeill, **Tommy Gemmell, Bobby Murdoch**
1968–69	**Billy McNeill**
1971–72	**Billy McNeill**
1976–77	Danny McGrain, **Pat Stanton**
1977–78	Johannes Edvaldsson, Peter Latchford, Roddie MacDonald
1978–79	**Roy Aitken**
1979–80	Peter Latchford, Murdo MacLeod
1980–81	**Pat Bonner**
1981–82	Pat Bonner, Murdo MacLeod, **Mark Reid**
1982–83	Pat Bonner, **Paul McStay**
1985–86	Roy Aitken
1986–87	Brian McClair
1987–88	Chris Morris, **Paul McStay**
1989–90	Pat Bonner
1990–91	Pat Bonner
1995–96	Gordon Marshall
2004–05	Neil Lennon, **John Hartson**

CLEAN SHEETS

	Player (years at club)	Clean Sheets	Games
1	Pat Bonner (1978–1994)	254	641
2	Charlie Shaw (1913–1925)	237	436
3	Davie Adams (1902–1912)	126	291
4	Ronnie Simpson (1964–1970)	90	188
5	Robert Douglas (2001–2005)	86	161+1
6	Peter Latchford (1975–1987)	82	275
	Joe Kennaway (1931–1940)	82	295
8	Jonathan Gould (1997–2003)	72	156+2
9	John Thomson (1926–1931)	66	188
10	Gordon Marshall Jnr (1992–1998)	63	136
11	John Fallon (1958–1972)	61	195
	Frank Haffey (1958–1964)	61	201
13	Evan Williams (1969–1974)	59	148
14	Artur Boruc (2005–2008)	52	137
15	John Bonnar (1946–1958)	50	180
16	Alistair Hunter (1973–1976)	43	91
	Dick Beattie (1954–1959)	43	156
18	Dick McArthur (1892–1903)	42	120
19	Peter Shevlin (1924–1927)	35	103
20	Willie Miller (1942–1950)	29	123
21	John Mulrooney (1911–1914)	26	51
22	Denis Connaghan (1971–1977)	23	56
23	Magnus Hedman (2002–2005)	22	37
24	Joe Cullen (1892–1897)	19	73
25	Stewart Kerr (1994–2001)	15	40+2
26	David Marshall (2000–2007)	13	47+3
27	Andrew McPherson (1902–1904)	9	32
	George Hunter (1949–1954)	9	38
29	Tom Sinclair (1906–1907)	6	6
	Willie Duncan (1910–1915)	6	9
	John Kelly (1929–1930)	6	10
	Carl Muggleton (1994–1994)	6	13
	Roy Baines (1976–1979)	6	16
	James Bell (1890–1891)	6	22
35	Allen McKnight (1986–1988)	5	17
36	James Foley (1934–1936)	4	6
	Tom Duff (1891–1892)	4	9
	Mark Brown (2007–2008)	4	10
	Javier Sanchez Broto (2003–2003)	4	9+1
	Dmitri Kharine (1999–2003)	4	10+1
	Robert McFarlane (1901–1902)	4	23
42	John Hughes (1922–1925)	3	5
	John Wallace (1932–1934)	3	18
	Andrew Bell (1951–1955)	3	28
45	Michael Dolan (1888–1888)	2	3
	Willie Donnelly (1900–1901)	2	5
	Alan Rough (1988–1988)	2	7
	John Falconer (1931–1934)	2	8
49	John Kennedy (1965–1967)	1	1
	Bernard McCreadie (1955–1957)	1	1
	Frank Collins (1921–1922)	1	2
	Jim Oliver (1909–1909)	1	2
	James McLaughlin (1888–1890)	1	3
	Tony Warner (1998–1999)	1	5
	Willie Dunning (1888–1889)	1	6
	Ian Andrews (1988–1990)	1	8
	Frank Connor (1960–1962)	1	8
	Robert Boyle (1912–1913)	1	10
59	Graham Barclay (1973–1977)	0	1
	Willie Goldie (1960–1961)	0	1
	Eamon McMahon (1953–1955)	0	1

CLEAN SHEETS (cont.)

Player	Clean Sheets	Games
Richard Madden (1962–1964)	0	1
Gordon Marshall Snr (1971–1972)	0	1
Davie Nicol (1927–1929)	0	1
John O'Brien (1895–1895)	0	1
Leigh R Roose (1910–1911)	0	1
Bobby Wraith (1968–1969)	0	1
John Doherty (1937–1939)	0	2
Charlie Kelly (1991–1993)	0	2
John Kelly (1888–1889)	0	2
David Robertson (1930–1931)	0	2
David Syme (1918–1919)	0	2
Joseph Coen (1931–1932)	0	3
Alex Devanny (1949–1952)	0	3
Willie Laurie (1919–1921)	0	3
Tom Doyle (1935–1938)	0	5
Rolando Ugolini (1944–1948)	0	5
John Docherty (1898–1900)	0	11

THE 100 GOALS CLUB

	Player	Total	League	LC	SC	Europe
1	Jimmy McGrory	468	395	0	73	0
2	Bobby Lennox	273	167	61	31	14
3	Henrik Larsson	242	174	10	23	35
4	Steve Chalmers	231	158	31	29	13
5	Jimmy Quinn	217	187	0	30	0
6	Patsy Gallacher	192	186	0	6	0
7	John Hughes	188	115	38	25	10
8	Sandy McMahon	177	130	0	47	0
9	Jimmy McMenemy	168	144	0	24	0
10	Kenny Dalglish	167	112	35	11	9
11	Adam McLean	148	128	0	20	0
12	Willie Wallace	134	88	21	12	13
13	Jimmy Johnstone	130	82	21	11	16
14	Tommy McInally	126	110	0	16	0
15	Charlie Nicholas	125	85	26	7	7
16	Dixie Deans	123	88	11	18	6
	Jimmy McColl	123	117	0	6	0
18	Harry Hood	121	74	22	13	12
	Brian McClair	121	99	9	11	2
20	Bobby Collins	117	81	26	10	0
21	John Campbell	113	88	0	25	0
22	John Hartson	110	89	7	8	6
23	Frank McGarvey	109	77	11	13	8
	Neil Mochan	109	81	12	16	0
25	Joe Cassidy	103	90	0	13	0
26	Bobby Murdoch	102	61	17	13	11
27	John Divers	101	79	8	11	3
28	Alec Thomson	100	87	0	13	0

TOP SCORER BY SEASON IN ALL COMPETITIONS

Season	Division	Player	Goals
1888–89		Willie Groves	10
1889–90		Willie Groves	1
1890–91	SFL	Peter Dowds	17
1891–92	SFL	Sandy McMahon	25
1892–93	SFL	Sandy McMahon	19
1893–94	Div I	Sandy McMahon	30
1894–95	Div I	Sandy McMahon	9
1895–96	Div I	Allan Martin	18
1896–97	Div I	Sandy McMahon	10
1897–98	Div I	George Allan	16
1898–99	Div I	Sandy McMahon	21
1899–1900	Div I	Sandy McMahon / Jack Bell	12
1900–01	Div I	Sandy McMahon / Johnny Campbell	13
1901–02	Div I	Johnny Campbell	12
1902–03	Div I	Johnny Campbell	15
1903–04	Div I	Jimmy Quinn	15
1904–05	Div I	Jimmy Quinn	21
1905–06	Div I	Jimmy Quinn	21
1906–07	Div I	Jimmy Quinn	30
1907–08	Div I	Jimmy Quinn	20
1908–09	Div I	Jimmy Quinn	29
1909–10	Div I	Jimmy Quinn	28
1910–11	Div I	Jimmy Quinn	17
1911–12	Div I	Jimmy Quinn	11
1912–13	Div I	Jimmy Quinn / Patsy Gallacher	11
1913–14	Div I	Patsy Gallacher	24
1914–15	Div I	Jimmy McColl	25
1915–16	Div I	Jimmy McColl	34
1916–17	Div I	Jimmy McColl	24
1917–18	Div I	Patsy Gallacher	17
1918–19	Div I	Jimmy McColl	17
1919–20	Div I	Tommy McInally	30
1920–21	Div I	Tommy McInally	30
1921–22	Div I	Tommy McInally / Joe Cassidy	18
1922–23	Div I	Joe Cassidy	32
1923–24	Div I	Joe Cassidy	25
1924–25	Div I	Jimmy McGrory	28
1925–26	Div I	Jimmy McGrory	42
1926–27	Div I	Jimmy McGrory	57
1927–28	Div I	Jimmy McGrory	53
1928–29	Div I	Jimmy McGrory	31
1929–30	Div I	Jimmy McGrory	35
1930–31	Div I	Jimmy McGrory	44
1931–32	Div I	Jimmy McGrory	28
1932–33	Div I	Jimmy McGrory	30
1933–34	Div I	Frank O'Donnell	27
1934–35	Div I	Jimmy McGrory	20
1935–36	Div I	Jimmy McGrory	50
1936–37	Div I	Jimmy McGrory	26
1937–38	Div I	John Crum	25
1938–39	Div I	John Divers	21
1939–40	Div I	John Divers / John Crum	2
1946–47	Div I	Tommy Kiernan	17
1947–48	Div I	Johnny Paton	10
1948–49	Div I	Jackie Gallacher	22
1949–50	Div I	John McPhail	21
1950–51	Div I	John McPhail	28
1951–52	Div I	Bobby Collins	13
1952–53	Div I	John McGrory / Bertie Peacock	11
1953–54	Div I	Neil Mochan	25
1954–55	Div I	Jimmy Walsh	24
1955–56	Div I	Neil Mochan	20
1956–57	Div I	Billy McPhail	17
1957–58	Div I	Sammy Wilson	32
1958–59	Div I	John Colrain	16
1959–60	Div I	Neil Mochan	22
1960–61	Div I	Steve Chalmers	26
1961–62	Div I	John Hughes	26
1962–63	Div I	John Hughes	21
1963–64	Div I	Steve Chalmers	38
1964–65	Div I	Steve Chalmers	26
1965–66	Div I	Joe McBride	43
1966–67	Div I	Steve Chalmers	36
1967–68	Div I	Bobby Lennox	41
1968–69	Div I	Willie Wallace	34
1969–70	Div I	Willie Wallace	24
1970–71	Div I	Harry Hood	33
1971–72	Div I	Dixie Deans	27
1972–73	Div I	Kenny Dalglish	41
1973–74	Div I	Dixie Deans	33
1974–75	Div I	Paul Wilson	22
1975–76	Prem Div	Kenny Dalglish	32
1976–77	Prem Div	Kenny Dalglish / Ronnie Glavin	26
1977–78	Prem Div	Joe Craig	16
1978–79	Prem Div	Tom McAdam	13
1979–80	Prem Div	John Doyle / George McCluskey	15
1980–81	Prem Div	Frank McGarvey	29
1981–82	Prem Div	George McCluskey	25
1982–83	Prem Div	Charlie Nicholas	48
1983–84	Prem Div	Brian McClair	31
1984–85	Prem Div	Brian McClair	23
1985–86	Prem Div	Brian McClair	26
1986–87	Prem Div	Brian McClair	41
1987–88	Prem Div	Andy Walker	32
1988–89	Prem Div	Mark McGhee	19
1989–90	Prem Div	Dariusz Dziekanowski	16
1990–91	Prem Div	Tommy Coyne	19
1991–92	Prem Div	Charlie Nicholas	25
1992–93	Prem Div	Andy Payton	15
1993–94	Prem Div	Pat McGinlay	12
1994–95	Prem Div	John Collins	12
1995–96	Prem Div	Pierre van Hooijdonk	32
1996–97	Prem Div	Jorge Cadete	33
1997–98	Prem Div	Henrik Larsson	19
1998–99	SPL	Henrik Larsson	37
1999–2000	SPL	Mark Viduka	27
2000–01	SPL	Henrik Larsson	53
2001–02	SPL	Henrik Larsson	35
2002–03	SPL	Henrik Larsson	44
2003–04	SPL	Henrik Larsson	41
2004–05	SPL	John Hartson	30
2005–06	SPL	John Hartson / Maciej Zurawski	20
2006–07	SPL	Jan Vennegoor of Hesselink	18
2007–08	SPL	Scott McDonald	31

HAT-TRICK HEROES

A list of all Celtic players ever to have scored a hat-trick of three or more goals in one match. Jimmy McGrory scoring eight and Dixie Deans scoring six in one match have both been counted as one hat-trick.

	Player	Total	Lge	LC	SC	Europe
1	Jimmy McGrory	55	48	0	7	0
2	Jimmy Quinn	20	17	0	3	0
3	Henrik Larsson	15	12	1	1	1
	Bobby Lennox	15	8	4	2	1
5	Steve Chalmers	14	11	3	0	0
6	Sandy McMahon	13	8	0	5	0
7	Patsy Gallacher	9	9	0	0	0
	John Hughes	9	7	1	0	1
	Joe McBride	9	6	3	0	0
	Jimmy McColl	9	8	0	1	0
11	Joe Cassidy	8	6	0	2	0
12	Dixie Deans	7	4	1	2	0
13	John Crum	6	3	0	3	0
	Brian McClair	6	6	0	0	0
	Tommy McInally	6	6	0	0	0
	John McPhail	6	5	0	1	0
	Charlie Napier	6	5	0	1	0
	Peter Scarff	6	6	0	0	0
	Willie Wallace	6	4	1	0	1
20	John Hartson	5	5	0	0	0
	Harry Hood	5	2	2	0	1
22	Neil Mochan	4	3	0	1	0
	George McCluskey	4	1	1	2	0
	Jimmy McMenemy	4	4	0	0	0
25	Joe Carruth	3	3	0	0	0
	Bobby Collins	3	3	0	0	0
	Kenny Dalglish	3	2	1	0	0
	John Divers	3	3	0	0	0
	Frank McAvennie	3	2	1	0	0
	Adam McLean	3	3	0	0	0
	Billy McPhail	3	0	2	1	0
	Bobby Murdoch	3	1	1	1	0
	Charlie Nicholas	3	2	1	0	0
34	Alec Bennett	2	2	0	0	0
	Harald Brattbakk	2	2	0	0	0
	Jorge Cadete	2	1	1	0	0
	John Campbell	2	2	0	0	0
	Tommy Coyne	2	1	0	1	0
	Peter Dowds	2	2	0	0	0
	Ronnie Glavin	2	1	0	1	0
	Tommy Johnson	2	2	0	0	0
	Andy McAtee	2	2	0	0	0
	Scott McDonald	2	2	0	0	0
	Tommy McDonald	2	2	0	0	0
	Mark McGhee	2	2	0	0	0
	Johnny Madden	2	1	0	1	0
	Allan Martin	2	2	0	0	0
	Hugh O'Donnell	2	1	0	1	0
	Chris Sutton	2	2	0	0	0
	Mark Viduka	2	2	0	0	0
	Jimmy Walsh	2	2	0	0	0
	Sammy Wilson	2	1	1	0	0
53	George Allan	1	1	0	0	0
	Bertie Auld	1	1	0	0	0
	John Bell	1	1	0	0	0
	Craig Bellamy	1	1	0	0	0
	John Browning	1	1	0	0	0
	Willie Buchan	1	1	0	0	0
	Mark Burchill	1	0	0	0	1
	Craig Burley	1	1	0	0	0
	Alec Byrne	1	1	0	0	0

HAT-TRICK HEROES (cont.)

	Player	Total	Lge	LC	SC	Europe
53 (cont.)	John Collins	1	1	0	0	0
	John Colrain	1	1	0	0	0
	Bobby Craig	1	1	0	0	0
	Joe Craig	1	0	0	1	0
	Danny Crainie	1	1	0	0	0
	Gerry Creaney	1	0	0	1	0
	Willie Crone	1	1	0	0	0
	Jimmy Delaney	1	1	0	0	0
	John Divers	1	1	0	0	0
	Johnny Divers	1	1	0	0	0
	Michael Dunbar	1	0	0	1	0
	Dariusz Dziekanowski	1	0	0	0	1
	Johannes Edvaldsson	1	1	0	0	0
	Willie Fernie	1	1	0	0	0
	William Fleming	1	1	0	0	0
	Willie Gallagher	1	1	0	0	0
	Sam Gilligan	1	1	0	0	0
	Thomas Gravesen	1	1	0	0	0
	Willie Groves	1	0	0	1	0
	Mike Haughney	1	0	1	0	0
	John Higgins	1	1	0	0	0
	Maurice Johnston	1	1	0	0	0
	George Livingstone	1	1	0	0	0
	Pat McCluskey	1	1	0	0	0
	Aiden McGeady	1	1	0	0	0
	James McGhee	1	1	0	0	0
	John McGrory	1	1	0	0	0
	Alan McInally	1	1	0	0	0
	Willie McOustra	1	1	0	0	0
	Paul McStay	1	0	0	1	0
	Lou Macari	1	1	0	0	0
	Tom Maley	1	0	0	1	0
	Shaun Maloney	1	0	1	0	0
	Bob Muir	1	1	0	0	0
	Frank Murphy	1	0	0	1	0
	Shunsuke Nakamura	1	1	0	0	0
	Frank O'Donnell	1	1	0	0	0
	Joe O'Kane	1	1	0	0	0
	Ebenezer Owers	1	1	0	0	0
	Andy Payton	1	0	1	0	0
	Stilian Petrov	1	1	0	0	0
	Willie Rennet	1	1	0	0	0
	Alec Thomson	1	1	0	0	0
	Bertie Thomson	1	0	0	1	0
	Jan Vennegoor of Hesselink	1	1	0	0	0
	Ross Wallace	1	0	1	0	0
	Jock Weir	1	1	0	0	0
	Maciej Zurawski	1	1	0	0	0

CELTIC FACTS AND FIGURES

(Only League, League Cup, Scottish Cup and European matches taken into consideration)

When the League started in 1890 a total of 18 matches were played. This eventually rose to a high of 44 and now stands at 38. Therefore more than one figure is given sometimes as, for example conceding 18 League goals in 38 games in 2001–02 deserves a mention although the record is 13 League goals in 18 games in 1897–98.

MOST GOALS SCORED IN A SEASON
184 in 1966–67
Home :-   110 in 1966–67
Away :-   80 in 1972–73

MOST LEAGUE GOALS SCORED IN A SEASON
116 in 1915–16
Home :-   71 in 1935–36
Away :-   53 in 1967–68

FEWEST GOALS SCORED IN A SEASON
43 in 1902–03
Home :-   20 in 1896–97
Away :-   19 in 1910–11

FEWEST LEAGUE GOALS SCORED IN A SEASON
36 in 1902–03 (22 games) & 37 in 1989–90 (36 games)
Home :-   19 in 1901–02 (9 games)
            20 in 1896–97 (9 games) & 1902–03 (11 games)
            21 in 1947–48 (15 games) & 1989–90 (18 games)
Away :-   14 in 1949–50 (15 games)

MOST GOALS CONCEDED IN A SEASON
82 in 1959–60
Home :-   34 in 1959–60
Away :-   54 in 1964–65

MOST LEAGUE GOALS CONCEDED IN A SEASON
59 in 1959–60
Home :-   31 in 1938–39
Away :-   39 in 1964–65

FEWEST GOALS CONCEDED IN A SEASON
16 in 1897–98 (20 games) & 1913–14 (45 games)
Home :-   3 in 1910–11 (21 games)
Away :-   9 in 1897–98 (11 games) & 1916–17 (19 games)

FEWEST LEAGUE GOALS CONCEDED IN A SEASON
13 in 1897–98 (18 games) & 18 in 2001–02 (38 games)
Home :-   3 in 1910–11
Away :-   6 in 1897–98 (9 games)
            8 in 1913–14 (19 games)

SEASONS WHEN SCORED IN EVERY MATCH
1892–93 (23 games)   1900–01 (25 games)

SEASONS WHEN SCORED IN EVERY LEAGUE MATCH
1892–93 (18 games)
1900–01 (20 games)
1901–02 (18 games)
2002–03 (38 games)

MOST MATCHES WHERE FAILED TO SCORE IN A SEASON
17 in 1989–90

MOST LEAGUE MATCHES WHERE FAILED TO SCORE IN A SEASON
15 in 1989–90

MOST MATCHES PLAYED IN A SEASON
61 in 1973–74 (34 Lge, 13 LC, 6 SC & 8 Eur)
61 in 2003–04 (38 Lge, 2 LC, 5 SC & 16 Eur)

CONSECUTIVE LEAGUE GOALSCORING RUNS
62 games from 7 October 1899 to 6 December 1902
(note – from 26 December 2001 to 13 November 2004 Celtic played 109 League matches and scored in all but one v Dunfermline on 9 August 2003)

LONGEST TIME WITHOUT SCORING A GOAL
4 games from 18 August 1934 to 1 September 1934
4 games from 16 April 1966 to 27 April 1966
4 games from 31 August 1991 to 14 September 1991
4 games from 19 December 1992 to 9 January 1993

LONGEST TIME WITHOUT SCORING A LEAGUE GOAL
4 games from 18 August 1934 to 1 September 1934
4 games from 24 March 1990 to 17 April 1990
4 games from 24 August 1991 to 14 September 1991
(note – in 1989–90 as well as 4 games without scoring, Celtic also had 3 separate runs of 3 League games without a goal)

LONGEST TIME WITHOUT SCORING A GOAL AT THE START OF A SEASON
3 games (297 minutes) in 1948–49

MOST GOALS SCORED IN A SCOTTISH CUP CAMPAIGN
37 in 1888–89 (first ever season)

FEWEST GOALS SCORED IN A SCOTTISH CUP CAMPAIGN
0 in 1923–24, 1967–68 & 1993–94

FEWEST GOALS SCORED IN A WINNING SCOTTISH CUP CAMPAIGN
7 in 1910–11

FEWEST GOALS CONCEDED IN A SCOTTISH CUP CAMPAIGN
0 in 1910–11

MOST GOALS CONCEDED IN A SCOTTISH CUP CAMPAIGN
13 in 1959–60

MOST GOALS CONCEDED IN A WINNING SCOTTISH CUP CAMPAIGN
9 in 1926–27, 1936–37 & 1953–54

MOST GOALS SCORED IN A LEAGUE CUP CAMPAIGN
41 in 1968–69 & 1982–83

FEWEST GOALS SCORED IN A LEAGUE CUP CAMPAIGN
0 in 1998–99

FEWEST GOALS SCORED IN A WINNING LEAGUE CUP CAMPAIGN
8 in 1999–2000

FEWEST GOALS CONCEDED IN A LEAGUE CUP CAMPAIGN
0 in 1997–98 & 1999–2000

MOST GOALS CONCEDED IN A LEAGUE CUP CAMPAIGN
17 in 1970–71 & 1972–73

MOST GOALS CONCEDED IN A WINNING LEAGUE CUP CAMPAIGN
13 in 1974–75

MOST GOALS SCORED IN A EUROPEAN CAMPAIGN
30 in 2002–03

FEWEST GOALS SCORED IN A EUROPEAN CAMPAIGN
1 in 1974–75, 1981–82 & 1996–97

FEWEST GOALS CONCEDED IN A EUROPEAN CAMPAIGN
2 in 1981–82, 1993–94 & 1999–2000

MOST GOALS CONCEDED IN A EUROPEAN CAMPAIGN
15 in 2002–03

MOST GAMES PLAYED IN A EUROPEAN CAMPAIGN
16 in 2003–04

LONGEST UNBEATEN LEAGUE RUN
62 games – between losing 2-0 away to Hearts on 13 November 1915 and losing 2-0 at home to Kilmarnock on 21 April 1917 (49 wins and 13 draws)

LONGEST RUN OF CONSECUTIVE LEAGUE WINS
25 games – between drawing 0-0 away to Dunfermline on 9 August 2003 (first League game of the season) and drawing 1-1 at home to Motherwell on 14 March 2004

LONGEST UNBEATEN HOME RUN
77 games – 22 August 2001 v Ajax CLQ 0-1 to 21 April 2004 v Aberdeen SPL 1-2

MOST CONSECUTIVE CLEAN SHEETS
13 in 1913–14

MOST CONSECUTIVE LEAGUE CLEAN SHEETS
10 in 1913–14 (earned 19 clean sheets in 20 League games) & 1921–22

MOST CONSECUTIVE LEAGUE CLEAN SHEETS FROM DEBUT
6 Carl Muggleton in 1993–94

MOST CONSECUTIVE LEAGUE CLEAN SHEETS FROM BEGINNING OF SEASON
6 in 1906–07

MOST CLEAN SHEETS IN A SEASON
32 in 1987–88 (17 at home 15 away)
Home :-   18 in 1921–22
Away :-   18 in 1966–67

MOST LEAGUE CLEAN SHEETS IN A SEASON
28 in 1987–88
Home:-   17 in 1921–22
Away :-   13 in 1913–14 & 1987–88

MOST CLEAN SHEETS IN A SEASON BY AN INDIVIDUAL
31 in 45 games by Charlie Shaw in 1913–14

FEWEST CLEAN SHEETS IN A SEASON
4 in 1901–02 (24 games)
6 in 1938–39 (43 games) & 1952–52 (41 games)

FEWEST LEAGUE CLEAN SHEETS IN A SEASON
2 in 1951–52 (30 games)
Home :-   1 in 1899–1900 (9 games), 1901–02 (9 games) & 1938–39 (19 games)
Away :-   0 in 1896–96 (9 games)
             1 in 1951–52 (15 games)

LONGEST LEAGUE RUN WITHOUT A CLEAN SHEET
22 games from 16 April 1958 to 2 January 1959

MOST GOALKEEPERS USED IN A SEASON
5 in 1998–99 & 2002–03

MOST GOALS CONCEDED IN A MATCH
8 by Joe Kennaway v Motherwell on 30 April 1937

LONGEST UNBROKEN RUN BY A GOALKEEPER
200 games by Charlie Shaw from Aug 1913 to Sep 1918

GOALKEEPERS EVER-PRESENT IN A SEASON

Cullen 1893–94 (23 games), McPherson 1902–03 (27), Adams 1904–05 (30), 1905–06 (33), 1907–08 (39), 1910–11 (40) Shaw 1913–14 (45), 1914–15 (38), 1915–16 (38), 1916–17 (38), 1917–18 (34), 1920–21 (45), 1923–24 (39) Thomson 1927–28 (44), Kennaway 1934–35 (42), Latchford 1977–78 (51), 1979–80 (54), Bonner 1981–82 (46), 1989–90 (48), 1990–91 (46), Marshall 1995–96 (47)

MOST GOALKEEPERS IN ONE MATCH

3 on 6 September 1947 in a League Cup section tie away to Dundee. Keeper Willie Miller was injured in the 12th minute and replaced by Bobby Hogg. Celtic trailed by 3-1 at half-time and Hogg was then replaced by centre-forward Joe Rae who managed to save a penalty kick! Celtic eventually lost 4-1.

HIGHEST SCORING CELTIC MATCHES WHERE TEN OR MORE GOALS HAVE BEEN SCORED

9-2 v Clyde (SC) 8 December 1888 (H)
9-1 v Vale of Leven (L) 5 May 1891 (H)
6-5 v Leith Athletic (L) 30 March 1895 (A)
11-0 v Dundee (L) 26 October 1895 (H)
9-1 v Clyde (L) 25 December 1897 (A)
9-2 v Clyde (L) 5 November 1898 (H)
8-3 v Partick Thistle (L) 3 December 1898 (A)
7-3 v Hibernian (L) 11 October 1919 (H)
9-1 v East Fife (L) 10 January 1931 (H)
7-3 v Falkirk (L) 17 April 1935 (H)
9-1 v Kilmarnock (L) 13 August 1938 (H)
8-3 v Burntisland Shipyards (SC) 21 January 1939 (A)
7-3 v Airdrieonians (L) 22 December 1956 (A)
7-3 v Stirling Albion (L) 13 December 1958 (H)
8-2 v St Mirren (LC) 17 August 1966 (H)
7-3 v Stirling Albion (L) 2 November 1966 (H)
10-0 v Hamilton Accies (LC) 11 September 1968 (H)
9-1 v Clyde (L) 4 September 1971 (H)
8-3 v Hamilton Accies (L) 3 January 1987 (H)
9-1 v Arbroath (LC) 25 August 1993 (A)

BIGGEST LEAGUE WIN

Home :-   11-0 v Dundee 26 October 1895
Away :-   9-1 v Clyde 25 December 1897

BIGGEST SCOTTISH CUP WIN

Home :-   8-0 v Cowlairs 22 September 1888
Away :-   7-0 v Arthurlie 8 January 1898
            8-1 v 6th GRV (Dalbeattie) 14 January 1899
Neutral :- 6-1 v Hibernian 6 May 1972 (Final)
            5-0 v Rangers 21 March 1925 (Semi-Final)
            5-0 v Hibernian 12 April 1980 (Semi-Final)

BIGGEST LEAGUE CUP WIN

Home :-   10-0 v Hamilton Accies 11 September 1968
Away :-   8-0 v Dumbarton 23 August 1975
            9-1 v Arbroath 25 August 1993
Neutral :- 7-1 v Rangers 19 October 1957 (Final)
            7-1 v Morton 11 October 1967 (Semi-Final)

BIGGEST EUROPEAN WIN

Home :-   9-0 v KPV Kokkola (EC)16 September 1970
Away :-   7-0 v Waterford (EC) 21 October 1970

BIGGEST LEAGUE DEFEAT

Home :-   0-5 v Hearts 14 September 1895
Away :-   0-8 v Motherwell 30 April 1937

BIGGEST SCOTTISH CUP DEFEAT

Home :-   0-3 v Rangers 28 February 1903
Away :-   0-3 v Dumbarton 20 December 1890
Neutral :- 0-4 v Rangers 14 April 1928 (Final)
            0-4 v St Mirren 4 April 1959 (Semi-Final)

BIGGEST LEAGUE CUP DEFEAT

Home :- 0-4 v Rangers 31 August 1955
Away :- 1-4 v Dundee 6 September 1947
    0-3 v Hibernian 30 August 1952
    2-5 v Aberdeen 22 August 1953
    0-3 v Dunfermline 15 September 1956
    3-6 v St Mirren 30 August 1958
    0-3 v Rangers 24 August 1963
Neutral :- 0-3 v Rangers 13 October 1951 (Semi-Final)
    1-4 v Partick Thistle 23 October 1971 (Final)

BIGGEST EUROPEAN DEFEAT

Home :- 0-3 v Paris Saint Germain (CWC) 2 November 1995
Away :- 0-5 v Artmedia Bratislava (CLQ) 27 July 2005

ATTENDANCES

RECORD LEAGUE ATTENDANCE

Home :- 83,500 v Rangers (3-0) 1 January 1938 note – often given as 92,000
Away :- 118,730 v Rangers (1-2) 2 January 1939 – Scottish League record attendance

RECORD SCOTTISH CUP ATTENDANCE

Home :- 80,840 v Hearts (2-1 aet) 22 February 1939
Away :- 95,000 v Rangers (0-2) 14 March 1953
Neutral :- 146,433 v Aberdeen (2-1) 24 April 1937 (Final) – record attendance for any club match in Europe

RECORD LEAGUE CUP ATTENDANCE

Home :- 75,000 v Rangers (3-1) 30 August 1967
    75,000 v Rangers (1-0) 24 August 1968
Away :- 95,000 v Rangers (0-2) 27 August 1949
Neutral :- 107,609 v Rangers (2-1) 23 October 1965 (Final) – record League Cup attendance

RECORD EUROPEAN ATTENDANCE

Home :- 133,961 v Leeds United (2-1) 15 April 1970 EC (played at Hampden Park) record attendance for
    any European club match
At Celtic Park :- 77,240 v Fiorentina (3-0) EC 4 March 1970
Away :- 115,000 v Real Madrid (0-3) EC 19 March 1980
Neutral :- 55,000 v Inter Milan (2-1) ECF 25 May 1967 at Estadio Nacional, Lisbon

RECORD MIDWEEK ATTENDANCE AT CELTIC PARK

80,840 v Hearts (2-1 aet) 22 February 1939 – Scottish Cup

SEASONS WITH MORE THAN ONE SIX FIGURE ATTENDANCE

3 – 1970–71
2 – 1953–54, 1962–63, 1965–66, 1969–70

LARGEST GROSS ATTENDANCE FOR HOME LEAGUE MATCHES

1,128,492 – 2000–01 Ave 59,394
1,113,543 – 2001–02 Ave 58,608
1,104,841 – 2005–06 Ave 58,150

Note:- Attendance records are as accurate as possible. In early days attendance figures were not always given. eg the record attendance for Celtic Park is often given as 92,000 on 1.1.38. That was the capacity of the ground at that time and the more reliable sources give an attendance of 83,500 for this match. Only recently have exact figures been given for attendances and not round figures as previously.

LIST OF ALL SIX-FIGURE ATTENDANCES

21 Mar 1925	v Rangers	SCSF	5-0	101,714
14 Apr 1928	v Rangers	SCF	0-4	118,115
11 Apr 1931	v Motherwell	SCF	2-2	104,803
15 Apr 1933	v Motherwell	SCF	1-0	102,339
24 Apr 1937	v Aberdeen	SCF	2-1	146,433
2 Jan 1939	v Rangers	L	1-2	118,730
16 Oct 1948	v Rangers	LC	1-2	105,000
21 Apr 1951	v Motherwell	SCF	1-0	131,943
27 Mar 1954	v Motherwell	SCSF	2-2	100,000
24 Apr 1954	v Aberdeen	SCF	2-1	129,926
23 Apr 1955	v Clyde	SCF	1-1	106,234
21 Apr 1956	v Hearts	SCF	1-3	132,842
23 Mar 1957	v Kilmarnock	SCSF	1-1	109,145
22 Apr 1961	v Dunfermline	SCF	0-0	113,328
4 May 1963	v Rangers	SCF	1-1	129,527
15 May 1963	v Rangers	SCFR	0-3	120,263
24 Apr 1965	v Dunfermline	SCF	3-2	108,800
23 Oct 1965	v Rangers	LCF	2-1	107,600
23 Apr 1966	v Rangers	SCF	0-0	126,599
29 Apr 1967	v Aberdeen	SCF	2-0	126,102
1 Nov 1967	v Racing Club	WCC	1-2	120,000
26 Apr 1969	v Rangers	SCF	4-0	132,870
11 Apr 1970	v Aberdeen	SCF	1-3	108,434
15 Apr 1970	v Leeds United	ECSF	2-1	136,505
24 Oct 1970	v Rangers	LCF	0-1	106,000
8 May 1971	v Rangers	SCF	1-1	120,000
12 May 1971	v Rangers	SCFR	2-1	103,000
6 May 1972	v Hibernian	SCF	6-1	106,000
5 May 1973	v Rangers	SCF	2-3	122,000
19 Mar 1980	v Real Madrid	EC	0-3	115,000
5 Nov 1986	v Dynamo Kiev	EC	1-3	107,000

THE LISBON LIONS

The team that won the 1967 European Cup by defeating Inter Milan 2-1 in the final are known throughout the footballing world as The Lisbon Lions. The starting XI of Simpson, Craig & Gemmell, Murdoch, McNeill & Clark, Johnstone, Wallace, Chalmers, Auld & Lennox only ever began eleven matches together (thirteen including friendlies against Tottenham Hotspur and Penarol). Here is the list of all their games as a starting XI.

14 Jan 1967	v St Johnstone (A)	L	4-0	19,000	Johnstone (63,69) Chalmers (86) Lennox (90)
19 Apr 1967	v Aberdeen (H)	L	0-0	33,000	
25 Apr 1967	v Dukla Prague (A)	ECSF	0-0	22,000	
29 Apr 1967	v Aberdeen (N)	SCF	2-0	126,102	Wallace (42,49)
6 May 1967	v Rangers (A)	L	2-2	78,000	Johnstone (41,74)
25 May 1967	v Inter Milan (N)	ECF	2-1	55,000	Gemmell (63) Chalmers (85)
12 Aug 1967	v Dundee United (H)	LC	1-0	54,000	Johnstone (90)
16 Aug 1967	v Rangers (A)	LC	1-1	94,168	Gemmell (38pen)
19 Aug 1967	v Aberdeen (H)	LC	3-1	50,000	Gemmell (48pen) Lennox (71) Auld (88pen)
30 Aug 1967	v Rangers (H)	LC	3-1	75,000	Wallace (78) Murdoch (83) Lennox (89)
20 Sep 1967	v Dynamo Kiev (H)	EC	1-2	54,000	Lennox (62)

The last time all eleven Lions appeared on a pitch at the same time was on 10 February 1968 when Celtic beat Motherwell 1-0 at Fir Park. John Hughes scored the only goal and was later replaced by Steve Chalmers, thus restoring the full Lions line up one last time.

CELTIC v INTER MILAN
25 May 1967
Estadio Nacional, Lisbon
Kick-off 5.30 p.m.

CELTIC	INTER MILAN
R Simpson	G Sarti
J Craig	T Burgnich
T Gemmell	G Facchetti
B Murdoch	G Bedin
B McNeill (c)	A Guarneri
J Clark	A Picchi (c)
J Johnstone	A Domenghini
W Wallace	S Mazzola
S Chalmers	M Bicicli
B Auld	R Cappellini
B Lennox	M Corso

	CELTIC	INTER
Shots at goal	43	4
Shots on target	12	3
Corners	10	0
Offside	8	1
Fouls committed	20	21

Manager   Manager
J Stein   H Herrera

Referee
K Tschenscher (Ger)

Attendance
55,000

Scorers
Mazzola 7 min (pen)
Gemmell 63 min
Chalmers 85 min

TRANSFER FEES

First 5-figure fee paid	£12,000 to Clyde in 1948 for Leslie Johnston
First 6-figure fee paid	£120,000 to Kilmarnock in 1978 for Davie Provan
First 7-figure fee paid	£1,000,000 to Hibernian in 1990 for John Collins
Highest fee paid	£6,000,000 to Chelsea in 2000 for Chris Sutton &
	£6,000,000 to Coventry City in 2001 for John Hartson

First 5-figure fee received	£10,000 from Blackpool in 1937 for Willie Buchan
First 6-figure fee received	£200,000 from Manchester United in 1973 for Lou Macari
First 7-figure fee received	£1,250,000 from West Ham United in 1989 for Frank McAvennie
Highest fee received	£6,500,000 from Aston Villa in 2006 for Stilian Petrov

Record fee for a transfer between Scottish clubs is £4,400,000 which Celtic paid Hibernian in 2007 for Scott Brown.

PLAYING RECORD

	Pld	W	D	L	F	A
Scottish League	3379	2025	696	658	7343	3587
SPL	376	280	51	45	888	303
Scottish Cup	516	363	81	72	1287	465
League Cup	404	267	53	84	963	437
European Cup/CL	128	63	22	43	203	136
Cup Winners' Cup	38	21	4	13	75	37
Inter-Cities Fairs Cup	6	1	3	2	9	10
UEFA Cup	69	33	13	23	113	67
World Club Championship	3	1	0	2	2	3
	4919	3054	923	942	10883	5045

TURNOVER

Season	Turnover (£)	% Wages/Turnover ratio
2006–07	75.237m	48.4
2005–06	57.411m	56.6
2004–05	62.168m	60.2
2003–04	69.020m	58.7
2002–03	60.569m	54.6
2001–02	56.892m	57.6
2000–01	42.007m	61.7
1999–00	38.579m	52.3
1998–99	33.840m	42.9
1997–98	27.821m	44.7
1996–97	22.190m	39.1
1995–96	16.000m	39.3
1994–95	10.368m	46.3
1993–94	8.736m	N/A

STADIUM STATS

Current capacity	**60,832**
Main Stand	7,850
North Stand	26,970
Jock Stein Stand	13,006
Lisbon Lions Stand	13,006

In 2002 Celtic Park was voted the UK's favourite sporting venue on the BBC's Radio 5 Live taking nearly 60% of the total vote.

1892	Celtic move to the current site.
1895	State of the art turnstiles are installed.
1898	The Grant Stand is built on the London Road side of the ground with padded seats and sliding windows. However condensation hampers vision and the windows are removed.
1904	A fire completely destroys the stand on the Janefield Street side of the ground.
1905	The ruined stand is replaced by a covered enclosure which would later become known as the Jungle.
1929	The Janefield Street pavilion is destroyed in a fire and the 'Grant Stand' is demolished. Celtic finish the season playing home matches away from Celtic Park. Incredibly the new stand is ready for the start of the new season.
1959	Celtic play under proper floodlights for the first time at home.
1966	The Jungle gets a new roof and concrete steps.
1971	The Main Stand gets a major renovation including a new roof.
1985	Undersoil heating is installed.
1988	To celebrate the centenary of the club a new red brick facade is built on the front of the stadium as well as new hospitality suites, restaurants and executive boxes.
1991	Two electronic scoreboards are installed at either end of the ground.
1993	It is farewell to the Jungle as a standing terracing as seats are installed.
1994	Fergus McCann takes over and immediately plans are in place to turn Celtic Park into a 60,000 all-seater stadium. Celtic play a full season at Hampden as work begins.
1995	The North Stand is opened.
1996	The Lisbon Lions Stand is opened.
1998	The Jock Stein Stand is opened and the redevelopment is complete.

The largest official attendance at the all seated Celtic Park is 60,632 who watched Celtic beat Manchester United 1-0 in the Champions League on 21 November 2006.

SUBSTITUTES

FIRST EVER SUBSTITUTE
Willie O'Neill v St Mirren (A) League Cup 3 Sep 1966 won 1-0 replacing Jimmy Johnstone

FIRST LEAGUE SUBSTITUTE
Steve Chalmers v Dundee (A) 24 Sep 1966 won 2-1 replacing Joe McBride

FIRST SCOTTISH CUP SUBSTITUTE
Willie Wallace v Elgin City (H) 18 Feb 1967 won 7-0 replacing Bobby Murdoch

FIRST EUROPEAN SUBSTITUTE
Willie Wallace v Red Star Belgrade (A) 27 Nov 1968 drew 1-1 replacing Steve Chalmers

FIRST SCOTTISH CUP FINAL SUBSTITUTE
John Clark v Rangers 26 April 1969 won 4-0 replacing Jim Brogan

FIRST LEAGUE CUP FINAL SUBSTITUTE
Steve Chalmers v Rangers 29 Oct 1966 won 1-0 replacing John Hughes

FIRST EUROPEAN CUP FINAL SUBSTITUTE
George Connelly v Feyenoord 6 May 1970 lost 1-2 aet replacing Bertie Auld

FIRST SCORING SUBSTITUTE
Steve Chalmers v Dundee (A) League 24 Sep 1966 won 2-1

FIRST SUBSTITUTE TO SCORE TWO GOALS
Willie Wallace v Elgin City (H) Scottish Cup 18 Feb 1967 won 7-0

FIRST AND SO FAR ONLY SUBSTITUTE TO SCORE THREE GOALS
Andy Payton v Arbroath (A) League Cup 25 Aug 1993 won 9-1

MOST SUBSTITUTE APPEARANCES
Bobby Lennox 81
Shaun Malony 69
Jackie McNamara 52
Andy Walker 50
Simon Donnelly 50

MOST GOALS SCORED AS A SUBSTITUTE
Bobby Lennox 11
George McCluskey 8
Gerry Creaney 8
Mark Burchill 8
Shaun Maloney 8

MOST SUBSTITUTE APPEARANCES IN ONE SEASON
Chris Killen 24 2007-08
Brian McLaughlin 21 1995-96
Liam Miller 21 2003-04
Shaun Maloney 20 2002-03

MOST GOALS SCORED AS A SUBSTITUTE IN ONE SEASON
George McCluskey 5 1980-81
Gerry Creaney 5 1991-92
Andy Payton 5 1993-94

MATCHES DECIDED BY PENALTY SHOOT-OUT (REGARDED AS DRAWS)
Inter Milan 1971-72 ECSF lost (Home)
Airdrieonians 1991-92 LC lost (Away)
Hibernian 1985-86 LC lost (Away)
Raith Rovers 1994-95 LCF lost (Neutral)
Aberdeen 1986-87 LC won (Away)
Valencia 2001-02 UEFA lost (Home)
Motherwell 1986-87 LCSF won (Neutral)
Partick Thistle 2002-03 LC won (Home)
Hearts 1989-90 LC won (Away)

Falkirk LC 2006–07 LC lost (Home)
Aberdeen 1989–90 SCF lost (Neutral)
Spartak Moscow 2007–08 CLQ won (Home)

SEASONS UNBEATEN IN THE LEAGUE
1897–98

SEASONS UNBEATEN AT HOME IN THE LEAGUE
1890–91
1891–92
1906–07
1907–08
1909–10
1911–12
1914–15
1919–20
1921–22
1925–26
1937–38
1949–50
1953–54
1965–66
1967–68
1972–73
1976–77
1983–84
2001–02
2002–03

SEASONS UNBEATEN AWAY IN THE LEAGUE
1916–17
1995–96
2003–04

INDIVIDUAL SCORING FEATS

50 GOALS IN A SEASON OR MORE
57	Jimmy McGrory 1926–27
53	Jimmy McGrory 1927–28
	Henrik Larsson 2000–01
50	Jimmy McGrory 1935–36

MOST LEAGUE GOALS IN A SEASON
50	Jimmy McGrory 1935–36

MOST GOALS IN A MATCH
8	Jimmy McGrory v Dunfermline (H) League 14 Jan 1928 won 9-0
6	Dixie Deans v Partick Thistle (H) League 17 Nov 1973 won 7-0
5	Sandy McMahon v Clyde (A) League 29 Aug 1891 won 7-2
5	John Madden v 5th KRV (H) Scottish Cup 17 Dec 1892 won 7-0
5	George Allan v Clyde (A) League 25 Dec 1897 won 9-1
5	Jimmy Quinn v Kilmarnock (H) League 23 Apr 1904 won 6-1
5	Jimmy McGrory v Aberdeen (H) League 23 Oct 1926 won 6-2
5	Jimmy McGrory v Dundee United (H) League 27 Nov 1926 won 7-2
5	Jimmy McGrory v Clyde (H) League 15 Jan 1927 won 7-0
5	Jimmy McGrory v East Fife (H) League 10 Jan 1931 won 9-1
5	John Crum v Albion Rovers (A) League 1 Oct 1938 won 8-1
5	Neil Mochan v St Mirren (H) Scottish Cup 29 Feb 1960 won 5-2
5	John Hughes v Aberdeen (H) League 30 Jan 1965 won 8-0
5	Bertie Auld v Airdrieonians (A) League 10 Mar 1965 won 6-0
5	Steve Chalmers v East Fife (H) League Cup 16 Sep 1965 won 6-0
5	Bobby Lennox v Partick Thistle (A) League Cup 31 Aug 1968 won 6-1
5	Steve Chalmers v Hamilton Accies (H) League Cup 11 Sep 1968 won 10-0
5	Bobby Lennox v Hamilton Accies (H) League Cup 11 Sep 1968 won 10-0

CHAIRMEN

John H McLaughlin	1897–1909
James Kelly	1909–1914
Tom White	1914–1947
Sir Robert Kelly	1947–1971
Desmond White	1971–1985
Tom Devlin	1985–1986
John McGinn	1986–1991
Kevin Kelly	1991–1994
Fergus McCann	1994–1999
Frank O'Callaghan	1999–2000
Brian Quinn	2000–2007
Dr John Reid	2007–present day

MANAGERS	Trophies won					
	Period	League Titles	Scottish Cup	League Cup	Europe	Total
By Committee	1888–1897	3	1	0	0	4
Willie Maley	1897–1940	16	14	0	0	30
Jimmy McStay	1940–1945	0	0	0	0	0
Jimmy McGrory	1945–1965	1	2	2	0	5
Jock Stein *	1965–1978	10	8	6	1	25
Billy McNeill	1978–1983	3	1	1	0	5
David Hay	1983–1987	1	1	0	0	2
Billy McNeill	1987–1990	1	2	0	0	3
Liam Brady **	1990–1992	0	0	0	0	0
Lou Macari	1992–1994	0	0	0	0	0
Tommy Burns ***	1994–1997	0	1	0	0	1
Wim Jansen	1997–1998	1	0	1	0	2
Jozef Venglos	1998–1999	0	0	0	0	0
John Barnes	1999–2000	0	0	0	0	0
Kenny Dalglish ****	2000–2000	0	0	1	0	1
Martin O'Neill	2000–2005	3	3	1	0	7
Gordon Strachan	2005–2008	3	1	1	0	5
		42	34	13	1	90

* Sean Fallon was manager for 1975–76 season while Jock Stein recovered from road accident
** Frank Connor was manager for 3 matches before Lou Macari's appointment
*** Billy Stark was manager for the last three matches of 1996–97 season
**** Kenny Dalglish was appointed manager on a caretaker basis until the end of the season after the sacking of John Barnes in February 2000

CLUB CAPTAINS

James Kelly	1888–1897
Dan Doyle	1897–1899
Sandy McMahon	1899–1903
Willie Orr	1903–1906
James Hay	1906–1911
Jim Young	1911–1917
Alec McNair	1917–1920
William Cringan	1920–1923
Charlie Shaw	1923–1925
Willie McStay	1925–1929
Jimmy McStay	1929–1934
Bobby Hogg	1934–1935
Willie Lyon	1935–1939
John McPhail	1948–1952
Sean Fallon	1952–1953
Jock Stein	1953–1955
Bobby Evans	1955–1957
Bertie Peacock	1957–1961
Duncan McKay	1961–1963
Billy McNeill	1963–1975
Kenny Dalglish	1975–1977
Danny McGrain	1977–1987

Roy Aitken	1987–1990
Paul McStay	1990–1997
Tom Boyd	1997–2002
Paul Lambert	2002–2004
Jackie McNamara	2004–2005
Neil Lennon	2005–2007
Stephen McManus	2007–present day

CELTIC v RANGERS STATS

League record v Rangers

	Pld	W	D	L	F	A
Home	144	61	41	42	227	180
Away	144	33	41	70	152	236
Neutral	1	1	0	0	2	1
	289	95	82	112	381	417

The neutral League match was the play-off for the title on 6 May 1905 played at Hampden Park after both clubs finished level on points. Goals from McMenemy and Hamilton gave Celtic a 2-1 win and the title. The match was refereed by an Englishman, Mr Kirkham of Preston after some poor refereeing performances in the previous meetings that season.

FIRST LEAGUE MEETING
21 March 1891 at Celtic Park 2-2 goals from Peter Dowds and John Campbell

FIRST LEAGUE MEETING AWAY
2 May 1891 2-1 goals from Johnny Madden and Peter Dowds

LEAGUE CLEAN SWEEPS
(After 1975–76 the teams met four times in the League)
1895–96 4-2 (A) & 6-2 (H)   1907–08 2-1 (H) & 1-0 (A)   1912–13 3-2 (H) & 1-0 (A)
1913–14 2-0 (A) & 4-0 (H)   1971–72 3-2 (A) & 2-1 (H)   1973–74 1-0 (A) & 1-0 (H)
2003–04 1-0 (A), 3-0 (H), 2-1 (A) & 1-0 (H)

LEAGUE HAT-TRICKS
1 Jan 1912 Jimmy Quinn 3-0 (H), 10 Sep 1938 Malcolm MacDonald 6-2 (H) & 3 Jan 1966 Steve Chalmers 5-1 (H)

BIGGEST HOME LEAGUE WIN
6-2 – 14 Dec 1895   4-0 – 1 Jan 1914   6-2 – 10 Sep 1938
5-1 – 3 Jan 1966   5-1 – 21 Nov 1998   6-2 – 27 Aug 2000

BIGGEST AWAY LEAGUE WIN
4-0 – 27 Sep 1897

LONGEST UNBEATEN LEAGUE RUN
8 – 1982 to 1984

LONGEST UNBEATEN HOME LEAGUE RUN
16 – 1980 to 1989

MOST LEAGUE WINS IN A ROW
6 – 1912 to 1914

MOST LEAGUE DRAWS IN A ROW
5 – 1902 to 1904

TOP LEAGUE GOALSCORERS v RANGERS
Sandy McMahon 15
Henrik Larsson 11
Jimmy McGrory 10
Jimmy Quinn 9

NUMBER OF CELTIC PLAYERS TO SCORE AGAINST RANGERS IN THE LEAGUE
156

Scottish Cup record v Rangers

	Pld	W	D	L	F	A
Home	13	11	1	1	28	13
Away	8	3	1	4	9	10
Neutral	25	8	6	11	33	36
	46	22	8	16	70	59

FIRST SCOTTISH CUP MEETING
6 September 1890 at Celtic Park 1-0 goalscorer Willie Groves

SCOTTISH CUP FINAL MEETINGS
15 :- 7 wins & 7 defeats – cup withheld after 2 draws in 1909

SEMI-FINAL MEETINGS
8 :- 3 wins & 5 defeats

BIGGEST SCOTTISH CUP WIN
5-0 :- 21 March 1925 semi-final at Hampden Park

LAST SCOTTISH CUP MEETING AT IBROX PARK
0-3 :- 7 March 1964

LAST SCOTTISH CUP WIN v RANGERS AWAY FROM CELTIC PARK
1-0 :- 20 May 1989 Cup final at Hampden Park goal from Joe Miller

TOP SCOTTISH CUP SCORERS v RANGERS
Jimmy Quinn 5
Sandy McMahon 4
Bobby Lennox 3

SCOTTISH CUP HAT-TRICKS v RANGERS
Jimmy Quinn – Scottish Cup Final 16 April 1904 won 3-2; first ever Cup Final hat-trick

NUMBER OF CELTIC PLAYERS TO SCORE AGAINST RANGERS IN THE SCOTTISH CUP
49

League Cup record v Rangers

	Pld	W	D	L	F	A
Home	14	9	0	5	21	18
Away	12	5	2	5	17	16
Neutral	19	6	0	13	29	31
	45	20	2	23	67	65

FIRST LEAGUE CUP MEETING
9 August 1947 at Ibrox 0-2

FIRST LEAGUE CUP MEETING AT CELTIC PARK
30 August 1947 2-0 goalscorers Jackie Gallacher and Johnny Paton

LEAGUE CUP FINAL MEETINGS
12 :- 4 wins & 8 defeats

SEMI-FINAL MEETINGS
6 :- 2 wins & 4 defeats

BIGGEST LEAGUE CUP WIN
7-1 :- 19 October 1957 – biggest ever win in a major British final

TOP LEAGUE CUP SCORERS v RANGERS
Bobby Lennox 5
Harry Hood 5
John McPhail 4
Willie Wallace 4

LEAGUE CUP HAT-TRICKS

Billy McPhail – 19 October 1957 Final won 7-1

Harry Hood – 5 December 1973 Semi-Final won 3-1; last hat-trick by a Celtic player against Rangers

NUMBER OF CELTIC PLAYERS TO SCORE AGAINST RANGERS IN THE LEAGUE CUP

38

CELTIC v RANGERS MISCELLANEOUS

A total of 182 different Celtic players have scored against Rangers. In fact 15 have scored against the Ibrox club in each of the three main competitions.

Between 1977 and 1991 Celtic and Rangers met five times in the Scottish Cup and Celtic won all five without conceding a goal.

Rangers' last win over Celtic at Celtic Park in the Scottish Cup was by 2-1 on 5 April 1998. However it was a semi-final tie and technically a neutral venue as the ticket allocation was split evenly. You have to go back eight games to 28 February 1903 when Rangers won 3-0 to find their last 'away' win in the Scottish Cup at Celtic Park.

When Celtic beat Rangers 4-0 in the 1969 Cup final, not only was it the Ibrox club's first Scottish Cup final defeat for 40 years, but also their biggest ever defeat in the final of this competition.

Jimmy Johnstone and John Collins hold the record of scoring in four consecutive matches against Rangers.

At the beginning of season 1971–72 Celtic visited Ibrox Park three times in less than a month and emerged victorious on all three occasions. Both League Cup sectional ties were played at Ibrox due to work being done at Celtic Park but the Bhoys still won 2-0 (14 Aug) and 3-2 (28 Aug). The first League meeting of the season between the two sides took place on 11 September which Celtic again won 3-2.

When Celtic completed the League double over Rangers in 1971–72 it was their first for 58 years. Both wins required last-minute headed goals by Jimmy Johnstone at Ibrox and Jim Brogan at Celtic Park.

On 2 April 1984 Paul and Willie McStay became the first and so far only brothers to score in the same Old Firm match, helping Celtic to a 3-0 victory.

Danny Crainie made the perfect start to his Old Firm debut when he scored in the first minute as Celtic beat Rangers 2-1 on 10 April 1982.

The fastest recorded goal in an Old Firm match was netted by Chris Sutton at Ibrox on 7 December 2002. It took all of 19 seconds for the big striker to open the scoring but Celtic still lost 2-3.

CELTIC v RANGERS

Overall record

	Pld	W	D	L	F	A
Home	171	81	42	48	276	211
Away	164	41	44	79	178	262
Neutral	45	15	6	24	64	68
	380	137	92	151	518	541

Home record

	Pld	W	D	L	F	A
League	144	61	41	42	227	180
Scottish Cup	13	11	1	1	28	13
League Cup	14	9	0	5	21	18
	171	81	42	48	276	211

Away record

	Pld	W	D	L	F	A
League	144	33	41	70	152	236
Scottish Cup	8	3	1	4	9	10
League Cup	12	5	2	5	17	16
	164	41	44	79	178	262

Neutral record

	Pld	W	D	L	F	A
League	1	1	0	0	2	1
Scottish Cup	25	8	6	11	33	36
League Cup	19	6	0	13	29	31
	45	15	6	24	64	68

MISCELLANEOUS

Henrik Larsson is the only player ever to be top scorer in Scotland's top division four years in a row (2000–01 to 2003–04). But for a broken leg in Lyon in 1999 it could easily have been six as he was also top scorer in 1998–99.

For four seasons in a row (1980–81 to 1983–84), four different Celtic players ended the season as Premier Division top scorer – 1980–81 Frank McGarvey (21), 1981–82 George McCluskey (21), 1982–83 Charlie Nicholas (29) and 1983–84 Brian McClair (23).

In the eleven seasons between 1995–96 and 2004–05, the top scorer in the Premier Division/SPL was a Celtic player ten times.

Celtic's first ever match was a friendly against Rangers on 28 May 1888. Celtic won 5-2 and the club's first ever goalscorer was Neil McCallum. McCallum also scored Celtic's first ever goal in a Scottish Cup final on 9 February 1889 but Third Lanark spoiled the fairytale start for the new club by winning 2-1.

Celtic's first ever League match was against Renton, who won 4-1, but they were later disqualified from the League and all their results were cancelled. Therefore Celtic's first ever 'official' League match was a 5-0 win away to Hearts on 23 August 1890. Celtic's first League goalscorer was Johnny Madden.

Celtic's first ever Scottish Cup tie was a 5-1 home win over Shettleston on 1 September 1888.

The club's first ever League Cup tie was a 2-4 defeat away to Hibernian on 21 September 1946.

Celtic have played in 53 Scottish Cup finals, winning 34 and losing 18. The Cup was withheld in 1909 after two draws against Rangers and the subsequent Hampden Riot.

Celtic have played in 26 League Cup finals, winning 13 and losing 13.

Between 21 August 1965 and 13 August 1969 Celtic were unbeaten in 39 League Cup matches, winning 37.

Celtic appeared in a record 14 League Cup finals in a row between 1964–65 and 1977–78.

Celtic appeared in a record 7 Scottish Cup finals in a row between 1968–69 and 1974–75.

Not only were Celtic the first Scottish club to win nine League titles in a row but they were also the first to win two outright, five, six, seven and eight in a row.

Celtic's full League record during the 9 in a row period between 1965–66 and 1973–74 was:-
Pld 306, won 235, drawn 45, lost 26, goals for 868, goals against 258, points 515.

Between 23 October 1926 and 15 January 1927 Jimmy McGrory scored five goals in a single match on three separate occasions.

On 15 April 1916 Celtic played two matches in one day. In the afternoon they beat Raith Rovers 6-0 at home and travelled to Motherwell in the evening and won 3-1.

Celtic have played 15 matches on Christmas Day winning 13, drawing 1 and losing 1.

For the first 30 years or so of the League Cup, the competition started with six group matches before moving on to a knockout basis. In 1972–73 Kenny Dalglish became the first and only player in history to score in all six matches.

On 29 September 1984 Peter Grant scored the first ever goal in a sponsored Celtic jersey. Celtic won 3-2 away to Dundee.

Between 1889–90 and 1951–52 Celtic did not lose a single cup replay.

Celtic's first goal of the 20th century was scored by Jack Bell in a 3-2 home win over Rangers on New Year's Day.

Celtic's first goal of the 21st century was scored by Mark Viduka in a 1-1 draw away to Kilmarnock on 22 January.

Celtic's first ever match in the famous green and white hoops was on 15 August 1903 at home to Partick Thistle. Goals from Alec Bennett and Jimmy McMenemy gave Celtic a 2-1 win.

In 1906–07 goalkeeper Tom Sinclair joined Celtic on loan from Rangers and played six games keeping six clean sheets.

In contrast, on 30 March 1895 keeper John O'Brien made his one and only appearance for Celtic away to Leith Athletic and despite conceding 5 goals Celtic still managed to win by scoring 6.

In 1908–09 Celtic won the League title despite playing the last eight games in eleven days, five of which they won.

On 26 September 1953 Bobby Collins scored a hat-trick of penalties as Celtic beat Aberdeen 3-0 at home.

On 21 February 1953 Charlie Tully scored direct from a corner kick away to Falkirk in the Scottish Cup. The referee ordered a re-take only for the bold Charlie to score again and help Celtic to a 3-2 win.

The first ever floodlit match at Celtic Park was on 12 October 1959 when Celtic lost 0-2 against Wolverhampton Wanderers in front of a crowd of 45,000.

Celtic full-back Willie O'Neill made his first team debut in the Scottish Cup final replay against Dunfermline on 26 April 1961 but the Pars ran out 2-0 winners.

On 26 October 1963 Celtic beat Airdrieonians 9-0 despite goalkeeper Frank Haffey missing a penalty.

Celtic played in the first Scottish Cup final to be televised live against Clyde in 1955. The match ended 1-1 with Clyde winning the replay 1-0.

Celtic also played in the first League Cup final to be televised live against Rangers in 1984 which the Ibrox club won 3-2.

Dixie Deans scored the first ever competitive goal on a Sunday in Scotland when he opened the scoring in a 6-1 win over Clydebank in the Scottish Cup. Dixie went on to score the first ever Sunday hat-trick as well.

Celtic were the first Scottish club to win a League and cup double once, twice and thrice.

In 1959 Celtic played 38 League matches and did not win 2 in a row.

On 24 January 1891 Celtic played a whole match with 10 men as Mick McKeown missed the train to the game. After opening the scoring Celtic eventually lost 1-3 to Vale of Leven.

In early 1973 Celtic missed five successive penalties in three League matches. Just to prove even the best players can miss from 12 yards the kicks were missed by Bobby Murdoch (2), Kenny Dalglish (2) and Harry Hood.

In 2005 Chris Sutton became the first Celtic player to miss a penalty kick in a Scottish Cup final (excluding shootouts), when he slipped as he struck the ball against Dundee United and scooped the ball over the bar. However Celtic still ran out 1-0 winners.

In the four Scottish Cup finals between 1972 and 1975 Celtic used four different goalkeepers – Evan Williams v Hibernian (6-1), Ally Hunter v Rangers (2-3), Denis Connaghan v Dundee United (3-0) and Peter Latchford v Airdrieonians (3-1).

The first time Celtic fielded a starting XI without a single Scot was against Dunfermline on 8 September 2001 in the SPL. Celtic won 3-1. The line up was:-

D Kharine (Russia)
J Valgaeren (Belgium)
D Agathe (France)
B Balde (Guinea)
O Tebily (Ivory Coast)
A Thompson (England)
N Lennon (N Ireland)
S Petrov (Bulgaria)
L Moravcik (Slovakia)
C Sutton (England)
H Larsson (Sweden)

The last time Celtic fielded a starting XI made up entirely of Scots was against Motherwell on 3 December 1994 at Hampden Park in the Premier Division. The match ended 2-2. The line up was:

G Marshall
T Boyd
T McKinlay
M Galloway
B O'Neil
P Grant
B McLaughlin
P McStay
W Falconer
A Walker
S Gray

Note:- Stuart Gray was born in Harrogate but played for Scotland at international level the same way for example, Tommy Coyne represented the Republic of Ireland but was born in Glasgow. Mike Galloway was born in Oswestry but played for Scotland.

Total Player Stats

Player	Period at club	LEAGUE Apps	Goals	TOTAL Apps	Goals
ADAMS, Davie	1902–1912	248	0	291	0
AGATHE, Didier	2000–2006	110 (11)	9	169 (12)	11
AIRLIE, Seton	1939–1947	6	3	6	3
AITKEN, Roy	1972–1990	483	40	670 (2)	53
ALLAN, George	1897–1898	17	15	19	16
ALLAN, Thomas	1910–1913	2	0	2	0
ALIADIERE, Jeremie	2005–2005	0	0	0 (2)	0
ANDERSON, Oliver	1937–1946	13	3	13	3
ANDREWS, Ian	1988–1990	5	0	8	0
ANNONI, Enrico	1997–1999	26	11	32	17
ANTHONY, Marc	1995–1999	0 (2)	0	0 (3)	0
ARCHDEACON, Owen	1982–1989	38 (38)	7	42 (45)	8
ARNOTT, Walter	1895–1895	1	0	1	0
ATKINSON, John	1909–1910	1	0	1	0
AULD, Bertie	1955–1971	197 (9)	50	257 (18)	79
BAILLIE, Joe	1945–1954	107	0	151	1
BAILLIE, Lex	1982–1991	27 (4)	1	30 (5)	1
BAINES, Roy	1976–1979	12	0	16	0
BALDE, Bobo	2001–2008	160 (1)	7	233 (1)	16
BARBER, Tom	1918–1919	5	0	5	0
BARCLAY, Graham	1973–1977	0	0	1	0
BARRIE, Jim	1930–1930	1	0	1	0
BATTLES, Barney	1895–1904	110	6	136	6
BAUCHOP, James	1906–1918	14	5	14	5
BEATTIE, Craig	2003–2007	18 (32)	13	22 (43)	16
BEATTIE, Dick	1954–1959	114	0	156	0
BELL, Andrew	1951–1955	25	0	28	0
BELL, James	1890–1891	15	0	22	0
BELL, John	1898–1900	35	16	46	23
BELLAMY, Craig	2005–2005	12	7	15	9
BENNETT, Alec	1903–1908	126	44	152	50
BERKOVIC, Eyal	1999–2000	29 (3)	9	34 (8)	12
BIGGINS, Wayne	1993–1994	4 (5)	0	4 (6)	0
BIRRELL, Jimmy	1938–1940	6	2	6	2
BJARNASON, Teddy	2004–2008	1	0	1	0
BLACK, John	1912–1914	4	1	4	1
BLACK, Willie	1904–1905	10	0	11	0
BLACKWOOD, John	1899–1900	1	0	1	0
BLAIR, Dan	1924–1927	3	0	3	0
BLAIR, John	1910–1911	1	0	1	0
BLESSINGTON, Jimmy	1892–1898	82	31	99	39
BLINKER, Regi	1997–2000	37 (11)	9	57 (16)	12
BODEN, Alec	1943–1956	122	2	158	2
BOGAN, Tommy	1946–1948	34	5	47	8
BONE, Jimmy	1974–1975	5 (2)	1	8 (3)	1
BONNAR, John	1946–1958	120	0	180	0
BONNER, Pat	1978–1994	483	0	641	0
BORUC, Artur	2005–2008	100	0	136	0
BOYD, Tom	1991–2002	296 (10)	2	391 (16)	2
BOYLE, James	1890–1893	9	0	9	0
BOYLE, John	1933–1938	10	0	10	0
BOYLE, Robert	1912–1913	10	0	10	0
BRADY, Alec	1891–1892	19	4	24	10
BRATTBAKK, Harald	1997–2000	27 (17)	12	39 (21)	20
BRESLIN, Pat	1899–1899	1	0	1	0
BRITTON, Gerry	1987–1992	0 (2)	0	0 (4)	0
BRODIE, John	1916–1919	2	1	2	1
BROGAN, Frank	1960–1964	37	0	48	0
BROGAN, Jim	1962–1975	208 (5)	6	332 (9)	9
BROTO, Javier Sanchez	2003–2003	7 (1)	0	9 (1)	0
BROWN, Hugh	1916–1921	98	2	98	2
BROWN, John	1911–1913	40	7	47	10
BROWN, Mark	2007–2008	9	0	10	0
BROWN, Scott	2007–2008	31 (3)	32 (2)	45 (3)	3

Player	Period at club	LEAGUE Apps	Goals	TOTAL Apps	Goals
BROWN, Willie	1916–1919	2	2	2	2
BROWNING, John	1911–1919	210	64	217	66
BUCHAN, Willie	1933–1937	120	38	134	45
BUCKLEY, John	1978–1983	0	0	1	0
BURCHILL, Mark	1997–2001	15 (34)	20	23 (39)	24
BURLEY, Craig	1997–1999	61 (3)	20	90 (3)	25
BURNS, John	1918–1920	13	3	13	3
BURNS, Tommy	1973–1989	325 (32)	52	467 (41)	82
BYRNE, Alec	1954–1963	70	22	100	30
BYRNE, Paul	1993–1995	24 (4)	4	28 (4)	4
CADDIS, Paul	2004–2008	0 (2)	0	2 (2)	0
CADETE, Jorge	1995–1997	32 (5)	30	44 (5)	38
CAIRNEY, Charles	1949–1950	1	0	1	0
CAIRNEY, James	1922–1923	3	0	4	0
CALDWELL, Gary	2006–2008	55 (1)	1	76 (3)	2
CALLACHAN, Harry	1925–1927	11	0	11	0
CALLAGHAN, Tommy	1968–1976	143 (14)	144 (14)	240 (24)	34
CAMARA, Henri	2004–2005	12 (6)	8	16 (10)	8
CAMARA, Mohammed	2005–2006	19	0	24	0
CAMERON, James	1932–1933	4	2	4	2
CAMPBELL, John	1890–1903	169	88	215	113
CAMPBELL, Robert	1905–1906	11	0	11	0
CANNON, Bernard	1947–1948	3	0	3	0
CANTWELL, Jack	1946–1947	8	5	9	5
CARLIN, James	1896–1897	1	0	1	0
CARROLL, Bobby	1957–1963	61	21	78	27
CARRUTH, Joe	1936–1945	39	27	42	29
CASCARINO, Tony	1990–1992	13 (11)	4	16 (13)	4
CASEY, Jim	1974–1980	6 (7)	0	15 (14)	1
CASSIDY, Jimmy	1892–1898	1	0	1	0
CASSIDY, Joe	1893–1895	28	13	36	17
CASSIDY, Joe	1912–1924	189	90	204	103
CATTANACH, Dave	1963–1972	10 (3)	1	15 (4)	1
CHALMERS, Paul	1979–1986	0 (4)	1 (4)	0 (4)	1
CHALMERS, Steve	1959–1971	253 (9)	158	391 (14)	231
CLARK, Joe	1912–1913	2	1	2	1
CLARK, John	1903–1903	2	0	2	0
CLARK, John	1958–1971	162 (1)	1	280 (4)	3
CLIFFORD, Hugh	1892–1893	5	0	5	0
COEN, Joseph	1931–1932	3	0	3	0
COLEMAN, James	1888–1888	1	0	1	0
COLEMAN, Tommy	1888–1895	7	2	18	2
COLLINS, Alec	1888–1888	0	0	2	0
COLLINS, Bobby	1949–1958	220	81	320	117
COLLINS, Frank	1921–1922	2	0	2	0
COLLINS, John	1990–1996	211 (6)	47	267 (6)	54
COLQUHOUN, John	1983–1985	25 (6)	4	30 (6)	5
COLRAIN, John	1957–1960	44	21	58	23
CONN, Alfie	1977–1979	34 (3)	10	51 (5)	13
CONNACHAN, James	1897–1898	1	0	1	0
CONNAGHAN, Denis	1971–1977	32	0	56	0
CONNELLY, George	1965–1978	129 (7)	5	241 (13)	13
CONNOLLY, Barney	1913–1919	13	4	13	4
CONNOLLY, Paddy	1921–1933	259	40	296	47
CONNOR, Frank	1960–1962	2	0	8	0
CONNOR, John	1932–1936	4	1	4	1
CONROY, Mike	1953–1960	7	0	8	0
CONROY, Mike	1978–1982	59 (9)	7	76 (16)	9
CONROY, Ryan	2006–2008	2	0	2	0
CONVERY, John	1997–2002	0 (1)	0	0 (1)	0
CONWAY, Jim	1957–1961	32	9	43	13
COOK, Willie	1930–1932	100	0	110	0
CORBETT, Willie	1940–1948	48	0	60	0
CORCORAN, Patrick	1918–1919	3	0	3	0

Player	Period at club	LEAGUE Apps	LEAGUE Goals	TOTAL Apps	TOTAL Goals
CORR, Barry John	1997–1997	0 (1)	0	0 (1)	0
CORRIGAN, Edward	1924–1926	4	0	4	0
COWAN, Joseph	1929–1931	1	1	1	1
COYLE, Ronnie	1979–1987	1 (1)	0	1 (1)	0
COYNE, Brian	1977–1979	0 (1)	0	0 (1)	0
COYNE, Tommy	1989–1993	82 (23)	43	104 (27)	52
CRAIG, Billy	1953–1957	8	0	9	0
CRAIG, Bobby	1962–1963	17	13	21	13
CRAIG, Jim	1963–1972	143 (4)	144 (4)	224 (7)	6
CRAIG, Joe	1976–1978	53 (1)	24	69 (4)	39
CRAIG, Michael	1993–1995	0	0	0 (1)	0
CRAIG, Robert	1906–1909	13	0	13	0
CRAIG, Tully	1919–1922	9	3	9	3
CRAINEY, Stephen	1997–2004	15 (10)	0	19 (13)	1
CRAINIE, Danny	1979–1983	17 (8)	7	19 (13)	8
CRAWFORD, Alec	1901–1902	10	3	10	3
CREANEY, Gerry	1987–1994	85 (28)	36	109 (33)	53
CRERAND, Pat	1957–1963	91	5	120	8
CRILLY, Willie	1922–1922	3	0	3	0
CRINGAN, Willie	1917–1923	202	9	214	10
CRONE, Willie	1913–1916	17	9	17	9
CROSSAN, Barney	1890–1891	8	3	15	7
CROZIER, James	1928–1929	2	0	2	0
CRUM, John	1932–1942	190	73	211	87
CULLEN, Joe	1892–1897	58	0	73	0
CUNNINGHAM, Johnny	1890–1892	7	0	8	1
CURLEY, Tom	1961–1965	1	0	1	0
CURRAN, John	1892–1894	21	0	26	0
CURRAN, John	1958–1962	4	0	4	0
CUSHLEY, John	1960–1967	30	0	41	0
DALGLISH, Kenny	1967–1977	200 (4)	112	313 (7)	167
DAVIDSON, Andrew	1913–1914	5	0	6	0
DAVIDSON, James	1892–1895	21	10	21	10
DAVIDSON, Robert	1898–1902	43	0	56	0
DAVIDSON, Vic	1968–1981	37 (2)	17	54 (12)	24
DAVITT, Michael	1935–1941	1	0	1	0
DAWSON, Daniel	1936–1938	17	3	20	3
DE ORNALES, Fernando	2000–2000	0 (2)	0	0 (2)	0
DEANS, John 'Dixie'	1971–1976	122 (4)	88	175 (8)	123
DELANEY, Jimmy	1933–1946	143	69	160	74
DEVANNY, Alex	1949–1952	1	0	3	0
DEVLIN, James	1890–1895	2	0	2	0
DEVLIN, John	1895–1895	2	1	2	1
DI CANIO, Paolo	1996–1997	25 (1)	12	35 (2)	15
DIVERS, Johnny	1893–1901	64	37	87	45
DIVERS, John	1932–1945	75	44	82	48
DIVERS, John	1956–1966	170	79	231	101
DOBBIN, Jim	1980–1984	1 (2)	0	5 (2)	1
DOCHERTY, James	1954–1954	1	0	2	0
DOCHERTY, Jim	1947–1950	2	0	2	0
DOCHERTY, John	1898–1900	11	0	11	0
DOCHERTY, Tommy	1948–1949	9	3	9	3
DODDS, Joe	1908–1923	351	28	378	30
DOHERTY, Hugh	1946–1947	3	0	4	0
DOHERTY, John	1937–1939	2	0	2	0
DOLAN, Frank	1890–1894	2	0	2	0
DOLAN, Michael	1888–1888	3	0	4	0
DONALDSON, Andy	1911–1912	17	6	17	6
DONATI, Massimo	2007–2008	22 (3)	3	34 (7)	4
DONLEVEY, Pat	1898–1898	1	0	1	0
DONNELLY, John	1956–1962	31	0	43	0
DONNELLY, Simon	1993–1999	113 (33)	31	146 (50)	43
DONNELLY, Willie	1900–1901	3	0	5	0
DONOGHUE, John	1926–1933	42	1	50	1

Player	Period at club	LEAGUE Apps	Goals	TOTAL Apps	Goals
DOUGLAS, Robert	2001–2005	107 (1)	0	161(1)	0
DOWDS, Peter	1889–1894	36	16	49	19
DOWIE, John	1977–1979	12 (2)	0	15 (3)	0
DOYLE, Dan	1891–1899	112	3	123	5
DOYLE, Frank	1926–1933	17	2	21	3
DOYLE, Johnny	1976–1981	82 (13)	15	123 (20)	37
DOYLE, Tom	1935–1938	5	0	5	0
DRUMMOND, James	1901–1902	4	1	4	1
DU WEI	2005–2006	0	0	1	0
DUBLIN, Dion	2006–2006	3 (8)	1	3 (9)	2
DUFF, Tom	1891–1892	8	0	9	0
DUFFY, John	1948–1954	2	0	2	0
DUFFY, Robert	1935–1947	4	0	4	0
DUNBAR, Michael	1888–1893	15	4	32	10
DUNBAR, Tom	1890–1898	51	3	60	4
DUNCAN, James	1951–1955	8	2	9	2
DUNCAN, Scott	1919–1919	2	0	2	0
DUNCAN, Willie	1910–1915	9	0	9	0
DUNN, Willie	1933–1935	9	2	9	2
DUNNING, Willie	1888–1889	0	0	6	0
DZIEKANOWSKI, Dariusz	1989–1992	42 (6)	10	60 (6)	22
EDVALDSSON, Johannes	1975–1980	120 (9)	26	183 (12)	38
ELLIOT, Barry	1995–2000	0 (1)	0	0 (1)	0
ELLIOT, David	1987–1990	2 (4)	0	2 (4)	0
ELLIOTT, George	1918–1925	1	0	1	0
ELLIOTT, Paul	1989–1991	52	2	66	5
EVANS, Bobby	1944–1960	384	10	535	10
FAGAN, Willie	1934–1936	12	9	12	9
FALCONER, John	1931–1934	7	0	8	0
FALCONER, Willie	1994–1996	33 (8)	5	38 (11)	8
FALLON, John	1958–1972	125	0	195	0
FALLON, Sean	1950–1958	177	8	254	13
FARRELL, Paddy	1896–1897	1	0	1	0
FERGUSON, George	1945–1948	5	0	5	0
FERGUSON, John	1895–1895	1	1	1	1
FERGUSON, Willie	1895–1897	25	11	27	12
FERNANDEZ, David	2002–2005	3 (8)	0	8 (12)	1
FERNIE, Willie	1948–1961	219	54	317	75
FILLIPI, Joe	1977–1979	30 (2)	0	41 (3)	0
FINDLAY, Robert	1900–1901	14	6	17	8
FISHER, James	1898–1900	10	3	10	3
FITZSIMMONS, John	1934–1938	5	0	5	0
FITZSIMMONS, Tom	1892–1892	1	0	1	0
FLANNAGHAN, M	1892	4	1	4	1
FLEMING, William	1924–1925	19	10	19	10
FOLEY, James	1934–1936	6	0	6	0
FORAN, Joseph	1890–1894	2	1	2	1
FOTHERINGHAM, Mark	1999–2003	2 (1)	0	2 (1)	0
FRASER, Bet	1948–1949	1	0	1	0
FULLARTON, Alex	1916–1917	1	0	1	0
FULTON, Steve	1987–1993	54 (22)	2	67 (28)	3
GALLACHER, Jackie	1943–1951	22	15	33	27
GALLACHER, Patsy	1911–1926	432	186	464	192
GALLAGHER, Antony	1893–1893	2	1	2	1
GALLAGHER, Charlie	1958–1970	107	17	171	32
GALLAGHER, Hugh	1889–1890	1	1	1	1
GALLAGHER, Jimmy	1929–1932	2	0	2	0
GALLAGHER, Paddy	1888–1893	30	0	45	1
GALLAGHER, Pat	1892–1893	2	0	2	0
GALLAGHER, Willie	1937–1949	29	0	39	3
GALLOWAY, Mike	1989–1996	113 (23)	8	146 (28)	10
GARDEN, William	1925–1926	1	0	1	0
GARNER, Willie	1981–1982	1	0	3	0
GARRY, Edward	1905–1907	6	1	6	1

Player	Period at club	LEAGUE Apps	Goals	TOTAL Apps	Goals
GEATONS, Charlie	1927–1941	286	11	319	11
GEDDES, John	1927–1929	2	0	2	0
GEERHIN, Pat	1910–1911	1	0	1	0
GEMMELL, Tommy	1961–1971	247	38	418	63
GIBSON, Andrew	1912–1912	2	1	2	1
GIBSON, Johnny	1976–1978	1 (2)	0	1 (3)	0
GILCHRIST, John	1919–1923	127	7	134	7
GILFEATHER, Eddie	1922–1926	2	0	2	0
GILGUN, Paddy	1924–1925	3	1	3	1
GILHOOLY, Pat	1896–1900	46	17	50	20
GILLESPIE, Gary	1991–1994	67 (2)	3	82 (2)	3
GILLIGAN, Sam	1903–1904	13	13	14	13
GLANCEY, Lawrence	1921–1923	1	0	1	0
GLASGOW, Sam	1920–1922	2	0	2	0
GLAVIN, Ronnie	1974–1979	100 (2)	36	147 (8)	50
GOLDIE, Hugh	1897–1899	25	0	27	1
GOLDIE, Peter	1952–1958	13	0	14	0
GOLDIE, Willie	1960–1961	1	0	1	0
GOODWIN, Jim	1997–2002	1	0	1	0
GORMAN, John	1967–1970	0	0	1	0
GORMLEY, Phil	1948–1950	1	0	1	0
GOULD, Jonathan	1997–2003	109 (1)	0	156 (2)	0
GRAHAM, John	1903–1904	4	0	4	0
GRANGER, John	1922–1925	13	0	13	0
GRANT, Peter	1982–1997	338 (26)	15	444 (34)	19
GRASSAM, Willie	1903–1903	2	0	2	0
GRAVESEN, Thomas	2006–2008	18 (4)	6	23 (10)	6
GRAY, Alec	1912–1918	13	5	14	5
GRAY, John	1900–1902	2	1	2	1
GRAY, Michael	2003–2004	2 (5)	0	4 (6)	0
GRAY, Stuart	1992–1994	19 (9)	1	23 (10)	1
GRAY, William	1927–1929	26	12	31	12
GROVES, Willie	1888–1898	4	3	18	16
GUPPY, Steve	2001–2004	22 (11)	0	32 (17)	0
HAFFEY, Frank	1958–1964	140	0	201	0
HALPIN, John	1978–1984	3 (4)	0	5 (10)	1
HAMILL, Micky	1918–1920	7	0	7	0
HAMILTON, Davie	1902–1912	221	53	260	60
HANCOCK, Steve	1970–1974	0	0	0 (1)	0
HANNAH, David	1996–1999	28 (14)	0	40 (21)	1
HANNAH, Robert	1974–1977	0 (2)	0	0 (2)	0
HARTLEY, Paul	2007–2008	33 (4)	0	48 (5)	1
HARTSON, John	2001–2006	125 (21)	89	171 (30)	110
HASTIE, John	1910–1912	16	3	19	4
HAUGHNEY, Mike	1949–1957	159	32	233	44
HAVERTY, Joe	1964–1964	1	0	1	0
HAY, Chris	1993–1997	9 (16)	4	9 (21)	5
HAY, David	1966–1974	106 (3)	6	190 (3)	12
HAY, James	1903–1918	214	14	255	19
HAYES, Martin	1990–1993	3 (4)	0	6 (4)	0
HAZLETT, George	1946–1948	21	0	23	0
HEALY, James	1924–1925	2	0	2	0
HEALY, Colin	1998–2003	16 (13)	17 (13)	27 (20)	3
HEDMAN, Magnus	2002–2005	26	0	37	0
HEMPLE, Sam	1952–1954	4	2	4	2
HENCHOZ, Stephane	2004–2004	2 (4)	0	4 (4)	0
HENDERSON, Adam	1897–1898	9	4	10	6
HENDERSON, Athol	1976–1977	0	0	1 (1)	0
HENDERSON, John	1895–1897	3	0	4	0
HENDERSON, Sam	1962–1968	2	0	2	0
HEPBURN, Anthony	1952–1954	6	0	6	0
HERON, Gil	1951–1952	1	0	5	2
HEWITT, John	1989–1992	9 (7)	0	12 (9)	0
HIGGINS, John	1950–1959	65	31	84	41

Player	Period at club	LEAGUE Apps	Goals	TOTAL Apps	Goals
HILL, John	1913–1913	2	0	2	0
HILLEY, Hugh	1921–1930	171	0	195	0
HINKEL, Andreas	2008–2008	16	1	19	1
HODGE, John	1899–1902	34	19	42	24
HOGG, Bobby	1931–1948	278	0	322	0
HOOD, Harry	1969–1976	161 (28)	74	263 (47)	121
HUGHES, John	1922–1925	5	0	5	0
HUGHES, John	1959–1971	233 (3)	115	377 (6)	188
HUGHES, John	1995–1996	31 (1)	2	46 (1)	2
HUGHES, Willie	1929–1936	94	11	104	12
HUNTER, Alistair	1973–1976	60	0	91	0
HUNTER, George	1949–1954	31	0	38	0
HUTCHINSON, Ben	2008–2008	0 (2)	0	0 (2)	0
HUTCHISON, Tom	1896–1896	2	0	2	0
HYNDS, Tom	1898–1902	28	2	31	2
JACK, Peter	1895–1895	1	0	1	0
JACK, John	1950–1959	48	0	68	0
JACKSON, Darren	1997–1999	13 (16)	3	22 (24)	7
JACKSON, John	1908–1919	27	4	27	4
JACKSON, Mike	1957–1963	57	23	74	30
JAROSIK, Jiri	2006–2008	24 (9)	5	35 (12)	7
JARVIS, George	1912–1919	7	0	7	0
JEFFREY, Bobby	1961–1963	5	0	8	0
JOHNSON, Tommy	1997–2001	23 (12)	18	30 (22)	25
JOHNSTON, Leslie	1948–1949	24	8	29	8
JOHNSTON, Maurice	1984–1987	97 (2)	52	125 (2)	71
JOHNSTONE, Jimmy	1961–1975	298 (10)	82	498 (17)	130
JOHNSTONE, Peter	1908–1917	211	23	233	25
JORDAN, Jackie	1946–1947	3	1	3	1
JUNINHO	2004–2005	9 (5)	1	14 (8)	1
KAPLER, Konrad	1947–1949	7	0	8	0
KAVANAGH, Peter	1929–1932	32	5	35	5
KAY, Roy	1977–1978	5	0	10	0
KEANE, Roy	2005–2006	10	1	12 (1)	1
KELLY, Charlie	1891–1893	2	0	2	0
KELLY, Frank	1918	2	0	2	0
KELLY, James	1888–1897	104	3	139	4
KELLY, John	1888	0	0	2	0
KELLY, John	1929–1930	9	0	10	0
KELLY, John C	1938–1941	1	0	1	0
KELLY, John	1939–1940	1	0	1	0
KELLY, Johnny	1960–1962	3	0	3	0
KELLY, Paddy	1995–1997	1	0	1	0
KENNAWAY, Joe	1931–1940	263	0	295	0
KENNEDY, Jim	1955–1965	170	0	241	2
KENNEDY, John	1965–1967	0	0	1	0
KENNEDY, John	1999–2008	19 (9)	1	31 (14)	1
KERR, Stewart	1994–2001	34 (1)	0	40 (2)	0
KHARINE, Dmitri	1999–2003	7 (1)	0	10 (1)	0
KIERNAN, Tommy	1945–1947	23	12	32	17
KILLEN, Chris	2007–2008	2 (18)	1	3 (24)	1
KING, Alex	1896–1900	56	11	62	13
KING, John	1895–1897	9	0	10	0
KIVLICHAN, Willie	1907–1911	76	20	92	27
KURILA, John	1958–1962	5	0	9	0
KYLE, James	1890	2	0	2	0
LAFFERTY, James	1951–1953	7	4	7	4
LAMB, Peter	1945–1947	1	0	1	0
LAMBERT, Paul	1997–2005	180 (13)	14	253 (21)	19
LARSSON, Henrik	1997–2004	218 (3)	174	312 (3)	242
LATCHFORD, Peter	1975–1987	186	0	275	0
LAURSEN, Ulrik	2002–2005	34 (6)	0	49 (9)	0
LAVERY, Dan	1948–1949	4	1	4	1
LAWRIE, Willie	1919–1921	3	0	3	0

Player	Period at club	LEAGUE Apps	Goals	TOTAL Apps	Goals
LAWSON, Paul	2004–2007	I (2)	0	I (3)	0
LEES, Walter	1892–1894	4	3	4	3
LEITCH, William	1923–1926	5	I	6	I
LENNON, Neil	2000–2007	212 (2)	3	300 (3)	3
LENNOX, Bobby	1961–1980	297 (50)	167	508 (81)	273
LIVINGSTONE, Dugald	1916–1921	44	0	47	0
LIVINGSTONE, George	1901–1902	17	4	23	7
LOCHHEAD, Ian	1958–1961	7	2	12	3
LONEY, Willie	1900–1913	254	28	305	30
LONGMUIR, Archie	1920–1921	10	6	10	6
LYNCH, Allan	1897–1899	2	0	2	0
LYNCH, Andy	1973–1980	124 (7)	15	184 (8)	25
LYNCH, Matt	1934–1948	48	3	63	3
LYNCH, Simon	1999–2005	2 (I)	3 (I)	3 (2)	3
LYON, Willie	1935–1944	146	16	163	17
McADAM, Tom	1977–1986	251 (7)	36	354 (11)	46
McALINDON, John	1948–1957	16	7	18	7
McALOON, Gerry	1946–1948	20	12	26	14
McARDLE, John	1926–1927	I	0	I	0
McARTHUR, Dan	1892–1903	104	0	120	0
McATEE, Andy	1910–1925	407	65	439	67
McATEER, Tom	1910–1912	24	4	28	5
McAULAY, Willie	1898–1898	I	I	I	I
McAULAY, Pat	1942–1950	78	4	109	4
McAVENNIE, Frank	1987–1993	82 (3)	37	103 (3)	50
McBRIDE, Joe	1965–1968	52 (3)	54	90 (3)	86
McBRIDE, John Paul	1995–2002	I (2)	0	I (3)	0
McCABE, Pat	1915–1916	2	0	2	0
McCAFFERTY, Willie	1902–1903	I	0	I	0
McCAHILL, Steve	1989–1992	6 (I)	0	8 (I)	0
McCALLUM, Denis	1926–1932	39	3	40	3
McCALLUM, Neil	1888–1892	20	12	33	19
McCALLUM, Willie	1890–1911	I	0	3	0
McCANN, Dan	1910–1911	7	I	7	I
McCANN, Eddie	1893–1893	I	0	I	0
McCANN, John	1893–1893	3	0	3	0
McCANN, Ryan	1998–2003	I	0	I	0
McCANN, William	1894–1895	3	0	3	0
McCARRISON, Dugald	1987–1993	I (3)	I	I (3)	I
McCARRON, Frank	1962–1967	I	0	I	0
McCARTHY, Mick	1987–1989	48	0	64	I
McCLAIR, Brian	1983–1987	86 (15)	99	119 (23)	121
McCLUSKEY, George	1973–1983	110 (32)	55	161 (46)	83
McCLUSKEY, John	1976–1979	0	0	0 (I)	0
McCLUSKEY, Pat	1969–1977	105 (11)	10	169 (22)	13
McCOLGAN, Dan	1925–1928	2	0	2	0
McCOLL, Jimmy	1913–1920	165	117	169	123
McCOLLIGAN, Brian	1997–2001	I	0	I	0
McCONDICHIE Andy	1995–1999	I	0	I	0
McCORMACK, Arthur	1911–1912	I	0	I	0
McCORMACK, Harry	1917–1919	2	I	2	I
McCREADIE, Bernard	1955–1957	I	0	I	0
McDERMOTT, Thomas	1901–1903	12	2	21	5
MacDONALD, Malcolm	1932–1945	134	31	147	36
MacDONALD, Roddy	1972–1981	160 (5)	21	248 (7)	33
McDONALD, John	1951–1953	0	0	2	2
McDONALD, Pat	1942–1947	9	0	14	0
McDONALD, Scott	2007–2008	35 (I)	25	49 (3)	31
McDONALD, Tommy	1947–1948	13	7	14	7
McDONALD, Willie	1893–1897	30	I	34	I
McDOWALL, Daniel	1950–1951	I	0	I	0
McELENY, Charlie	1893–1897	30	I	34	I
McELHANEY, Ralph	1895–1895	2	0	2	0
McEVOY, Pat	1917–1921	10	0	10	0

Player	Period at club	LEAGUE Apps	Goals	TOTAL Apps	Goals
McFARLANE, John	1919–1929	268	12	304	14
McFARLANE, Robert	1901–1902	17	0	23	0
McGARVEY, Frank	1980–1985	159 (9)	77	226 (19)	109
McGEADY, Aiden	2001–2008	91 (30)	21	119 (43)	24
McGEE, Robert	1923–1924	1	0	1	0
McGHEE, James	1890–1908	10	4	10	4
McGHEE, Joe	1929–1932	5	2	6	2
McGHEE, Mark	1985–1989	62 (26)	27	80 (35)	34
McGILLIVRAY, Charlie	1932–1933	4	2	4	2
McGINLAY, Pat	1993–1994	44 (3)	11	54 (5)	13
McGINN, James	1893–1894	2	0	2	0
McGINNIGLE, Willie	1918–1919	1	0	1	0
McGLINCHEY, Michael	2005–2008	0 (1)	0	0 (1)	0
McGONAGLE, Peter	1926–1936	286	8	325	9
McGONAGLE, Tommy	1931–1932	1	0	1	0
McGOWAN, Paul	2005–2008	0 (1)	0	0 (1)	0
McGRAIN, Danny	1967–1987	433 (8)	434 (8)	653 (10)	7
McGREGOR, Alec	1914–1916	1	0	1	0
McGREGOR, Tom	1910–1919	77	0	80	0
McGROGAN, Vincent	1925–1925	5	0	6	0
McGRORY, Jimmy	1921–1937	378	395	445	468
McGRORY, John	1946–1953	38	3	58	11
McGUGAN, Paul	1980–1987	45 (4)	2	54 (4)	2
McGUIRE, Dougie	1984–1988	0 (2)	0	0 (4)	0
McGUIRE, Jimmy	1948–1950	14	0	18	0
McILROY, James	1950–1956	11	3	12	3
McILVENNY, Harry	1895–1905	9	1	11	2
McINALLY, Alan	1984–1987	38 (28)	17	51 (37)	23
McINALLY, Arthur	1917–1918	1	0	1	0
McINALLY, Jim	1980–1984	0 (1)	0	2 (1)	0
McINALLY, John	1934–1937	9	5	9	5
McINALLY, Tommy	1919–1925	188	110	213	126
McINTOSH, James	1909–1910	8	0	11	0
MacKAY, Duncan	1955–1964	162	0	236	0
MacKAY, Malcolm	1993–2002	32 (5)	4	45 (7)	6
McKAY, Johnnie	1919–1921	10	6	10	6
McKECHNIE, Jim	1984–1986	1 (1)	0	1 (1)	0
McKEOWN, Mick	1888–1891	14	0	30	0
McKINLAY, Tosh	1994–1999	87 (13)	0	123 (18)	0
McKNIGHT, Allen	1986–1988	12	0	17	0
McLAREN, James	1888–1896	3	0	16	2
McLAUGHLIN	1892–1893	1	0	1	0
McLAUGHLIN, Brian	1971–1977	3 (4)	1	12 (8)	2
McLAUGHLIN, Brian	1992–1999	38 (37)	5	50 (48)	5
McLAUGHLIN, George	1923–1924	1	0	1	0
McLAUGHLIN, James	1888–1890	0	0	3	0
McLAUGHLIN, Jim	1947–1948	2	0	2	0
McLAUGHLIN, Paul	1989–1991	2 (1)	0	4 (1)	0
McLEAN, Adam	1917–1928	367	128	408	148
McLEAN, Davie	1907–1909	28	13	28	13
McLEAN, Finlay	1904–1905	15	4	15	4
McLEAN, Lachlan	1909–1910	3	0	3	0
MacLEOD, Murdo	1978–1987	274 (7)	55	386 (9)	82
McLEOD, Donald	1902–1908	131	0	155	0
McMAHON, Eamon	1953–1955	1	0	1	0
McMAHON, Pat	1967–1969	2 (1)	2	5 (1)	5
McMAHON, Sandy	1890–1903	174	130	217	177
McMANUS, Peter	1895–1895	1	0	1	0
McMANUS, Stephen	1999–2008	111	13	147 (1)	16
McMASTER, John	1913–1923	204	6	218	6
McMENEMY, Jimmy	1902–1920	456	144	515	168
McMENEMY, John	1925–1928	15	2	16	2
McMILLAN, Duncan	1945–1949	18	0	25	0
McMILLAN, Thomas	1952–1954	0	0	2	0

Player	Period at club	LEAGUE Apps	Goals	TOTAL Apps	Goals
McNAIR, Alec	1904–1925	548	9	604	9
McNAIR, Willie	1905–1906	1	0	1	0
McNALLY, Mark	1987–1995	112 (10)	3	129 (13)	4
McNALLY, Owen	1927–1930	11	4	11	4
McNAMARA, Jackie	1972–1976	19 (3)	2	40 (8)	5
McNAMARA, Jackie	1995–2005	221 (16)	10	307 (42)	15
McNAMEE, John	1959–1964	27	0	38	0
McNEILL, Billy	1957–1975	486	21	790	35
McNEIL, Hugh	1900–1901	2	0	2	0
McOUSTRA, Willie	1899–1902	23	8	30	11
McPHAIL, Billy	1956–1958	33	14	57	40
McPHAIL, John	1941–1956	142	58	204	92
McPHERSON, Andrew	1902–1904	27	0	32	0
McPHERSON, James	1890–1894	0	0	1	0
McQUILKEN, Jamie	1991–1995	4 (1)	0	4 (1)	0
McSTAY, Jimmy	1920–1934	409	6	472	8
McSTAY, Paul	1981–1997	509 (6)	57	671 (6)	72
McSTAY, Willie	1912–1929	399	37	446	39
McSTAY, Willie	1979–1987	55 (12)	2	77 (13)	2
McVITTIE, Matt	1953–1959	33	11	44	14
McWILLIAMS, Bobby	1928–1932	7	0	7	0
McWILLIAMS, Ian	1977–1978	1978 1978	0	3 (1)	0
MACARI, Lou	1966–1973	50 (8)	27	89 (13)	57
MACKIE, Peter	1976–1979	1 (3)	0	2 (4)	0
MACKLE, Tommy	1959–1961	3	1	5	2
MADDEN, Johnny	1889–1897	92	33	118	49
MADDEN, Richard	1962–1964	1	0	1	0
MAHE, Stephane	1997–2001	74 (3)	4	107 (3)	5
MAIR, Matt	1901–1902	1	0	1	0
MALEY, Tom	1888–1891	2	0	9	6
MALEY, Willie	1888–1897	75	0	96	1
MALLAN, Jimmy	1942–1953	90	0	117	0
MALLOY, Willie	1925–1928	7	1	8	1
MALONEY, Shaun	1999–2007	51 (53)	26	69 (69)	37
MARSHALL, David	2000–2007	34 (1)	0	47 (3)	0
MARSHALL, Gordon	1971–1972	0	0	1	0
MARSHALL, Gordon	1992–1998	101	0	136	0
MARSHALL, Harry	1899–1903	29	4	46	4
MARSHALL, Scott	1999–1999	1 (1)	0	1 (1)	0
MARTIN, Allan	1895–1896	17	18	18	18
MARTIN, Lee	1994–1996	19	0	20	0
MATHIE, Alex	1987–1991	7 (4)	0	8 (4)	0
MAXWELL, Hugh	1964–1965	8	0	8	0
MEECHAN, Frank	1952–1959	86	0	116	0
MEECHAN, Peter	1895–1897	25	1	25	1
MELROSE, Jim	1983–1984	20 (9)	7	31 (16)	11
MILLAR, Alex	1935–1938	9	0	9	0
MILLER, Andrew	1920–1924	5	1	5	1
MILLER, Joe	1987–1993	113 (31)	27	150 (42)	33
MILLER, Kenny	2006–2007	21 (12)	7	28 (18)	11
MILLER, Liam	1997–2004	13 (12)	2	19 (24)	5
MILLER, Willie	1942–1950	94	0	123	0
MILLS, Hugh	1935–1936	1	0	1	0
MILLSOPP, John	1948–1952	19	2	26	2
MILNE, Roy	1940–1952	108	0	133	0
MITCHELL, John	1906–1913	89	0	95	0
MITCHELL, Ronald	1946–1949	1	0	1	0
MITCHELL, William	1918–1919	5	0	5	0
MJALLBY, Johan	1998–2004	132 (12)	13	184 (14)	15
MOCHAN, Neil	1953–1960	191	81	268	109
MOIR, James	1898–1903	34	0	38	0
MORAN, Martin	1898–1909	3	0	3	0
MORAVCIK, Lubomir	1998–2002	75 (19)	29	103 (26)	35
MORRIS, Chris	1987–1992	156 (6)	8	203 (7)	9

Player	Period at club	LEAGUE Apps	LEAGUE Goals	TOTAL Apps	TOTAL Goals
MORRISON, Alex	1907–1907	1	0	1	0
MORRISON, John	1929–1941	161	1	178	1
MORRISON, Tommy	1895–1897	15	1	16	1
MORRISON, William	1951–1953	1	0	1	0
MOWBRAY, Tony	1991–1995	78 (3)	5	100 (3)	5
MOYES, Davie	1978–1983	19 (5)	0	29 (7)	0
MUGGLETON, Carl	1994–1994	12	0	13	0
MUIR, Bob	1903–1904	20	4	25	7
MULROONEY, John	1911–1914	42	0	51	0
MULVEY, Mick	1892–1893	4	4	4	4
MUNRO, Dan	1905–1910	30	6	36	6
MUNRO, Frank	1977–1978	14 (1)	0	21 (1)	0
MURDOCH, Bobby	1959–1973	287 (4)	61	480 (4)	102
MURPHY, Frank	1933–1946	144	46	161	50
MURPHY, James B	1920–1923	35	0	38	0
MURPHY, James F	1921–1924	6	2	7	2
MURRAY, Michael	1892–1893	2	0	2	0
MURRAY, Patrick	1902–1903	11	2	16	3
MURRAY, Steve	1973–1976	62 (1)	11	100 (1)	21
NAKAMURA, Shunsuke	2005–2008	91 (5)	21	117 (7)	24
NAPIER, Charlie	1928–1935	176	82	200	92
NAYLOR, Lee	2006–2008	65	1	93	1
NELSON, John	1897–1897	1	0	1	0
NICHOL, Willie	1911–1912	16	8	16	8
NICHOLAS, Charlie	1979 1996	159 (28)	85	209 (40)	125
NICOL, Davie	1927–1929	1	0	1	0
O'BRIEN, Jim	2005–2008	0 (1)	0	0 (2)	0
O'BRIEN, John	1895–1895	1	0	1	0
O'BYRNE, Fergus	1893–1894	7	0	7	0
O'CONNOR, John	1888–1892	1	0	2	0
O'DEA, Darren	2006–2008	12 (8)	2	19 (12)	3
O'DONNELL, Frank	1930–1935	78	51	83	58
O'DONNELL, Hugh	1932–1935	75	20	90	27
O'DONNELL, Phil	1994–1999	76 (14)	16	101 (20)	21
O'HARA, Don	1959–1962	7	1	9	1
O'KANE, Joe	1914–1926	20	13	20	13
O'LEARY, Pierce	1984–1988	38 (2)	1	44 (7)	1
O'NEIL, Brian	1989–1997	92 (28)	8	119 (36)	10
O'NEILL, Felix	1910–1912	1	0	1	0
O'NEILL, Hugh	1937–1940	5	0	5	0
O'NEILL, John	1993–1995	0 (1)	0	0 (1)	0
O'NEILL, Willie	1959–1969	49 (1)	0	79 (3)	0
O'ROURKE, Peter	1895–1897	9	0	9	0
O'SULLIVAN, Pat	1945–1947	4	0	4	0
OLIVER, Jim	1909–1909	2	0	2	0
ORR, Jim	1895–1898	7	0	7	0
ORR, Willie	1897–1908	165	17	212	23
OWERS, Ebenezer	1913–1914	13	8	16	9
PATERSON, George	1932–1946	175	9	195	10
PATON, Johnny	1942–1952	52	11	72	16
PATON, Roy	1957–1961	0	0	1	0
PAYTON, Andy	1992–1993	20 (16)	15	27 (19)	20
PEACOCK, Bertie	1949–1961	318	32	453	50
PEARSON, Stephen	2004–2007	22 (34)	6	36 (40)	7
PERRIER DOUMBE, Jean	2007–2008	5 (1)	0	7 (1)	1
PETROV, Stilian	1999–2006	215 (13)	55	288 (23)	64
PETTA, Bobby	1999–2005	36 (16)	0	56 (24)	3
POWER, Pat	1894–1895	1	0	1	0
PRATT, David	1919–1921	22	0	22	0
PRENTICE, David	1928–1930	6	1	6	1
PRESSLEY, Steven	2007–2008	19	1	24 (1)	2
PRICE, Billy	1961–1964	51	0	74	0
PRICE, James	1918–1921	6	0	6	0
PROVAN, Davie	1978–1987	192 (14)	28	287 (16)	41

Player	Period at club	LEAGUE Apps	Goals	TOTAL Apps	Goals
QUINN, Frank	1946–1948	6	0	7	0
QUINN, Jimmy	1901–1915	273	187	331	217
QUINN, Jimmy	1964–1975	23 (5)	1	35 (6)	1
QUINN, Robert	1943–1947	6	0	9	0
RAE, Joe	1942–1948	1943 1948 11	25	12	
REID, Ian	1953–1957	4	1	4	1
REID, Mark	1977–1985	120 (4)	5	170 (7)	12
RENNET, Willie	1949–1951	14	4	15	4
REYNOLDS, Jack	1897–1898	4	1	4	1
REYNOLDS, Jerry	1889–1895	74	0	99	0
RIBCHESTER, Willie	1916–1919	2	0	2	0
RIEPER, Marc	1997–1998	37	2	48	3
RILEY, Joseph J	1928–1930	10	2	10	2
RIORDAN, Derek	2006–2008	8 (16)	5	13 (19)	8
RISETH, Vidar	1998–2001	54 (2)	3	70 (3)	5
RITCHIE, Andy	1973–1976	5 (4)	1	5 (5)	1
ROBERTSON, David	1930–1931	2	0	2	0
ROBERTSON, Graham	1929–1931	34	1	37	1
ROBERTSON, William	1909–1910	3	0	4	0
ROBSON, Barry	2008–2008	9 (6)	2	10 (6)	3
ROGAN, Anton	1986–1991	115 (12)	4	148 (13)	5
ROLLO, Alec	1948–1954	37	1	59	2
ROOSE, Leigh R	1910–1911	0	0	1	0
ROSS, Andrew	1898–1900	1	0	1	0
ROUGH, Alan	1988–1988	5	0	7	0
ROWAN, Jim	1952–1956	2	1	2	1
RUSSELL, Davie	1896–1899	71	12	84	12
RYAN, Vincent	1953–1958	22	3	22	3
SAMARAS, Georgios	2008–2008	5 (11)	5	5 (16)	6
SANDERSON, Robert	1908–1909	2	0	2	0
SCARFF, Peter	1928–1933	97	51	112	55
SCHEIDT, Rafael	1999–2000	1 (3)	0	2 (4)	0
SCOTT, Robert	1893–1899	1	0	1	0
SEMPLE, Willie	1907–1909	8	2	8	2
SHARKEY, Jim	1954–1957	23	8	27	9
SHAW, Charlie	1913–1925	420	0	436	0
SHAW, Hugh	1906–1906	1	0	1	0
SHEA, Danny	1919–1920	1	0	1	0
SHEPHERD, Tony	1983–1989	16 (12)	3	22 (16)	3
SHERIDAN, Cillian	2006–2008	0 (2)	0	0 (3)	0
SHEVLANE, Chris	1967–1968	2	0	3	0
SHEVLIN, Peter	1924–1927	86	0	103	0
SHIELDS, Jimmy	1939–1947	3	0	3	0
SHIELDS, Paul	2000–2003	0 (1)	0	0 (1)	0
SIMPSON, Ronnie	1964–1970	118	0	188	0
SINCLAIR, Graeme	1982–1985	45 (6)	1	65 (10)	1
SINCLAIR, Tom	1906–1907	6	0	6	0
SINCLAIR, Tommy	1927–1928	2	0	2	0
SIRREL, Jimmy	1945–1949	13	2	18	2
SLATER, Malcolm	1958–1960	5	1	5	1
SLATER, Stuart	1992–1993	40 (4)	3	50 (6)	3
SLAVEN, Pat	1897–1897	1	0	1	0
SLAVIN, Jim	1992–1996	3	0	3	0
SMITH, Barry	1991–1995	14 (5)	0	15 (5)	0
SMITH, Eric	1953–1960	95	13	130	20
SMITH, Hugh	1930–1934	25	1	27	1
SMITH, Jamie	1997–2005	12 (31)	2	23 (40)	5
SMITH, Mark	1986–1987	3 (3)	0	5 (3)	0
SNEDDON, Alan	1977–1981	66	1	100	1
SNO, Evander	2005–2008	10 (20)	1	20 (19)	1
SOLIS, Jerome	1931–1932	9	3	9	3
SOMERS, Peter	1897–1910	186	52	219	62
STANTON, Pat	1976–1978	37	0	44	0
STARK, Billy	1987–1990	58 (6)	17	74 (10)	25

Player	Period at club	LEAGUE		TOTAL	
		Apps	Goals	Apps	Goals
STEIN, Jock	1951–1957	106	2	148	2
STEWART, Tom	1918–1918	1	0	1	0
STORRIER, Dave	1898–1901	34	0	40	0
STRANG, William	1903–1905	2	0	2	0
STUBBS, Alan	1996–2001	101	4	138	6
SULLIVAN, Dominic	1979–1983	83 (7)	10	109 (10)	12
SUTTON, Chris	2000–2006	127 (3)	62	192 (6)	85
SYLLA, Mohammed	2001–2003	19 (19)	20 (19)	28 (36)	5
SYME, David	1918–1919	2	0	2	0
TAYLOR, David	1918–1920	5	0	5	0
TAYLOR, William	1948–1951	14	4	17	4
TEBILY, Olivier	1999–2002	29 (9)	0	41 (11)	2
TELFER, Paul	2005–2007	56 (1)	1	71 (2)	1
TEMPLETON, Bobby	1906–1907	29	5	36	5
THOM, Andreas	1995–1998	57 (13)	14	84 (17)	27
THOM, James	1895–1895	1	0	1	0
THOMAS, Danny	1895–1895	1	0	1	0
THOMPSON, Alan	2000–2007	146 (37)	37	207 (20)	51
THOMSON, Alec	1922–1934	392	82	451	100
THOMSON, Bertie	1929–1933	113	22	131	30
THOMSON, John	1926–1931	163	0	188	0
THOMSON, William	1895–1895	1	0	1	0
TIERNEY, Con	1930–1932	7	0	7	0
TONER, Willie	1948–1951	2	0	2	0
TOWIE, Tom	1892–1893	0	0	5	2
TRAVERS, Paddy	1911–1912	18	5	22	8
TRAYNOR, John	1983–1986	3 (1)	0	3 (1)	0
TRODEN, Paddy	1895–1895	1	0	1	0
TULLY, Charlie	1948–1959	216	30	319	43
TURNBULL, David	1927–1928	2	0	2	0
TURNBULL, Tom	1899–1900	11	0	11	0
TURNER, Paddy	1963–1964	7	0	14	0
UGOLINI, Rolando	1944–1948	4	0	5	0
VALGAEREN, Joos	2000–2005	112 (4)	7	169 (9)	10
VAN HOOIJDONK, Pierre	1995–1997	66 (2)	44	87 (5)	56
VARGA, Stanislav	2003–2006	79 (1)	10	114 (2)	14
VATA, Rudi	1992–1996	33 (12)	4	44 (12)	4
VEGA, Ramon	2000–2001	18	2	26	4
VENNEGOOR OF HESSELINK, Jan	2006–2008	48 (5)	28	70 (6)	38
VIDUKA, Mark	1998–2000	36 (1)	30	47 (1)	35
VIRGO, Adam	2005–2008	3 (7)	0	4 (8)	0
WALKER, Andy	1987–1996	112 (38)	49	145 (50)	69
WALLACE, John	1932–1934	15	0	18	0
WALLACE, Ross	2002–2006	18 (19)	19 (19)	24 (28)	4
WALLACE, Willie	1966–1971	135 (6)	88	217 (15)	134
WALLS, James	1903–1903	4	0	5	0
WALSH, Frank	1947–1949	10	3	10	3
WALSH, Jimmy	1949–1956	108	45	144	58
WARNER, Tony	1998–1999	3	0	3	0
WATSON, Charlie	1919–1922	18	4	18	4
WATSON, Hugh	1901–1905	49	0	58	1
WATSON, Phil	1902–1903	3	0	3	0
WATTERS, Jackie	1937–1947	9	4	10	5
WDOWCZYK, Dariusz	1989–1994	112 (4)	4	142 (5)	6
WEIR, Donald	1948–1952	6	1	7	2
WEIR, James	1907–1910	82	1	96	1
WEIR, Jock	1948–1952	81	26	106	37
WEIR, John	1978–1982	11	1	14	1
WELFORD, Jim	1897–1900	38	0	44	0
WELSH, Frank	1971–1976	4 (1)	0	4 (1)	0
WHITEHEAD, George	1913–1913	7	2	7	2
WHITELAW, Robert	1930–1934	17	0	18	0
WHITNEY, Tom	1931–1933	4	1	4	1
WHITTAKER, Brian	1983–1984	10	2	16	3

Player	Period at club	LEAGUE Apps	Goals	TOTAL Apps	Goals
WHYTE, Derek	1985–1992	211 (5)	7	270 (5)	8
WHYTE, Frank	1951–1956	7	0	9	0
WIEGHORST, Morten	1995–2002	59 (24)	10	79 (34)	16
WILLIAMS, Evan	1969–1974	82	0	148	0
WILSON, Alex	1905–1907	14	0	14	0
WILSON, James	1913–1919	47	0	47	0
WILSON, Mark	2006–2008	34 (4)	0	42 (5)	0
WILSON, Paul	1967–1978	97 (36)	30	168 (49)	55
WILSON, Peter	1923–1934	344	14	395	15
WILSON, Sammy	1957–1959	48	26	70	46
WRAITH, Bobby	1968–1969	0	0	1	0
WRIGHT, Ian	1999–2000	4 (4)	3	5 (4)	3
YOUNG, Ian	1961–1968	84	2	133	3
YOUNG, James	1918–1918	1	0	1	0
YOUNG, Jim	1903–1917	392	14	443	14
YOUNG, John	1908–1911	3	0	3	0
ZURAWSKI, Maciej	2005–2008	42 (13)	22	53 (19)	30

Index